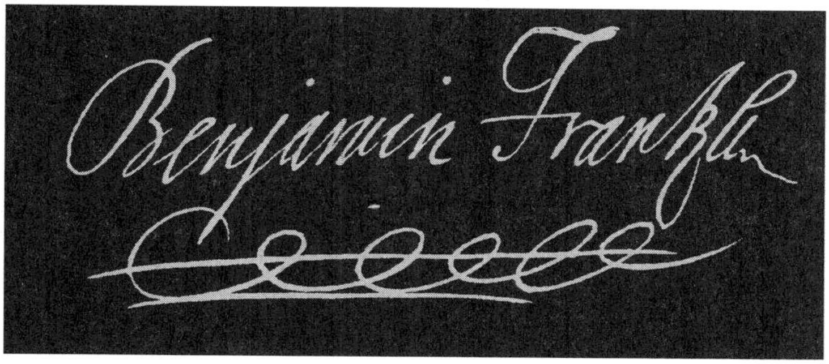

Benjamin Franklin
A Biographical Companion

A painting by Duplessis, 1928

Benjamin Franklin
A Biographical Companion

Jennifer L. Durham

ABC-CLIO
BIOGRAPHICAL
COMPANION

Library of Congress Cataloging-in-Publication Data

Durham, Jennifer L.
  Benjamin Franklin, a biographical companion / Jennifer L. Durham.
    p. cm.—(ABC-CLIO biographical companion)
  Includes bibliographical references and index.
  1. Franklin, Benjamin, 1706-1790—Encyclopedias. 2. Statesmen—
United States—Biography—Encyclopedias. I. Title. II. Series.
E302.6.F8D88 1997 973.3'092—dc21 97-41976

ISBN 0-87436-931-2

ISBN 0-87436-931-2 (alk. paper)

03 02 01 00 99 98 97   10 9 8 7 6 5 4 3 2 1 (cloth)

ABC-CLIO, Inc.
130 Cremona Drive, P.O. Box 1911
Santa Barbara, California 93116-1911

This book is printed on acid-free paper ∞ .
Manufactured in the United States of America

For Mark

ABC-CLIO BIOGRAPHICAL COMPANIONS

Benjamin Franklin, by Jennifer L. Durham

Forthcoming

Susan B. Anthony, by Judith E. Harper
Thomas Jefferson, by David Brown

JOIN, or DIE.

CONTENTS

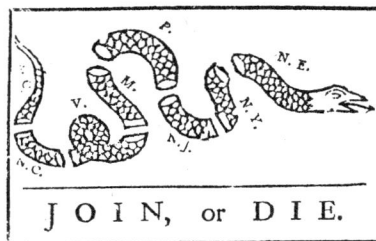

JOIN, or DIE.

Benjamin Franklin or particular aspects of his varied life have been the subjects of innumerable biographies and analytical works. In nearly every case, the picture of Franklin's life they present is given in chronological order. While a chronological format is useful and enables a reader to trace Franklin's life as it unfolded month by month, it does not easily facilitate an understanding of the particular interests and relationships that occupied him over long periods of time. Franklin's ability to pursue four or five divergent interests at once further complicates a search for information of Franklin's involvement in particular areas. It is hoped that the information in this volume, arranged by subject matter rather than by chronology, conveys in an accessible form how specific events of Franklin's life and times unfolded, how his particular interests and ideas developed, and how his relationships with other people progressed.

The alphabetical entries in this volume generally fall into four categories: writings, people, events, and interests. The reader will generally gain a better understanding of a certain topic by looking also at the related entries listed at the end of each. Franklin's extensive role in the American Revolution is necessarily divided into many entries. The reader will find descriptions of some of Franklin's most important scientific and philosophical contributions in the entries on his correspondents, to whom Franklin first described them. Among these are Sir John Pringle, John Bartram, Peter Collinson, Dr. John Fothergill, Jared Eliot, Cadwallader Colden, James Bowdoin, Dr. Joseph Priestley, Lord Kames, Dr. Benjamin Rush, Dr. Jacques Barbeu-Dubourg, and Dr. Jan Ingenhousz. The entries on individuals and events highlight Franklin's relationship with them and are not intended as comprehensive biographies and histories. Most of the individuals in the entries were accomplished in areas outside of their friendships with Franklin and are themselves the subjects of entire works.

A final note: The writings of Franklin quoted in the entries and in the appendix are, for the most part, from Albert Henry Smyth's *The Writings of Benjamin Franklin,* a respected collection published in the United States between 1905 and 1907. Franklin's pieces cited at the end of each entry can almost always be found in other collections of his writings as well. The pieces are listed as they appear in *The Papers of Benjamin Franklin,* edited by Leonard W. Labaree et al. (1959–), as these volumes provide the best explanatory notes. When not available in English in *The Papers,* preference is given to Smyth and *Benjamin Franklin: Writings,* edited by J. A. Leo Lemay (1987).

ACKNOWLEDGMENTS

I would like to thank the following for their advice, assistance, and support: Mark Moore; Mom, Dad, and Michael; Todd Hallman, Liz

Kincaid, and Martha Whitt at ABC–CLIO; the staff at the Northwest Regional and Cameron Village libraries, Raleigh, North Carolina; and the staff at the Walter R. Davis Library, University of North Carolina; the Franklin Institute.

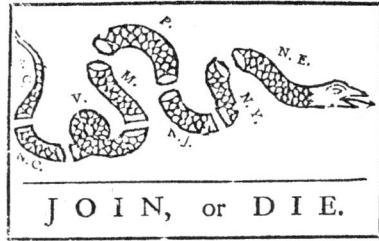

JOIN, or DIE.

More than 200 years after his death, Benjamin Franklin continues to be remembered as one of America's foremost statesmen, scientists, and inventors. His voluminous letters, articles, pamphlets, and journals, along with his own inclination to preserve them, have enabled numerous historians to piece together a fairly detailed picture of his life and accomplishments. It is hoped that the information in this volume, arranged by subject matter rather than by chronology, will convey in an accessible form how specific events of his life and times unfolded, how his ideas developed, and how his relationships with others progressed.

By all accounts, Franklin was even tempered, witty, and pleasant, and both optimistic and realistic. He expressed himself forcefully on paper, though less eloquently in speech, whether before public bodies or among groups of people. Strangers thought him silent and reserved, and friends commented on his economical use of words. Born in Boston, the fifteenth of 17 children in a family of modest circumstances, Franklin had less than two years of formal schooling. From a young age, he read voraciously and tried to compensate for his lack of schooling by educating himself. His natural sagacity, combined with his most cherished virtues, industry and frugality, began to lift him out of his poor circumstances almost as soon as he ran away to Philadelphia.

In 1730 he married Deborah Read Rogers, whose husband had deserted her.

Many have speculated on the nature of Franklin's relationships with other women. He wrote in his *Autobiography* of the period before he married her: "[T]hat hard-to-be-governed passion of youth hurried me frequently into intrigues with low women that fell in my way, which were attended with some expense and great inconvenience, besides a continual risk to my health by a distemper which of all things I dreaded, though by great good luck I escaped it." Some think that his illegitimate son, William, had been born to Deborah before she and Franklin were married; nobody has ever been able to determine the identity of William's mother with certainty. However, there is no solid evidence that Franklin was anything more than open and flirtatious with other women after he married.

He became something of a father figure to many younger women in America, England, and France—Catharine Ray Greene, Mary (Polly) Stevenson Hewson, the daughters of Jonathan Shipley, and Anne-Louise Brillon de Jouy—many who affectionately called him "papa." Franklin delighted in writing to Polly and Georgiana Shipley on matters of natural philosophy, and his letters to them are among his most interesting writings. Older women befriended him as well. Polly's mother, Margaret Stevenson, was Franklin's landlady on Craven Street in England and one of his dearest friends. Long after his wife's death, Franklin proposed in France to Madame Helvétius, the widow of the philosopher Claude-Adrien Helvétius,

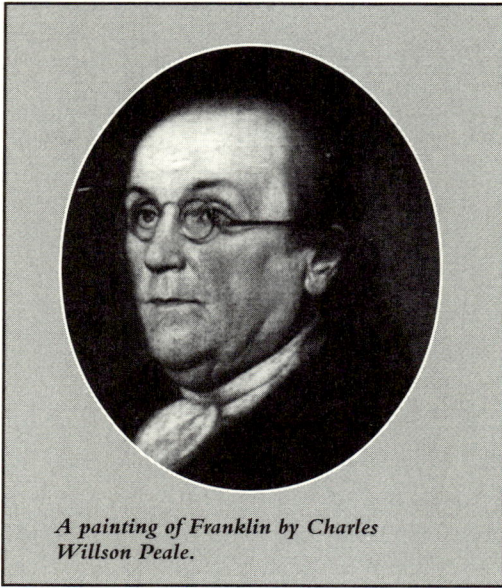

A painting of Franklin by Charles Willson Peale.

In 1757 the Pennsylvania Assembly sent Franklin to England as its agent to petition for the right to tax proprietary lands. A new phase of an old dispute between the Assembly and Pennsylvania's proprietors, Thomas and Richard Penn, had erupted during the French and Indian War (1754–1763). The Penns refused to pay taxes on their vast estates, and the Assembly refused to appropriate money for defense unless the Penns paid their share of it. The Penns appointed the governor and instructed him to veto any bills that did not exempt their estates from taxation. Franklin settled immediately into his new role in England. He moved into a house on Craven Street with Mrs. Stevenson and Polly and lived pleasantly there for the rest of his years in England. Dr. John Fothergill, Peter Collinson, and William Strahan, with whom Franklin had corresponded for years, were delighted to finally meet him. The Royal Society had elected him a member the year before he arrived in England, and he attended its meetings. With his son, Richard Jackson, and Sir John Pringle, Franklin traveled around Europe. These diversions balanced out the frustrating position in which he found himself as an agent for the American colonies. He ably worked for the repeal of the Stamp Act and unsuccessfully opposed other acts of Parliament that placed taxes and restrictions on the colonies, particularly Massachusetts.

although it is not known how seriously he intended the offer. In any case, the proposal and her refusal seem not to have damaged their friendship. With the exception of the women he met in France after his wife's death, these friendships were well known to Mrs. Franklin, who frequently sent them greetings and gifts.

Although he remained an American through and through, Franklin readily adapted to his environment in the three different countries in which he lived during his life. He lived as an increasingly eminent citizen in Philadelphia for 30 years. His printing business, which included *Poor Richard's Almanack* and the *Pennsylvania Gazette,* grew very successful. In the Pennsylvania Assembly he served as clerk, then member, and then speaker. The Junto, the American Philosophical Society, the Library Company of Philadelphia, the Academy of Philadelphia (later the University of Pennsylvania), and the Pennsylvania Hospital were all founded during this period and owed their existence to Franklin. With William Hunter, and later John Foxcroft, he held the highest position in America in the royal post office. Under their leadership, the colonial post office, for the first time in history, sent profits to England.

Franklin returned twice to Philadelphia (1762–1764 and 1775–1776) and in 1776 was dispatched to France, where he spent the next nine years as a commissioner from the United States. He settled in Passy outside of Paris, where he enjoyed a whole village of friends and pleasing company. Already known for his invention of the lightning rod, he was heralded too as a guardian of liberty and lavished with honors wherever he went. Portraits, prints, busts, and other likenesses of him rendered his face "as well known as that of the moon." It was "universally believed in France, England, and all Europe," John Adams complained, "that [Franklin's] electric wand has accomplished all this revolution." All of these honors Franklin neither played up nor played down, but took in stride. He associated chiefly with the residents of Passy—the Chaumonts (his landlords), the Brillons, and the Le Veillards—and a circle of friends centering on Madame Helvétius in the neighboring village of Auteuil.

Franklin's prominent presence in France significantly helped the United States and contributed to its success in the Revolutionary War. As much as he hated asking others for money, one of his chief duties as minister plenipotentiary to France was to persuade the French to finance the American Revolution. He worked with the French foreign minister, the Comte de Vergennes, who trusted Franklin and generally tried to grant his requests on behalf of the United States. It is doubtful that Vergennes or France would have been as generous had they been working solely with any of the other American commissioners, who were not nearly as well known or well liked. Franklin recommended foreign officers, organized exchanges of prisoners of war, oversaw the sale of prize ships, and helped persuade France to enter into an alliance with the United States. After the war, Franklin, John Adams, and John Jay negotiated the peace treaty with England.

Franklin's role in the American Revolution is all the more remarkable when his age is taken into consideration. At 70, he was the oldest signer of the Declaration of Independence. He risked an uncomfortable November voyage to France as a commissioner for the United States when he was nearly 71, and would likely have been executed for treason had the British captured him. Throughout his seventies, he handled the war business in France and negotiated treaties with foreign powers after the hostilities ceased. In 1787, at age 81, he served as the oldest delegate to the Constitutional Convention.

It might have been expected that the American Revolution would divide Franklin from his English friends, but the rift was strongest closer to home. William Franklin, his only living son and the royal governor of New

Franklin as portrayed by Benjamin West.

Jersey, remained loyal to England. He was arrested, became the president of a loyalist association, and later moved to England. Franklin and his son corresponded faithfully before the war, but their differences over the Revolution estranged them. In his will, Franklin left him "no more of an estate he endeavored to deprive me of," his land in Nova Scotia. Joseph Galloway, Franklin's longtime friend and political ally in the Pennsylvania Assembly, also became a loyalist. From England, the Shipleys, Benjamin Vaughan, Dr. Fothergill, Mrs. Stevenson, Polly Hewson, and even William Strahan, who was not as pro-American as the others, all remained Franklin's devoted friends.

Wherever he lived, Franklin most enjoyed his philosophical pursuits and longed for more time to devote to them during periods of heavy involvement in public affairs. Soon after he moved to Philadelphia, he formed the Junto, a philosophical discussion club that endured for almost 40 years. Later he conceived the American Philosophical Society as an American counterpart to European academies such as the Royal Society of London. While he lived in London, he enjoyed meeting with the Honest Whigs, a club that met every other week at a coffeehouse for dinner, drink, and discussion. Franklin attended the Royal Society's meetings when he lived in England, and the meetings of the French Academy of Sciences during his years in France. With the Freemasons, he was active in the St. John's Lodge in Philadelphia and in the Nine Sisters Lodge in France. Some of the groups were oriented more toward politics, and others focused on matters of science.

Personal letters from Franklin to his many correspondents contain a good portion of his scientific and philosophical writings. Correspondents such as Peter Collinson in England published his letters on electricity, sometimes without asking his permission. It was the publication and translation of these letters that led to Franklin's election to the prestigious Royal Society and the performance of his experiments by M. Delor before a gratified Louis XV. Although Franklin wrote letters later on that he knew his correspondents would publish, he seems not to have taken the time to publish many scientific writings himself.

Though he enjoyed experimenting and hypothesizing, Franklin believed that knowledge was useless unless it was applied to something practical. His experiments with pointed bodies and electricity led to his invention of the lightning rod, which would thereafter save buildings and lives. Potential uses of electricity in treating paralytics and the mentally ill also interested him. When he discovered that boats travel faster in deep water than in shallow water in canals, he wondered whether the additional swiftness would justify the expense of building deeper canals. Franklin experimented with oil on rough water and thought that it might be used to calm waters to enable ships to land on islands bounded with rough waves. He refused to patent or profit from his inventions—the lightning rod, the Franklin Stove, the pit-coal stove, the armonica—and believed "that, as we enjoy great advantages from the inventions of others, we should be glad of an opportunity to serve others by any in-

vention of ours; and this we should do freely and generously."

In all of his pursuits, writing was Franklin's most important tool. The *Pennsylvania Gazette,* which he began to publish in 1729, enabled him to promote public projects such as the Pennsylvania Hospital. He viewed the *Gazette* and his *Poor Richard's Almanack* in part as tools for instructing the public. As a printer, he printed pamphlets of his own writings that called for a volunteer militia to defend the province, influenced public opinion in favor of increasing the amount of paper money in circulation, and called for justice against a gang of rioters who murdered a band of peaceful Indians. While he lived in England he wrote biting satires on British policy toward America to English newspapers in an attempt to influence public opinion against the harsh measures Parliament took against the colonies. "These odd ways of presenting matters to the public view sometimes occasion them to be more read, talked of, and more attended to," he wrote to Thomas Cushing in 1773, referring to his "Rules by Which a Great Empire May Be Reduced to a Small One." In Passy, he set up a private press and charmed his French acquaintances with his humorous bagatelles. He did, however, he told Thomas Jefferson, avoid writing documents that were subject to the scrutiny of public bodies.

It is significant to note that in the enormous volume of his writings there is not one completed book. Despite repeated pleas by Benjamin Vaughan, Louis-Guillaume Le Veillard, and the Shipleys, Franklin only brought his *Autobiography* to the year 1757. His activities as a colonial agent in England and as a statesman during the American Revolution belong to later periods and are missing from his never-completed and most widely read work. He told his own story through letters, articles, pamphlets, and journals. The other book he long intended to write, *The Art of Virtue,* was never finished.

Public controversies bored and disgusted Franklin, and he rarely responded to his political and scientific accusers. One's time, he thought, was always employed more productively in discovering something useful than arguing with others. With his knack for looking at the positive side of everything, he spoke to others of the usefulness of enemies, even if he privately felt injury from their attempts to discredit him. "I have, as you observe, some enemies in England," he wrote to John Jay in 1784, "but they are my enemies as an American; I have also two or three in America, who are my enemies as a minister; but I thank God there are not in the whole world any who are my enemies as a man; for by His grace, through a long life, I have been enabled so to conduct myself, that there does not exist a human being who can justly say, 'Ben. Franklin has wronged me.'"

Throughout his varied pursuits, Franklin carefully attended to the needs of his family and assisted his relatives. He oversaw the education of his daughter and son, Sally and William, taking the latter to England to finish his studies in law. When they were grown, he directed the education of one grandson, Benjamin Franklin Bache, and tried unsuccessfully to obtain a political post for another, William Temple Franklin. He sent Bache to Geneva and then had him instructed in printing by some of France's foremost printers. Another grandson, William Bache, attended school in America at Franklin's expense. Temple served as his grandfather's secretary in France. Franklin set up Benjamin Bache in a printing house in Philadelphia and his nephew, Benjamin Mecom, in a printing house in Antigua (a decision he came to regret). Franklin's favorite sibling, Jane Mecom, kept him up-to-date on the family he had run away from in Boston. After their brother Peter died in 1766, Jane was Franklin's only remaining sibling, and Franklin supported her as they grew older.

Franklin always took special pleasure in children, even in his old age. He enjoyed the company of Polly Hewson's children in England and missed their "cheerful prattle" when they left after a winter visit to Passy.

Little Maria Jay, daughter of John Jay, also grew fond of Franklin in France. When John Adams was about to set sail for America from France, Franklin delivered letters for 11-year-old John Quincy Adams to his friends and wrote a short letter to "Master Johnny" wishing him a pleasant voyage. Franklin arrived in Philadelphia in 1785 to a house full of grandchildren, who were very fond of their grandfather.

Although he identified himself as a deist, at least in his youth, Franklin generally avoided arguing about his religious beliefs and preferred not to enter into theological discussions. He befriended clergy of widely divergent persuasions—Priestley, who became a Unitarian; Shipley, the bishop of St. Asaph; and the Reverend George Whitefield, the Anglican revivalist. Religion for Franklin was neither dogma nor mysticism but a vehicle by which to instill public and private morality. He believed that the Christian religion and the moral teachings of Jesus best served this purpose, and he aided churches of many denominations and always paid his subscription to the local Presbyterian church. Yet in his adult life he rarely attended church himself and did not believe in the central tenet of Christianity—the divinity of Jesus.

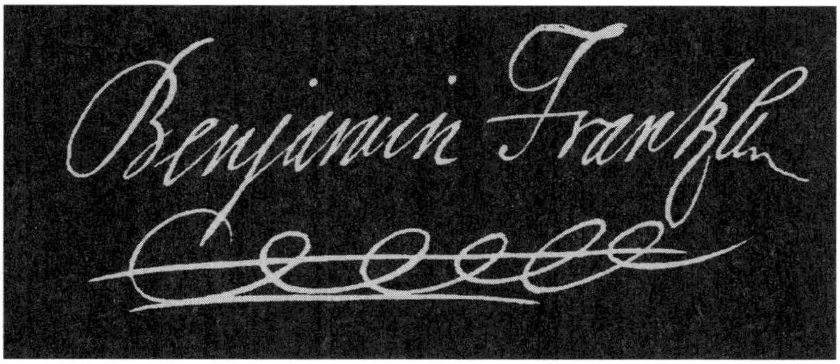

Benjamin Franklin
A Biographical Companion

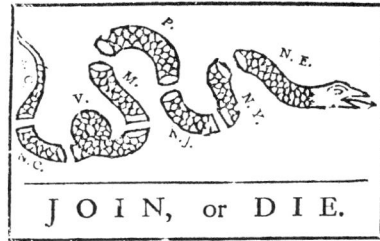

JOIN, or DIE.

A

An Account of Negotiations in London for Effecting a Reconciliation between Great Britain and the American Colonies

Franklin spent part of 1774 and 1775 immersed in secret negotiations with British government officials in a final attempt to avert war. On his voyage home to Philadelphia in 1775 he wrote down the details of these important negotiations for his son William, who was then the governor of New Jersey and soon to become a loyalist. The *Account* chronicles his dealings with Lords Chatham (William Pitt), Dartmouth, Howe, Hyde, Stanhope, and Camden, all of whom sympathized, to varying degrees, with American grievances. Lords Chatham and Camden were the most accommodating, while the others favored mild conciliatory measures that remained unsatisfactory to Americans.

The negotiations had not been Franklin's idea. In 1774 he had been the object of public denunciation as a result of the Oliver-Hutchinson letters affair, and he felt that his influence with Parliament was minimal. Moreover, there was relatively little real support for American grievances in Parliament, and he doubted that much more could be done to repair the growing breach. His friend Dr. John Fothergill, along with David Barclay, a merchant with great interest in American trade, briefly gave him a glimmer of hope that differences between Britain and its American colonies might be worked out.

Most members of Parliament who wanted to pursue conciliatory measures were less concerned about the actual complaints of Americans than about the possibility that the British Empire would break up. Parliament had passed strict measures against Massachusetts, and some of its members began to grow concerned that the measures did not force its colonists into submission as expected, but only strengthened their resolve to resist.

Franklin spoke to Lord Chatham, assuring him that he had never heard anyone in America, drunk or sober, express a desire for independence from England. Franklin's assurance pleased Lord Chatham, who had presided over Britain's victory in the French and Indian War and took a great interest in preserving and expanding the British Empire. Around that time, Lord Howe's sister invited Franklin to play chess with her, and she began feeling around for Franklin's sentiments on conciliation. David Barclay contacted Franklin about devising measures that would prevent a war. Franklin was skeptical, but he agreed to meet with Barclay and Fothergill. Barclay had connections to Lord Hyde, and Fothergill to Lord Dartmouth, the secretary of state for America.

Fothergill urged a reluctant and skeptical Franklin to draw up a plan for reconciliation, in order that it might be presented to some of England's moderate ministers. He was reluctant to act without the instructions of Congress and skeptical that his plan would do any good. Nevertheless, he drew up "Hints for Conversation upon the Subject of Terms That Might Probably Produce a Durable Union between Britain and the Colonies."

Its stipulations were that: the tea destroyed in the Boston Tea Party was to be paid for by the colonies; Britain was to repeal the Tea Act and repay the colonies for all duties that had been collected on tea; the Navigation Acts were to be reenacted in the colonies, with a Crown-appointed naval officer in each colony to see that they are observed; acts that placed restraints on colonial manufacturing were to be reconsidered; all tax money raised on trade-regulating acts were to be applied for public use of the colonies and paid into their respective treasuries; the collectors would come from the colonies, not England; no requisition from colonists was to be made by Britain in time of peace; no troops were to be forcibly quartered in colonies; established rules were to govern requisitioning in time of war; Castle William, which had been taken by the British, was to be restored to Massachusetts; no fortresses were to be built by the British without the consent of the colonial legislature; the Massachusetts and Quebec Acts were to be repealed, and Canada was to have a free government; judges were to be appointed on good behavior and paid by colonial assemblies; if the salaries were paid by Crown, it must be at the pleasure of the Assembly; governors were to be supported by the assemblies; if Britain would give up its monopoly on American commerce, the colonies would aid Britain monetarily in time of peace; Parliament was formally to disown Henry VIII's act of treason in American colonies (which allowed England to try American colonists charged with crimes in Britain); American admiralty courts were to be reduced to the same powers they had in England; and Parliament was to give up all claims of internal legislation in the colonies.

After some rewording of the articles (though less than Fothergill and Barclay thought was necessary), Fothergill presented them to Lord Dartmouth, and Barclay to Lord Hyde. Instructions soon arrived from Congress to the American agents in London—Franklin, Arthur Lee, William Bollan, Thomas Life, Edmund Burke, and Charles Garth—instructing them to present an American petition outlining colonial grievances to the king and perhaps to publicize it.

Franklin was told that the king had received the petition and had promised to give it to Parliament. Barclay, meanwhile, had spoken with Lord Hyde and suggested that his "Hints" be presented later. Franklin met with Lord Howe, who also asked him to draw up conciliatory measures that could be presented should any of the Congress's petition prove unacceptable. Franklin showed the Congress's petition to Lord Chatham, who was very impressed with the document and initially objected only to the demand that England keep no standing armies in the colonies during times of peace without the consent of the legislatures. Lord Camden also reacted positively to the petition.

Lord Howe had obtained a copy of the "Hints" and was disappointed to find out that Franklin had authored them. He asked Franklin to draw up another plan that might prove more acceptable to England. "This to me," Franklin said, "was what the French call 'spitting in the soup.'" However, Franklin complied and drew up another plan, which he doubted would be any more satisfactory to Britain. Mrs. Howe copied it so it would not be in his handwriting.

After speaking with members of the ministry, Howe was pessimistic about being able to accommodate the American requests. He asked Franklin whether he would personally be willing to pay for the tea lost in the Boston Tea Party. Fothergill had given Franklin's "Hints" to Lord Dartmouth, who rejected some and thought that others might be acceptable. In January 1775 Lord Chatham introduced a motion in the House of Lords to remove British troops from Boston. Lord Camden approved, and so did a few others, but, Franklin said, "all availed no more than the whistling of the winds."

Lord Chatham drew up a plan of conciliation to present to Parliament, and he asked Franklin, who admired him, for his input. The plan, as feared, was a disaster at the House of Lords. When Lord Chatham introduced it, Lord Dartmouth said it would require consideration, and Lord Sandwich opposed the mere introduction of the plan. Lord Sandwich surmised that it had been drawn up by an American (it had been written entirely by Lord Chatham) and glared at Franklin. "I kept my countenance as immoveable as if my features had been made of wood," Franklin wrote. Lord Dartmouth later sided with his colleagues who did not want even to consider the plan, and Lord Chatham rose with an eloquent defense of the plan and of Franklin. Franklin was not sure if he was more embarrassed by Lord Sandwich's abuse or by Lord Chatham's excessive compliments.

Franklin was disgusted with the system of hereditary legislators in the House of Lords and marveled at their disrespectful treatment of Lord Chatham, "the first statesman of the age, who had taken up this country when in the lowest despondency, and conducted it to victory and glory, through a war with two of the mightiest kingdoms in Europe." In addition, he was appalled by their failure to consider the plan. This, said Franklin, "made their claim of sovereignty over three millions of virtuous, sensible people in America seem the greatest of absurdities, since they appeared to have scarce discretion enough to govern a herd of swine."

After the debacle at the House of Lords, Franklin thought the negotiations had ended. However, Barclay wanted another meeting with Franklin and Fothergill. He told Franklin that several of his "Hints" were under consideration. Barclay thought that Franklin had more power than any other person to help achieve a peace, and that rewards might be in store for him if he helped to bring it about. Barclay's insinuations did not tempt Franklin, who believed that "the ministry . . . would rather give [him] a place in a cart to Tyburn [where prisoners were hung on the gallows], than any other place whatever." It appeared that Parliament would not waver on its belief in its right to alter colonial constitutions, and Franklin said that no agreement could be reached until they gave up that idea. At another meeting, Barclay presented a draft of another plan. Franklin promised to consider it and was asked to involve other colonial agents. Only the agents of Massachusetts, Franklin, Bollan, and Lee, would be concerned in the matter. Franklin, who thought it might be useful to send a commissioner to America, drafted a joint petition for Bollan and Lee to sign as well as a letter from himself to Lord Dartmouth proposing that commissioners go to America. Some "remarks" and "hints for further conversation" were also written.

Lord Howe, who thought he might be chosen as a commissioner, again desired to meet with Franklin and asked for his assistance should England decide to send commissioners. Franklin wanted to know exactly what propositions to appease America were in the making and said that he would help only if they were reasonable. Howe promised to reward Franklin's help, but Franklin said he was not interested in a potential reward and asked again about specific propositions the British planned to offer. Lord Howe asked him to speak to Lord Hyde, but the latter soon became skeptical of a potential reconciliation, and Franklin decided not to go. Back in the House of Lords, Lord North, the prime minister, introduced a watered-down conciliatory measure that was approved.

Upon hearing of his wife's death, Franklin wanted to sail home as quickly as possible. Lord Howe proposed to go with him and urged him again to visit Lord Hyde. Lord Hyde was surprised that Lord North's measure was not satisfactory to Franklin, who objected to Parliament's idea that it had the right to alter colonial constitutions. The negotiations ended, and even the mediators Barclay and Fothergill were fed up with the British ministers.

Franklin attended the House of Lords before he left, only to hear slander of his fellow countrymen. Thoroughly disgusted, he wrote "A Memorial to Lord Dartmouth," which contained strong language about the British blockade of Boston and a new plan to close northern fisheries to Massachusetts. "I do hereby give notice," he warned, "that satisfaction will probably one day be demanded for all the injury that may be done and suffered by the execution of such act." His friend Thomas Walpole convinced him not to present it. A few days before Franklin left for Philadelphia, Fothergill asked him to tell their American friends that any pretenses of conciliation offered by Britain were hollow.

Franklin had been America's most prominent and influential agent in England before the war. The failure of these negotiations, undertaken largely in secret, only strengthened his growing sentiments for independence. Little more than a year after he sailed home to Philadelphia, he signed the Declaration of Independence.

Related entries:
Boston Tea Party
Colonial Agent
Continental Congresses
Fothergill, Dr. John
Franklin, William
Great Britain
Oliver-Hutchinson Letters Affair
Revolutionary War

Suggestions for further reading:
"To William Franklin: Journal of Negotiations in London," March 22, 1774 (Labaree et al., vol. 21).

Adams, John (1735–1826)

Of all the men commonly thought of as the "Founding Fathers," John Adams worked more closely with Franklin than any other. His diary is filled with colorful, though not always respectful, accounts of Franklin during the years of the American Revolution. Adams was born in 1735 in Braintree, Massachusetts. He attended Harvard College and later studied law. He was admitted to the bar in 1758, and in 1770 he took the unpopular job of defending the British soldiers charged with five murders in the Boston Massacre. In 1764 he married Abigail Quincy Smith, and the couple had five children, including John Quincy Adams, who, like his father, would become president.

Adams was an orator and frequent writer during the years surrounding the Revolutionary War. In 1765 he denounced the Stamp Act in his "Braintree Instructions," and his "Novanglus" essays in 1774 and 1775 supported American resistance to coercive British policies. Adams was a delegate to both Continental Congresses and served with Franklin in the second. With Thomas Jefferson, Robert R. Livingston, and Roger Sherman, both served on the committee that drafted the Declaration of Independence. Both also served on the committee responsible for designing the U.S. seal and the Committee of Secret Correspondence, which sought out foreign agents who might be friendly to America.

In September 1776 Congress appointed Adams, Franklin, and Edward Rutledge as commissioners to negotiate with Lord Howe on Staten Island. On the way, Adams and Franklin stayed in an overcrowded hotel, cramped in a tiny room and forced to share a bed. When Adams started to shut the window for fear of the night air, Franklin said, "Oh! Don't shut the window, we shall be suffocated." Adams left the window open and "had so much curiosity to hear his reasons that I would run the risk of a cold. The Doctor then began a harangue upon air and cold, and respiration and perspiration, with which I was so amused that I soon fell asleep, and left him and his philosophy together . . . the

Portrait of John Adams. Frontispiece in **The Boston Magazine,** *1784. Stipple engraving.*

last few words I heard were pronounced as if he was more than half asleep."

Congress appointed Franklin, Arthur Lee, and Silas Deane as commissioners to France at the end of 1776. When Deane was recalled in 1778, Adams was sent to take his place. The Adamses lived outside of Paris at Passy with Franklin, and their son John Quincy attended school with Franklin's grandson, Benjamin Franklin Bache. Franklin found time to write a letter to young John Quincy in 1779: "Benjamin [Franklin's grandson] whom you so kindly remember, would have been glad to hear of your welfare, but he is gone to Geneva. As he is destined to live in a Protestant country, and a republic, I thought it best to finish his education where the proper principles prevail." Adams and his wife disliked the French and did not care for Franklin's friends.

Adams was present when Franklin and Voltaire were introduced at the French Academy of Sciences just before the latter's death in 1778. "[T]here presently arose a general cry that M. Voltaire and M. Franklin should be introduced to each other," Adams recorded in his diary. "This was done, and they bowed and spoke to each other. This was no satisfaction; there must be something more."

Franklin and Voltaire took each other by the hand. "The two aged actors upon this great theater of philosophy and frivolity then embraced each other, by hugging one another in their arms, and kissing each other's cheeks, and then the tumult subsided."

The perpetual quarrels between Arthur Lee, Ralph Izard, and Franklin exasperated Adams, and he wrote to Congress suggesting that it revoke the joint commission and appoint a sole commissioner. Arthur Lee had wanted the position, but Congress appointed Franklin. The appointment relieved Adams, who thought Franklin was the best choice on account of his reputation, and he readily turned his papers over to Franklin on his request.

Adams returned to France in 1780 with a commission to negotiate any possible peace terms, and he left his errand unknown to Franklin. He wrote letters to the Comte de Vergennes, the French foreign minister, without consulting Franklin. Vergennes was offended by Adams's letters and refused to deal with him any further, and he asked Franklin to transmit the letters to Congress. Franklin wrote to Samuel Huntington in 1780: "Mr. Adams has given offense to the court here, by some sentiments and expressions contained in several of his letters written to the Count de Vergennes." Franklin did not share Adams's distrust of the French: "He thinks . . . that America has been too free in expressions of gratitude to France . . . and that we should show spirit in our applications. I apprehend that he mistakes his ground, and that this court is to be treated with decency and delicacy." Franklin thought Adams meant to act for the good of America, but was mistaken in his belief that "a little apparent stoutness, and greater air of independence and boldness in our demands, will procure us more ample assistance." Adams spent much of the next two years in Holland, trying to procure a loan for the United States, while Franklin kept him up-to-date by letter.

When Adams arrived in Paris for the negotiations of the Treaty of Paris in 1783, conducted by himself, John Jay, and Franklin, he feared the worst in working with Franklin. Jay and Adams distrusted France and feared that Franklin trusted the French too much. "Between two as subtle spirits in the world," Adams wrote in his diary, "the one malicious, the other, I think honest, I shall have a delicate, a nice, a critical part to act. Franklin's cunning will be to divide us; to this end he will provoke, he will insinuate, he will intrigue, he will maneuver. My curiosity will at least be employed in observing his invention and his artifice." Adams and Jay were convinced that the commissioners should disobey their instructions from Congress and conduct the negotiations without consulting Vergennes, and Franklin consented. Contrary to Adams's expectations, the negotiations proceeded smoothly, and he admitted afterward in his diary that Franklin's sagacity and reputation had been useful in the negotiations and that he had worked harmoniously with Adams and Jay throughout the discussions. After the preliminary articles were signed, Franklin complained to Robert R. Livingston about Adams's hostile attitude toward the French court and toward himself. "I am persuaded, however," he wrote, "that he means well for his country, is always an honest man, often a wise one, but sometimes, and in some things, absolutely out of his senses."

Whatever Adams's personal feelings for Franklin, which seem to have been mixed, he generally kept them out of the important diplomatic business at hand. Adams's political career was far from over when Franklin died in 1790. He served as George Washington's vice president and became the second U.S. president (1797–1801). He carried on extensive correspondence with Thomas Jefferson, and both died on the same day, July 4, 1826, exactly 50 years after the adoption of the Declaration of Independence.

Related entries:
Continental Congresses
Declaration of Independence
France
Izard, Ralph
Jay, John
Jefferson, Thomas
Lee, Dr. Arthur
Revolutionary War
Treaties of Amity and Commerce
Treaty of Paris, 1783
Vergennes, Comte de (Charles Gravier)
Weissenstein, Charles de

Suggestions for further reading:
Adams, John. 1850. *The Works of John Adams, Second President of the United States.* Boston: Little, Brown.
"To John Quincy Adams," April 21, 1779 (Labaree et al., vol. 29).
"To Robert R. Livingston," July 22, 1783 (Smyth, vol. IX).
"To Samuel Huntington," August 9, 1780 (Smyth, vol. VIII).

Albany Plan of Union

*I*n 1754 the Lords of Trade in England ordered a congress held in Albany, New York, in which representatives of the American colonies were to meet with the chiefs of the Six Nations, a confederacy of Iroquois tribes, and discuss plans to defend their territories. War with France over American territory was almost certain. Governor James Hamilton of Pennsylvania appointed Franklin and the Assembly's speaker, Isaac Norris, to join Secretary Richard Peters and Thomas Penn as commissioners to the congress. "In our way thither," Franklin wrote in his *Autobiography,* "I projected and drew up a plan for the union of all the colonies under one government, so far as might be necessary for defense, and other important general purposes." He thought that some sort of colonial union was essential to the colonies' success in a war in North America. When he arrived in New York, Franklin showed his plan to James Alexander, Archibald Kennedy, and his correspondent Cadwallader Colden, who offered their suggestions.

When Franklin offered his plan to the congress, he found that others had come with similar schemes. The delegates voted unanimously in favor of a colonial union and appointed a committee composed of one member from each state to consider the various plans. The committee chose to proceed with Franklin's. The original plan called for a Crown-appointed governor-general, who was to be a military man with veto power over the acts of a grand council. The grand council was to consist of one member from each of the smaller colonies, and two or more from the larger ones, apportioned according to the amount of money they paid into a general treasury. The congress was to meet each year in the capitals of the various colonies. Taxes on liquor, licenses for public houses, and taxes on "superfluities" like tea would fund the congress's needs, allowing each colony to pay according to its own wealth. The governor-general and the grand council were to have responsibility for Indian treaties, purchases of Indian land that fell outside of proprietary grants, establishment of new settlements, raising of troops, building of forts, protection of trade, and the equipping of ships to protect the coasts from privateers in wartime.

After some amendments and lengthy debate, the Albany Congress voted unanimously to adopt Franklin's plan. In the amended plan, the governor-general was retitled to president-general and appointed and paid by the Crown. An act of Parliament would carry the scheme into execution to prevent colonies from pulling out of the union at random. The number of representatives from each colony ranged from two from New Hampshire and Rhode Island to seven from Massachusetts and Virginia, and they were to be reapportioned every three years. The grand council was to meet once every year, and more often than that if necessary. The president-general could call the council in an emergency with the consent of seven members. Among the duties of the proposed colonial government were the negotiation of Indian treaties, jurisdiction over purchases of Indian lands that fell outside of colonial boundaries as well as over new settlements

on those lands, and the raising of troops and equipping of fleets for the defense of the colonies.

However, the plan was universally rejected once it left the Albany Congress. Colonial assemblies feared a loss of sovereignty to an intercolonial government, and England chose another approach. Colonial governors and their councils were to meet and organize the military. The funds were to come from England, and Parliament would levy a tax on the colonists after the war to repay the money. The governor of Pennsylvania liked the Albany plan, but one of Franklin's political enemies in the Assembly scheduled its consideration for a day on which he was to be absent.

In December 1754 Franklin corresponded with Governor William Shirley of Massachusetts about the two plans. He adamantly opposed the taxation of the colonies by Parliament—an issue that would contribute to the American Revolution more than 20 years later. Franklin advised Shirley that Parliament's taxing Americans without their consent would prove to be bad policy: "where heavy burthens have been laid on them, it has been found useful to make it, as much as possible, their own act. . . ." Laying taxes on the colonists without their consent, Franklin argued, was like "treating them as a conquered people and not as true British subjects." Franklin liked Shirley's suggestion of introducing American representatives into Parliament. In 1774 John Adams included portions of Franklin's responses to Shirley in his "History of the Dispute with America."

"I am still of the opinion it would have been happy for both sides [of] the water if [the Albany Plan] had been adopted," Franklin wrote many years later in his *Autobiography*. "The colonies, so united, would have been sufficiently strong to have defended themselves; there would then have been no need of troops from England; of course, the subsequent pretense for taxing America, and the bloody contest it occasioned, would have been avoided."

Related entries:
    Articles of Confederation
    Colden, Cadwallader
    French and Indian War
    Native Americans

Suggestions for further reading:
    Masur, Louis P., ed. 1993. *The Autobiography of Benjamin Franklin.* Boston: Bedford Books of St. Martin's Press.
    "Papers Relating to a Plan of Union of the Colonies, Adopted by the Commissioners Assembled at Albany in July, 1754" (Smyth, vol. III).
    "Three Letters to Governor Shirley," 1754–1755 (Smyth, vol. III).

American Philosophical Society

*I*n May 1743, while living in Philadelphia, Franklin drew up "A Proposal for Promoting Useful Knowledge among the British Plantations in America," which established the initial framework for the formation of the American Philosophical Society. He believed there was a need for those in the colonies who had useful and advantageous insights to have a means of communicating them. The distance separating people in the colonies made it difficult for them to share ideas, and Franklin wanted to create a means for "virtuosi or ingenious men" to get together for discussion or to share their thinking by correspondence. Any useful insights they had could be pursued further and might lead to discoveries that would benefit the British colonies or "mankind in general."

Franklin sought to bring together men of science for this purpose. This idea was not new to him—in 1727, he had formed the Junto, a local group smaller and more political in scope than he envisioned for the American Philosophical Society. He circulated his proposal for a new group among friends with whom he corresponded about scientific subjects. Philadelphia was to serve as the center, and ten members were always to reside there. The ten should be composed of a president, treasurer, secretary, and seven

others who represented specific branches of study. Only the "chemist" category was not represented in the list of the society's original members that Franklin sent to Cadwallader Colden in 1744. They were: John Bartram, a botanist; Dr. Thomas Bond, a medical doctor; Thomas Godfrey, a mathematician; William Parsons, a geographer; Samuel Rhodes, a mechanician (a specialist in mechanical design); Dr. Phineas Bond, a natural philosopher; William Coleman, treasurer; Thomas Hopkinson, president; and Franklin, who served as secretary. Members from the other colonies were soon added.

Franklin envisioned improvements in agriculture, horticulture, mechanical inventions, mining, brewing, mapping, mathematics, manufacturing, animal breeding, and "all philosophical experiments that let light into the nature of things, tend to increase the power of man over matter, and multiply the conveniences or pleasures of life." The society was also to keep contact with others in Europe, such as the Royal Society of London.

The society did not take off right away. In 1745 Franklin complained, "The members of our Society here are very idle gentlemen. They will take no pains." In 1768 the original American Philosophical Society merged with the American Society but kept its name. Franklin was elected the first president of the new institution in 1769, while he was in England. From across the ocean, he sent books, papers, pamphlets, and other items of interest that people donated to the society. Franklin also sent *Memoirs* and *Philosophical Transactions* from prestigious European academies and societies. In 1774 the Comte de Buffon donated a preliminary copy of his *Natural History of Birds.*

The society had continued to elect Franklin president during his long absence in Europe and welcomed him back to Philadelphia with an address in 1785. "Sir," the address said, "it reflects honor on philosophy, when one, distinguished by his deep investigations, and many valuable improvements in it, is known to be equally distinguished for his philanthropy, patriotism, and liberal attachment to the rights of human nature."

Many of Franklin's papers were read at the society before and after his return. "On the Theory of the Earth" was read in 1782. A paper entitled "Loose Thoughts on a Universal Fluid," which Franklin wrote in 1784 in France, was read before the Society in 1788. His "Description of a New Stove for Burning of Pitcoal, and Consuming All Its Smoke," which he wrote on his return voyage from France in 1785, was read in 1786. In contrast to the many doctors in the society, he had little formal education, but he was by far its most famous and influential member in his lifetime. He also succeeded in getting many of his European friends elected to the society. The physicist Jean-Baptiste Le Roy was elected in 1773, Dr. Jacques Barbeu-Dubourg in 1775, and Dr. Jan Ingenhousz in 1786.

For most of Franklin's life, the society had no permanent home and met at various locations. After Franklin's return to Philadelphia in 1785, it met in his home, to which he had added a large meeting room. In 1789 the society finally built a permanent home, in part with the help of Franklin's funds.

The American Philosophical Society became a prestigious institution and still exists today. Among its many members have been Albert Einstein, John James Audubon, Thomas Jefferson (who served as its third president), and Charles Darwin. It now holds a large number of Franklin's original writings.

Related entries:
Barbeu-Dubourg, Dr. Jacques
Bartram, John
Colden, Cadwallader
Collinson, Peter
French Academy of Sciences
Hopkinson, Thomas and Francis
Ingenhousz, Dr. Jan
The Junto
Pringle, Sir John
Royal Society of London
Rush, Dr. Benjamin

Suggestions for further reading:
"Address of the American Philosophical Society," 1785 (Smyth, vol. X).
"A Proposal for Promoting Useful Knowledge," 1743 (Labaree et al., vol. 2).
"To Cadwallader Colden," April 5, 1744 (Labaree et al., vol. 2).

Armonica

Franklin loved music and played several instruments himself, including the violin, the harp, and the guitar. He recalled in his *Autobiography* sitting and listening to his father sing and play psalm tunes as a child.

The most detailed description of Franklin's musical invention, the armonica, is found in a letter to Giambatista Beccaria, an Italian scientist who had publicized Franklin's work in electricity in his country, dated July 13, 1762. Franklin told him that his armonica was well suited for Italian music and sent him instructions on how to construct it.

The concept of the armonica was based on the tones obtained by running a wet finger around the rim of a glass. Franklin told Beccaria that Richard Puckeridge, of Ireland, first put a number of these glasses together on one table and "tuned" them by filling them with various amounts of water. Puckeridge died in a fire, and his instrument was also destroyed, but a member of the Royal Society of London constructed another, improved version.

Franklin had not heard Puckeridge's original instrument, but he was pleased with the later model. "Being charmed with the sweetness of its tones," he wrote, "and the music he produced from it, I wished only to see the glasses disposed in a more convenient form, and brought together in a narrower compass, so as to admit of a greater number of tones, and all within reach of hand to a person sitting before the instrument. . . ." Franklin began experimenting, and he came up with his final product in 1761 or 1762.

The glasses on his armonica ranged from three to nine inches in diameter, were shaped as hemispheres, and were of varying thicknesses. There were 23 sizes and 37 total glasses, each having an open neck. Thirty-seven

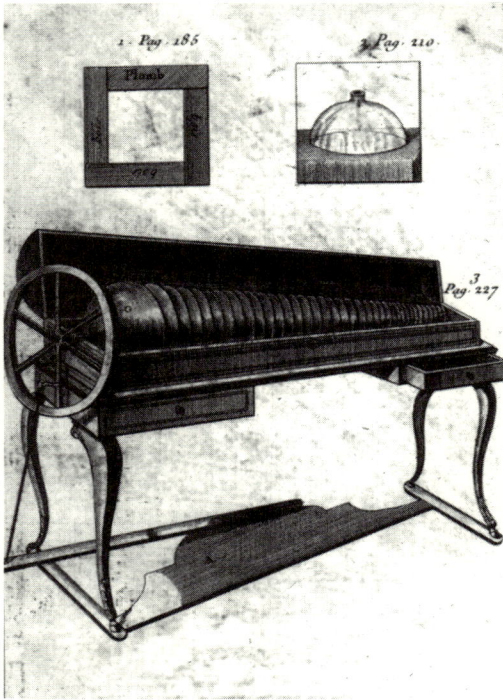

Armonica designed by Benjamin Franklin, 1762.
Engraving by Martinet in **Oeuvres de M.**
Franklin, *1773, plate 7.*

glasses, Franklin said, were enough to cover three octaves. They were arranged in the instrument so that the glasses ran from largest to smallest.

Each glass should be chosen for a particular note and tuned by grinding it down from the neck toward the brim and testing the glass against the corresponding note on a tuned harpsichord. This was a one-time chore; glasses would never have to be tuned again. Once all of the glasses were tuned, they were to be affixed onto an iron spindle in a case about three feet in length and 3 to 11 inches in width. The spindle tapered in diameter from 1 inch to 1/4 inch. It ran horizontally down the case and turned on brass pins at both ends. The largest end of the instrument was to be toward the left hand, and the smallest toward the right. An 18-inch wheel fixed on a square shank served to even the motion when the spindle was turned. The largest glass sounded a low G, and the smallest sounded a high G, spanning three octaves. The glass for

each note was to be painted a different color, and semitones were white.

Franklin described how each glass was affixed to the spindle: "[E]very glass when fixed shows about an inch of its brim, (or three quarters of an inch, or half an inch, as they grow smaller) beyond the brim of the glass that contains it; and it is from these exposed parts of each glass that the tone is drawn, by laying a finger upon one of them as the spindle and glasses turn round."

The instrument was to be played by turning the glasses with one's foot and placing the fingers on them as they turned. They needed to be wetted every once in awhile; the players' fingers should be soaked in water before playing and perhaps dusted with a small amount of chalk. The glasses should rotate away from the player's fingers.

Franklin was very pleased with his armonica and liked its sweet tones, which could be amplified or diminished with varying amounts of finger pressure. His instrument, which he did not patent, became popular in Europe for a short time, and the famous composers Mozart and Beethoven wrote music for it. The first performances on the armonica were given by Marianne Davies in 1762. It was first introduced in America in 1764, and Franklin taught some of his acquaintances how to play it.

Related entries:
Brillon de Jouy, Anne-Louise Boivin d'Hardancourt
Franklin, Peter
Kames, Lord (Henry Home)

Suggestions for further reading:
"Directions for Drawing Out the Tone from the Glass Armonica," 1779 (Labaree et al., vol. 31).
"To Giambatista Beccaria," July 13, 1762 (Labaree et al., vol. 10).

The Art of Virtue

Virtue was a subject with which Franklin concerned himself for most of his life. He never finished the book he had long intended to write called *The Art of Virtue*. His intention for the book, he explained to Lord Kames in 1760, was "to explain and enforce this doctrine, that vicious actions are not hurtful because they are forbidden, but forbidden because they are hurtful, the nature of man alone considered; that it was, therefore, everyone's interest to be virtuous who wished to be happy even in this world...." It was Franklin's belief that many people wanted to be virtuous, but they did not know how to effect the necessary changes in their lives to behave virtuously. He therefore proposed to write a book explaining in detail how to acquire missing virtues and retain those that people already had—a process that was an art.

His plan to write the book was conceived in 1732, around the time he decided to try to attain moral perfection for himself. At first he thought it would be easy to identify proper modes of behavior and to adhere to them, but he soon found himself falling short. On the basis of his reading at the library, he made a list of virtues, each with a brief description. The virtues were not "without religion," but they were presented in such a way that they would not offend any sect. There were originally 12 virtues on his list: temperance, silence, order, resolution, frugality, industry, sincerity, justice, moderation, cleanliness, tranquillity, and chastity. On the suggestion of a friend, who told Franklin that he was generally considered insolent and prideful when he expressed his opinions, he added humility as a thirteenth.

Mastering one virtue became the object of each week. He began to grade himself on his performance of each virtue every day, placing a black spot next to each area in which he believed he fell short. After finishing 13 weeks, each step building on the others, he would start over again. The 52 weeks in one year would allow four courses of this cycle. To help himself achieve order, he made a daily schedule.

Franklin described how he conquered pride in pursuit of humility—at least its outward appearance. Instead of using words that implied a firm opinion, such as "certainly" and "undoubtedly," he began to temper his opinions with softer phrases like "I imagine" or "I conceive." Franklin found that the new appearance of modesty eased his conversation and rendered his opinions more acceptable to his fellows. Pride, he believed, was the most difficult vice to contain: "[E]ven if I could conceive that I had completely overcome it, I should probably be proud of my humility."

Also spurred by Franklin's experiment with his own behavior was his plan for establishing a "united party for virtue," which would include people who adhered to the 13 virtues and believed in a creed he had written. The creed expressed belief in the immortality of the soul and one universal God who created all things, rewards virtue, punishes vice, and requires worship. The party was to be called "The Society of the Free and Easy" and kept secret until it became widespread. Members were to strive to be free of vice and debt. The scheme, however, never materialized.

Though he had intended from 1733 almost until his death to write *The Art of Virtue,* he never did. He wrote to Lord Kames about his intention to finish it in 1760 and 1761, and his friend Benjamin Vaughan encouraged him to finish the work in 1783. With respect to his success in his strivings to become virtuous in his life, he wrote, "In truth, I found myself incorrigible with respect to order; and now I am grown old, and my memory bad, I feel very sensibly the want of it. But, on the whole, though I never arrived at the perfection I had been so ambitious of obtaining, but fell far short of it, yet I was, by the endeavor, a better and a happier man than I otherwise should have been if I had not attempted it...."

Related entries:
    Kames, Lord (Henry Home)
    Religious Beliefs
    Vaughan, Benjamin

Suggestions for further reading:
Masur, Louis P., ed. 1993. *The Autobiography of Benjamin Franklin*. Boston: Bedford Books of St. Martin's Press.
Rogers, George L., ed. 1986. *Benjamin Franklin's The Art of Virtue: His Formula for Successful Living*. Eden Prairie, MN: Acorn Publishing.
"To Lord Kames," May 3, 1760 (Labaree et al., vol. 9).

Articles of Confederation

After the Declaration of Independence was written and signed in 1776, the colonies had already fixed their revolutionary course of action in response to the injustices they believed they suffered at the hands of the British. A plan of government for the colonies was also needed.

Even before then, the subject of uniting the colonies had been a pressing issue. Franklin had already expended some effort trying to unite the colonies under a plan of union around the time of the French and Indian War (1754). He believed the colonies should have some form of governmental unity so that they could effectively defend themselves from external threats. He drew up a scheme for union in 1754, which the Albany Congress adopted but colonial assemblies and England never accepted. In 1754 the French and the Indians threatened the colonies; now the British threatened them.

In 1775 Franklin read his "Proposed Articles of Confederation" to the Committee of the Whole of Second Continental Congress. Under his plan the colonies would be bound in "a firm league of friendship with each other"; the aims of the league were to provide common defense, to preserve security of liberty and property, to ensure the safety of people, and to provide for general welfare.

Franklin's plan would have established a Congress with limited powers to regulate matters between the colonies, such as interstate commerce and money, and to handle negotiations with foreign countries. It also would have forbidden any individual colony from starting wars with or entering into agreements with Indians without the Congress's approval. However, individual colonies would still retain their own constitutions and almost exclusive authority for making their own laws. Other colonies would also be allowed to apply to join the new union: the Floridas, St. John's, Quebec, the West India Islands, the Bermudas, and Ireland. The articles were to be binding unless the British remedied some of the colonies' grievances, including the burning of Charlestown and the presence of British troops in America.

Although the colonies were highly dissatisfied with British rule, they were generally reluctant to establish a strong central government in America, and that sentiment was reflected in Franklin's draft. Most members of Congress were not yet ready to fix themselves on a course of independence. Congress did not adopt his plan, but it considered new articles the following year that bore some similarity to Franklin's.

In June 1776 a committee appointed by Congress came up with a first draft of the Articles. A final version passed in November 1777, but it was not ratified by all of the states until 1781. The Articles of Confederation became the governing document of the newly named United States of America that year, until 1789 when enough states had adopted the current Constitution.

The final version of the Articles was similar to Franklin's proposal in some ways. Franklin had proposed "The United Colonies of North America" as a name for the union; the new document called the country "The United States of America." The concept of a "league of friendship" between the colonies was retained, as was the heavy emphasis on states' rights. The Articles were more detailed than Franklin's, however. They explicitly reserved "sovereignty, freedom, and independence, and every power, jurisdiction, and right, which is not by this Confederation expressly delegated to the United States" for the individual states.

Delegates to the Congress were appointed by state legislatures in whatever ways the individual legislature saw fit. States could not enter into alliances with other countries without the consent of Congress, and Congress was to settle boundary disputes between states. However, the Articles placed restrictions on congressional authority. Congress could not enter into a war, determine the value of money, appropriate money, or appoint a commander in chief without the approval of nine states. While Franklin's articles would have allowed any of several British colonies into the union upon application, the invitation was extended only to Canada in the Articles of Confederation.

The Articles were short-lived, and a new Constitution replaced them in 1789.

Related entries:
Albany Plan of Union
Constitutional Convention
Continental Congresses
Declaration of Independence
Revolutionary War

Suggestions for further reading:
"Proposed Articles of Confederation," July 1775 (Labaree et al., vol. 22).

Astronomy

Although astronomy was not Franklin's chief area of study in the sciences, he maintained a scholarly interest in the heavens throughout his life and corresponded with some of his era's leading astronomers. Franklin's curiosity about the skies was evident from a young age. On his voyage from London to Philadelphia in 1726 he kept a journal in which he described a partial solar eclipse on September 14, in which "at least ten parts of twelve of [the sun] were hid from our eyes," and a partial lunar eclipse

on September 30: "It began with us about eleven last night, and continued till near two this morning, darkening her body about six digits, or one half; the middle of it being about half an hour after twelve, by which we may discover that we are in a meridian of about four hours and a half from London, or 67 1/2 degrees of longitude, and consequently have not much above one hundred leagues to run."

Franklin told James Bowdoin in 1753, "[T]he improvement of geography and astronomy is the common concern of all polite nations. . . ." Having received some letters about an upcoming transit of the planet Mercury across the Sun, Franklin printed 50 copies of them as "Letters Relating to a Transit of Mercury over the Sun, Which Is to Happen May 6th, 1753" and distributed them among his friends in America. He planned to observe the event with a three-foot reflecting telescope.

Franklin kept his scientific friends in America, England, and France up-to-date on astronomical events, and he often transmitted information between them. In 1767 he reported to John Canton at the Royal Society that a comet with a long tail had been visible in France; he thought it to be in the constellation of Taurus and on its way toward the Sun. He sent John Winthrop in America a telescope from London in 1769. It had been delayed by the increased demand for instruments needed to view an upcoming transit of Venus. Franklin also told Winthrop that Nevil Maskelyne, royal astronomer in England, wished that an experienced American astronomer would observe the transit at Lake Superior. His friends in the colonies sent their accounts of astronomical events to him in England, some of which were read at the Royal Society. Cadwallader Evans and Winthrop sent accounts of planetary transits, as did the Reverend John Ewing (1732–1802).

Although Franklin's chief area of scientific expertise was electricity, he read new papers on astronomy with interest. In 1773 he and Humphry Marshall exchanged letters about prevailing theories on sunspots. Franklin related to Marshall a new theory put forth by Dr. Alexander Wilson (1714–1786). Wilson asserted that the Sun was a solid ball of combustible material, but that only the surface burned. He supposed that sunspots might be caused when an explosion causes the burning parts to be blown away from a particular area, and the part thereby uncovered, which was not yet on fire, appeared as a spot. (Scientists still have much to learn about sunspots, but they now believe that they are cool regions on the Sun affected by the Sun's magnetic field.) Scientists in Franklin's time were just beginning to connect sunspots with the aurora borealis, or northern lights, another subject in which he took great interest.

The astronomer William Herschel, who was German-born but lived in England, was elected to the Royal Society (of which Franklin was also a member) in 1781. Herschel discovered the planet Uranus that same year and named it "Georgium Sidus" after George III. After the discovery of the planet, he also located two of its moons. In 1787 he sent a catalog of 1,000 new nebulae he had discovered to Franklin, who shared it with the American Philosophical Society. Franklin wrote to him that year to thank him for the gift and congratulate him on the discovery of the moons: "You have wonderfully extended the power of human vision, and are daily making us acquainted with the regions of the universe totally unknown to mankind in former ages."

Related entries:
Aurora Borealis
Electricity
French Academy of Sciences
Navigation
Royal Society of London

Suggestions for further reading:
"To James Bowdoin," February 28, 1753 (Labaree et al., vol. 4).
"To Nevil Maskelyne," February 12, 1770 (Labaree et al., vol. 17).
"To William Herschel," May 18, 1787 (Smyth, vol. IX).

Aurora Borealis

*T*he aurora borealis, or northern lights, are moving, multicolored lights that appear in the northern polar regions of the Earth. Modern scientists believe that they are caused when sunspots contribute high-energy atomic particles to the solar wind. These atomic particles enter the Earth's lower Van Allen radiation belt. The excess particles are discharged into the atmosphere around the Earth's north and south magnetic polar regions. When the particles collide with gas molecules, the molecules release electromagnetic radiation, causing the lights. The intensity of the northern lights is directly related to the 11-year sunspot cycle.

The phenomenon of the northern lights interested Franklin for many years, although he never offered more than "suppositions" and "conjectures" on the subject. His thoughts on the aurora borealis have now been discredited, but they were eagerly listened to by other scientists of his time. His contemporaries were only beginning to discern the connection between sunspots and the northern lights.

Franklin's conjectures on thunder-gusts, sent to Peter Collinson in 1749, contained a short consideration of the aurora borealis. When a canal filled with water is opened on one end, he said, the motion of the water starts at that end. Even though the water moves from the close end toward the open end, motion begins at the open end, and "so the electrical fire discharged into the polar regions, perhaps from a thousand leagues length of vaporized air, appears first where 'tis first in motion, i.e., in the most northern part, and the appearance proceeds southward, though the fire really moves northward. This is supposed to account for the aurora borealis."

In 1752 he wrote to Cadwallader Colden that he supposed there could be a region of fire, as the ancients thought, above the Earth's atmosphere. Some of this region could reach low enough to electrify the highest clouds in the Earth's atmosphere. Or, he thought, the aurora borealis could be currents of the fluid in the region of fire that could be seen when they moved. "There is no end to conjectures," he said.

Franklin wrote to Jean–Baptiste Le Roy in 1772 expressing his support for an upcoming French expedition to the North Pole. "I hope your philosophers on that voyage will be able to discover more clearly the cause of the aurora borealis, and a passage round the north of America," he said. While he was in the middle of procuring foreign aid for the American army during the Revolutionary War, Franklin authored a paper on the northern lights entitled "Aurora Borealis: Suppositions and Conjectures towards Forming an Hypothesis for Its Explanation."

His argument in the paper was as follows: air that has been heated becomes rarefied and specifically lighter than other air. Heated air rises, and the surrounding cooler air takes its place. Air above a certain height is so rare that it is almost a vacuum. Air heated between the Earth's tropics rises continuously, and northerly and southerly winds from cooler regions blow cooler air in. The lighter, hotter air floats above the cooler air, moving northward and southward and descending between the two poles to take the place of the cooler air that has moved toward the tropics. In this manner, the air in the Earth's atmosphere continues to circulate. Moisture rising from the tropics forms clouds that are charged with electricity. The electricity is normally absorbed by the Earth when it is released through rain, snow, hail, and lightning. However, as ice is a poor conductor and ice covers the polar regions, the Earth cannot absorb the electricity. The thin atmosphere of the Earth, almost a vacuum, is much closer to the ground at the poles than in other regions. As a vacuum is a good conductor, electricity accumulated on the ice runs through the atmosphere above, producing the lights.

This paper, the most detailed explanation of the northern lights that Franklin offered, was read before the French Academy of Sciences in Paris in 1778.

Related entries:
   Astronomy
   Electricity
   French Academy of Sciences
   Meteorology

Suggestions for further reading:
   "Suppositions and Conjectures on the Aurora Borealis," 1778 (Labaree et al., vol. 19).
   "To Jean–Baptiste LeRoy," April 20, 1772 (Smyth, vol. V).

Autobiography

Although Franklin was a prolific writer of letters, pamphlets, essays, papers, and journals, the only book he ever began to write was his *Autobiography*. He started the project between July 30 and August 13, 1771, at the country home at Twyford, England, of his friend Jonathan Shipley, the bishop of St. Asaph. It was originally addressed to his only surviving son, William, and began:

> Dear Son: I have ever had pleasure in obtaining any little anecdotes of my ancestors. You may remember the inquiries I made among the remains of my relations when you were with me in England, and the journey I undertook for that purpose. Imagining it may be equally agreeable to you to know the circumstances of my life, many of which you are yet unacquainted with, and expecting the enjoyment of a week's uninterrupted leisure in my present country retirement, I sit down to write them for you.

Franklin also thought that his descendants might like to know the means by which he raised himself from poverty to success. The first portion of the work was written for the benefit of his posterity, but after receiving encouraging letters from friends, he broadened the focus for the rest of the narrative. He believed that the events of his life and the courses of action he took led to success, for the most part, and might benefit and instruct others. Many years later, he told Benjamin Vaughan that he planned to omit "facts and transactions" that would not be of benefit to a young reader.

The portion of the *Autobiography* that he finished was written in four parts—the first at the Shipleys' home in 1771, the second in France in 1784 and 1785, the third in Philadelphia in 1788, and the fourth in Philadelphia in 1789 and 1790. During the last years of his life, Franklin frequently promised impatient friends in three countries that he would keep writing—particularly Louis-Guillaume Le Veillard, Abel James, Benjamin Vaughan, and the Shipleys. What he completed of the *Autobiography* recounts his life through 1757, the year that he traveled to England, when his political career in Europe began. The straightforward and optimistic narrative was one of the first prominent pieces of American literature. It includes accounts of his childhood, efforts at self-improvement, marriage, printing career, philosophical endeavors, and political activity. Franklin's *Autobiography* has remained a popular piece of early American literature and is still widely read today.

The part of the manuscript he had completed at the Shipleys' went with him to Philadelphia in 1775 but remained in an ill-fated trunk of papers that Franklin left with Joseph Galloway before he went to France in 1776. The trunk was plundered in the midst of the turmoil surrounding the Revolution. A copy of the first portion of the manuscript fell into the hands of his friend Abel James, who wrote to him in France and encouraged him to continue it. Benjamin Vaughan wrote to him in 1783, "Your history is so remarkable, that if you do not give it, somebody else will certainly give it; and perhaps so as nearly to do as much harm, as your own management of the thing might do good." He promised his friends he would

work on it during his voyage home to Philadelphia in 1785, but he wrote three scientific essays instead.

Franklin did not want accounts of his life to be published while he was still alive. Matthew Carey wrote to him in 1786 to ask for his permission to publish a history of his life in the *Columbian Magazine,* and for the portion of his *Autobiography* he had already written. Franklin responded with a request not to print it and did not send his autobiographical papers.

Despite the persistent urging of people like Vaughan and Le Veillard, Franklin never completed the *Autobiography;* political obligations and painful illness overrode his intentions. Before he died, he sent copies of the first three parts to friends in England and France. In the last few months of his life, he wrote a brief fourth part that never made it into the first editions of the book. Just before his death, he gave a partial copy of the manuscript to Thomas Jefferson—the only American who was not a relation known to have received any of the *Autobiography* before Franklin passed away.

After Franklin's death in 1790, the *Autobiography* was published in several incomplete editions and poor translations in Europe, including a version published by William Temple Franklin in 1818. All of these omitted the short fourth section that Franklin wrote in 1789 and 1790. The work was not published in its entirety until 1868, by John Bigelow.

Related entries:
    Collected Works
    France
    Franklin, William
    Franklin, William Temple
    Jefferson, Thomas
    Shipley, Jonathan
    Vaughan, Benjamin

Suggestions for further reading:
    "Franklin's Draft Scheme of the Autobiography" (Smyth, vol. I).
    Masur, Louis P., ed. 1993. *The Autobiography of Benjamin Franklin.* Boston: Bedford Books of St. Martin's Press.

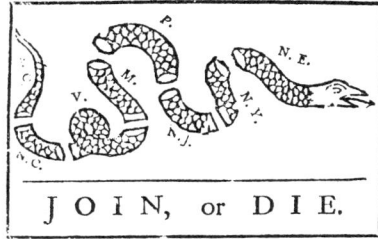

JOIN, or DIE.

Bache, Benjamin Franklin (1769–1798)

Benjamin Franklin Bache was the eldest child of Franklin's daughter, Sarah, and her husband, Richard Bache. He was born in Philadelphia while his grandfather was in England, and for the first six years of his life Franklin heard only accounts of him from Philadelphia. When Congress sent Franklin to France in 1776, he took seven-year-old Bache and his other grandson, William Temple Franklin, aged 17. He enrolled Bache in a boarding school, where, for a short time, young Benjamin attended with young John Quincy Adams.

"I have a great deal of pleasure in Ben," Franklin told his son-in-law in 1779. "He is a good, honest lad, and will make, I think, a valuable man." Franklin decided to send Bache to Geneva to study: "As I intend him for a Presbyterian as well as a republican, I have sent him to finish his education at Geneva. He is much grown, in very good health, draws a little . . . learns Latin, writing, arithmetic, and dancing, and speaks French better than English," Franklin wrote to his daughter. Samuel Cooper Johonnot, the grandson of his friend from Boston, Samuel Cooper, also attended school in Geneva. Franklin wrote to Bache occasionally from France, encouraging him to remain diligent in his studies.

After four years in Geneva, Bache returned to France, where Franklin had him instructed in printing. He thought about sending him to England under the care of his friend Mary Hewson, but that plan never materialized. "I have determined to give him to a trade that he may have something to depend on," Franklin wrote to his son-in-law in 1784, "and not be obliged to ask favors or offices of anybody." Bache had the best instructors— Philippe-Denis Pierres (1741–1808), who taught him typography, and François-Ambroise Didot (1730–1804) of the famous Didot printing family. In addition, Bache learned at Franklin's private printing press in Passy, outside of Paris.

Bache returned to the United States with his grandfather in 1785 and attended college, after which Franklin set him up in a printing house and let him manage it under his supervision. In 1789 Bache copied Franklin's *Autobiography* and sent it to Louis-Guillaume Le Veillard in France. Bache and his cousin Temple were present when their grandfather died. Franklin left him all of his printing materials, some of his books, and his share in the Library Company. Bache became the editor of the Anti-Federalist *Aurora and General Advertiser* in Philadelphia and was arrested for libel under the Adams administration. He died before his trial.

Related entries:
Bache, Richard

Bache, Sarah Franklin
France
Printing

Suggestions for further reading:
Fay, Bernard. 1933. *Bernard Fay's The Two Franklins: Fathers of American Democracy.* Boston: Little, Brown.
Smith, Jeffery Alan. 1990. *Franklin and Bache: Envisioning the Enlightened Republic.* New York: Oxford University Press.
Tagg, James. 1991. *Benjamin Franklin Bache and the "Philadelphia Aurora."* Philadelphia: University of Pennsylvania Press.
"To Benjamin Franklin Bache," August 19, 1779 (Labaree et al., vol. 30).
"To Benjamin Franklin Bache," January 25, 1782 (Smyth, vol. VIII).

Bache, Richard (1737–1811)

Richard Bache, born in Yorkshire, moved to Philadelphia from New York and married Franklin's daughter, Sarah (Sally), in 1767. Franklin had been in England since 1764, and, not anticipating his return to Philadelphia anytime soon, he left the marriage in the hands of his wife. "I know very little of the gentlemen or his character, nor can I at a distance," he wrote to her in June 1767. "I hope his expectations are not great of any fortune to be had with our daughter before our death. I can only say, that if he proves a good husband to her, and a good son to me, he shall find me as good a father as I can be."

Four years after Bache and Sarah wed, Bache traveled to England, where he visited relatives and sought Franklin's assistance in obtaining a political post. Franklin, who had until this time known little more of him than his wife's approving words and his son's suspicions, liked Richard and found his relatives pleasant and agreeable. As to his business, he advised Richard to keep the £1,000 he had brought with him and set up a store in Philadelphia. After the visit, Franklin explained to his daughter, "I am of the opinion, that almost any profession a man has been educated in, is preferable to an office held at pleasure, as rendering more independent,

more a freeman, and less subject to the caprices of superiors." He told Deborah that Richard could set up a store in a room in their house and gave him £200 sterling. Franklin also thought it best for Sally to stay with her mother.

When Franklin returned to Philadelphia in 1775, he lived with the Baches. Bache, serving in the post of controller, helped him restructure the post office that replaced the unpopular royal post office. Bache continued in the post office when Franklin was dispatched to France in 1776. Franklin took the Baches' eldest son, Benjamin, to France with him, sent him to school in Geneva, and had him instructed in printing. He told Bache in 1781 that one foreign education was enough for his sons and had him send the next, William, to school in America at his expense. Franklin wanted William to learn French, mathematics, and acquire "a perfect knowledge of accounts."

After Franklin returned once again to Philadelphia in 1785, he lived the rest of his life with his daughter and son-in-law. Bache served as a director of the Bank of North America, which obtained a restoration of its charter under Franklin's presidency of the Supreme Executive Council of Pennsylvania. Upon Franklin's death, the Baches received a large portion of his Philadelphia property. Franklin bequeathed his land in the Ohio region to Richard and canceled a bond of £2,172 and five shillings. Franklin had only one request in return—that Richard free his slave, Bob, upon his death. The Baches had seven children: Benjamin, William, Betsy, Louis, Deborah, Richard, and Sarah.

Related entries:
Bache, Benjamin Franklin
Bache, Sarah Franklin
Franklin, Deborah Read Rogers
Post Office

Suggestions for further reading:
"To Richard Bache," June 2, 1779 (Labaree et al., vol. 29).
"To Richard Bache," September 13, 1781 (Smyth, vol. VIII).

Bache, Sarah Franklin
(1743–1808)

Franklin's only daughter, Sarah (Sally), was born in 1743 and baptized in the Christ Church in Philadelphia. At age seven, she was, Franklin thought, "a fine girl, and is extremely industrious with her needle, and delights in her book. She is of a most affectionate temper, and perfectly dutiful and obliging to her parents, and to all."

When the Pennsylvania Assembly sent Franklin to England in 1757, and again in 1764, Sally stayed in Philadelphia with her mother, who refused to cross the ocean. Franklin sent her clothing and books from England and encouraged his wife to attend to her education. Franklin and his wife had Sally studying French and music. In 1758 Franklin expressed concern about her poor spelling. "I hope she continues to love going to church," Franklin told his wife, "and would have her read over and over again the *Whole Duty of Man,* and the *Lady's Library.*"

Before he left for England in 1764, Franklin wrote to Sally from New York and encouraged her to attend church faithfully, as he had many political enemies who would watch for missteps in her behavior. "The acts of devotion in the common prayer book," he told her, "are your principal business there; and if properly attended to, will do more towards mending the heart than sermons generally can do. For they were composed by men of much greater piety and wisdom, than our common composers of sermons generally can do." Franklin advised her to study her arithmetic and bookkeeping.

Franklin and his friend William Strahan joked for years about arranging a marriage between Sally and the Strahans' son. Around 1760 Strahan offered a serious proposal, but Deborah Franklin refused to let her daughter move to England, or to move there herself. Sally married Richard Bache seven years later, during another period when Franklin lived in England. Franklin, who did not meet

Sarah Bache, daughter of Benjamin Franklin. Engraving.

Bache until four years later, hoped he was not after money and instructed his wife to fit Sally out with no more than £500 worth of clothes and furniture. Franklin met his son-in-law in 1771 when Bache visited his relatives in England, and he was pleased with the entire Bache family.

Franklin lived in Philadelphia with his daughter and son-in-law in 1775 and 1776, until he sailed for France as an American commissioner. Bache helped Franklin reorganize the colonial post office in 1775 and served as controller. The war made it difficult for Franklin and his daughter to correspond, and few of their letters got through. The Baches removed to the country when the British occupied Philadelphia in 1777 and 1778, and when they returned, they found books, musical instruments, a portrait of Franklin, and some of Franklin's electrical instruments missing. Franklin, who repeatedly complained about the needless consumption of superfluities in America during the war, wrote a response to two of Sally's letters in 1779: "I was charmed with the account you gave me of your industry, the table-cloths of your own spinning . . . but the latter part of the paragraph, that you had sent for linen from France, because weaving and flax are grown dear, alas, that dissolved the charm; and your sending for long black pins, and lace, and feathers! disgusted me as much as if you had put salt into my strawberries." Franklin sent her the things she asked for that were "useful and necessary," but left out the other things she had requested. "If you wear your cambric ruffles as I do," Franklin told her, "and take care not to mend the holes, they will come in time to be lace; and feathers, my dear girl, may be had in America from every cock's tail." In 1784 Franklin sent his daughter a lengthy explanation of the absurdity of hereditary titles, as well as the reasons for his dislike of the bald eagle as the U.S. emblem.

When Franklin returned to Philadelphia in 1785 he lived with his daughter's family for the remainder of his life. Sally nursed him when he was ill, and her children delighted him. "I too," Franklin wrote in 1788 to Mather Byles, a Boston minister who credited Franklin's lightning rod with saving his and his daughters' lives, "have a daughter who lives with me and is the comfort of my declining years, while my son is estranged from me by the part he took in the late war, and keeps aloof, residing in England, whose cause he espoused; whereby the old proverb is exemplified; 'My son is my son till he take him a wife; But my daughter's my daughter all the days of her life.'"

Franklin left the majority of his estate to Mr. and Mrs. Bache. He made separate provisions for his daughter, explaining: "[M]y intention is, that the same shall be for her sole and separate use, notwithstanding her coverture, or whether she be covert or sole. . . . This provision for my daughter is not made out of any disrespect I have for her husband."

Related entries:
Bache, Benjamin Franklin
Bache, Richard
Franklin, Deborah Read Rogers
Last Will and Testament
Society of the Cincinnati
United States Seal and Emblem

Suggestions for further reading:
"To Mrs. Sarah Bache," January 26, 1784 (Smyth, vol. IX).
"To Sarah Bache," June 3, 1779 (Labaree et al., vol. 29).
"To Sarah Franklin," November 8, 1764 (Labaree et al., vol. 11).

Bagatelles

Franklin wrote his "bagatelles" largely for the amusement of his friends in France. Mostly a collection of humorous anecdotes and satires (some written in English and some in French), some copies were printed on his own press in his home at Passy, near Paris. His first was "The Ephemera, an Emblem of Human Life" (1778), which he addressed to Madame Brillon. Franklin wrote it in honor of a day spent at Moulin Joli, where he observed the skeletons of "a kind of little fly, called an ephemera, whose successive generations, we were told, were bred and expired within the day." Franklin jokingly recorded the philosophical soliloquy of "an old gray-headed" fly, sitting by himself on a leaf. "What now avails all my toil and labor, in amassing honey-dew on this leaf, which I cannot live to enjoy! What the political struggles I have been engaged in, for the good of my compatriot inhabitants of this bush, or my philosophical studies for the benefit of our race in general!" the fly pondered. "Our present race of ephemerae will in a course of minutes become corrupt, like those of other and older bushes, and consequently as wretched. . . . "

To Madame Brillon Franklin also wrote "The Whistle" (1779). "In my opinion, we might all draw more good from [the world] than we do, and suffer less evil, if we would take care not to give too much for whistles," Franklin wrote. The whistle in question was one he said he had purchased as a boy of seven. He had given all of his money for the whistle, come home, and blown it around the house. When his family told him he had paid four times more for it than it was worth, Franklin grew upset, "and the reflection gave me more chagrin than the whistle gave me pleasure." Many people, Franklin thought, paid too much for their whistles: "As I grew up, came into the world, and observed the actions of men, I thought I met with many, very many, who gave too much for the whistle. . . . When I see a beautiful, sweet-tempered girl married to an ill-natured brute of a husband, What a pity, say I, that she should pay so much for a whistle!" People brought misery on themselves by "false estimates they have made on the value of things, and by their giving too much for their whistles."

To Madame Helvétius in 1778, Franklin wrote about an imaginary meeting with her late husband in the Elysian fields after her refusal of Franklin's marriage proposal (which may or may not have been a serious one). "Vexed by your barbarous resolution, announced so positively last evening, to remain single all your life in respect to your dear husband, I went home, fell on my bed, and believing myself dead, found myself in the Elysian fields," he began. There, Franklin met her late husband, who had taken another wife. If Franklin would wait around, he could see her; but in the meantime, he advised him that he might have engaged the help of the Abbé Morellet or the Abbé de La Roche to win his former wife's heart. Monsieur Helvétius's new wife turned out to be none other than Deborah Franklin, Franklin's wife, who had passed away in 1774. Franklin's "A Dialogue between Franklin and the Gout" (1780; *see* Medicine for a discussion of this bagatelle) was written with both Madame Helvétius and Madame Brillon in mind.

In "The Levée" and "Proposed New Version of the Bible," both written in 1779, in the midst of the American Revolution, Franklin played on the Book of Job to mock monarchy as a form of government. As Satan had appeared with the sons of God at his court, or levée, to accuse Job, so modern company assembled on levées to accuse their fellows before their princes. It was normal for a king to ask someone whom he had not seen at his court for a long time how he had spent his time since his last appearance. "Thus Satan being asked whence he cometh? answers, 'From going to and fro in the earth, and walking up and down in it.' And being further asked, whether he had considered the uprightness and fidelity of the prince's servant Job," Franklin continued, "he immediately displays all the malignance of the designing courtier, by answering with another question: 'Doth Job serve God for naught? Hast thou not given him immense wealth, and protected him in the possession of it? Deprive him of that, and he will curse thee to thy face.'" Satan's behavior, Franklin wrote, was comparable to, "In modern phrase, take away his places and his pensions, and your Majesty will soon find him in the opposition." The moral of the Book of Job, Franklin said, was not to trust a single person with the government of a state. If God himself would let Satan's accusations against Job go unanswered and ruin him for a time, the best of human princes, blinded by the devices of "artful, interested, and malicious courtiers," would inevitably do much worse.

Franklin continued this line of thought in his "Proposed New Version of the Bible," in which he jokingly suggested updating the Bible to modern language. He portrayed God as a king, and Satan as a member of his ministry, and he modified a few verses in the first chapter of Job as an example. Franklin changed verse 9 from "Then Satan answered the Lord, and said, Doth Job fear God for naught?" to "And Satan answered, Does your Majesty imagine that his good conduct is the effect of mere personal attachment and affection?"

To the Abbé de La Roche, Franklin sent a drinking song on happiness that he had written many years earlier. In this song the singer looks for happiness in love, riches, and power, until the chorus convinces the singer that happiness exists in friends and wine. It began:

Singer:
Fair Venus calls; her voice obey,

In beauty's arms spend night and day.
The joys of love all joys excel,
And loving's certainly doing well.
Chorus:
Oh! No!
Not so!
For honest souls know,
Friends and a bottle still bear the bell.

Franklin sent the Abbé Morellet a bagatelle arguing that wine was a divine gift, meant to be enjoyed by mankind. The piece was accompanied by drawings of animals bending their heads to the ground to drink the waters of the Earth, as their design required of them, and drawings of the human elbow, which Franklin asserted was exactly designed to accommodate the lifting of the wine glass to a person's mouth.

"The Morals of Chess" was composed in 1779 "to correct (among a few young friends) some little improprieties in the practice of it," and to show "that it may, in its effects on the mind, be not merely innocent, but advantageous, to the vanquished as well as the victor." Life itself was like a game of chess, and playing chess could sharpen qualities that a person needed in order to function well. A chess player needed to use "foresight, which looks a little into futurity, and considers the consequences that may attend an action"; "circumspection, which surveys the whole chessboard, or scene of action"; and "caution, not to make our moves too hastily." Chess, Franklin asserted, taught players not to be discouraged by present circumstances, as favorable changes could arise without warning.

The game should be played as agreeably as possible, Franklin continued, "and every action or word that is unfair, disrespectful, or that in any way may give uneasiness, should be avoided. . . . " To promote this harmonious atmosphere, Franklin offered a number of suggestions. First, if players agree strictly to follow the rules, then they must stick to them. Second, if they agree not to follow the rules, and "one party demands indulgences,

he should then be willing to allow them to the other." Third, players should make no false moves to gain an advantage over an opponent or to get themselves out of trouble. Fourth, a player should not hurry a slow opponent. Fifth, a player was not to disarm his opponent's carefulness by pretending to have made bad moves and lost the game. Sixth, a player should not boast after defeating his opponent. Seventh, spectators should remain silent: "If you have a mind to exercise or show your judgment, do it in playing your own game, when you have an opportunity, not in criticizing, or meddling with, or counseling the play of others." Finally, "If the game is not to be played rigorously, according to the rules above mentioned, then moderate your desire of victory over your adversary, and be pleased with one over yourself."

Franklin wrote "The Handsome and Deformed Leg" in 1780. "There are two sorts of people in the world," it began, "who with equal degrees of health, and wealth, and the other comforts in life, become, the one happy, and the other miserable." The latter sort always sour their company, offend others, and "make themselves everywhere disagreeable." Their behavior was not bestowed on them by nature, but acquired through imitation, and therefore curable. A philosopher-friend, Franklin wrote, had determined to avoid sour company and developed a test to measure dispositions. One of his legs was deformed, and the other handsome. "If a stranger, at the first interview, regarded his ugly leg more than his handsome one, he doubted him. If he spoke of it, and took no notice of the handsome leg, that was sufficient to determine my philosopher to have no further acquaintance with him."

"Apologue" was written sometime after the peace treaty concluded between the United States and England and was meant as an attack on demands for compensation by American loyalists. Franklin portrayed George III as "Lion," who through the support of his "faithful dogs" (American colonies) had expanded his dominions and "become the terror of his enemies." His evil counselors—tigers, leopards, and panthers—were turned loose on the dogs, and condemned them without hearing them. Some of the dogs (loyalists) "derived from a mixture with wolves and foxes, corrupted by royal promises of great rewards, deserted the honest dogs and joined their enemies." Now that the war was over, the corrupted dogs demanded the royal promises. "A council of beasts was held to consider their demand." Only the horse disagreed with the unanimous decision of the wolves and foxes that royal promises should be kept. In the end, "the council had sense enough to resolve—that the demand be rejected."

Although Franklin wrote most of the bagatelles for his friends in France, he penned "The Art of Procuring Pleasant Dreams" (1786) for Catherine Shipley, a daughter of his friend in England, Bishop Jonathan Shipley. For pleasant dreams, Franklin prescribed a physical regimen involving fresh air in one's bedroom, thin and porous bedclothes, exercise before meals, and temperance. "[I]ndolence, with full feeding, occasions nightmares and horrors inexpressible; we fall from precipices, are assaulted by wild beasts, murderers, and demons, and experience every variety of distress," Franklin said. Taking the proper steps to ensure good health would generally procure good dreams, but there were exceptions, for example, "when the person who desires to have pleasant dreams has not taken care to preserve, what is necessary above all things, a good conscience."

In "A Petition of the Left Hand, To Those Who Have the Superintendency of Education," Franklin humorously presented the unfortunate plight of the left hand in a society that taught people to use their right hands: "From my infancy," the left hand complained, "I have been led to consider my sister as being of a more elevated rank. I was suffered to grow up without the least instruction, while nothing was spared in her education. She had masters to teach her writing, drawing, music, and other accomplishments; but if by chance

I touched a pencil, a pen, or a needle, I was bitterly rebuked; and more than once I have been beaten for being awkward, and wanting a graceful manner."

Franklin's bagatelles, originally intended for the private amusement of his friends, were not published as a collection until 1818 in William Temple Franklin's volumes of Franklin's writings.

Related entries:
Brillon de Jouy, Anne-Louise Boivin d'Hardancourt
France
Helvétius, Anne-Catherine de Ligniville d'Autricourt
Printing
Shipley, Catherine and Georgiana (Hare-Naylor)

Suggestions for further reading:
"Apologue," 1783 (Smyth, vol. VIII).
"The Art of Procuring Pleasant Dreams," 1786 (Smyth, vol. X).
"The Handsome and Deformed Leg," 1780 (Smyth, vol. VIII).
"The Levée," 1779 (Smyth, vol. VII).
"The Morals of Chess," 1779 (Smyth, vol. VII).
"To Madame Brillon: The Ephemera," September 20, 1778 (Labaree et al., vol. 27).
"On Wine" (Lemay 1987).
"A Petition of the Left Hand" (Smyth, vol. X).
"Proposed New Version of the Bible," 1779 (Smyth, vol. VII).
"The Whistle," 1779 (Smyth, vol. VII).

Barbeu-Dubourg, Dr. Jacques (1709–1779)

Dr. Jacques Barbeu-Dubourg was a loyal friend and admirer of Franklin's and played an important part in publicizing his electrical experiments in France. Barbeu-Dubourg was a medical doctor and a member of several prestigious European academies—the Medical Society of London, the Academy of Sciences at Stockholm, the Royal Society of Montpellier, and the Royal Society of Medicine. In 1772 Barbeu-Dubourg began work on translating Franklin's "Experiments and Observations on

Electricity" from English to French. The translation appeared the following year with a complimentary preface written by Barbeu-Dubourg, and it did well in France. He translated and published some of Franklin's other writings as well.

Barbeu-Dubourg was interested in discussing almost anything Franklin cared to write about. They exchanged letters on the causes of colds, the treatment of smallpox, electricity, and magnetism. In response to Barbeu-Dubourg's description of a new smallpox treatment, Franklin told him about his daily habit of "bathing" in cold air: "With this view I rise almost every morning, and sit in my chamber without any clothes whatever, half an hour or an hour, according to the season, either reading or writing." Franklin believed that this practice contributed to his overall health.

Franklin answered Barbeu-Dubourg's inquiries on the musical instrument he invented, the armonica, and explained to him how to play it. In 1773 Barbeu-Dubourg asked Franklin if killing animals with electricity would make the meat more tender. Franklin, who had tried to kill a turkey by shocking it in 1750 and nearly electrocuted himself instead, recommended the practice less for its utility than for its humanity (the shock causes almost instant death). He warned Barbeu-Dubourg that "the operator must be very circumspect, lest he should happen to make the experiment on his own flesh, instead of that of the fowl."

Franklin also had a friend in Barbeu-Dubourg regarding the growing troubles between England and America in the 1770s. "I see with pleasure," Franklin wrote to him in 1770, "that we think pretty much alike on the subject of English America." He complained to Barbeu-Dubourg about Parliament's taxation of the colonies. After the war started, Barbeu-Dubourg suggested to the American Congress that it would be wise to send commissioners to France. Franklin, along with Arthur Lee and Silas Deane, were chosen as commissioners. When

Franklin arrived in France, Barbeu-Dubourg introduced him to the Comte de Vergennes, with whom he would work closely throughout the war and the subsequent peace negotiations.

Franklin had recommended Barbeu-Dubourg as a member of the American Philosophical Society to his friend Joseph Galloway in 1773, and Barbeu-Dubourg was elected in 1775. He died of a fever in 1779, after which Franklin published some of his writings at his press in Passy.

Related entries:
American Philosophical Society
Electricity
France
Medicine
Revolutionary War

Suggestions for further reading:
"To Jacques Barbeu-Dubourg," July 28, 1768 (Labaree et al., vol. 15).
"To Jacques Barbeu-Dubourg," March 10, 1773 (Labaree et al., vol. 20).
"To Jacques Barbeu-Dubourg," October 2, 1770 (Labaree et al., vol. 17).

Bartram, John (1699–1777)

The eminent American botanist John Bartram was a close friend of Franklin's for many years and an original member of the American Philosophical Society (as its botanist). He and Franklin shared correspondents in England and America—Peter Collinson, Dr. John Fothergill, Cadwallader Colden, and Jared Eliot. In addition, Bartram corresponded with the famed Swedish botanist Carolus Linnaeus (1707–1778) and other prominent European naturalists.

Bartram was a native of Pennsylvania, orphaned at age 13, and self-taught in botany and medicine. He traveled extensively through the American colonies and Canada identifying new plants and wildlife, making maps, and recording his observations. Franklin read his best-known work, *Observations on the Inhabitants, Climate, Soil, Rivers, Productions, and Other Matters Worthy of Notice, Made by John Bartram in His Travels from Pennsylvania to Onondaga, Oswego, and the Lake Ontario* (1751). Bartram established the first botanical garden (which still exists and is maintained by the city of Philadelphia) in America near Philadelphia.

Franklin consulted Bartram on questions relating to botany and animals, in which he was always interested. According to one account, Franklin found a basket that formerly held imported goods floating in a creek, and he noticed sprouts growing out of the basket. He planted some of the sprouts, which grew into yellow willow trees, the first in America. He took notes on a strange animal that had been killed in the garden of a Maryland inn where he stayed, and he relayed the description to Bartram. Bartram identified the animal Franklin had never seen as a groundhog. In 1755 Franklin sent Jared Eliot some "living letters" of Bartram's, among which were "at least twenty folio pages, large paper well-filled, on the subjects of botany, fossils, husbandry, and the first creation."

While Franklin lived in England, he sent Bartram seeds across the Atlantic. Among them were Chinese rhubarb seeds, used for medicinal purposes, the first to grow under cultivation in America. Franklin also sent oats, Swiss barley, "green dry peas, highly esteemed here as the best for making pea soup," Chinese beans that were used in making a cheese in China (with an account of how the cheese was made), rice, Chinese Tallow Tree, cabbage turnips (kohlrabi), and Scotch cabbage. The kohlrabi and Scotch cabbage were probably first introduced to America by Franklin and Bartram. Bartram sent American seeds to Collinson in England and in 1764 sent "a very curious collection of specimens of all the uncommonly valuable plants and trees of North America to the King." With assistance from Franklin and Collinson, Bartram was appointed American Botanist to King George III the following year.

In 1769 Franklin urged Bartram to "now decline your long and dangerous peregrinations in search of new plants, and remain safe and quiet at home, employing your leisure hours in a work that is much wanted, and which no one besides is so capable of performing; I mean the writing of a natural history of our country." During one of his trips, Bartram and his son, William, discovered a small fall-flowering tree native to Georgia and named it after Franklin—*Franklinia alatamaha*. The tree is now extinct in the wild and exists only in cultivation.

Related entries:
American Philosophical Society
Colden, Cadwallader
Collinson, Peter
Eliot, Jared
Fothergill, Dr. John

Suggestions for further reading:
Jenkins, Charles F. 1933. "The Historical Background of Franklin's Tree." *Pennsylvania Magazine of History and Biography*, vol. LVII, pp. 193–208.
"To John Bartram," August 22, 1772 (Labaree et al., vol. 19).
"To John Bartram," February 10, 1773 (Labaree et al., vol. 20).
"To John Bartram," January 9, 1769 (Labaree et al., vol 16).
"To John Bartram," January 11, 1770 (Labaree et al., vol. 17).
"To John Bartram," July 9, 1769 (Labaree et al., vol. 16).
"To John Bartram," July 17, 1771 (Labaree et al., vol. 18).

Bifocal Glasses

While he was living in France, Franklin invented bifocal glasses to solve his own vision problems. Though he did not do the work of cutting them himself, he came up with the concept of combining two different kinds of glass in one pair of spectacles. He had been carrying around two pairs of glasses, one for reading and the other for general vision. The constant changing of the glasses frustrated him, and he ordered a pair cut with half of each kind of glass in the same circle. The top half of the glass in each eye helped him to see distant objects, and the bottom half helped him see closer objects. He wrote to his friend George Whatley in 1785: "This I find more particularly convenient since my being in France, the glasses that serve me best at table to see what I eat, not being the best to see the faces of those on the other side of the table who speak to me; and when one's ears are not well accustomed to the sounds of a language, a sight of the movements in the features of him that speaks helps to explain; so that I understand French better by the help of my spectacles."

Related entry:
France

Suggestion for further reading:
"To George Whatley," May 23, 1785 (Smyth, vol. IX).

Boston Tea Party

O ne of the most famous and influential events in American Revolutionary War history, the 1773 Boston Tea Party was an act of resistance to British restrictive policies in Massachusetts. Franklin was in England as an agent of several colonies during the incident, and it forced him to bear much of the resulting outrage in Britain. The British Parliament had repealed acts of taxation against which the colonists had objected except the tea tax, which it retained as an example of its authority to tax Americans. It was this principle that Franklin and many other Americans resented. Franklin told his friend William Strahan in England that the preamble to the act, which maintained Parliament's right to tax the colonists and claimed that the money was for the benefit of colonial governments and justice, was "unnecessary, unjust, and dangerous."

Parliament had considered many ways to alter the tea tax, including reducing it to make

English tea cheaper than any other foreign tea. Franklin complained to Thomas Cushing in the Massachusetts Assembly, "They have no idea that any people can act from any other principle but that of interest; and they believe that 3d in a lb. of tea, of which one does not perhaps drink 10 in a year, is sufficient to overcome all the patriotism of an American."

It was in part this resentment of the tea tax that led to the Boston Tea Party. In 1773 the British granted the East India Company a monopoly on tea exported to the American colonies. Three ships of East India tea arrived in Boston in late 1773. Massachusetts colonists had been trading tea illegally and not buying British tea in resistance to the tea tax, but now there was the added irritation of the monopoly granted to the East India Company's tea merchants in America. Company agents were forced to resign in many American towns, and shipments of tea were turned back or put into storage. Boston, however, was an exception. When Governor Thomas Hutchinson refused to send the tea back, a group of men led by Samuel Adams dressed themselves as Mohawk Indians, entered three anchored British ships, and threw all of their tea into the harbor on December 16, 1773.

Although Franklin resented the tea tax as much as other Americans, he was disturbed at the destruction of the tea. He had written satires of British policy toward her colonies to London papers in an effort to change public opinion, testified before Parliament on the colonies' behalf, and expended a lot of his energy in other endeavors to bring about a reconciliation between England and America. Although he grew increasingly cynical about the possibility of reaching any agreement, he found his work all the more difficult after the tea dumping. An outraged Parliament passed a measure that closed the port of Boston.

The Committee of Correspondence from the Massachusetts Assembly sent Franklin, its agent, an account of the destruction. Franklin

Casting tea overboard in Boston Harbor. Engraving in Harper's Monthly, *Volume IV, 1851.*

wrote back to them urging them to make reparations and told them "I am truly concerned as I believe all considerate men are with you, that there should seem to any a necessity for carrying matters to such an extremity, as, in a dispute about public rights, to destroy private property." He later heard rumor that "Messrs. [John] Hancock and [Samuel] Adams were seen at the head of the mob that destroyed the tea, openly encouraging them." If he believed the report, he would not acknowledge it to others.

At the end of 1774 and the beginning of 1775, reparations for the destroyed tea were a central issue in the negotiations that took place between Franklin and members of Parliament. Franklin offered to pay for the tea out of his own pocket, without knowing whether or not he would be reimbursed, if Parliament would repeal the Massachusetts Acts. By then, Franklin maintained that the closing of Boston's port had caused Boston more damage than Bostonians had caused with the tea incident, and that any offer to pay for it was a gesture of goodwill. The deal never materialized, however, and Franklin sailed home to Philadelphia.

Related entries:
  An Account of Negotiations in London for Effecting a Reconciliation between Great Britain and the American Colonies
  Colonial Agent
  Great Britain
  Revolutionary War
  Stamp Act

Suggestions for further reading:
  "From Thomas Cushing," December 10, 1773 (Labaree et al., vol. 20).
  "To Thomas Cushing," March 22, 1774 (Labaree et al., vol. 21).

Bowdoin, James II (1726–1790)

Franklin's Boston correspondents included John Winthrop, the Reverend Samuel Cooper, Josiah Quincy, and James Bowdoin, the last of whom was a scientist and eminent statesman. The wealthy Bowdoin family was involved in banking and shipping and owned a large quantity of land. James Bowdoin II was a member of the American Academy of Arts and Sciences and an ardent proponent of American independence from England during the Revolutionary period.

Bowdoin became interested in Franklin's electrical experiments after Franklin began conducting them in 1746. In 1751 Franklin sent a letter to him introducing his neighbor, Ebenezer Kinnersley, who traveled to Boston in 1751 to lecture on electricity. He sent Leyden jars to Bowdoin for his own experimentation and for the local college in 1753. The two corresponded on magnetism, astronomy, electricity, and other subjects. From London in 1758, Franklin described to Bowdoin "an easy, simple contrivance . . . for keeping rooms warmer in cold weather than they generally are, and with less fire." The mechanism consisted of an iron frame and metal plate inserted into a chimney at the bottom. "Drawing it out, so as to leave a space between its further edge and the back, of about two inches," Franklin wrote, "this space is sufficient for the smoke to pass; and so a large part of the funnel being stopped by the rest of the plate, the passage of warm air out of the room, up the chimney, is obstructed and retarded, and by that means much cold air is prevented from coming in through the crevices, to supply its place." He also suggested a method for keeping meat, butter, and milk cool in the summer—wrapping them in wet linen and hanging them in the fireplace. The air passing through the chimney would evaporate the water and keep the food cool, he supposed, if one kept wetting the linen.

With the increase in political tension between England and America, the subject of their correspondence turned to politics in the late 1760s. Bowdoin was a member of the council in Massachusetts, and Franklin acted as an agent for the Massachusetts House of Representatives in England beginning in 1770. Bowdoin shared Franklin's alarm over Parliament's taxes and restrictions on the colonies, particularly his own province of Massachusetts. "The eyes of all Christendom are now upon us, and our honor as a people is become a matter of the utmost consequence to be taken care of," Franklin wrote to him from London in 1775. "If we tamely give up our rights in this contest, a century to come will not restore us in the opinion of the world; we shall be stamped with the character of dastards, poltroons, and fools; and be despised and trampled upon, not by this haughty, insolent nation only, but by all mankind."

Bowdoin served as governor of Massachusetts from 1785 to 1787, during roughly the same period that Franklin served as the president of the Supreme Executive Council of Pennsylvania, and he was instrumental in quelling Shays's Rebellion in 1786 and 1787. With leisure from retirement facing them a year later, Franklin proposed that they renew their philosophical correspondence and sent him conjectures on the Earth and magnetism. Franklin thought that the Earth might have existed for some time before it became magnetic, and that the Earth's iron ore might have acquired magnetic properties from an external source. Franklin proposed to Bowdoin: "May not a magnetic power exist throughout our system, perhaps through all systems, so that if men could make a voyage in the starry regions, a compass might be of use? And may not such universal magnetism, with its uniform direction, be serviceable in keeping the diurnal revolution of a planet more steady to the same axis?" Franklin further speculated that since the presence of stronger magnets can change the poles of weaker magnets, a passing comet or other magnetic force in ancient times might have changed the Earth's magnetism and caused an upheaval.

Bowdoin and Franklin died in the same year, 1790. Bowdoin College, in Maine, bears his name.

Related entries:
Colonial Agent
Electricity
Kinnersley, Ebenezer
Revolutionary War

Suggestions for further reading:
Kershaw, Gordon E. 1991. *James Bowdoin II: A Patriot and Man of the Enlightenment.* Lanham, Md.: University Press of America.
"To James Bowdoin," December 13, 1753 (Labaree et al., vol. 5).
"To James Bowdoin," February 25, 1775 (Labaree et al., vol. 21).
"To James Bowdoin," January 24, 1752 (Labaree et al., vol. 4).
"To James Bowdoin: Queries and Conjectures Relating to Magnetism and the Theory of the Earth," May 31, 1788 (Smyth, vol. IX).

Bradford, Andrew

See **The Busy-Body; Printing.**

Brillon de Jouy, Anne-Louise Boivin d'Hardancourt (1744–1824)

Franklin, who was nearly 71 years old and a widower when he moved to Passy, a village outside of Paris, gained a reputation for flirting with French women soon after his arrival. Two in particular grew close to him during his stay from 1776 to 1785: Madame Helvétius and Madame Brillon. The latter was wealthy, married to a French treasury official who was 24 years older than she, and considered by many the best female musician and composer in France. She was emotional, imaginative, romantic, and prone to bouts of depression—traits that are evident in the hundreds of letters she and Franklin exchanged.

The Brillons' and Franklin's mutual neighbor in Passy, Louis-Guillaume Le Veillard, first introduced Franklin to Madame Brillon. Franklin and his grandson Temple soon developed a habit of visiting the Brillons on Wednesdays and Saturdays, where they talked, ate dinner, drank tea, and played chess. Although many rumors have surfaced about Franklin's romantic involvement with Madame Brillon, there is no evidence to suggest that anything more than a deep and playful friendship developed between them. Outside observers recorded what they thought were indiscretions, one of them being her habit of sitting on Franklin's knee. They were flirtatious and affectionate toward one another, but she resisted the romantic overtures that Franklin made (whether in jest or not). She preferred, instead, to think of him as her father and always addressed him as "papa" in her letters.

She, who played the harpsichord and the piano, composed music for him and, with her two daughters, often entertained him with it. Franklin called their performances "my opera, for I rarely go to the opera at Paris." Madame Brillon's "March of the Insurgents" was composed in honor of the 1777 American victory over Major General Burgoyne in Saratoga. Franklin wrote bagatelles for her—including "The Ephemera" (1778) and "The Whistle (1779). Madame Brillon's husband, who was for a time more interested in their daughters' governess, Mlle. Juppin, than his wife, seems not to have minded the affection between her and Franklin. He enjoyed Franklin's company and

sometimes wrote short notes at the end of his wife's letters to him.

Franklin responded to Madame Brillon's verses, "Le Sage et la Goutte," with his "Dialogue between the Gout and Mr. Franklin" (1780), written when illness kept them both confined to their quarters. "The Gout" faulted "Mr. F" for riding to and from Madame Brillon's in his carriage instead of walking, and suggested that the carriage should be used to transport older peasants who toiled all day instead of himself.

Madame Brillon did not speak English, so Franklin wrote to her in French. She sometimes made corrections to the grammar in his letters. When he complained that his French was lacking, she replied that only a heart was needed to write to a friend, "and you combine with the best heart, when you wish, the soundest moral teaching, a lively imagination, and that droll roguishness which shows that the wisest of men allows his wisdom to be perpetually broken against the rocks of femininity."

Some of their letters were playful, others serious, and still others philosophical. They discussed the afterlife and the Ten Commandments, and Franklin confessed that he had trouble obeying the commandment not to covet one's neighbor's wife. Madame Brillon endeavored to improve his soul. Franklin became one of her confidantes when she discovered what others already knew—that her husband was romantically involved with Mlle. Juppin. He encouraged her to forgive and not seek revenge. Madame Brillon was devastated, threw her daughters' governess out, and fell ill as a result of the emotional stress.

Franklin wished to marry his grandson, William Temple Franklin, to one of the Brillon's daughters, Cunégonde. Madame Brillon wrote to Franklin that the family could not accept the offer: ". . . [W]e like your son, and believe that he has all that is necessary to make a man distinguished, and to render a woman happy. But he cannot reasonably decide to remain in this country;

his property, his profession, and his duty bind him to his country." Temple later became involved with their other daughter, Aldegonde, and then with a neighbor's wife, Blanchette Caillot, who bore him an illegitimate child.

When Madame Brillon was away from Passy, she complained of her missed Wednesday and Saturday gatherings with Franklin. In 1781, on the recommendation of her doctor, who recommended a change of scenery to alleviate her illness and depression, she and her family moved to Nice. After her return in 1783, she and Franklin saw less of one another but kept up their correspondence. Madame Brillon was grieved when Franklin returned to Philadelphia in 1785 and said her good-byes three days before he departed, as she could not bear the pain of watching him leave. She and Franklin continued to write until the end of his life.

Portrait of Edmund Burke. Mezzotint by James Watson, 1770, after a painting by Joshua Reynolds.

Related entries:
Bagatelles
France
Helvétius, Anne-Catherine de Ligniville d'Autricourt
Medicine

Suggestions for further reading:
Lopez, Claude-Anne. 1966. *Mon Cher Papa: Franklin and the Ladies of Paris.* New Haven, Conn.: Yale University Press.
"Social Life in France" (Smyth, vol. X, chap. XI).

Burke, Edmund (1729–1797)

When tensions between the American colonies and the British began to run high before shots were fired in the Revolutionary War, Americans had relatively few friends in the British Parliament. One notable exception was the philosopher and politician Edmund Burke, a friend of Franklin's and a sympathizer with complaints of unfair taxation expressed by American colonists. Franklin was in England working for the repeal of the Stamp Act (passed in 1765), a goal with which Burke sympathized, when the latter was elected to the House of Commons as a Whig in 1765.

Burke was Irish and had attended Trinity College in Dublin. His father was a Protestant and his mother Catholic. He moved to London in 1750. In 1756 his *Vindication of Natural Society* was published, and *Origin of Our Ideas of the Sublime and Beautiful* was published the following year. Burke was an eloquent writer and speaker, and both of these attributes helped him in his long political career. He worked as a secretary for the Whig Marquess of Rockingham the year he was elected to the House of Commons.

Burke defended the interests of American colonists with speeches such as "On American Taxation" (1774), and he was an agent for New York before the war. In American history, he is perhaps most famous for a speech he made to the English House of Commons, "On Conciliation with the Colonies," in 1775. He spoke just after Franklin set sail for America, urging England to extend adequate rights to the colonists in order to maintain peace. Colonists who were granted the same rights as English citizens would remain staunchly loyal to England, he asserted. Burke's speech was unpopular in the House of Commons, and resolutions he introduced, including one in favor of American authority over its own taxation, were voted down decisively. However, news of Burke's speech reached across the Atlantic to the grateful Second Continental Congress.

Burke reported a conversation he had with Franklin before the latter sailed from London to America in 1775. He noted that Franklin was more open than usual and was frustrated with the prospect of war and division between the colonies and England (Labaree et al. 1982). Correspondence between Burke and Franklin ceased during the Revolutionary War, but it resumed in 1781 when Burke wrote an amiable letter on behalf of British Major General John Burgoyne, who was to be exchanged for Henry Laurens. "I may indeed with great truth assure you," Burke wrote, "that your friendship has always been an object of my ambition; and that if an high and very sincere esteem for your talents and virtues could give me a title to it, I am not wholly unworthy of that honor."

Burke was involved in many political issues outside of the American colonies. He was instrumental in the 1785 impeachment of Warren Hastings, the governor-general of the East India Company's holdings. After Franklin's death, Burke wrote *Reflections on the Revolution in France* (1790), which expressed his objections to the revolution—some of them being the accompanying violence and attacks on religion—and sparked a rebuttal from Thomas Paine, *The Rights of Man*.

Related entries:
Continental Congresses
Paine, Thomas
Revolutionary War
Stamp Act

Suggestions for further reading:
"From Edmund Burke to Benjamin Franklin," 1781 (Smyth, vol. VIII).
"To Edmund Burke," October 15, 1781 (Smyth, vol. VIII).

The Busy-Body

"The Busy-Body" was a pseudonym used by both Franklin and Joseph Breintnal (a friend of Franklin's from the Junto) for a series of letters to Andrew Bradford's *American Weekly Mercury* early in 1729. Franklin had planned in 1728 to establish a newspaper after he broke from his former boss, Samuel Keimer, and set up a printing house with Hugh Meredith. A journeyman, George Webb, sought employment under Franklin and Meredith. They could not afford to hire him, but Franklin mistakenly trusted him with knowledge of the plans to create a newspaper. Franklin asked Webb not to tell Keimer, but he did anyway. Keimer quickly announced his own scheme for a newspaper, *The Universal Instructor in All Arts and Sciences and Pennsylvania Gazette*. "I resented this," Franklin said in his *Autobiography*, "and, to counteract them, as I could not yet begin our paper, I wrote several pieces of entertainment for Bradford's paper, under the title of 'The Busy-Body'. . . . By this means, the attention of the public was fixed on that paper, and Keimer's proposals, which we [Franklin and Breintnal] burlesqued and ridiculed, were disregarded."

Franklin's Busy-Body was a self-appointed identifier of virtue and even the most trifling vices, offering praise where it was due and criticism where it was merited. Busy-Body number four complained of the annoying habit people have of overextending their visits with others. A fictitious woman named "Patience" complained to the Busy-Body about her neighbor's habit of staying in her store for too long and allowing her mischievous children to destroy her merchandise. The Busy-Body sympathized with her annoyance and related a Turkish custom of perfuming beards at the end of a visit. A visitor knew it was near time to leave after the perfuming, and the Busy-Body recommended the institution of a modified version of this custom. Busy-Body number eight expounded on the futility of searching for legendary hidden treasures while leaving potentially successful businesses unattended. In letter number three, the Busy-Body presented Cato, with whom he claimed to be acquainted, as a model for virtue. "It was not an exquisite form of person, or grandeur of dress, that struck us with admiration. . . . I believe long habits of virtue have a sensible effect on the countenance." Cato was contrasted to Cretico: "Thou sour philosopher! Thou cunning statesman! Thou art crafty, but far from being wise. When will thou be esteemed, regarded, and beloved like Cato?"

Although Keimer proceeded with his paper, poor management, small readership, and debt caused it to fail within a year. He sold it to Meredith and Franklin, who turned it into the popular and successful *Pennsylvania Gazette*.

Related entries:
The Junto
Pennsylvania Gazette
Printing

Suggestions for further reading:
"The Busy-Body—No. 1," 1729 (Labaree et al., vol. 1).
"The Busy-Body—No. 2," 1729 (Labaree et al., vol. 1).
"The Busy-Body—No. 3," 1729 (Labaree et al., vol. 1).
"The Busy-Body—No. 4," 1729 (Labaree et al., vol. 1).
"The Busy-Body—No. 5," 1729 (Labaree et al., vol. 1).
"The Busy-Body—No. 8," 1729 (Labaree et al., vol. 1).

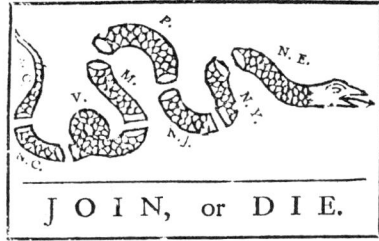

JOIN, or DIE.

C

Canada

Before the English and the French began to colonize Canada, the vast territory was occupied by Indian tribes and Eskimos. The first European explorers in modern history arrived around the late 1400s and early 1500s. Larger numbers of French settlers arrived in the 1600s. Quebec was founded by the French in 1608, and it became Canada's first permanent settlement. The French set up many fur-trading enterprises in Canada.

French fur trading and territorial claims, which reached down into the Ohio River valley, were sources of conflict between the French colonists in Canada and the English settlers in New England, who wished to expand their settlements westward. The French and the British fought sporadically over territory from the late 1600s to the mid-1700s.

A treaty in 1713 gave Britain Nova Scotia, Newfoundland, and territory around the Hudson Bay. In 1745 American colonists, still under the British Crown, took a French fort in Louisbourg, Cape Breton Island, but the French regained it under the Treaty of Aix-la-Chapelle in 1748. The territorial disputes reached their height in 1754, when the French and Indian War broke out. The British eventually defeated the French in 1760, and in 1763 the Treaty of Paris ceded all of Canada to England.

During the three-year span between the defeat of the French in Canada and the treaty that gave the territory to the British, disputes arose over whether England should ask for the small island of Guadeloupe or the vast Canadian territory from the French. One objection to obtaining Canada was that putting it under British rule would require immigration on a scale that the British population could not support.

Others, including Franklin, saw a great opportunity for the expansion, wealth, and security of the British Empire. He argued that no further immigration from England would be necessary, because there were a sufficient number of people already living in the New World to grow into a large population. He estimated that the inhabitants of the northern colonies doubled in population every 25 years. Increased population meant increased trade with Britain.

Security was another issue. He did not believe that hostility toward the colonies from the French would cease with a treaty. Having Canada under British rule would, on the other hand, provide the necessary protection. These were all points he argued, with Richard Jackson, in a pamphlet written in 1760 called "The Interest of Great Britain Considered." (He had also written the much less serious "Humorous Reasons for Restoring Canada" in the *London Chronicle* the previous year.)

After the British gained control of Canada, Franklin was enlisted to help establish a mail route between New York and Quebec. In March 1763 he embarked on a lengthy journey with John Foxcroft, who with Franklin was joint deputy postmaster general in America, to examine mail routes already in existence and report the findings to England.

At the time of the French defeat, the American colonists were still loyal to the British Crown. However, new problems with remaining French Canadian settlers arose before the Revolutionary War broke out in 1776. In 1775 a committee on which Franklin was serving learned that the French settlers did not support the colonies in their disputes with England. Along with Charles Carroll, John Carroll, and Samuel Chase, he set out on a journey to Canada to try to sway them otherwise. However, the Canadians, both British and French, remained in sentiment loyal to Britain. Franklin, who was ill and saw little prospect of success, returned to Philadelphia.

After the Americans had won the Revolutionary War, Franklin, during treaty negotiations with the British, proposed that Canada be given to the new United States, but his suggestion never came to fruition, and Canada remained in British hands. Thousands of loyalists who lived in the American colonies moved to Canada after the war.

Both before and after the war, some had wanted Canada to join a union of American colonies. Franklin extended such an invitation to British Canada in his "Proposed Articles of Confederation" (written in 1775 and not adopted). The Articles of Confederation that were adopted as the new form of American government in 1781 also had a provision for allowing Canada to join the colonies.

Related entries:
Albany Plan of Union
Articles of Confederation
Continental Congresses
French and Indian War
Jackson, Richard
Post Office
Treaty of Paris, 1783

Suggestions for further reading:
"The Interest of Great Britain Considered,"
April 17, 1760 (Labaree et al., vol. 9).

Childhood

Much of what is known about Franklin's childhood is recorded in his *Autobiography.* He was born on January 17, 1706, to Josiah and Abiah Franklin in Boston. He was the youngest son of 17 children but had two younger sisters. His siblings were: Elizabeth, Samuel, Hannah, Josiah, Anne, and two brothers named Joseph who both died soon after they were born, all by Josiah's first wife, Anne; and John, Peter, Mary, James, Sarah, Ebenezer, Thomas, Lydia, and Jane by Abiah Folger Franklin. After searching records in England later in his life, he found that he was the youngest son of a youngest son for five generations back.

His father was a tallow chandler, and his mother was Josiah's second wife. Franklin attended school from the time he was eight years old until he was ten and never received any further formal education. Franklin's early eagerness to read and the opinions of his father's friends convinced Josiah Franklin that his son would make a good scholar, and he at first resolved to devote him to the church. Franklin excelled at the grammar school, but his father decided that he could not afford to send him to college and put him in a school for writing and mathematics instead. Franklin did well in writing at the school, run by George Brownell, but poorly in math.

For recreation, Franklin was fond of the water. He learned to swim at a young age, and he fished and canoed. His father sometimes sang and played the violin in the evenings, and at the dinner table he encouraged "some ingenious or useful topic for discourse, which might tend to improve the minds of his children." So little attention was given to etiquette and the food on the table that Franklin sometimes could not remember what he had eaten a few hours after dinner. Franklin learned to read early and spent what spare money he had on books. From his father's library, he read divinity books, Daniel Defoe's *An Essay on Projects* (1695), Cotton

Mather's *Essays to Do Good* (1710), and Plutarch's *Lives.* On Sundays the Franklins attended church.

His father removed him from school altogether at age 10 and kept him home to help him with his business—cutting wick for the candles, working at the shop, and doing other chores. Franklin did not like the tallow-chandling trade, and his father began to search for another. His other son Josiah had run away to sea, and Franklin's father feared that Franklin would run too if he did not find a profession that was more acceptable for his promising son. He began to take Franklin for walks to see other tradesmen at work. He decided that his son might like to become a cutler, and Franklin went to live with his cousin Samuel, a cutler and son of his uncle Benjamin, for a short time. However, monetary disagreements between his father and his cousin brought him home again. At age 12 he was apprenticed to his brother James, a printer who later published the *New England Courant.* Franklin liked printing much more than tallow-chandling and signed a contract to remain until he was 21.

With his new position, Franklin gained much-desired access to more books, and he sometimes stayed up all night reading. A local tradesman, Matthew Adams, allowed Franklin to borrow books from his library. For a brief time, he dabbled in poetry, which his brother James encouraged. James printed some of the poems and sent his brother to sell them, and they met with some success. "This flattered my vanity," Franklin said, "but my father discouraged me by ridiculing my performances, and telling me verse-makers were generally beggars."

Franklin sometimes disputed with his friend John Collins for sport. When his father found a series of letters written between them arguing over the propriety of educating women, he sat his son down and criticized his manner of arguing. His father complimented him on his spelling and punctuation but encouraged him to improve his

The birthplace of Benjamin Franklin. Wood engraving in **Harper's Weekly,** *1872.*

writing. After this, Franklin began to teach himself how to write more fluently by trying to reproduce stories from the *Spectator.* He jotted down the main ideas of the stories and tried to write them again himself, and then he compared his to the originals. Perceiving that he needed to expand his vocabulary, he wrote the stories out in verse, which he believed would help him learn and master the use of more words. To help himself learn how to mold thoughts into convincing arguments, he purposely mixed up material he had jotted down and tried to arrange them in the best order a few weeks later.

Having read a book with examples of the Socratic method, Franklin said, "I was charmed with it, adopted it, dropped my abrupt contradiction and positive argumentation, and put on the humble inquirer and doubter." He became proficient in arguing with this method. Among the other changes in Franklin's thinking during his teens were growing doubts about religious doctrines with which he had grown up. Franklin also tried to correct his failures in mathematics. He went through an arithmetic book and taught himself a small amount of geometry from navigation books.

James began to publish the *New England Courant* in 1721 (when Franklin was 15), and

Franklin helped him compose types, print the newspapers, and sell them. In 1722 he wrote 14 humorous letters signed "Mrs. Silence Dogood" and secretly submitted them to the paper. Soon after his ruse was uncovered, he began to fight frequently with James. Franklin ran away to New York, and then to Philadelphia, in 1723.

Related entries:
Dogood, Mrs. Silence
Franklin, James
Printing

Suggestions for further reading:
Masur, Louis P., ed. 1993. *The Autobiography of Benjamin Franklin*. Boston: Bedford Books of St. Martin's Press.
Tourtellot, Arthur Bernon. 1977. *Benjamin Franklin, the Shaping of Genius: The Boston Years*. Garden City, N.Y.: Doubleday.

Colden, Cadwallader (1688–1776)

*L*ike Franklin and many of his other correspondents, Cadwallader Colden was a man of varied interests and accomplishments. A native of Ireland, Colden moved to Philadelphia and then to New York, where he was active in the government and eventually became lieutenant governor. He authored *History of the Five Indian Nations* (1727) and *Principles of Action in Matter* (1752). Franklin met him on a road in 1743 and began to correspond with him about many different subjects.

Franklin kept Colden up-to-date on the progress of the American Philosophical Society, which he conceived that same year. Colden's interest in nature led him to classify the plants around his home according to a new system invented by the Swedish botanist Carolus Linnaeus (1707–1778). He was encouraged by reported successes of pokeweed as a cure for cancer. Colden also invented a new method of printing, called stereotyping, and wrote to his printer friend Franklin to ask his opinion of it.

Impressed with Franklin's invention of the Pennsylvania fireplace, Colden sent his pamphlet describing it to the naturalist Johann F. Gronovius, and Gronovius indicated that he would have it translated into Dutch. Franklin offered to publish Colden's "Explication of the First Causes of Motion in Matter, and of the Cause of Gravitation" at his own expense. Franklin told him, "If I can be the means of communicating anything valuable to the world, I do not always think of gaining, nor even of saving, by my business; but a piece of that kind, as it must excite the curiosity of all the learned, can hardly fail of bearing its own expense." Colden and Franklin also traded letters on meteorology. When Colden sent Franklin some of his suppositions on the pores of the skin—that there were vessels that perspired as well as absorbed—Franklin was very pleased and designed an experiment to test the one objection he had—that simply the direction of a small vessel, where it joins a larger artery or vein, sufficed to produce perspiration and absorption.

Colden's *History of the Five Indian Nations* was published in England, and Franklin read it with approval. Shipments of the book arrived in the colonies, and Franklin sought ways to distribute and sell them. Because of Colden's knowledge of the Indian nations, Franklin consulted him in 1754 when the Albany Congress met with the purpose of orchestrating a colonial union. Franklin drafted a Plan of Union (it was never adopted) and asked Colden to offer suggestions.

Outside of science, the two men were both involved in the politics of their respective states. When French privateers threatened Pennsylvania in 1747, Franklin wrote to Colden to ask if Pennsylvania might borrow cannon from New York until the ones they had ordered arrived from overseas. Colden became the lieutenant governor, and then the governor, of New York. Franklin was later elected to the Pennsylvania Assembly. Colden died in 1776.

Colden Cadwallader, shown in a stipple engraving by Scoles.

Related entries:
Albany Plan of Union
American Philosophical Society
Bartram, John
Collinson, Peter
Pennsylvania Assembly
Volunteer Militia

Suggestions for further reading:
"From Cadwallader Colden," June 20, 1754 (Labaree et al., vol. 5).
New York Historical Society. 1918–1937. *The Letters and Papers of Cadwallader Colden.* New York: New York Historical Society.
"To Cadwallader Colden," August 15, 1745 (Labaree et al., vol. 3).

Collected Works

According to one of Franklin's editors, "Franklin preserved all his papers. . . . Every letter written to him, every rough draft and copy of a letter written by him, every visiting card, and every invitation to dinner or to a Masonic lodge meeting was saved and cherished, and went to swell the tremendous aggregate of his collection of papers." Even before he died, some of his friends began to publish small collections of these papers. These consisted largely of his scientific and political writings. *Experiments and Observations on Electricity* was published in London in 1751 and succeeded by a supplemental edition two years later. Thomas-François Dalibard translated it into French. In 1769 another, more comprehensive, English edition appeared in London, which Franklin's friend Dr. Jacques Barbeu-Dubourg translated into French. Another of Franklin's longtime friends, Benjamin Vaughan, published an edition of Franklin's *Political, Miscellaneous, and Philosophical Pieces* in London in 1779. When Franklin died he bequeathed the majority of his papers to his grandson, William Temple Franklin.

After a lengthy delay, Temple published three volumes of his grandfather's writings as *Memoirs of the Life and Writings of Benjamin Franklin* (London, 1818). Jared Sparks edited the next major collection, entitled *The Works of Benjamin Franklin* (Boston, 1840). Many modern scholars consider this collection to be inadequate because of the liberties Sparks took in altering the text. John Bigelow edited a subsequent edition of Franklin's works in ten volumes, *The Complete Works of Benjamin Franklin* (New York, 1887–1889). In 1907 Albert Henry Smyth completed publishing the ten-volume *The Writings of Benjamin Franklin* (New York, 1905–1907), considered by most to be the best and most accurate collection to that date. In 1959 scholars began putting together *The Papers of Benjamin Franklin,* a comprehensive set including not only Franklin's own writings but also many letters written to him by others and thorough editorial notes. Shorter and less comprehensive collections of Franklin's writings have also appeared. Many of the original Franklin manuscripts are held at the American Philosophical Society in Philadelphia, Yale University, the Library of Congress, and the University of Pennsylvania. Numerous other public and private collections containing Franklin's manuscripts are maintained around the world.

EXPERIMENTS
AND
OBSERVATIONS
ON
ELECTRICITY,

MADE AT

Philadelphia in *America*,

BY

Mr. BENJAMIN FRANKLIN,

AND

Communicated in several Letters to Mr. P. COLLINSON,
of *London*, F. R. S.

LONDON:

Printed and sold by E. CAVE, at *St. John's Gate*. 1751.
(Price 2s. 6d.)

Title page of Benjamin Franklin's "Experiments and Observations on Electricity," published in London in 1751.

Even the extensive collected works that now exist necessarily exclude some of Franklin's papers. Many have been lost or destroyed over the years. A large trunk of his early writings perished during the Revolutionary War after he left them with his old political ally Joseph Galloway. The trunk was broken into and the papers inside of it destroyed. Richard Bache, Franklin's son-in-law, tried to recover what he could of the trunk's contents, but most were lost. Other manuscripts have been destroyed by fires, people who came into possession of them but did not know their value, mice (which ruined many of Franklin's letters to his sister, Jane Mecom), and a variety of other causes.

Related entries:
Barbeu-Dubourg, Dr. Jacques
Collinson, Peter
Fothergill, Dr. John
Franklin, William Temple
Galloway, Joseph
Vaughan, Benjamin

Suggestions for further reading:
Bigelow, John, ed. 1887–1889. *The Complete Works of Benjamin Franklin*. New York pub.?.
Franklin, William Temple, ed. 1817–1818. *Memoirs of the Life and Writings of Benjamin Franklin*. London: H. Colburn.
Labaree, Leonard W., et al., eds. 1959–. *The Papers of Benjamin Franklin*. New Haven: Yale University Press.
Smyth, Albert Henry, ed. 1905–1907. *The Writings of Benjamin Franklin*. New York: Macmillan.
Sparks, Jared, ed. 1836–1840. *The Works of Benjamin Franklin*. Boston: Hilliard, Gray, and Company.

Collinson, Peter (1694–1768)

Franklin considered his longtime friend Peter Collinson "a most benevolent, worthy man, very curious in botany and other branches of natural history, and fond of improvements in agriculture. . . . " Collinson was an English Quaker, a scientist, and a merchant who was interested in the American colonies. He began corresponding with Franklin in 1747 and was one of the principal recipients of Franklin's descriptions of his electrical experiments. For more than 30 years he purchased and chose books in England for the Library Company of Philadelphia with the money it raised.

It was Collinson who sent a Leyden jar to the Library Company as a gift in 1746, touching off the electrical experiments that led to Franklin's invention of the lightning rod. Franklin had seen electrical experiments "imperfectly performed" in Boston and jumped at the opportunity to conduct his own. Franklin kept Collinson up-to-date on his experiments and sent him letters that described them in detail. Collinson, who was a member of the Royal Society of London, succeeded in having Franklin's papers read before the society. They were initially laughed at and not even printed in the society's *Philosophical Transactions*. Dr. John Fothergill, however, thought that they should be printed, and Collinson found a printer. Franklin's papers were published as "Experiments and Observations on Electricity," with a preface by Fothergill.

Although electricity was the chief subject of their correspondence, Franklin and Collinson also wrote about other areas of scientific interest as well as political matters in the colonies. In 1751 Franklin asked for Collinson's assistance in gaining the position of deputy postmaster general of America. Franklin sent him a description of a whirlwind he and his son had followed in 1755. The best descriptions of the magic squares and magic circles that Franklin invented are also found in letters to Collinson. Collinson also corresponded with mutual friends of his and Franklin's—most notably the botanist John Bartram and Jared Eliot. Bartram, an original member of the American Philosophical Society that Franklin conceived in 1743, often sent Collinson seeds from American plants to try in England.

Franklin met Collinson in 1757, when the Pennsylvania Assembly sent him to England to push for the right to tax proprietary lands. In addition to their association with the Royal Society of London, Collinson and Franklin both passed time at meetings of the Honest Whigs, an informal philosophical discussion club that met in a London coffeehouse every two weeks.

After Collinson's death in 1768, his son, Michael Collinson, published an account of his life. Franklin heard of his plans to write the account and sent him some details about his father's life that he thought Michael might not have known. He told him that Collinson had donated "valuable presents" and procured others from his friends for the subscription library founded in 1730. He conducted business for the library in London, handling the purchase, shipping, and choice without taking payment for it.

Related entries:
Bartram, John
Colden, Cadwallader
Electricity
Eliot, Jared

Fothergill, Dr. John
Honest Whigs
Library Company of Philadelphia
Magic Squares/Magic Circles
Meteorology
Pennsylvania Assembly
Post Office
Royal Society of London

Suggestions for further reading:
Brett-James, Norman G. 1926. *The Life of Peter Collinson.* London: E. G. Dunstan.
"To Peter Collinson," March 28, 1747 (Labaree et al., vol. 3).

Colonial Agent

*T*he Pennsylvania Assembly sent Franklin to England as its agent in 1757, and then again in 1764. Its members entrusted him with petitioning for the Assembly's right to tax proprietary lands in Pennsylvania, and then with presenting a petition to the king to assume the government of the province from the proprietaries. However, as England's Parliament continued to introduce taxes and other restrictive measures in America, larger, intercolonial worries soon overshadowed these provincial concerns. In addition to the petition for the change in government that Franklin carried with him in 1764, the Assembly had also instructed him to oppose the impending Stamp Act. The act passed, and Franklin soon immersed himself in working for its repeal. Franklin's clear and competent testimony before the House of Commons in favor of repealing the Stamp Act in 1766 won him respect in other American provinces. Three other colonies— Georgia in 1768, New Jersey in 1769, and Massachusetts in 1770—appointed him as their agent as well. In reality, though not officially, he served as a spokesman for all of the colonies.

Massachusetts voted Franklin £600 per year for his services as agent, although the governor refused to allow its payment. New

Franklin's Examination by the House of Commons in London, 1766. *Reproduction of a painting by Charles E. Mills, c. 1920.*

Jersey's payment, though smaller, was always prompt. Georgia had appointed him at £100 per year, but his accounts with that province still remained unsettled in 1785. He was eventually given the right to 3,000 acres of Georgia land, which he bequeathed to his grandson, William Temple Franklin.

Franklin attended to the routine affairs of each colony, such as their statues when they came to the Board of Trade, but the affairs of Massachusetts consumed a greater amount of his time and caused him more frustration than those of the other three colonies combined. Many of England's politicians looked upon Massachusetts as the ringleader of rebellion in the colonies, and Parliament came down harder on that province than on any other. In 1770 the Committee of Correspondence, consisting of Thomas Cushing, Samuel Adams, and James Otis, wrote to Franklin to inform him of his appointment and acquaint him with "the state and circumstances of the province, and the grievances we labor under, the redress of which will require your utmost attention and application." When Franklin called on Lord Hillsborough, the secretary of state for America, to inform him of the appointment, Lord Hillsborough refused to recognize his agency because the governor (Thomas Hutchinson) had not assented. "[H]is Lordship, whose countenance

changed at my naming that province," Franklin reported to the Reverend Samuel Cooper, "cut me short by saying, with something between a smile and a sneer, 'I must set you right there Mr. Franklin, you are not agent.'"

Lord Hillsborough's successor, Lord Dartmouth, allowed Franklin to function as an agent. He had little effect in that position, however, as resentment against Massachusetts grew steadily in England. Franklin reported on the deteriorating state of affairs chiefly to Cooper and Cushing in Boston. He accurately predicted to the Committee of Correspondence in 1771: "I think one may clearly see, in the system of customs to be exacted in America by act of Parliament, the seeds sown of a total disunion of the two countries, though, as yet, that event may be at a considerable distance."

In 1772 Franklin mysteriously obtained a handful of letters written by Hutchinson and Andrew Oliver, who by then had become lieutenant governor of Massachusetts. Hutchinson and Oliver represented Massachusetts in negative terms and suggested that England send troops to the province. As the agent for Massachusetts, Franklin transmitted the letters to Boston to acquaint a few notable people with this likely source of their grievances. The letters, which were not supposed to go beyond those few people, were eventually published and caused an uproar. Massachusetts instructed Franklin to present its petition for the removal of Oliver and Hutchinson. The Lords of the Committee for Plantation Affairs summoned Franklin to the Cockpit part of Whitehall, in January 1774, on the pretense of considering the petition. When he returned later with counsel, Alexander Wedderburn, counsel for Oliver's and Hutchinson's agent (Israel Mauduit) denounced Massachusetts, Franklin, and his conduct in obtaining the letters. Most of the Lords in attendance accompanied Wedderburn's tirade with laughter and applause.

Between the humiliation he suffered at the Cockpit and the outrage in England over the Boston Tea Party (December 16, 1773), Franklin lost what little influence he had on behalf of Massachusetts. He reported to Cushing on March 22, 1774: "The violent destruction of the tea seems to have united all parties here against our province, so that the bill now brought into Parliament for shutting up Boston as a port till satisfaction is made, meets with no opposition." Parliament punished Massachusetts with the "Intolerable Acts" of 1774, which ignited anger in all 13 colonies. The Boston Port Act closed Boston's port, and the Massachusetts Government Act altered the province's constitution and allowed only one town meeting per year. The Quartering Act required Massachusetts inhabitants to house British soldiers in uninhabited buildings, and the Impartial Administration of Justice Act allowed British officials charged with capital crimes to stand trial in England. When Franklin left England in 1775 Parliament was considering a bill to deprive Massachusetts of the right to use fisheries in Nova Scotia and Newfoundland. Just before he sailed, Franklin drew up a memorial to Lord Dartmouth declaring his objections to the continuance of the port blockade, and that satisfaction might one day be demanded for the restriction from the fisheries. A friend, Thomas Walpole, convinced him not to present it.

Franklin's efforts as a colonial agent to bring about a redress of American grievances had failed. He arrived home in Philadelphia in time to sit in the Second Continental Congress, the body that adopted the Declaration of Independence.

Related entries:
Adams, John
Boston Tea Party
Great Britain
Oliver-Hutchinson Letters Affair
Revolutionary War
Stamp Act

Suggestions for further reading:
"The House of Representatives of Massachusetts to Benjamin Franklin," 1770 (Cushing, vol. II).
"The House of Representatives of Massachusetts to Benjamin Franklin," June 19, 1771 (Cushing, vol. II).
Morgan, David T. 1996. *The Devious Dr. Franklin, Colonial Agent: Benjamin Franklin's Years in London*. Macon, Ga.: Mercer University Press.
"To Thomas Cushing," March 22, 1774 (Labaree et al., vol. 21).

Constitutional Convention

When the Articles of Confederation proved to be unacceptable to the newly independent United States, the states convened a Constitutional Convention to revise the form of the government. Many, including George Washington, believed that a stronger central government was needed to unite the colonies. A farmer's rebellion in Massachusetts led by Daniel Shays also contributed to the calls for reforms. Shays and his mob demanded lower taxes and new protective legislation, and they prevented several courts in Massachusetts from sitting in 1786. The mob was on its way to the federal arsenal in Springfield when it was turned back by an American militia force, and it was soon broken up.

The purpose of the convention, which convened on May 14, 1787, was at first to revise the Articles of Confederation. Soon, however, it decided to draw up an entirely new plan of government. At age 81, Franklin was the oldest delegate. He and George Washington, who served as president, were the convention's most prominent members, and both were generally silent during the proceedings. Although Franklin suffered perpetually from a bladder stone, he attended faithfully. Notably absent from the convention were John Adams, Thomas Jefferson, John Jay, Samuel Adams, and Patrick Henry.

Franklin offered relatively little to the Constitution itself. His significant speeches were written out beforehand and, because it was painful for him to stand, sometimes read by others. His most important contributions were not the ideological framework or the wording of the Constitution but his flexibility and his ability to calm warring factions during heated debate. He brought with him a lifetime of experience in political controversy and negotiation as well as international renown as an American philosopher and inventor.

One of the points to which Franklin objected was the matter of paying elected government officials. While he was in England, he became disgusted with the bribery and vote buying of members of Parliament and with the system of hereditary legislators in the House of Lords. He believed that public office was a position of service that should be earned on merit and not be used for gain. On June 2, 1787, he delivered his opinion on salaries: "[T]here are two passions which have a powerful influence in the affairs of men. These are ambition and avarice; the love of power and the love of money. Separately, each of these has great force in prompting men to action; but when united in view of the same object, they have in many minds the most violent effects." Franklin blamed the sectarianism, involvement in wars, and other troubles of the British government on these factors. He believed that even starting out with moderate salaries would lead to higher ones in the future, as rulers would inevitably vote themselves raises.

Nine days later the convention heard Franklin's opinion on the explosive issue of proportional representation. Smaller states pushed for equal representation in a national legislature, fearing that proportional representation would render their influence insignificant. Larger states argued for proportional representation, because their greater populations would allow them more representatives. Franklin favored proportional representation in a single house.

Other issues to which Franklin objected were an unchecked veto power for the executive (which he thought should consist of more than one person), the limitation of voting rights to freeholders, and long waiting periods for the naturalization of foreigners.

On June 28 Franklin presented a motion to begin each session of deliberation with a prayer. The convention seemed to be at a standstill and unable to settle many issues. Franklin offered a potential solution to the stalemate: "I have lived, sir, a long time; and the longer I live, the more convincing proofs I see of this truth, that God governs in the affairs of men. And if a sparrow cannot fall to the ground without his notice, is it probable that an empire can rise without his aid?" Roger Sherman seconded his motion, but Franklin reported that only three or four delegates thought it necessary to open with prayers.

Franklin was elected on July 2 to the Grand Committee, which consisted of one delegate from each state and was charged with finding a solution to the raging debate over representation. He had initially objected to two houses and to equal representation; the other delegates leaned toward two houses and had yet to reach an agreement on representation. According to many sources, it was Franklin who suggested that one house contain an equal number of representatives from each state, while the other would be composed of a number of representatives proportional to the population of each state.

Franklin had not initially supported many of the final provisions of the Constitution. However, once the convention agreed on a draft, he encouraged the delegates to sign it. "I confess that I do not entirely approve of this Constitution at present," he said, "but, sir, I am not sure I shall never approve it. . . . " Franklin said he doubted that another convention could produce a better constitution than this one had. He urged the delegates to promote the Constitution in their respective states, regardless of any objections they had to specific provisions. The delegates to the convention signed the new Constitution on September 17, 1787. It was sent to Congress and all of the states' legislatures. Franklin recommended the new Constitution to Pennsylvania's General Assembly the following morning.

A heated controversy soon emerged over the new document. Views were divided into two camps: the Federalists and the Anti-Federalists. The Federalists Alexander Hamilton, James Madison, and John Jay wrote a series of papers supporting the new Constitution, which are now known as the *Federalist Papers*. Anti-Federalists included Patrick Henry, George Mason, and Elbridge Gerry (Mason and Gerry had refused to sign the original document, and Henry had objected to the convention altogether).

Franklin stayed away from the public debate for the most part, but his chief contribution to it was "A Comparison of the Conduct of the Ancient Jews and of the Anti-Federalists in the United States of America," printed in the *Federal Gazette* in 1788. He compared the attitude of the Israelite tribes who were rescued from Egypt to that of the Anti-Federalists—neither were wholly satisfied with the form of government given to them, and various motives spurred "discontented, restless spirits" among each of the tribes (colonies) to oppose the new government given to them. "I beg I may not be understood to infer," he concluded, "that our General Convention was divinely inspired . . .

merely because that Constitution has been unreasonably and vehemently opposed; yet I must own I have so much faith in the general government of the world by Providence, that I can hardly conceive a transaction of such momentous importance . . . should be suffered to pass without being in some degree influenced, guided, and governed by that omnipotent, omnipresent, and beneficient Ruler, in whom all inferior spirits live, and move, and have their being." Pennsylvania ratified the Constitution on December 12, 1787. Nine of the 13 states had ratified the Constitution by June 1788. It became a binding document in 1789.

Related entries:
 Articles of Confederation
 Washington, George

Suggestions for further reading:
 Carr, William George. 1990. *The Oldest Delegate: Franklin in the Constitutional Convention*. Newark, N.J.: University of Delaware Press.
 "A Comparison of the Conduct of the Ancient Jews and of the Anti-Federalists in the United States of America," 1787 (Smyth, vol. IX).
 "Motion for Prayers in the Convention," June 28, 1787 (Smyth, vol. IX).
 "Proposal for Consideration in the Convention for Forming the Constitution of the United States," 1787 (Smyth, vol. IX).
 "Speech in a Committee of the Convention; On the Proportion of Representation and Votes," 1787 (Smyth, vol. IX).
 "Speech in the Constitutional Convention, at the Conclusion of Its Deliberation," 1787 (Smyth, vol. IX).
 "Speech in the Convention; On the Subject of Salaries," 1787 (Smyth, vol. IX).
 Stevens, Richard B., ed. 1984. *The Declaration of Independence and the Constitution of the United States*. Washington, D.C.: Georgetown University Press.

Continental Congresses

The First Continental Congress, with representatives from all colonies except Georgia, convened in Philadelphia on

September 5, 1774, to consider a course of action in response to the "Intolerable Acts" that Parliament had passed in response to the Boston Tea Party. Peyton Randolph of Virginia served as its president. The First Congress established the Continental Association, an agreement among the colonies to boycott British trade, and instructed Committees of Safety to enforce the boycott. Franklin was in London for the duration of Congress, and he and other American agents—Paul Wentworth, William Bollan, Arthur Lee, Thomas Life, Edmund Burke, and Charles Garth—were charged with presenting the Congress's "Declaration of Rights and Grievances" to the king.

The first Congress adjourned in October 1774 and agreed to meet the following year on May 10 in Philadelphia if necessary. Franklin reported to Charles Thomson in the interim, on March 13, 1775, that "the petition of the Congress has lain upon the table of both houses ever since it was sent down to them among the papers that accompanied it from above, and has had no particular notice taken of it; our petition to be heard in support of it, having been . . . rejected with scorn in the Commons. . . . " Lord Camden, according to Franklin, spoke highly of America, and particularly of Congress, to the House of Lords. Lord Chatham (William Pitt) thought, in Franklin's words, "taking the whole together, and considering the members of Congress as the unsolicited, and unbiased choice of a great, free, and enlightened people; their unanimity, their moderation, and their wisdom, he thought it the most honorable assembly of men, that had ever been known; that the histories of Greece and Rome gave us nothing equal to it."

Hostilities between America and Britain had already begun at Lexington and Concord when the delegates convened again in May 1775. Franklin arrived in Philadelphia from England just five days before the Congress opened, and the Pennsylvania Assembly chose him as a delegate the next day. Other delegates included George Washing-

ton, Thomas Jefferson, and John Adams. Congress and the Assembly both put Franklin to work on a myriad of committees. On May 29 he was appointed to a committee to establish a new post office, and Franklin, who had been a deputy postmaster general of America in the royal post office, served as its chairman. Franklin drew up a plan, which was adopted and which established the current postal system in the United States, and was appointed postmaster general. He gave his salary of $1,000 per year to aid soldiers wounded in action. Franklin was chairman of the Committee of Safety for Pennsylvania, which was responsible for organizing the colony for defense and handling a variety of military matters. Other congressional committees on which Franklin served dealt with Indian affairs, printing American paper money, seeking sources of saltpeter, commerce, design of the U.S. seal, consideration of Lord North's conciliatory motion in Parliament, and captured ships. As a member of the Committee of Secret Correspondence, he sought out potential agents for America in foreign countries. To this end Franklin wrote to Charles W. F. Dumas in Holland, Dr. Jacques Barbeu-Dubourg in France, and Don Gabriel of Bourbon in Spain. The committee sent Silas Deane to France.

In July Franklin read his proposed "Articles of Confederation and Perpetual Union" to the Congress, but these were largely ignored, and Congress adopted other Articles of Confederation in 1777, which were not ratified until 1781. In October Franklin, Thomas Lynch, and Benjamin Harrison met with Washington in Cambridge to determine the state and needs of the Continental army and establish rules for prize ships and prisoners of war. In the spring of 1776 Congress sent Franklin, along with Charles Carroll, Samuel Chase, and the Reverend John Carroll (who was a Jesuit priest) on a futile mission to Canada, where they were to try to procure support for the colonies. On May 10, 1776, exactly one year after the Second Congress convened, the delegates voted to recommend that the states form their own governments. The harsh Canadian weather strained Franklin's health, few Canadians were inclined to help the colonies, and he had returned to Philadelphia by June. He arrived in time to serve as president of the convention that formed Pennsylvania's constitution and to sit on the committee—with Thomas Jefferson, John Adams, Robert R. Livingston, and Roger Sherman—that drafted the Declaration of Independence.

Another of Franklin's roles as a delegate to Congress was his participation in the last-minute, but futile, negotiations with Lord Howe with Adams and Edward Rutledge. On May 3, 1776, Lord Howe and his brother, General William Howe, were appointed as commissioners to seek reconciliation with the colonies. Lord Howe, with whom Franklin had already negotiated secretly and unsuccessfully in England, arrived at Staten Island in July and sent Franklin a letter. Franklin told Lord Howe that his mission would prove fruitless, as he offered peace on the condition that the colonies submit, and Congress ignored Howe's overtures. The Battle of Long Island ensued, after which Lord Howe sent the captured American General John Sullivan to Congress with a request that it send commissioners. On September 7 Congress appointed Franklin, Adams, and Rutledge "to be sent to know whether Lord Howe has any authority to treat with persons authorized by Congress for that purpose, on behalf of America, and what that authority is, and to hear such propositions as he shall think fit to make respecting the same." On September 11 the commissioners met on Staten Island, where Howe offered them nothing but peace if the colonies submitted and a questionable promise to consider revising the "offensive acts of Parliament."

On September 26 Congress appointed Franklin as a commissioner to France, along with Arthur Lee, who was in London, and Deane, already in France. Before he left, he lent Congress between £3,000 and £4,000. Franklin wrote to Congress frequently from France, keeping its members up-to-date on American affairs. Congress sent bills to France to be paid with the French money that Franklin and the other commissioners were instructed to seek. In 1781, after the Articles of Confederation were ratified, the Congress of the Confederation replaced the Second Continental Congress.

Related entries:
> Adams, John
> Articles of Confederation
> Declaration of Independence
> France
> Jay, John
> Jefferson, Thomas
> Lee, Dr. Arthur
> Revolutionary War
> United States Seal and Emblem
> Washington, George

Suggestions for further reading:
> "Correspondence and Interview with Lord Howe," 1776 (Smyth, vol. VI).
> Ford, Worthington Chauncy, ed. 1904–1937. *Journals of the Continental Congress, 1774–1789.* Washington, D.C.: U.S. Government Printing Office.
> "Intended Vindication and Offer from Congress to Parliament," July 18, 1775 (Labaree et al., vol. 22).

Craven Street Gazette

During his stay in England, Franklin lived on Craven Street in the home of Mrs. Margaret Stevenson. Mrs. Stevenson, a widow, and her daughter Mary (Polly) were dear friends to him. In 1770, between the meetings and events on his calendar, he found a little bit of time for humor. Franklin's English cousin Sally had moved into the Craven Street home, and when she traveled to Rochester with Mrs. Stevenson for a few days, Franklin recorded daily events during their absence in a mock newspaper he called the *Craven Street Gazette.*

In the news stories, Margaret Stevenson was "Queen Margaret" who had gone to Rochester with her "first maid of honor, Miss

Franklin." Franklin characterized himself as a "great person (so called from his enormous size)." Polly and her husband William Hewson, who had both stayed home, were the new administration. Combining humor from his experience printing newspapers and the daily politics in which he was immersed in England, Franklin reported on the daily happenings in the Craven Street home. Thus, Franklin admitted everyone's failure to attend church one Sunday, September 23: "Notwithstanding yesterday's solemn order of council, nobody went to church today. It seems the great person's broad-built bulk lay so long abed, that the breakfast was not over till it was too late to dress."

The *Craven Street Gazette* also contained letters to the publisher, written by "Indignation" and "A Hater of Scandal." "Indignation" complained that the great person was "half-starved on the blade-bone of a sheep" on account of "the most careless, worthless, thoughtless, inconsiderate, corrupt, ignorant, blundering, foolish, crafty, and knavish ministers, that ever got into a house and pre-tended to govern a family and provide a dinner." "A Hater of Scandal" responded with a defense of the new ministry and an attack on the great person's ingratitude. To complete the newspaper, Franklin included an account of no recent marriages, an obituary for all the mice that died "in the back closet and elsewhere," and a report of the stocks: "Biscuit—very low. Buckwheat and Indian meal—both sour. Tea, lowering daily—in the canister. Wine, shut."

Related entries:
Franklin, Sarah (Sally)
Hewson, Mary (Polly) Stevenson
Stevenson, Mrs. Margaret

Suggestion for further reading:
"The Cravenstreet Gazette," September 22–26, 1770 (Labaree et al., vol. 17).

Cushing, Thomas

See **Colonial Agent.**

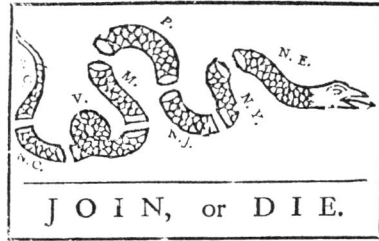

JOIN, or DIE.

D

Dartmouth, Earl of

See **An Account of Negotiations in London for Effecting a Reconciliation between Great Britain and the American Colonies; Colonial Agent; Great Britain.**

Dashwood, Sir Francis (Lord Le Despencer) (1708–1781)

Franklin met the infamous Sir Francis Dashwood, also known as Lord Le Despencer, through the post office in England. Franklin first visited his home at Wycombe at Buckinghamshire in 1772 and had nothing but positive things to say about him to his son. Dashwood was infamous in England for his involvement with the Knights of St. Francis of Wycombe, a cultic sect he had founded in 1745, also known as the Medmenham Club. The sect's members included the Earl of Sandwich, Paul Whitehead (who bequeathed his heart to Dashwood), John Wilkes, and Lord Bute. The secretive sect met in a restored Cistercian abbey and carried on orgies and mock religious rituals. A scandal erupted when Wilkes grew disillusioned with the group and exposed its activities. By the time Franklin befriended him, the club was defunct and Dashwood was outwardly more respectable.

He was very wealthy and a member of Parliament. The two enjoyed one another's company. In 1772 Franklin spent 16 days "most agreeably" at Dashwood's, and he told his son in 1773 that Dashwood was "on all occasions very good to me, and seems of late very desirous of my company."

During one of his visits to Dashwood's in 1773 Franklin and the rest of the company enjoyed a good laugh over his "Edict by the King of Prussia," a satire on British policy in America. Whitehead often looked through the papers early in the morning for news of interest. According to Franklin's account, he came running into the room and said that the King of Prussia had claimed a right to Britain's kingdom. Whitehead began to read the satire aloud, and everybody was taken in at first. About halfway through the reading, he caught on, looked at Franklin, and exclaimed, "I'll be hanged if this is not some of your American jokes on us!" At the end of the reading, the company laughed, and the piece was cut out and placed in Dashwood's collection.

The same year, Dashwood undertook the abridgment of the Book of Common Prayer, the Liturgy of the Church of England. He asked Franklin to assist him with the catechism and the reading and singing of psalms. Franklin complied and also wrote the preface. Characteristic of Franklin's tendency to use as few words as possible, the catechism was reduced to only two questions: "What is your duty to God? What is your duty to your neighbor?" He amended the psalms by taking out repetitions and passages that he believed contradicted Christian doctrines of forgiveness and doing good to enemies. Franklin sailed for Philadelphia in 1775 and learned of Dashwood's death in 1781.

Related entries:
Great Britain
Religious Beliefs
Revolutionary Writings

Suggestions for further reading:
Kemp, Betty. 1967. *Sir Francis Dashwood: An Eighteenth Century Independent.* New York: St. Martin's Press.
"To William Franklin," October 6, 1773 (Labaree et al., vol. 20).

Davenport, Sarah Franklin (1699–1731)

Sarah Franklin Davenport was Franklin's older sister, Josiah Franklin's fifth child by his second wife. She married Joseph Davenport but died in 1731. Franklin sold some watches for her husband some time around 1729. Josiah Davenport, their son, sought Franklin's assistance on more than one occasion, and he was reluctant to give it. When one of Josiah's many businesses failed, he asked Franklin for help. Franklin sent him four dozen maps to sell in his store in February 1773 but declined to help him further on account of the trouble he had with another nephew, Benjamin Mecom. "I have been hurt too much by endeavoring to help cousin Ben Mecom," he wrote. "I have no opinion of the punctuality of cousins. They are apt to take liberties with relations they would not take with others, from a confidence that a relation will not sue them." William Franklin asked his father later that year to try to procure a post for Josiah from Lord North, a request that "vexed" Franklin. Franklin was on poor terms with much of

the British government and did not want to have a relation of his involved in the American customs system, which he hated. He thought that William, who was the governor of New Jersey, could use other channels to obtain a position for Josiah if he wanted to. As with some of his other siblings, Franklin left Sarah's descendants £50 sterling to divide among themselves in his will.

Related entry:
Mecom, Jane Franklin

Suggestions for further reading:
"To Jane Mecom," June 19, 1731 (Labaree et al., vol. 1).
"To Josiah Davenport," February 14, 1773 (Labaree et al., vol. 20).
"To Sarah Davenport," 1730 (Labaree et al., vol. 1).
"To William Franklin," July 14, 1773 (Labaree et al., vol. 20).

Death

Sometime before April 5, 1790, Thomas Jefferson visited Franklin and found him emaciated and bedridden but in good humor. He was eager to hear anything Jefferson could tell him about the French Revolution and the fate of his friends in France. In the days before he died on April 17, Franklin was feverish and breathed with difficulty. He suffered from an attack of pleurisy. After a brief respite from pain, an abscess in his lungs burst. With his grandsons William Temple Franklin and Benjamin Franklin Bache at his side, he died on the night of April 17.

Franklin's body was buried in the graveyard of the Christ Church on April 21, next to those of his wife and his son Francis Folger, who had died in childhood. Members of the clergy, government, judicial system, American Philosophical Society, University of Pennsylvania, and many other groups attended his funeral. An estimated 20,000 people watched as the pallbearers carried his body to his grave. The pallbearers included the mayor, the chief justice of Pennsylvania, and the governor. His death was officially mourned in the House of Representatives, the French National Assembly, the French Academy of Sciences, the American Philosophical Society, Yale College, and other places.

Franklin had written his own epitaph early in his life:

The body of B Franklin Printer
(Like the Cover of an Old Book
Its Contents torn out
And stript of its Lettering & Gilding)
Lies here, Food for Worms.
But the Work shall not be lost;
For it will, (as he believ'd) appear once more,
In a new and more elegant Edition
Revised and corrected
By the author.

However, in his will, he requested that "Benjamin and Deborah Franklin 1790" appear on his tombstone, and the later request was adhered to.

Related entry:
Last Will and Testament

Suggestion for further reading:
"The Life of Benjamin Franklin," pp. 486–493 (Smyth, vol. X).

Declaration of Independence

I n 1776 the fever for independence from Britain grew profuse in the American colonies. Spurred by a long series of British restrictions, including an order to blockade colonial ports and cut off trade, the Second Continental Congress voted on July 2, 1776, to declare the colonies' independence from England. Franklin had been in Europe for most of the period between 1757 and 1775, but he returned to Philadelphia in time to participate in the Second Congress.

The Second Continental Congress convened in May 1775 in Philadelphia. The First Continental Congress, which had convened in 1774, had forwarded a list of grievances to King George III, and the king did not respond. The Second Congress sent another in July 1775, which also came to nothing. To add to the Americans' outrage, King George hired German mercenaries to fight in the colonies. Frustration was more intense at the Second Congress, which created a colonial army, currency, and post office before it declared independence. Fighting with the British had already begun.

Thomas Paine's popular pamphlet *Common Sense* was printed at the beginning of 1776, and support for independence was quickly growing. Richard Henry Lee, a delegate to the Congress from Virginia, introduced a resolution on June 7, 1776, that the colonies were independent from Britain and absolved of all political connection to it. A final vote on the resolution was postponed until after the coming recess, but the Congress was confident enough in its success to appoint a committee (June 10) to draw up a declaration of independence in the meantime. Five men were chosen for the task: Franklin, Robert R. Livingston, Roger Sherman, John Adams, and Thomas Jefferson, who was chosen by the committee to author the document.

Jefferson worked tirelessly on a draft, and when he had finished he sent it to both Adams and Franklin for editing and revision. Both men made small changes. Changes attributed to Franklin include: rephrasing "deluge in blood" to "destroy us," referring to the practice of hiring foreign mercenaries to fight against the colonies; and rewording "power" to "despotism" in Jefferson's phrase, "evinces a design to subject them to arbitrary power" (Boyd 1950).

Jefferson then presented it to the whole committee, which made few changes. It was given next to the Congress on June 28, 1776,

The first announcement of the Declaration of Independence, July 4, 1776, outside Independence Hall, with Hancock, Franklin, Jefferson, Adams, Livingston, and Sherman on the steps. Engraving by Davis Garber, 1874.

where it received some additional revisions. The most significant alteration was the elimination of Jefferson's biting criticism of the slave trade, to which, according to Jefferson, South Carolina and Georgia objected. On July 4 the Declaration of Independence was ratified.

Jefferson kept track of the changes his draft underwent during the congressional discussion of the document, and they are recorded in his *Autobiography*. In a letter many years later (1818), Jefferson wrote of an anecdote that Franklin had related to him upon viewing his frustration with all of the changes made to his original draft. Franklin told him that he avoided writing documents that were subjected to the scrutiny and revision of public bodies because of an incident that occurred when he was young. When the time came for a hatter friend to open his own shop, Franklin said, the hatter determined to make

a nice sign to hang on the door. After submitting his preliminary idea for the sign's inscription to a number of friends for editing, only the hatter's name remained from the ten-word original phrase (Van Doren 1938).

After it was ratified, the declaration was immediately printed by John Dunlap. This first printed set of declarations became known as the Dunlap Broadsides. Although it was ratified, the document was not signed by anyone except John Hancock and Charles Thomson on July 4. New York had abstained from the July 4 vote and did not vote to accept independence until July 9, after which an official copy was ordered. The signing of the official copy began on August 2, 1776, and some delegates who could not be present signed it later. A few delegates to the Congress did not sign it at all. Franklin's signature is one of the 56 on the document. Just before the signing, as legend has it, John

Hancock (whose large signature on the document is famous) said, "We must be unanimous. We must all hang together." Franklin is said to have replied, "We must indeed all hang together, or, most assuredly, we shall all hang separately."

The Declaration of Independence and other political documents from that era, such as George Mason's Virginia Declaration of Rights (adopted June 12, 1776), reflected the ideas of Enlightenment philosophers such as John Locke (1632–1704). In his *Two Treatises of Government,* Locke wrote about the inherent rights of man. "The liberty of man, in society," he said, "is to be under no other legislative power, but that established, by consent, in the commonwealth; nor under the dominion of any will, or restraint of any law, but what that legislative shall enact, according to the trust put in it."

The first section of the Virginia declaration asserted that all men are free and independent, and have inherent rights, "of which, when they enter into a state of society, they cannot, by any compact, deprive or divest their posterity; namely, the enjoyment of life and liberty, with the means of acquiring and possessing property, and pursuing and obtaining happiness and safety."

The beginning of the Declaration of Independence proclaimed "unalienable rights" of "life, liberty, and the pursuit of happiness." It went on to say that the "long train of abuses and usurpations" the colonists had suffered at the hands of the British required the colonies to dissolve the political bonds between them. The abuses cited against the king were many: not allowing colonial governors to pass laws of immediate importance; dissolving houses of representatives; trying to restrict the population of the colonies; obstructing justice; creating new offices and sending new officers to fill them, which drained the colonies of substance; keeping standing armies among them in a time of peace; quartering soldiers among them without their consent; imposing taxes on them without their consent; restricting their trade; capturing Ameri-

cans at sea and forcing them to turn on their fellow citizens; and inciting insurrections in the colonies and bringing Indians against them.

Furthermore, King George III "has plundered our seas, ravaged our coasts, burnt our towns, and destroyed the lives of our people. He is at this time transporting large armies of foreign mercenaries to complete the works of death, desolation and tyranny, already begun with circumstances of cruelty and perfidy scarcely paralleled in the most barbarous ages, and totally unworthy of the head of a civilized nation. . . . A prince whose character is thus marked by every act which may define a tyrant, is unfit to be the ruler of a free people."

The original Declaration of Independence, which has faded considerably, is today kept at the National Archives Building in Washington, D.C.

Related entries:
  Adams, John
  Boston Tea Party
  Continental Congresses
  Jefferson, Thomas
  Paine, Thomas
  Revolutionary War
  Stamp Act

Suggestions for further reading:
  Boyd, Julian P., ed. 1950. "Notes of Proceedings in the Continental Congress"; "The Declaration of Independence," in *The Papers of Thomas Jefferson.* Princeton, N.J.: Princeton University Press.
  Van Doren, Carl. 1945. "John Thompson, Hatter" in *Franklin's Autobiographical Writings.* New York: Viking Press
  Stevens, Richard B., ed. 1984. *The Declaration of Independence and the Constitution of the United States.* Washington, D.C.: Georgetown University Press.

"A Dissertation on Liberty and Necessity, Pleasure and Pain"

*I*n 1724 Franklin traveled to London with his friend James Ralph and subsequently obtained work as a journeyman printer. The following year, he read William

Wollaston's *The Religion of Nature Delineated* while he composed it for printing. His perusal of Wollaston's work, with which he disagreed, prompted him to write a response, "A Dissertation on Liberty and Necessity, Pleasure and Pain."

The short work evidences Franklin's "thoughts of the general state of things in the universe" as a young man of 19, and not the philosophy he held at the end of his life. In 1779, recalling his essay in a letter to his friend Benjamin Vaughan, he said he had written a subsequent piece that used as its basis the assertion that almost all men throughout history have used prayer at one time or another. The second essay, he said, examined another side of the same question discussed in the first—the doctrine of fate. However, the second essay was never printed, and he lost the manuscript. Franklin soon abandoned examinations of this sort: "The great uncertainty I found in metaphysical reasonings disgusted me, and I quitted that kind of reading and study for others more satisfactory." He wrote in his *Autobiography* that publishing the pamphlet had been a mistake.

Franklin printed 100 copies of his work but later burned most of them. One copy was read by a surgeon and author of the *Infallibility, Dignity, and Excellency of Humane Judgment* (1710), William Lyons, who was impressed by it and introduced Franklin to some of his friends.

Franklin's essay was divided into two main parts, the first on "liberty and necessity" and the other on "pleasure and pain." His argument began with the premise that there was an all-powerful, all-good, and all-wise God who made the universe. He argued that evil cannot exist under the rulership of a God with these qualities, and that things that are supposed by people to be evil ultimately work for the good and success of the universe. Creatures in God's creation cannot operate against his will, because nothing can.

In order to know which is best to be done," he wrote, "and which not, it is requisite that we should have at one view all the intricate consequences of every action with respect to the general order and scheme of the universe, both present and future; but they are innumerable and incomprehensible by any thing but Omniscience. As we cannot know these, we have but as one chance to ten thousand, to hit on the right action; we should then be perpetually blundering about in the dark, and putting the scheme in disorder; for every wrong action of a part, is a defect or blemish in the order of the whole. Is it not necessary then, that our actions should be overruled and governed by an all-wise Providence?" (Lemay 1987)

This premise Franklin carried into the next section on pleasure and pain. Pain and uneasiness were, he argued, the root of all action in the universe. If they were removed, life would grind to a halt. Furthermore, pleasure was what fulfilled the desires caused by pain and uneasiness. The amount of pleasure that satisfied uneasiness and pain was equal to the amount of pain endured.

Related entry:
Religious Beliefs

Suggestions for further reading:
"A Dissertation on Liberty and Necessity, Pleasure and Pain," 1725 (Labaree et al., vol. 1).
Masur, Louis P., ed. 1993. *The Autobiography of Benjamin Franklin.* Boston: Bedford Books of St. Martin's Press.
"On the Providence of God in the Government of the World," 1732 (Labaree et al., vol. 1).
"To Benjamin Vaughan," November 9, 1779 (Labaree et al., vol. 31).

Dogood, Mrs. Silence

Franklin signed the fictitious name "Mrs. Silence Dogood" to a series of 14 humorous letters written to the *New En-*

gland Courant, a newspaper owned by his brother James. It was probably taken from two titles of Cotton Mather's writings: *Silentius* and *Essays to Do Good,* the latter of which Franklin said had influenced him at an early age.

Franklin, who was at the time 16 years old and apprenticed to James, wrote the letters without his brother's knowledge. He got the idea of writing them from some of James's friends, who wrote similar small submissions for the paper. Franklin put them under the door at night, and during the day James and his friends, who enjoyed the letters, tried to figure out who authored them. Being just a teenager, he was pleased to learn that they supposed the author to be a learned man.

Mrs. Dogood wrote about many unrelated subjects: her childhood, popular apparel of the time, Harvard College, drunkenness, pride, women, religion, and other topics. In the first letter, published on April 2, 1722, Franklin introduced her as the daughter of immigrants who had set sail from London and moved to New England. She was born on the ship on the voyage over; her father was swept off of it by a wave that came out of nowhere, and he died the same day she was born. Later Mrs. Dogood recounted that she had been apprenticed to a minister and learned from him math, writing, sewing, and reading. She had access to the minister's library, which she took advantage of.

Franklin used the Dogood letters to parody Harvard College and poets, the subjects of two of the most biting and witty of his submissions to the *Courant.* In the fourth letter (May 14, 1722), Mrs. Dogood recounted a dream she had while resting under an apple tree, just after pondering the merits and drawbacks of educating her son. She dreamed she was let into the "temple of learning" as a spectator, who, having got past the gates attended by "riches and poverty," observed learning dressed in black and sitting atop a throne "in an awful state." English sat on her right; Latin, Greek, and Hebrew, who rarely showed their faces, on

her left. The students were sent there because many parents "consulted their own purses instead of their children's capacities ... [and] a great many, yea, the most part of those who were traveling thither, were little better than dunces and blockheads. Alas! alas!" Most students, Mrs. Dogood said, were content to sit at the bottom of the steps leading to learning's throne "with idleness and her maid ignorance."

Letter number seven mocked writers of elegies, and Mrs. Dogood presented guidelines (which she attributed to her late husband) for writing them. The subject of the elegy was to be chosen as follows:

> Take one of your neighbors who has lately departed this life; it is no great matter at what age the party died, but it will be best if he went away suddenly, being killed, drowned, or froze to death. Having chose the person, take all his virtues, excellencies, &c. and if he have not enough, you may borrow some to make up a sufficient quantity: To these add his last words, dying expressions, &c. if they are to be had; mix all these together, and be sure you strain them well. Then season all with a handful or two of melancholly expressions, such as, dreadful, deadly, cruel cold death, unhappy fate, weeping eyes, &c. . . .

In other letters, Mrs. Dogood asserted that men were generally more prone to vice than women, attacked religious hypocrites, examined the pros and cons of drinking alcohol, proposed that organizations be established to aid widows and virgins who had passed their prime for marrying, and made fun of women's hoop-petticoats, "the most immodest and inconvenient of any the art of woman has invented." She complained, "These monstrous topsy-turvy mortar-pieces are neither fit for the church, the hall, or the kitchen; and if a number of them were well mounted on Noddles-Island, they would look more like engines of war for bombarding the town, than ornaments of the fair sex." She said she did not have much hope of persuading women to stop wearing them, but she hoped they would at least shrink in size (June 11, 1722).

Franklin eventually ended his charade by telling his brother and friends that he had written the letters. He speculated that this might have led to the enmity that formed between him and his brother during his apprenticeship. Some readers in the town expressed their disappointment that Silence Dogood had quit writing.

Related entries:
Franklin, James
Printing

Suggestions for further reading:
"The Dogood Papers," 1722 (Smyth, vol. II).
Masur, Louis P., ed. 1993. *The Autobiography of Benjamin Franklin*. Boston: Bedford Books of St. Martin's Press.

Douse, Elizabeth Franklin (1677–1759)

The eldest of Josiah Franklin's 17 children, Elizabeth Franklin Douse was Franklin's half sister and nearly 30 years his senior. She was born to Josiah and Anne (Child) Franklin in England, along with Samuel Franklin and Hannah Franklin (Cole), and moved to Boston in 1683. Franklin was happy to find when he went to England a relation (Mary Franklin Fisher, daughter of Franklin's uncle Thomas) who remembered Elizabeth and two other children before they set sail for America. In 1721 Elizabeth married her second husband, Richard Douse, a shipmaster, after the death of her first husband, Captain Joseph Berry.

In 1757 Franklin wrote to his youngest sister, Jane Mecom, concerned for Elizabeth's living situation. "When they have long lived in a house, it becomes natural to them," he said, "they are almost as closely connected with it, as the tortoise with his shell; they die, if you tear them out of it; old folks and old trees, if you remove them, it is ten to one that you kill them; so let our good old sister be no more importuned on that hand." Elizabeth outlived all of her 16 younger siblings except Franklin, Peter, and Jane (Mecom), and died in 1759, while Franklin was overseas.

Related entry:
Mecom, Jane Franklin

Suggestions for further reading:
"To Jane Mecom," April 19, 1757 (Labaree et al., vol. 7).
"To John Franklin," August 6, 1747 (Labaree et al., vol. 3).

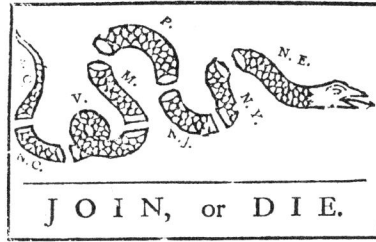

JOIN, or DIE.

E

Education

As a child, Franklin had less than two years of formal education, but he actively sought to educate himself. Throughout his life, he read voraciously, attended philosophical discussion clubs and meetings at academies, conducted scientific experiments, and corresponded with others about a broad range of subjects in natural philosophy. Although he lacked formal education, he received a multitude of honorary degrees from colleges in England and America. In July 1753 he received an honorary master of arts from Harvard College. In September 1753 he was awarded an honorary master of arts from Yale College. In April 1756 he received an honorary master of arts degree from William and Mary College. The University of St. Andrews made him an honorary doctor of laws in 1759, and Oxford University awarded him an honorary doctorate of civil laws in 1762.

Franklin wanted young boys in Philadelphia to have the opportunity to gain the formal education he lacked. In 1743 he drafted a proposal for establishing an academy, as an opportunity for education was one of two things he felt were missing in Pennsylvania (the other was adequate defense). He approached Reverend Richard Peters (1704–1775), who was unemployed, about serving as the superintendent. Peters declined, how-

ever, and Franklin did not know of another person fit for the job. The project came to a halt until 1749, when Franklin began to circulate a proposal among his friends (many from the Junto). He published his "Proposals Relating to the Education of Youth in Pennsylvania" as a pamphlet and distributed it among the "principal inhabitants" without charge.

Franklin proposed that "some persons of leisure and public spirit apply for a charter, by which they may be incorporated, with power to erect an academy for the education of youth, to govern the same, provide masters, make rules, receive donations, purchase lands, etc., and to add to their number, from time to time such other persons as they shall judge suitable." The members of the corporation were to be actively interested in the students. Franklin suggested that a house be provided for the academy. It should have a library, a garden, a meadow, an orchard, and a field. The library should contain maps of all countries, globes, mathematical instruments, equipment for experiments in natural philosophy and mechanics, and prints. The rector, who would oversee the tutors, was to be a man of good understanding, moral, diligent, patient, and proficient in languages and sciences.

The students of the academy were to be boys between the ages of 8 and 16. Franklin thought they should eat together, plainly, temperately, and frugally, and have plenty of

The University of Pennsylvania. Wood engraving in **American Magazine**, *1836.*

exercise. "[T]hings that are likely to be most useful and most ornamental" were most important to learn, Franklin thought. Instructors would teach them handwriting, drawing, mathematics, accounting, geometry, astronomy, and grammar. The curriculum should include works of John Tillotson (1630–1694), Joseph Addison (1672–1719), Alexander Pope (1688–1744), Algernon Sidney (1622–1683), and Cato (234–149 B.C.). The academy was to place emphasis on proper reading and writing techniques, which students could learn by writing letters to one another, making abstracts of what they read, rewriting pieces in their own words, and repeating and delivering speeches.

Franklin envisioned educating young boys by "universal history," which would give students "a connected idea of human affairs. [I]f history be made a constant part of their reading," he wrote, "such as the translations of the Greek and Roman historians, and the modern histories of ancient Greece and Rome, &c. May not almost all kinds of useful knowledge be that way introduced to advantage, and with pleasure to the student?" Geography, chronology, ancient customs, morality, oratory, natural history, mechanical history, the advantages of public religion and of religious character, and "the excellency of the Christian religion above all others ancient or modern" were all part of Franklin's scheme. Practical application should accom-

pany their reading—while students read natural history, they should visit successful farms and garden themselves.

After people had the chance to read Franklin's "Proposals," he began to solicit subscriptions for the academy. The subscriptions totaled £5,000, and the subscribers chose 24 trustees. Franklin served as president of the board of trustees from 1749 to 1756. Tench Francis and Franklin drafted constitutions for the academy. The same year, they were able to hire teachers and a house and open the school. The number of students soon exceeded the house's capacity, and with Franklin's help, the academy moved into the debt-ridden building that was originally constructed as a permanent speaking platform for speakers of any religion when Reverend George Whitefield came to town. By the terms of the agreement, a large hall of the house remained open for speakers, and a free school for poor children was established as well. The Philadelphia Academy and Charitable School obtained the building, paid its debts, and purchased some additional land. The trustees of the academy were incorporated, and the school grew with the help of donations of money and land from Britain, the proprietaries, and the Assembly.

Franklin elaborated further on his intentions for education in "Idea of an English School" (1750), which was printed with the text of a sermon delivered by Peters at the academy's opening. He maintained that students should be able to write legibly and pronounce and divide syllables. He divided the program into six classes. The first class was to emphasize English grammar, vocabulary, and spelling. In the second class, students would learn to read with proper pronunciation and meaning and focus on understanding what they read: "[T]hey often read as parrots speak, knowing little or nothing of the meaning. And it is impossible a reader should give the due modulation to his voice, and pronounce properly, unless his understanding goes before his tongue, and makes him master of the sentiment." The third class placed emphasis on proper speaking and rhetoric, and the students were to begin reading history—chronologies, natural history, and mechanical history.

Students in the fourth class were to concentrate on composition, morality, more history, and geography. Franklin suggested that students write letters to one another on a variety of subjects, and "in these they should be taught to express themselves clearly, concisely, and naturally, without affected words or high-flown phrases." Class number five was to continue developing composition skills, moving from writing letters to writing essays and verse. Writing verse, Franklin thought, taught students how to vary their expressions. In addition, the fifth class was to study logic and reasoning and continue studying history. Finally, the sixth class continued its studies from the previous classes but was now to be introduced to "the best English authors," Pope, Jonathan Swift (1667–1745), Addison, Tillotson, John Milton (1608–1674), and John Locke (1632–1704). In addition, they were to read translations of Homer (8th century B.C.), Horace (65–8 B.C.), and Virgil (70–19 B.C.). Students were to spend part of the day with a writing teacher, part with a math teacher, and the remainder with the teacher of the English school.

The building was 70 feet wide and 100 feet long and had three stories, with an observatory. In 1751 the academy paid the rector, who taught Greek and Latin, £200 per year; the English master £150 per year; the math professor £125 per year; and assistant tutors £60 each per year. The trustees tried to keep salaries high to attract quality instructors. Franklin was fairly involved in the academy's affairs while he lived in Philadelphia. Among the trustees a controversy over the role of the English and Latin schools persisted over the years. Franklin had envisioned a well-rounded English education—progressive for its time—but some of the subscribers favored a Latin school and a more classical education. In 1789 Franklin wrote "Observations Relative to the Intentions of the Original Founders of the Academy in Philadelphia," in which he defended the English school. The academy was renamed the University of Pennsylvania in 1779 and still exists today.

Related entries:
Kinnersley, Ebenezer
Pennsylvania Assembly

Suggestions for further reading:
Cloyd, David Excelmons. 1902. *Benjamin Franklin and Education: His Ideal of Life and His System of Education for the Realization of That Ideal.* Boston: D. C. Heath.
"Idea of the English School, Sketched Out for the Consideration of the Trustees of the Philadelphia Academy," 1751 (Labaree et al., vol. 4).
Meyerson, Martin, and Dilys Pegler Winegrad. 1978. *Gladly Learn and Gladly Teach: Franklin and His Heirs at the University of Pennsylvania, 1740–1976.* Philadelphia: University of Pennsylvania Press.
"Observations Relative to the Intentions of the Original Founders of the Academy in Philadelphia," June 1789 (Smyth, vol. X).
"Proposals Relating to the Education of Youth in Pennsylvania," 1749 (Labaree et al., vol. 3).
"To Samuel Johnson," August 9, 1750 (Labaree et al., vol. 4).
"To Samuel Johnson, D.D.," August 23, 1750 (Labaree et al., vol. 4).

Electricity

Aside from his extensive role in the American Revolution, Franklin is perhaps best known for his work in electricity and the invention of the lightning rod. In 1745 Peter Collinson, one of Franklin's London correspondents, sent a glass tube used in electrical experiments—a Leyden jar—as a gift to the Library Company of Philadelphia. Just before he received this gift Franklin had observed electrical experiments in Boston "imperfectly performed" by Dr. Adam Spencer. After the glass tube arrived at the Library Company he tried to repeat the experiments he had witnessed. "My house was continually full for some time with

The Philosopher and His Kite. *(Franklin's experiment with a kite and a key in a thunderstorm).* *Engraving by Henry S. Sadd.*

persons who came to see these new wonders," Franklin wrote in his *Autobiography*. He had more glass tubes blown so that others could perform the experiments, and he hired his unemployed neighbor, Ebenezer Kinnersley, to show them. Franklin composed two different lectures for Kinnersley "in which the experiments were arranged in such order and accompanied with explanations in such method as the foregoing would assist in comprehending the following."

Franklin sent letters to Collinson and others in London describing the experiments they had performed with his gift. The central item in Franklin's experiments was the Leyden jar, invented by Pieter van Musschenbroek in 1745. The stoppered jar was constructed of glass, and a wire extended through the stopper to water inside the jar. Tinfoil coated both the inside and the outside of the jar. To charge the jar, one held it in one hand and brought the wire into contact with an electrical device. Franklin amended the design by filling the jar with granulated lead instead of water. He found that lead was easier to warm and to keep warm and dry in humid air. A member of the Junto, Philip Syng, designed an electrical device that enabled one to charge the jars with less difficulty.

In the first description Franklin sent to Collinson of his experiments, written in 1747, he related a new discovery (which he credited to Thomas Hopkinson, the original president of the American Philosophical Society), which was that pointed bodies both draw off and throw off electrical fire. To show that pointed bodies throw off electricity, he placed an iron shot on the mouth of a glass bottle and hung a cork ball by a piece of silk thread from the ceiling, so that the cork rested on the side of the shot. When the shot was electrified, it repelled the cork ball. When he held a long, slender bodkin 6 to 8 inches from the shot, the shot no longer repelled the cork. To show that a pointed body drew off electricity, he took the blade out of the bodkin and fixed it in a stick of wax. When he placed the blade in the same position near the shot, the repulsion remained, but if he slid his finger up the wax so it touched the blade, the cork was immediately attracted to the shot.

Some of Franklin's experiments were entertaining. In one of them, he suspended above a table a fake spider, its body constructed of cork and its legs of thread, with lead to add weight. Franklin and his fellow experimenters placed an upright wire 2 to 3 inches from the spider on the table underneath it. "[T]hen we animate him, by setting the electrified phial at the same distance on the other side of him; he will immediately fly to the wire of the phial, bend his legs in touching it; then spring off, and fly to the wire on the table . . . playing with his legs against both, in a very entertaining manner, appearing perfectly alive to persons unacquainted."

One of Franklin's most important contributions to the understanding of electricity was his study of positive and negative—or plus and minus—charges, and he was the first to use those terms. Before his work, scientists believed that two different kinds of electricity existed, vitreous and resinous. Franklin adhered to a single-fluid theory, which hypothesized that electricity was a single fluid. Electric fluid, Franklin thought, was found in varying amounts in different bodies. The fluid could pass from one body to another when one was charged positively and the other charged negatively. Matter without electricity repelled itself, and electric fluid repelled itself and attracted matter. On the Leyden jar, he found, "At the same time that the wire and the top of the bottle . . . is electrised positively or plus, the bottom of the bottle is electrised negatively or minus, in exact proportion; i.e., whatever quantity of electrical fire is thrown in at the top, an equal quantity goes out of the bottom" (1747).

In a letter to Peter Collinson in 1749 Franklin speculated on the relationship between electricity and lightning. "As electrified clouds pass over a country, high hills and high trees, lofty towers, spires, masts of ships, chimneys . . . as so many prominencies and points, draw the electrical fire, and the cloud discharges there," he thought. "Dangerous, therefore, is it to take shelter under a tree, during a thunder-gust. It has been fatal to many, both men and beasts." In November 1749 he noted several characteristics that were common to both lightning and electricity: "1. Giving light. 2. Color of the light. 3. Crooked direction. 4. Swift motion. 5. Being conducted by metals. 6. Crack or noise in exploding. 7. Subsisting in water or ice. 8. Rending bodies it passes through. 9. Destroying animals. 10. Melting metals. 11. Firing inflammable substances. 12. Sulphureous smell."

Franklin's work with pointed bodies and electricity, coupled with his equation of lightning with electricity, led directly to his invention of the lightning rod. In 1750 he wrote to Collinson, "[M]ay not the knowledge of this power of points be of use to mankind, in preserving houses, churches, ships, &c. from the stroke of lightning, by directing us to fix on the highest parts of those edifices, upright rods of iron made sharp as a needle, and gilt to prevent rusting, and from the foot of those rods a wire down the outside of the building into the ground? . . . "

Thomas-François Dalibard performed the first test of Franklin's suggestion in France, where he set up a 40-foot iron rod outside of Paris. In May 1752 Dalibard's observers witnessed sparks from the rod when a thunder cloud passed overhead. M. Delor, who had performed Franklin's experiments for Louis XV, repeated Dalibard's experiment with a 99-foot rod at his home in Paris. (Louis XV, after watching the experiments, instructed the Abbé Mazéas to write a letter to the Royal Society, with gratitude to Franklin for his discoveries in electricity and the lightning rods that prevented the terrible effects of storms.) He likewise observed sparks when a thundercloud passed over it. Members of the Royal Society of London also performed experiments with metal rods. The following year, a Swedish physicist, G. W. Richmann, died in St. Petersburg while performing the experiment, the news of which disturbed Franklin.

Franklin, during this time, devised another method of drawing fire from clouds. Sometime in 1752 he performed his famous experiment with a kite and a key. After he conducted the trial successfully, he wrote a description of the experiment to draw "the electric fire from the clouds." He constructed his kite from two strips of cedar formed into a cross, with a handkerchief stretched over them. He fastened a sharp, pointed wire to the top of the kite that extended at least a foot above it. To the end of the kite string, he fastened a silk ribbon, and a key was fastened where the silk ribbon joined the kite string. The holder of the kite was to stand in a doorway to prevent the silk ribbon from getting wet. "[W]hen the rain has wet the kite and the twine, so that it can conduct the electric fire freely, you will find it stream out plentifully from the key on the approach of your knuckle," Franklin instructed. Franklin found that the electricity from the key would charge a vial, and that the electrical experiments he conducted could be performed with this electricity, thereby demonstrating "the sameness of the electric matter with that of lightning." The famous story of Franklin's own performance of the kite experiment comes from Dr. Joseph Priestley's *History of Electricity* (1767). Franklin and his son William, in June 1752, stood in a shed in a field during a storm. They raised the kite into the storm, and at first there seemed to be no evidence of electricity in the kite. However, as the kite continued in the air, Franklin noticed loose threads on the string standing erect. He touched the key with his knuckle and received a shock.

Collinson had, during this time, had some of Franklin's letters to him on the experi-

ments read at the Royal Society of London, whose members dismissed them as inconsequential. One paper, in which Franklin equated lightning with electricity, was sent to Dr. John Mitchell, read at the Society, and laughed at. However, with the encouragement of Dr. John Fothergill, Collinson had the letters published. The first edition, entitled "Experiments and Observations on Electricity, Made at Philadelphia in America" (1751), was an 86-page pamphlet with a preface by Fothergill.

The pamphlet flopped in England, but a French philosopher, the Comte de Buffon, convinced Dalibard to undertake a good French translation. The Abbé Nollet, who had himself performed many electrical experiments and developed theories on electricity, believed that the letters were a production of his enemies and doubted the existence of any Franklin at Philadelphia. Nollet then wrote a series of letters criticizing Franklin's theories and defending his own. Franklin never responded publicly, and Nollet's theories later fell into disrepute. Franklin's letters were translated into many languages and widely read in Europe, and they made him famous.

The Royal Society of London began to take a belated interest in the experiments they had earlier dismissed. Dr. William Watson, who had conducted many experiments in electricity, summarized Franklin's writings on the subject, and they appeared in the Society's *Philosophical Transactions*. "[T]hey soon made me more than amends for the slight with which they had before treated me," Franklin wrote in his *Autobiography*. "Without my having made any application for that honor, they chose me as a member, and voted that I should be excused the customary payments, which would have amounted to twenty-five guineas; and ever since have given me their *Transactions* gratis." The Royal Society awarded Franklin the Sir Godfrey Copley medal in 1753 and elected him in 1756.

Back in America, the preface to Franklin's *Poor Richard's Almanack* for 1753 contained instructions for securing homes with lightning rods. The first lightning rods in America were raised in Philadelphia, though the exact date is uncertain. In September 1752 Franklin placed a lightning rod on top of his house in order to conduct experiments with it. He placed a second rod that was connected to the ground about 6 inches away and attached a bell to each rod. Then he hung a small ball by a silk thread between the two bells, so that the ball struck either bell when it was attracted to it. The bells sometimes rang under a dark cloud with no thunder and lightning. Sometimes a flash of lightning caused them to stop ringing, and sometimes it caused them to start ringing.

In 1753 Franklin experimented with the electrical charge of clouds. He charged one vial with lightning and another with his electric glass globe. He hung a cork ball on a silk thread from the ceiling between the wires and observed the behavior of the ball. From the first experiment, he concluded that the clouds had a negative charge. Subsequent trials showed that the clouds usually had a negative charge but sometimes had a positive charge. He further concluded that lightning struck from the ground to the clouds, and not the other way around.

Franklin performed many other experiments in electricity, far too numerous to describe in full. In 1749 he constructed what he called an electrical battery. He discovered that electricity magnetized needles, and he used electricity to ignite gunpowder. In 1755 he electrified a silver pint can and lowered a cork into the can. He found that the cork was not attracted to the inside of the can, and when he pulled it out, it had not received any charge. "The fact is singular," Franklin wrote to Dr. John Lining. "You require the reason: I do not know it." Later, Franklin deduced that the mutual repulsion of the can's inner opposite sides prevents the accumulation of an electric atmosphere on them and forces it to stand outside. This experiment was a predecessor to the important discovery that electrical repulsion varies inversely with the square of the distance between charges, proved by Priestley around 1766.

The experiments that Franklin conducted encouraged his scientific acquaintances and correspondents to try their own. Among them were James Alexander of New York, the Dutch physician Dr. Jan Ingenhousz, James Bowdoin in Boston, and Dr. Joseph Priestley, who wrote his *History of Electricity* in 1767. In Italy, Giambatista Beccaria conducted experiments and agreed with Franklin's theories, and he later became one of Franklin's correspondents.

In 1772 Franklin was appointed to a committee in the Royal Society for determining the best method of protecting British arsenals at Purfleet. A dissenter on the committee, Benjamin Wilson, believed that blunt rods were preferable to pointed rods, which the rest of the committee, including Franklin, recommended. Pointed rods were installed on the royal palace and at the arsenals. However, after the American Revolution broke out, George III ordered the pointed rods on the royal palace replaced with blunt ones. Humorous rhymes, such as the following, circulated in London:

> While you, great George, for knowledge hunt
> And sharp conductors change for blunt
> The Empire's out of joint.
> Franklin another course pursues
> And all your thunder heedless views
> By keeping to the point.
> (Smyth 1907)

Franklin always sought to apply the knowledge he gained from his experiments in practical ways. He performed electrical experiments on turkeys and chickens, believing that instant death from an electric shock was a more humane way of killing them, and that electricity rendered the meat more tender. He found that the shock from two large, thin, 6-gallon glass jars, when charged, would kill chickens but only knock turkeys out for

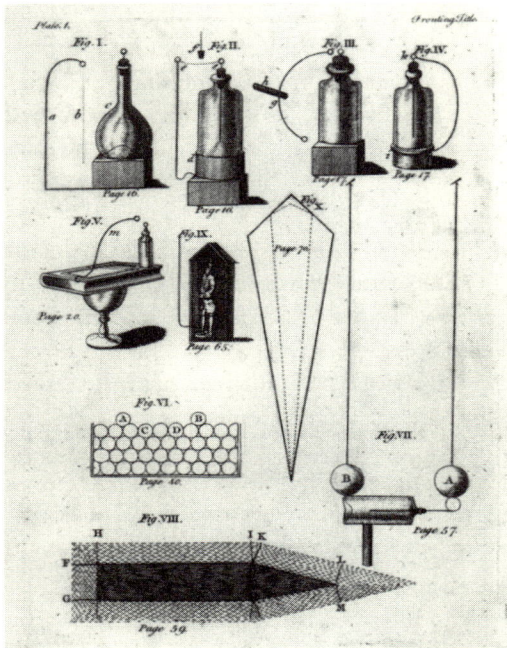

Benjamin Franklin's electrical apparatus, c. 1751. Engraving in Benjamin Franklin's, "Experiments and Observations on Electricity," 1774, plate 1.

Suggestions for further reading:
"Additional Experiment," September 27, 1750 (Labaree et al., vol. 4).
"Electrical Experiments," March 14, 1755 (Labaree et al., vol. 5).
"Experiments Supporting the Use of Pointed Lightning Rods," August 18, 1772 (Labaree et al., vol. 19).
"Franklin: Answers to Queries from Dr. Ingenhousz," 1780 (Labaree, et. al., vol. 32).
"Of Lightning, and the Method (Now used in America) of Securing Buildings and Persons from Its Mischievous Effects," 1767 (Labaree et al., vol. 14).
"To John Mitchell," April 29, 1749 (Labaree et al., vol. 3).
"To Peter Collinson," September 1, 1747 (Labaree et al., vol. 3).
"To Peter Collinson," October 18, 1748 (Labaree et. al., vol. 3).
"To Peter Collinson," April 29, 1749 (Labaree et al., vol. 3).
"To Peter Collinson," 1753 (Labaree et al., vol. 5).

15 minutes. Three additional jars killed a ten-pound turkey. During one of these experiments, Franklin accidentally shocked himself instead of the turkey with the charge of two jars. He said it seemed as if he had received a universal blow throughout his body, and he trembled violently for a few seconds. He did not recover his senses until a few minutes later. The only lingering symptoms were numbness in his arms and back that lasted the rest of the day, a swelling on top of his head where he had received the shock, and a soreness in his chest for about a week. Potential medical uses for electricity also interested Franklin. He conducted experiments on paralytics and, at Ingenhousz's suggestion, recommended to a French surgeon using electricity on mentally ill patients.

The chief years of Franklin's electrical research were the late 1740s and early 1750s, after which he was generally too busy with public affairs to devote as much time to study as he would have liked. However, he continued to conduct experiments as time allowed.

Eliot, Jared (1685–1763)

Jared Eliot was the grandson of John "Apostle" Eliot (1604–1690), the American minister who devoted much of his time to proselytizing Native Americans in Massachusetts. The younger Eliot graduated from Yale College, became rector of Killingworth, Connecticut, and was a fellow of the Royal Society. He corresponded with Franklin about a wide variety of subjects in natural philosophy, and the two had mutual friends or correspondents in John Bartram, Hugh Roberts (of the Junto), and Peter Collinson.

Eliot was a physician and a minister, and he was particularly interested in agriculture. In 1748 he wrote "An Essay on Field Husbandry in New England." Franklin sent him accounts of agricultural experiments that he conducted on his 300-acre farm near Burlington, New Jersey, purchased around 1748. He found that he could grow more than 60 bushels of Indian corn per acre on a portion of meadow that had been ditched and mowed. He sowed 30 acres with red clover and herd grass in August, and found that the red clover came up in four days, and the herd grass in six days. The more densely he sowed the seed, he found, the better the plants fared in frost. On 1 acre, Franklin sowed 12 pounds of red clover seed, and on another, two bushels of rye grass seed and 5 pounds of red clover seed. "[T]he rye grass seed failed," he told Eliot, "and the red clover heaves out much for want of being thicker." Franklin also found that the herd grass had shallower roots and was less affected by the frost than the red clover, although he had previously guessed that the red clover's extensive root system would render it more hardy.

Franklin and Eliot also considered the origin of springs. Franklin agreed that most springs arose from "rains, dews, or ponds, on higher grounds, yet possibly some, that break out near the tops of high hollow mountains, may proceed from the abyss, or from water in the caverns of the earth, rarefied by its internal heat, and raised in vapor, till the cold region near the tops of such mountains condenses the vapor into water again. . . . "This water creates a spring, Franklin conjectured, and runs down the side of a mountain.

Among the other subjects on which they corresponded were northeastern storms, ditching, Schuyler's copper mines in New Jersey, trade winds, bubbles, oil, the academy that Franklin founded in Philadelphia, and a tariff law in Connecticut. Franklin objected to the tariff law, which placed a 5 percent duty on goods imported from other colonies. The Connecticut consumer, he argued in 1747, would end up bearing the burden of the duty, which he thought was in reality "only another mode of taxing your own people." The law might possibly stimulate manufacturing in Connecticut, if that colony began to manufacture goods it normally imported from other colonies. But a duty on goods from other colonies would likely create resentment, Franklin thought, and perhaps spur other colonies to levy duties on goods they imported from Connecticut. Finally, he thought that the law would prove difficult to enforce, as Connecticut would have to expend considerable resources to stop smugglers and prevent them from underselling the lawful goods.

Related entries:
Bartram, John
Collinson, Peter
The Junto

Suggestions for further reading:
Thoms, Herbert. 1967. *Jared Eliot, Minister, Doctor, Scientist, and His Connecticut.* Hamden, Conn.: Shoe String Press.
"To Jared Eliot," July 16, 1747 (Labaree et al., vol. 3).
"To Jared Eliot," 1749 (Labaree et al., vol. 3).
"To Jared Eliot," May 3, 1753 (Labaree et al., vol. 4).

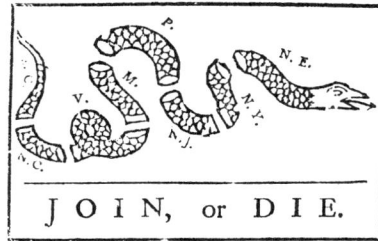

JOIN, or DIE.

Fire

Fire fascinated Franklin throughout his life, and that interest motivated him both to study it and to design measures to prevent the destruction it causes. In his inquiries into the nature of fire he speculated on why different substances were good or poor conductors of fire. He thought of fire as a fluid that penetrated other bodies and dissipated their parts, some more easily than others. Every living being, he thought, contains a small quantity of the fluid called "fire," and it provides them with their body warmth. Too much of it produces a burning sensation; he also thought that "all the fire emitted by wood and other combustibles when burning existed in them before in a solid state, being only discovered when separating."

He recounted in his *Autobiography:* "I wrote a paper (first to be read in Junto, but it was afterward published) on the different accidents and carelessnesses by which houses were set on fire, with cautions against them, and means proposed of avoiding them. This was much spoken of as a useful piece, and gave rise to a project, which soon followed it, of forming a company for the more ready extinguishing of fires, and mutual assistance in removing and securing the goods when in danger."

Franklin had also written a letter to the *Pennsylvania Gazette* in 1735 signed "A. A."

offering suggestions for fire safety measures. His letter included suggestions for both private prevention and public regulation: removing wooden moldings on the sides of fireplaces, which caught fire easily; imposing regulations on certain buildings, such as bake houses; taking more care in the removal of coals; and better and more frequent chimney cleanings, to be achieved by licensing chimney sweepers and charging them fines for fires that result from poor sweeping. He also advised that the town take up an orderly approach to fire fighting, which involved companies of men working under the direction of a fire warden when fires broke out.

Members of the subsequently formed Union Fire Company (1736) agreed to keep leather buckets, strong bags, and baskets ready to use in the event of fire, and also to hold monthly meetings for the purpose of discussing new ideas about fires. Requests for membership in the new fire company soon grew so numerous that additional companies formed. The fire companies proved to be very valuable and continued to operate in the colonies.

Those who missed monthly meetings were required to pay a fine, which went toward the purchase of "fire-engines, ladders, fire-hooks, and other useful implements." In 1752 Franklin was also elected to the board of directors of the first fire insurance company in the colonies. Writing at the end of his life, Franklin noted that since the fire-fighting companies formed, fire had never destroyed more than two houses at once in Philadelphia.

Related entries:
Franklin Stove
The Junto

Suggestions for further reading:
"Loose Thoughts on a Universal Fluid," June 25, 1784 (Smyth, vol. IX).
Masur, Louis P., ed. 1993. *The Autobiography of Benjamin Franklin.* Boston: Bedford Books of St. Martin's Press.
"On Protection of Towns from Fire," February 4, 1734/1735 (Labaree et al., vol. 2).
"To John Lining," April 14, 1757 (Labaree et al., vol. 7).

Fothergill, Dr. John (1712–1780)

Dr. John Fothergill was a Scottish Quaker and longtime friend of Franklin's. He pursued almost as many interests as Franklin did. By profession Fothergill was a medical doctor—and Franklin's personal physician when he fell ill with a cold upon his arrival in London in 1757.

Fothergill took an early interest in Franklin's papers that equated lightning with electricity. These notions, which are now known to be true, were laughed at when first introduced to the Royal Society of London. Fothergill, however, thought that they were valuable and suggested that they be printed. He wrote a preface to the resulting pamphlet. Botany was another of his areas of study; he corresponded frequently with his and Franklin's mutual friend John Bartram in America and kept a large botanical garden. In his *Autobiography* Franklin described him as "a great promoter of useful projects." He proposed to Fothergill what he thought would be a more efficient method of keeping the streets of London and Westminster clean. Both men were members of the Royal Society and a philosophical club called the "Honest Whigs" in London.

Outside of science, Fothergill was a political negotiator with an optimistic outlook and a desire for the peaceful resolution of disputes. In two different sets of circumstances he served as a mediator in negotiations in which Franklin was involved. The first talks took place in 1757, when Franklin arrived in England to push for the Pennsylvania Assembly's right to tax proprietary lands. Fothergill advised Franklin to take the Assembly's grievances to the proprietors themselves before he went to the government. He arranged an ill-fated meeting between Franklin and the proprietors at the home of Thomas Penn, the proprietor with the largest holdings.

Fothergill served as a mediator, along with David Barclay, between Franklin and British ministers during Franklin's final attempt to reconcile England with her colonies in 1774 and 1775. He had written a pamphlet urging the repeal of the Stamp Act during that controversy and sympathized with American grievances. At first he was optimistic that some sort of compromise could be worked out between the two parties and urged Franklin to draw up a plan of reconciliation. According to Franklin, "The good doctor, with his usual philanthropy, expatiated on the miseries of war; that even a bad peace was preferable to the most successful war. . . . " By the end of the failed negotiations, however, Fothergill had grown disgusted with the British government. He advised Franklin to tell their friends in America that "whatever specious pretenses are offered, they are all hollow . . . to get a larger field on which to fatten a herd of worthless parasites is all that is regarded."

Fothergill did not live to see the conclusion of the war. He died in December 1780. In 1783 Franklin ordered two sets of Fothergill's works from the Quaker physician John Coakley Lettsom, who had collected them. After Fothergill's death, Franklin wrote of him, "I think a worthier man never lived."

Related entries:
American Philosophical Society

An Account of Negotiations in London for
Effecting a Reconciliation between Great
Britain and the American Colonies
Bartram, John
Collinson, Peter
Electricity
Great Britain
Revolutionary War
Royal Society of London

Suggestions for further reading:
Fox, R. Hingston. 1919. *Dr. John Fothergill and
His Friends: Chapters in Eighteenth Century Life.*
London: Macmillan.
Lettsom, John Coakley. 1786. *Memoirs of John
Fothergill.* London: C. Dilly.
"To John Fothergill," March 14, 1764
(Labaree et al., vol. 11).
"To John Fothergill," June 19, 1780 (Labaree
et al., vol. 32).
"To William Franklin: Journal of Negotiations
in London" (Labaree et al., vol. 21).

*Benjamin Franklin's first audience in France at
Versailles, March 20, 1778. Etching by Daniel
Chodowiecki, 1784.*

France

*I*n 1767 Franklin visited France with
Sir John Pringle, during which both
were presented to Louis XV. Almost ten years
later, he returned to France as a commissioner
from the Second Continental Congress.
Franklin, at age 70, brought with him his two
grandsons, William Temple Franklin and Benjamin Franklin Bache, aged 17 and 7, respectively. Already famous for his lightning rod,
he became a hero almost as soon as he arrived in France.

It quickly became fashionable in Paris to
own a likeness of Franklin. Friends convinced
him to sit for portraits and busts, which they
commissioned and paid for. He obliged them,
even though he disliked sitting still for hours
on end. Clay medallions, Franklin wrote to
his daughter in 1779, "with the pictures, busts,
and prints (of which copies upon copies are
spread everywhere), have made your father's
face as well known as that of the moon, so
that he durst not do anything that would
oblige him to run away, as his phiz [face]
would discover him wherever he should venture to show it." Franklin preferred simple
dress to Paris fashions. "Figure to yourself an

old man," he wrote to Polly Hewson in 1779,
"with grey hair appearing under a martin
fur cap, among the powdered heads of Paris.
It is this odd figure that salutes you, with
handfuls of blessings on you and your dear
little ones."

The official duties associated with the war
took up a large portion of Franklin's time in
France. As one of the commissioners (with
Arthur Lee, Silas Deane, and later John
Adams), and later the sole minister plenipo-
tentiary, he procured loans from France, paid
Congress's bills, oversaw the sale of prize ships,
recommended foreign officers, orchestrated
exchanges of prisoners of war, and negoti-
ated treaties. After the United States signed a
treaty of alliance with France in 1778,
Franklin went to the French court every
Tuesday. In the business of the war, he dealt
chiefly with the Comte de Vergennes, the
French foreign minister. John Jay, Henry
Laurens, and Thomas Jefferson joined him in
France after the war.

After a two-month stay at the Hôtel
d'Hambourg in Paris, Franklin found per-

Benjamin Franklin as Ambassador from the Congress of America to the Court of France. Etching after the medal first done by Manufacture Nationale des Sèvres, 1778.

manent lodging at the more removed Hôtel Valentinois in Passy with Jacques-Donatien Le Ray de Chaumont, who refused to accept any rent from Franklin and his American associates during the war. Chaumont, a thorough businessman, was engaged in commerce with America and bought and sold American prize ships. Deane, and later Adams, lived at Passy with Franklin; Lee found lodging elsewhere.

Franklin's neighbors in Passy became his closest friends and enthusiastically supported the American cause. Louis-Guillaume Le Veillard managed Les Nouvelles Eaux de Passy, a source of bottled mineral water, which wealthier Parisians drank instead of the polluted water from the Seine River. Le Veillard helped Franklin with his French, and his son, Louis, became a close friend of Temple Franklin. Madame Le Veillard and their daughter, Geneviève, were among the many French women who grew to love and admire Franklin. Le Veillard urged Franklin even more persistently to finish his *Autobiography* than did Benjamin Vaughan in England, and Franklin sent both of them copies of the unfinished book before he died. When Franklin left, Le Veillard gave him a supply of his mineral water, and Franklin wrote from

Philadelphia in 1786: "[W]e are now drinking every day *les eaux épurées de Passy* with great satisfaction. . . . " Le Veillard became mayor of Passy during the French Revolution and died on the scaffold in 1794.

The Brillons, who lived next door to the Le Veillards, entertained Franklin on Wednesdays and Saturdays with dinner, chess, tea, and music. Of the women Franklin befriended, Madame Brillon was one of the two closest to him, along with Madame Helvétius. Franklin unsuccessfully tried to arrange a marriage between Temple and one of the Brillons' daughters. The Brillons declined, and Temple fathered an illegitimate son, Théodore, by a neighbor's wife, Blanchette Caillot. Théodore died of smallpox as an infant.

Madame Helvétius lived in the neighboring village of Auteuil, and at her small estate she hosted some of France's most eminent philosophers. She was the widow of the philosopher Claude-Adrien Helvétius (1715–1771). Franklin spent Saturday afternoons in her salon, often in philosophical discussions with the Abbé de La Roche, the Abbé Morellet, and Pierre-Jean-Georges Cabanis, who either lived near or on her estate. Though it is not known whether or not he intended it seriously, Franklin proposed to Madame Helvétius, and she refused him on the same grounds on which she had refused a proposal from the economist Anne-Robert-Jacques Turgot (1727–1781)—she vowed not to remarry in memory of her late husband.

Among Franklin's other acquaintances in France was the Duc de La Rochefoucauld, a fellow Mason of the Nine Sisters Lodge whom Franklin convinced to translate the American constitutions into French. The Comtesse d'Houdetot, who lived at Sannois, welcomed Franklin in 1781 with an elaborate celebration that included extravagant praises of Franklin, America, and liberty in verse. Madame d'Houdetot, admired by philosopher Jean-Jacques Rousseau (1712–1778), was "Sophie" in his *Confessions*. After the company ate, Franklin planted a Virginia

Franklin's return from Europe. Painting by Charles Mills, c. 1920.

locust tree. Madame de Forbach, Dowager-Duchess of Deux-Ponts, gave Franklin a "fine crab-tree walking stick, with a gold head curiously wrought in the form of a cap of liberty," which he bequeathed to George Washington.

Franklin, never at home without his scientific and philosophic pursuits, had been a member of the French Academy of Sciences since 1772 and attended its meetings in Paris regularly. At one of them, he was ceremoniously introduced to the French philosopher Voltaire. Félix Vicq d'Azyr, physician to Marie Antoinette, started the Royal Society of Medicine in 1776, and Franklin was the first foreign associate elected (1777). Of the members of the Academy, he already knew Jean-Baptiste Le Roy, who took an early interest in his work in electricity. He observed the work of the chemist Antoine-Laurent Lavoisier (1743–1794), who was the first to name oxygen and hydrogen as the compo-

nents of water. In 1784 Franklin and other members of the Academy investigated and discredited the "animal magnetism" theories of Friedrich Anton Mesmer (1734–1815). Among those on the committee that investigated Mesmer were Lavoisier, Le Roy, and Joseph-Ignace Guillotin, who, though he did not invent the guillotine, later promoted its use as a more humane method of execution than others. Franklin, who had been a Freemason for his entire adult life, became a member and grand master of the Nine Sisters Lodge, where he escorted Voltaire in for his initiation.

On the private press that Franklin set up in Passy, he printed official documents, short pieces that he wrote to influence European opinion in favor of America, and his humorous bagatelles for French acquaintances. He contacted some of France's foremost printers, some of whom instructed his grandson, Benjamin Bache. François-Ambroise Didot

(1730–1804) took Bache on as an apprentice, and during his apprenticeship Bache lived at the Le Roys.

Franklin's French friends could not bear to see him leave in 1785. Madame Helvétius, the Chaumonts, and the Brillons vainly tried to convince him to spend the rest of his life in France and offered him a place in their homes. Louis XVI gave Franklin a customary miniature of himself set in diamonds as a departing gift. Franklin rode from Passy to Le Havre in one of the royal litters. Temple, Bache, and Franklin's grandnephew, Jonathan Williams, returned to America with him. Le Veillard accompanied Franklin all the way to Southampton, and Madame Helvétius sent a desperate letter after him begging him to return. Franklin sailed from Southampton on July 28, 1785. He kept in touch with all of his French friends until his death in 1790.

Related entries:
Adams, John
Barbeu-Dubourg, Dr. Jacques
Brillon de Jouy, Anne-Louise Boivin d'Hardancourt
Electricity
Freemasonry
French Academy of Sciences
French Revolution
Helvétius, Anne-Catherine de Ligniville d'Autricourt
Izard, Ralph
Jay, John
Jefferson, Thomas
Journal of the Negotiation for Peace with Great Britain
Lee, Dr. Arthur
Revolutionary War
Treaties of Amity and Commerce
Treaty of Alliance with France
Treaty of Paris, 1783
Vergennes, Comte de (Charles Gravier)

Suggestions for further reading:
Aldridge, Alfred Owen. 1957. *Franklin and His French Contemporaries.* New York: New York University Press.
Dull, Jonathan R. 1982. *Franklin the Diplomat: The French Mission.* Philadelphia: American Philosophical Society.
Hale, Edward, and Edward E. Hale, Jr., 1969. *Franklin in France: From Original Documents, Most of Which Are Now Published for the First Time.* New York: B Franklin.
Lopez, Claude-Anne. 1966. *Mon Cher Papa: Franklin and the Ladies of Paris.* New Haven, Conn.: Yale University Press.
Schoenbrun, David. 1976. *Triumph in Paris: The Exploits of Benjamin Franklin.* New York: Harper & Row.
"To Sarah Bache," June 3, 1779 (Labaree et al., vol. 29).

Franklin, Abiah Folger (1667–1752)

Franklin's mother, Abiah Folger, was the youngest daughter of Peter Folger, an early, multitalented settler of Nantucket. Her mother, Mary Morrils, was an indentured servant whom Peter purchased and later married. Abiah married Josiah Franklin after his first wife, Anne, died in childbirth. "My mother . . . had an excellent constitution: she suckled all her ten children," Franklin wrote in his *Autobiography.* "I never knew either my father or mother to have any sickness but that of which they died, he at 89, and she at 85 years of age. They lie together at Boston, where I some years since placed a marble over their grave. . . . "

After Franklin ran away from home in 1723, he saw little of his parents. The correspondence between Franklin and his mother relates mainly to family life—Franklin's wife and children in Philadelphia, and his siblings in Boston and elsewhere. In 1738 he tried to allay her fears about his involvement with the Freemasons: "I know of no way of giving my mother a better account of them than she seems to have at present. . . . I must entreat her to suspend her judgment till she is better informed, unless she will believe me, when I assure her that . . . [they] have no principles or practices that are inconsistent with religion and good manners."

Abiah outlived her husband, who died in 1744, by eight years, and Franklin composed an elaborate inscription for their tombstone (*see* Franklin, Josiah).

Related entry:
  Franklin, Josiah

Suggestions for further reading:
  "To Abiah Franklin," April 12, 1750 (Labaree et al., vol. 3).
  "To Abiah Franklin," September 7, 1749 (Labaree et al., vol. 3).
  "To Josiah and Abiah Franklin," April 13, 1738 (Labaree et al., vol. 2).

Franklin, Benjamin (1650–1727)

Franklin's uncle Benjamin was one of his father's three brothers. "I was named after this uncle," he wrote in his *Autobiography,* "there being a particular affection between him and my father." Benjamin was a silk dyer from England, "an ingenious man," pious, and something of a politician. He enjoyed listening to sermons and took volumes of notes on them in his own shorthand. In England Benjamin and Josiah had been nonconformists, while their older brothers Thomas and John remained loyal to the Church of England. Josiah emigrated to Boston with his young family, and Benjamin eventually followed him.

Benjamin, a widower who had also lost all but one of ten children, lived with Josiah's family for a time. He liked the young nephew who bore his name and agreed with Josiah that Franklin might make a good scholar. He proposed to give Franklin his volumes of sermon notes to get him started. Later, when Josiah sought another trade for his restless son, Franklin briefly went to stay with Benjamin's son Samuel, a cutler.

Another of Benjamin's hobbies was writing verse, which, to Josiah's dismay, had a brief influence on Franklin in his youth. Before he moved to Boston, he sent verses to his nephew from England. Many years later, Franklin found the widow of a cousin (Jane Franklin Page) in England who gave him letters that his uncle Benjamin had written to

his late wife. One of them contained a poem that formed an acrostic of her name. Franklin sent the poem to his own sister Jane, along with a critique of his uncle's religious beliefs contained in the verses:

Illuminated from on high,
And shining brightly in your sphere,
Ne'er faint, but keep a steady eye,
Expecting endless pleasures there;
Flee vice as you'd a serpent flee;
Raise faith and hope three stories higher,
And let Christ's endless love to thee
Ne'er cease to make thy love aspire.
Kindness of heart by words express,
Let your obedience be sincere,
In prayer and praise your God address,
Nor cease, till he can cease to hear.

The phrase "three stories higher," signifying faith, hope, and charity, seemed to him obscure. Franklin advised his sister not to stay on the ground floor of faith or the next of hope, but to get up to charity as soon as she could: "[F]or in truth the best room in the house is charity. For my part I wish the house was turned upside down; 'tis so difficult (when one is fat) to go up stairs. . . . " In the line "kindness of heart by words express," Franklin said he would change "words" to "deeds," because "the world is too full of compliments already" and lacking in good works.

In 1771 Franklin was fortunate to come across a multivolume set of political pamphlets his uncle had collected and left in England before he moved to America. A book dealer whom Franklin knew in England approached him offering to sell the set, which contained an ordered collection of political pamphlets with their titles and costs in the fronts of the volumes, and notes in the margins of some of the pamphlets. Franklin examined them and determined that the collector was none other than his uncle Benjamin. The book dealer had no idea that the collector was Franklin's uncle and had offered the volumes to him simply as a curiosity he might be interested in. Franklin wrote to his cousin Samuel (his uncle's grandson) in Boston to tell him of the good fortune.

Related entries:
Franklin, Josiah
Franklin, Samuel
Mecom, Jane Franklin
Religious Beliefs

Suggestions for further reading:
Masur, Louis P., ed. 1993. *The Autobiography of Benjamin Franklin.* Boston: Bedford Books of St. Martin's Press.
"To Jane Mecom," September 16, 1758 (Labaree et al., vol. 8).
"To Samuel Franklin," July 12, 1771 (Labaree et al., vol. 18).

Franklin, Deborah Read Rogers (1708–1774)

Deborah Franklin's first impression of her famous husband was of a young, sloppily dressed runaway carrying two bread rolls and eating a third. It was 1723, the year Franklin moved to Philadelphia. "Thus I went up Market Street as far as Fourth Street, passing by the door of Mr. Read, my future wife's father; when she, standing at the door, saw me, and thought I made, as I certainly did, a most awkward, ridiculous appearance," Franklin said in his *Autobiography.* As fate would have it, Franklin lodged at the Read household while he worked for Samuel Keimer, one of the two printers in town. Deborah soon changed her opinion of Franklin, and their courtship began.

Franklin, however, left for England in 1726 following what turned out to be an empty promise from Governor William Keith to help him purchase equipment and meet London printers. Although he had planned to marry Deborah when he returned, he obtained work, decided that he might not come home, and wrote to Deborah not to expect him—a decision he later regretted. In his absence, she married a potter named John Rogers, who Franklin said was, apart from his industry, "a worthless fellow." It was rumored that Rogers had another wife. Deborah, miserable, parted with him and wanted nothing more to do with him. Debt-ridden, Rogers fled to the West Indies and was never heard from again.

When Franklin returned to Philadelphia, he felt ashamed of himself for the way he had treated her. He was still on friendly terms with the Read family and went to visit them on occasion. "I pitied poor Miss Read's unfortunate situation, who was generally dejected, seldom cheerful, and avoided company. I considered my giddiness and inconstancy when in London as in a great degree the cause of her unhappiness. . . . " Deborah's mother blamed herself for her daughter's misery, as she had objected to her marrying Franklin before he left for London.

Romance again budded between Franklin and Deborah, and after overcoming a few obstacles, the two married in 1730. One of those obstacles was the confusion surrounding Deborah's former husband, and another was perhaps the mysterious illegitimate son (William) that Franklin fathered around that time. They feared that her former husband's creditors would call on them to collect his debts. "None of the inconveniences happened," Franklin wrote in 1771, and she proved a good and faithful helpmate, assisted me much by attending the shop; we throve together, and have ever mutually endeavored to make each other happy."

Franklin and Deborah had at least two children together—three if she was the mysterious mother of William. Francis Folger was born in 1732 but died four years later of smallpox. Sarah (Sally) was not born until 1743. Various relations of Franklin and Deborah lived with them at times. Deborah's widowed mother lived with them until her death in 1762 and sold ointments and salves. When Franklin bought a house in 1751, he moved the post office there, and Deborah helped him with the postal work.

Benjamin Franklin as a youth, in front of a doorway with a young woman, Deborah Read. Painting published by Dill and Collins Company, July 31, 1923.

From 1730 to 1757 Franklin was only gone from her for relatively short periods. "[W]e are grown old together," he told Catharine Ray in 1755, "and if she has any faults, I am so used to 'em that I don't perceive 'em. . . . Indeed, I begin to think she has none, as I think of you." However, the Pennsylvania Assembly chose him as an agent to sail to England and push for the right to tax the vast proprietary estates in 1757. From that year until 1775, he was home for about two years. Although Franklin wanted to take the family with him, Deborah insisted on remaining in Philadelphia because she was terrified of the water. William went with his father to England, and Sally stayed at home with her mother.

Deborah was different from her husband in many ways. Her outlook was less optimistic than Franklin's, and she reportedly had a temper (although scarcely a hint of it is found in Franklin's writings). She did not share her husband's intellectual interests, could not write well, and concerned herself chiefly with her family. There is none of the imagination or intellectual content in Franklin's letters to her that he exchanged with other women like Polly Hewson and Madame Brillon.

Franklin and his wife wrote profusely to one another during the first period of their marriage that he spent in England. He usually addressed her as "My Dear Child." She managed their affairs in Philadelphia, and he lodged in the home of Mrs. Margaret Stevenson and her daughter Mary (Polly), who helped him pick out some of the many gifts he sent to his wife and his daughter. "'Tis true," Franklin wrote to her in 1758, "the regard and friendship I meet with from persons of worth, and the conversation of ingenious men, give me no small pleasure; but at this time of life, domestic comforts afford the most solid satisfaction, and my uneasiness at being absent from my family, and longing desire to be with them, make me often sigh in the midst of cheerful company."

Franklin returned in 1762 but set sail for London again in 1764. It was the last he was to see his wife. He wrote less frequently during this stay in London, and Deborah grew increasingly lonely when he kept promising to return but never did. Deborah suffered some consequences of Franklin's increasingly high-profile career. When angry Philadelphians, under the misconception that Franklin had helped to pass the Stamp Act (1765), threatened their new house, relatives came to defend her. In 1767 Richard Bache had proposed to their daughter, and Franklin left it up to Deborah to give her consent: "It seems now as if I should stay here another winter, and therefore I must leave it to your judgment to act in the affair of your daughter's match, as shall seem best. If you think it a suitable one, I suppose the sooner it is completed the better." Franklin was still in England when his daughter's first child, Benjamin Franklin Bache, was born. Franklin was embroiled in secret and futile negotiations with British government officials when Deborah suffered a stroke on December 14, 1774. She died five days later.

Related entries:
Bache, Benjamin Franklin
Bache, Richard
Bache, Sarah Franklin
Franklin, Francis Folger
Franklin, William
Great Britain
Pennsylvania Assembly
Post Office
Stamp Act

Suggestions for further reading:
Masur, Louis P., ed. 1993. *The Autobiography of Benjamin Franklin.* Boston: Bedford Books of St. Martin's Press.
"To Mrs. Deborah Franklin," June 22, 1767 (Labaree et al., vol. 14).
"To Deborah Franklin," June 27, 1760 (Labaree et al., vol. 9).

Franklin, Elizabeth

See **Douse, Elizabeth Franklin.**

Franklin, Francis Folger (1732–1736)

Francis Folger Franklin was the son of Franklin and Deborah, born two years after they married. He died at the age of four from smallpox. There had been a great controversy at the time over the safety and effectiveness of smallpox vaccinations. Franklin was known to be an ardent supporter of the practice, and false rumors circulated that Francis Folger had died from an inoculation. Franklin always regretted that he had not had his son inoculated in time. After the child's death, William Franklin remained his father's only son, and Deborah (unless she was William's mother, whose identity is unknown) was left childless until their daughter was born in 1743.

The child did not die without having his portrait painted, and he remained on his famous father's mind. Franklin wrote to his sister in 1772: "All who have seen my grandson agree with you in their accounts of his being an uncommonly fine boy, which brings often afresh to my mind the idea of my son Franky, though now dead thirty-six years, whom I have seldom seen equaled in every thing, and whom to this day I cannot think of without a sigh."

Related entries:
Bache, Sarah Franklin
Franklin, Deborah Read Rogers
Franklin, William

Suggestions for further reading:
Masur, Louis P., ed. 1993. *The Autobiography of Benjamin Franklin.* Boston: Bedford Books of St. Martin's Press.
"To Mrs. Jane Mecom," January 13, 1772 (Labaree et al., vol. 19).

Franklin, James (1697–1735)

Franklin's older brother, James, brought a press and letters from London and set up a printing shop in Boston in 1717. When Franklin was 12, his father prevailed upon him to apprentice himself to his brother, beginning his long career in printing. Working under James in 1718, Franklin composed his first known writings, the ballads "The Lighthouse Tragedy" and "On the Taking of Teach or Blackbeard the Pirate." The brothers printed them, and James sent Franklin around town to sell them. In 1719 James began to print the *Boston Gazette* (which he printed for less than a year), and in 1721 he began to publish the *New England Courant.*

The *Courant* was only the fourth newspaper in America, and James filled its pages with satires and burlesques of rival "dull" newspapers and local officials. In 1722 Franklin decided to try his hand at humor and secretly contributed a series of 14 letters using disguised handwriting and the pseudonym "Mrs. Silence Dogood." Among the *Courant*'s victims was Cotton Mather, whom its writers mercilessly criticized for promoting smallpox inoculations. Mather and his father, Increase Mather, condemned the paper as profane, immoral, sacrilegious, and scandalous.

Franklin and his brother began to quarrel frequently. Franklin resented James for treating him harshly, as he would have treated any other apprentice, and expected more leniency from a brother than James gave. Their disputes often landed in front of their father, who generally sided with Franklin. "But my brother was passionate, and had often beaten me, which I took extremely amiss; and, thinking my apprenticeship very tedious, I was continually wishing for some opportunity of shortening it," Franklin wrote in his *Autobiography.* "I fancy his harsh and tyrannical treatment of me might be a means of impressing me with that aversion to arbitrary power that has stuck to me through my whole life."

The opportunity to free himself came after the Massachusetts Assembly threw James in jail for criticizing local officials. Franklin was examined, admonished, and released. In spite of his disagreements with James, the

Benjamin Franklin selling his ballads on the streets of Boston. Painting by C. E. Mills, 1914.

Assembly's action angered Franklin. The management of the paper fell into his young but able hands, and he "made bold to give our rulers some rubs in it, which my brother took very kindly, while others began to consider me in an unfavorable light, as a young genius that had a turn for libeling and satyr." The Assembly released James but soon forbade him to publish the *Courant*. To circumvent this restriction, the brothers dissolved Franklin's indentures, for the purpose of proving legally that Franklin was not James's apprentice, and secretly drew up new ones. The paper appeared with Franklin's name as publisher for the next few months.

When the brothers began to argue again, Franklin made use of the dissolved indentures and claimed his freedom. James prevailed upon other local printers not to hire him, and Franklin ran away to New York, then Philadelphia. "It was not fair in me to take this advantage . . . but the unfairness of it weighed little with me, when under the impressions of resentment for the blows his passion too often urged him to bestow upon me, though he was otherwise not an ill-natured man: perhaps I was too saucy and provoking," Franklin recalled. When Franklin returned to Boston in 1724 to seek his father's assistance in setting up a printing business in Pennsylvania, he visited James at his printing house. Franklin was dressed well and openly displayed his newfound prosperity before his brother's journeymen. James took great offense at the show and later declared to their mother that he would never forgive Franklin.

In 1727 James moved to Newport. He began to print an almanac, *Poor Robin,* and later the *Rhode Island Gazette.* Franklin visited James at Newport and reconciled with him in 1733. James, in poor health, requested that Franklin take his son, James Jr., in the event of his death and instruct him in printing. Franklin complied when James died two years later, sending the boy to school and then helping him get started in printing. "Thus it was that I made my brother ample amends for the service I had deprived him of by leaving him so early," Franklin wrote.

Related entries:
  Childhood
  Dogood, Mrs. Silence
  Printing

Suggestions for further reading:
  Masur, Louis P., ed. 1993. *The Autobiography of Benjamin Franklin.* Boston: Bedford Books of St. Martin's Press.
  "The Printer to the Reader," February 11, 1723 (Labaree et al., vol. 1).

Franklin, Jane

See **Mecom, Jane Franklin.**

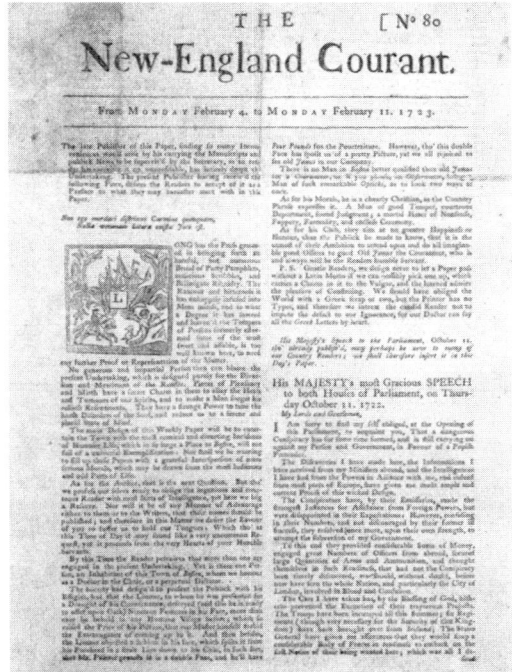

The **New England Courant,** *number 80, 1723 (The first issue to carry Benjamin Franklin's name as a printer). Facsimile.*

Franklin, John (1690–1756)

John Franklin was Franklin's oldest full brother, the first child of Josiah Franklin's second wife. He married Mary Gooch, and, after her death, Elizabeth Gooch Hubbard. John and Peter Franklin learned their father's tallow-chandling trade and John was the most prosperous of all the Franklin children, aside from Franklin. John's green "Crown Soap" was a popular item in Boston and Philadelphia and object of family pride. Franklin described a brief visit with John in Newport on his way to Philadelphia: "The sloop putting in at Newport, Rhode Island, I visited my brother John, who had been married and settled there some years. He received me very affectionately, for he always loved me." A friend of his brother's, hearing that Franklin was going to Pennsylvania, asked him to collect a debt owed him there. The deed

later caused Franklin "a good deal of uneasiness," as he gave much of the money to his alcoholic friend John Collins and worried that he would be called upon to pay it.

It was for John that Franklin designed a flexible catheter in 1752. John, ill with a bladder stone, had apparently written that he desired to have one. Franklin quickly designed one and took his directions to a silversmith to have it made. John and his wife later moved to Boston, where he served as the postmaster from 1754 to 1756. He died in 1756, the year before Franklin traveled to England as an agent for the Pennsylvania Assembly. His wife succeeded him as postmaster.

Related entries:
  Franklin, Josiah
  Franklin, Peter
  Medicine

Suggestions for further reading:
  Masur, Louis P., ed. 1993. *The Autobiography of Benjamin Franklin.* Boston: Bedford Books of St. Martin's Press.

"To John Franklin," December 8, 1752 (Labaree et al., vol. 4).
"To John Franklin," May 1745 (Labaree et al., vol. 3).

Franklin, Josiah (1655–1744)

Josiah Franklin, Franklin's father, was born in 1655 in England. His original home was the small Franklin farm at Ecton, Northamptonshire, which had been in the family for hundreds of years. He left his home to serve as an apprentice to his elder brother John, a dyer at Banbury in Oxfordshire. He was the youngest of Thomas Franklin's four sons, Thomas, John, Benjamin, and Josiah. The Franklins were historically Protestants, even through the reign of the Catholic Queen Mary. During her rule the family kept a Bible fastened open under a stool to hide it. The two eldest sons of Thomas Franklin, Thomas and John, remained loyal to the Church of England. Benjamin (for whom Franklin was named) and Josiah, however, were nonconformists. These two brothers would remain close, and Benjamin later lived with Josiah's family in Boston.

Whether for religious or economic reasons, Josiah left England and sailed across the Atlantic in 1683. He brought with him his wife Anne and their three children, Elizabeth, Samuel, and Hannah. The 17-week voyage brought them to America, and they settled in Boston. He soon found that he could not support his young family with the dyeing trade he had learned, so he turned to tallow-chandling and soap-boiling.

Josiah's wife Anne died in childbirth after having borne seven children. Josiah remarried within a year. His second wife, Abiah Folger, gave him ten more children, including Benjamin, the couple's youngest son. By the time Benjamin was six years old, Josiah had moved the family and the shop to a house at the corner of Union and Hanover Streets, marked by the sign of the blue ball. Josiah was a typical hard-working Protestant in Boston. He belonged to and was very active in the Old South Church, took great interest in his family, and found apprenticeships for all of his sons. Discussion and the exchange of ideas took precedence over etiquette at the dinner table. Josiah had a small collection of books, including Plutarch's *Lives* and writings by Cotton Mather.

He originally hoped to give Franklin to church service and sent him to grammar school when he was 8 years old. Although Franklin excelled, Josiah determined that he could not afford to send him to college and moved him to another school owned by George Brownell. Franklin did not do as well at the new school and was soon put to work at his father's trade, "cutting wick for the candles, filling the dipping mold and the molds for cast candles, attending the shop, going of errands, &c." Franklin disliked the work, and Josiah searched for another trade that would suit his son. His eagerness to find a new trade for his son was in part motivated by a fear that Franklin would run away to sea as his other son Josiah had. At the age of 12, Franklin was bound to his older brother James, a printer.

There were traits in Franklin that Josiah did not like. Franklin did not share his father's religious beliefs or his devotion to public worship. He showed an early inclination toward writing poetry, which Josiah feared would not earn him an adequate living. Franklin ran away to New York at the age of 17, and he soon moved to Philadelphia and acquired work. He returned to his father less than a year later with a letter of recommendation from the governor, who wanted Benjamin to set up his own business. Josiah felt that Benjamin was too young and refused to support the enterprise, but he was proud of his work and allowed him to return.

Nevertheless, Franklin respected his father. He described him in his *Autobiography* as a man who

had an excellent constitution of body, was of middle stature, but well set and very strong. He was ingenious, could draw prettily, was skilled a little in music and had a clear pleasing voice, so that when he played psalm tunes on his violin and sung withal as he sometimes did in an evening after the business of the day was over, it was extremely agreeable to hear. He had a mechanical genius too, and on occasion was very handy in the use of other tradesmen's tools. But his great excellence lay in a sound understanding, and solid judgment in prudential matters, both in private and public affairs.

Josiah did not see much of his youngest son after he ran away from Boston as a youth. He died in 1744, at the age of 89. Franklin composed the inscription for the gravestone marking his parents' burial site:

Josiah Franklin
And Abiah his Wife
Lie here interred.
They lived lovingly together in
Wedlock
Fifty-five Years.
Without an Estate or any gainful
Employment,
By constant Labour and Industry,
With God's Blessing,
They maintained a large Family
Comfortably;
And brought up thirteen Children,
And seven Grandchildren
Reputably.
From this Instance, Reader,
Be encouraged to Diligence in thy
Calling,
And distrust not Providence.
He was a pious & prudent Man,
She a discreet and virtuous Woman.
Their youngest Son,
In filial Regard to their Memory,
Places this Stone.
J.F. born 1655—Died 1744 Ætat 89.
A.F. born 1667—died 1752 Ætat 85.

Related entries:
Childhood
Franklin, Abiah Folger
Franklin, Benjamin
Franklin, James
Franklin, John
Franklin, Peter

Suggestions for further reading:
Masur, Louis P., ed. 1993. *The Autobiography of Benjamin Franklin.* Boston: Bedford Books of St. Martin's Press.
"To Josiah and Abiah Franklin," April 13, 1738 (Labaree et al., vol. 2).
"To Josiah and Abiah Franklin," September 6, 1744 (Labaree et al., vol. 2).

Franklin, Lydia

See **Scott, Lydia Franklin.**

Franklin, Mary

See **Homes, Captain Robert and Mary Franklin.**

Franklin, Peter (1692–1766)

Peter Franklin was one of Franklin's elder brothers, the second son of Josiah Franklin by his second wife. He was born on November 22, 1692, and later moved to Newport, Rhode Island. Their father taught Peter and his brother John his own tallow-chandling and soap-boiling trade. Franklin sold the products they made in his own shop, and Peter and John carried Franklin's merchandise.

Franklin wrote some interesting letters to his brother. In 1760 he speculated on the origin of salt in the ocean. He disagreed with his contemporaries who believed that salt in the ocean only comes from dissolved minerals and rock salts: "I own I am inclined to a different opinion, and rather think all the water on this globe was originally salt, and that the fresh water we find in springs and rivers, is the produce of distillation." The Sun causes pure water to evaporate from the ocean, forming clouds that produce rain, which in turn produces rivers and springs, he thought.

In 1762 Peter was asked by an acquaintance to obtain Franklin's opinion on how to protect powder magazines from lightning. Franklin advised him to erect a mast near the magazine, with an iron rod fastened to it and reaching 15 to 20 feet above it. The rod was to be at least one inch thick, to be pointed at the top, and to reach far enough down into the earth to hit water. Franklin also advised his brother on improved storage methods that would keep the powder dry.

Peter was interested in music and sent Franklin a ballad he had written. Franklin replied, "I like your ballad, and think it well adapted for your purpose of discountenancing expensive foppery, and encouraging industry and frugality." Peter requested that Franklin find someone to compose music for his words, and although Franklin disliked prevailing musical preferences in England, he promised to find someone to do the work. Franklin complained, "[A] modern song . . . neglects all the proprieties and beauties of common speech, and in their place introduces its defects and absurdities as so many graces." As proof of his assertions, Franklin critiqued George Frideric Handel's (1685–1759) "The Additional Favorite Song in Judas Maccabeus." Among the faults he reckoned in Handel's composition were unnecessary screaming, incorrect emphasis on words, stuttering, drawling, and unintelligibleness. Franklin enclosed the entire song for Peter and advised him to "read the words without repetitions. Observe how few they are, and what a shower of notes attend them."

By 1766 Peter had moved to Philadelphia and taken the position of deputy postmaster general of Philadelphia (a position that both Franklin and his son William had both held). That year, Franklin's wife wrote to him in England and told him that his brother was ill. Peter had been Franklin's only living brother when he died in July 1766, at the age of 74. Franklin wrote a letter of condolence to Peter's wife of nearly 50 years. Concerned for her welfare, he offered to set up their adopted son in a printing house, in partnership with her. A printing project in Antigua with his nephew, Benjamin Mecom, had failed, and Franklin asked his wife to have Mecom's materials delivered to Mary Franklin, Peter's widow.

Related entries:
Electricity
Franklin, Abiah Folger
Franklin, John
Franklin, Josiah
Franklin, William

Suggestions for further reading:
"To Mary Franklin," August 26, 1766 (Labaree et al., vol. 13).
"To Peter Franklin," [date unknown] (Labaree et al., vol. 11).
"To Peter Franklin," May 7, 1760 (Labaree et al., vol. 9).
"To Peter Franklin," 1762 (Labaree et al., vol. 10).

Franklin, Samuel (1721–1775)

Franklin was fond of his relation in Boston, Samuel Franklin, who was the grandson of his uncle Benjamin, for whom Franklin was named. Franklin had briefly stayed with Samuel's father (Samuel Sr., a cutler) as a youth, when his own father thought that Franklin might learn cutlery. Franklin wrote to Samuel periodically from England, primarily to update him on interesting information he found about their relatives in England. There were few Franklins left who still bore the family name—Thomas Franklin, a widower and grandson of John Franklin, the brother of Franklin's father Josiah and Samuel's grandfather Benjamin. Thomas, a dyer of Lutterworth in Leicestershire, had only one daughter, Sarah

(Sally), who lived with Franklin at Craven Street for a time and later married James Pearce. In addition, there were women who had married and taken their husbands' surnames. Eleanor Franklin Morris was a daughter of Hannah Franklin, the sister of both Franklin's father and Samuel's grandfather. Hannah Franklin Walker, who had three sons, was a granddaughter of John Franklin, Franklin's uncle.

Franklin also wrote to Samuel about the volumes of political pamphlets collected by his uncle Benjamin (Samuel's grandfather) before he moved to Boston. In 1771 a book dealer in England, who knew nothing of Franklin's relation to the collector, approached him with a set of volumes that "contained all the principal pamphlets and papers on public affairs, that had been printed here from the Restoration down to 1715." After examining them, Franklin realized that his uncle Benjamin, Samuel's grandfather, had been the collector.

Related entries:
Childhood
Franklin, Benjamin
Franklin, Sarah (Sally)

Suggestions for further reading:
"To Samuel Franklin," July 12, 1771 (Labaree et al., vol. 18).
"To Samuel Franklin," July 17, 1767 (Labaree et al., vol. 14).
"To Samuel Franklin," June 8, 1770 (Labaree et al., vol. 17).

Franklin, Sarah

See **Bache, Sarah Franklin.**

Franklin, Sarah (Sally)

Franklin met Sally Franklin (life dates not known), a distant cousin in England, after he sought out his English rela-tives in Banbury at Ectonshire. Her father, Thomas Franklin, was the grandson of Franklin's uncle, John Franklin. In 1766 Thomas brought his 13-year-old daughter to town to see Franklin, and Margaret Stevenson (Franklin's friend and landlady at Craven Street) convinced him to let her stay under her care for "schooling and improvement" while Franklin traveled to Germany. "When I returned, I found her indeed much improved, and grown a fine girl. She is sensible, and of a sweet, obliging temper," Franklin wrote to his wife later that year. Both he and Mrs. Stevenson were fond of Sally. Thomas, a widower, pressed Franklin to take his only child to America when he returned, but Franklin did not like the idea, and, he explained to his wife, "the care of educating other people's children is a trust too weighty for us as we grow old." Franklin did not return to Philadelphia until 1775, and by that time Sally had married James Pearce, "a substantial young farmer at Ewell . . . a very sober, industrious man. . . . "

Related entry:
Franklin, Samuel

Suggestions for further reading:
"To Deborah Franklin," October 11, 1766 (Labaree et al., vol. 13).
"To Samuel Franklin," June 8, 1770 (Labaree et al., vol. 17).

Franklin, State of

Toward the end of Franklin's life, buildings, towns, counties, and even a short-lived state bearing his name began to spring up in the colonies. In 1784 a group of former North Carolinians declared themselves a separate state. William Cocke wrote to Franklin to tell him that they had named their new state "Franklin" in his honor. Franklin, having heard the state called "FrankLand," had not realized that it had been named after him. The General Assembly of North Carolina had ceded that state's western land to the Congress, and the inhabitants of those lands formed themselves into a separate state. However, North Carolina repealed the act the following year and later tried to resume governing the western lands. John Sevier, a representative of the new state, wrote to Franklin to ask for his support in reclaiming their government. Franklin distanced himself from the dispute and would only encourage the disgruntled citizens to follow through with their intention to submit the matter to Congress for resolution. The state later became Tennessee.

Related entry:
Articles of Confederation

Suggestions for further reading:
"The Life of Benjamin Franklin," pp. 483–486 (Smyth, vol. X).
"To William Cocke," August 12, 1786 (Smyth, vol. IX).

Franklin, William
(c.1730–1814)

William Franklin was Franklin's illegitimate son, born sometime around 1730. His mother's true identity has never been discovered, although some suggest that Deborah Franklin conceived him out of wedlock. It was for William that Franklin began his *Autobiography,* which he never finished. Until they were divided by the Revolutionary War, Franklin maintained a close relationship with his son.

After the couple's son Francis Folger died of smallpox at the age of four, William remained Franklin's only son. As a youth he was fairly ambitious and involved with his father's activities. He helped Franklin fly the kite in his famous electrical experiment. At age 15, he tried to run away on a privateer, but his father retrieved him from the ship. In 1746 he went on a military campaign to Canada as an ensign during King George's War. He became clerk of the Pennsylvania Assembly in 1751, was appointed postmaster

of Philadelphia in 1753, and was promoted to controller the following year—all positions his father had held. In 1755 he helped his father procure wagons and supplies for General Edward Braddock's ill-fated campaign to Fort Duquesne. William also studied law under Franklin's future political partner in the Assembly, Joseph Galloway.

William went with his father to England when the Pennsylvania Assembly sent him across the water in 1757. He attended school, helped his father, and received an honorary master of arts degree from Oxford University at the same time that Franklin received an honorary doctor of laws degree. He studied law and was admitted to the bar. In 1760 he fathered an illegitimate son, William Temple, who eventually came to live with Franklin and the Stevensons at the Craven Street house. In 1762 he was appointed royal governor of New Jersey, a position he retained until the Revolution erupted. After an unsuccessful attempt by his father to pair him with Polly Stevenson and a broken engagement to Elizabeth Graeme, William married Elizabeth Downes, the daughter of a Barbados planter.

While he served as governor he maintained faithful correspondence with Franklin, who kept him informed of activities and politics in England. Both were involved in the Grand Ohio Company, which was trying to obtain 20 million acres of western land from the Crown. Tension mounted in their relationship when Franklin returned to America in 1775. He was an ardent patriot who supported American independence; William maintained his loyalty to England. Franklin tried in vain to persuade his son to join the move for independence. The New Jersey Assembly ordered William's arrest in 1776. Despite his arrest and confinement until 1778, he remained loyal to England throughout the war. Elizabeth Franklin died after she fled to New York, overcome by her husband's arrest and imprisonment. He later became the president of an association of loyalists. William moved to England in 1782, where he lived the rest of his life. He married Mary D'Evelyn in 1788.

After the war, father and son reconciled briefly. Franklin wrote to him in 1784:

> I received your letter . . . and am glad to find that you desire to revive the affectionate intercourse that formerly existed between us. It will be very agreeable to me; indeed nothing has ever hurt me so much and affected me with such keen sensations as to find myself deserted in my old age by my only son; and not only deserted, but to find him taking up arms against me, in a cause, wherein my good fame, fortune and life were all at stake. . . . This is a disagreeable subject. I drop it. And we will endeavor, as you propose mutually to forget what has happened relating to it, as well as we can.

William saw his father for the last time in England in 1785, when Franklin was en route to Philadelphia from France. The younger Franklin was more forgiving of his father than his father was of him. Resentment toward William remained. In his will, Franklin left him his land in Nova Scotia and explained, "the part he acted against me in the late war, which is of public notoriety, will account for my leaving him no more of an estate he endeavored to deprive me of." William was shocked at the will, but whatever his resentment he rarely spoke ill of his father after his death. His relationship with his own son was strained, and William essentially wrote Temple out of his will. In 1792 Richard and Sarah Bache visited him in England. Mary Franklin died in 1811, and William followed her three years later.

Related entries:
  Bache, Richard
  Bache, Sarah Franklin
  Franklin, Deborah Read Rogers
  Franklin, Francis Folger
  Franklin, William Temple
  French and Indian War
  Grand Ohio Company

Engraving of William Temple Franklin, son of Benjamin Franklin.

Revolutionary War
Volunteer Militia

Suggestions for further reading:
  Randall, Willard Sterne. 1984. *A Little Revenge: Benjamin Franklin and His Son.* Boston: Little, Brown.
  Skemp, Sheila L. 1990. *William Franklin: Son of a Patriot, Servant of a King.* New York: Oxford University Press.
  "To William Franklin," August 16, 1784 (Smyth, vol. IX).

Franklin, William Temple (1760–1823)

William Temple Franklin was Franklin's grandson by his illegitimate son William. William Temple, who was also illegitimate, was born in London in 1760 to an unknown mother. Unlike his father, who remained staunchly loyal to England during the American Revolution, William Temple supported the move for independence. He spent the troubled years of the war working for his famous grandfather in France.

"Temple," as Franklin called his grandson, served as his grandfather's secretary during the war. Some of his political enemies in

Congress objected to having the son of a loyalist on the congressional payroll doing Franklin's work. Franklin complained to his son-in-law, Richard Bache, in 1779, "Methinks it is rather some merit, that I have rescued a valuable young man from the danger of being a Tory, and fixed him in honest republican Whig principles; as I think, from the integrity of his disposition, his industry, his early sagacity, and uncommon abilities for business, he may in time become a great service to his country. It is enough that I have lost my son; would they add my grandson?"

Franklin was very pleased with Temple's work. He felt somewhat guilty for keeping his grandson away from studying law, but he was too valuable to Franklin as a secretary and as an attendant when he fell ill. For much of his time in France, Temple was the only family Franklin had around him. Benjamin Franklin Bache, another grandson, went to school in Geneva. William Franklin had been arrested in America and later became president of a loyalist association. Franklin's wife had passed away, and his daughter and her family remained in America.

When the Congress resolved to present the Marquis de Lafayette with a sword as an expression of its gratitude for his services, Temple had the honor of taking it to him. Lafayette offered to make him his aide. The Congress did not pay Temple for his duties as secretary for several years; Franklin paid him instead and wrote to Robert R. Livingston in Congress for reimbursement in 1782. Temple's salary had been 3,400 livres ($650) for December 1776 through 1777; 4,000 livres ($800) for 1778; 4,800 livres ($900) for 1779; and 6,000 livres ($1,500) for 1780. After the war ended Temple served as the secretary for the American peace commissioners during treaty negotiations, in spite of John Adams's protest.

Temple accompanied Franklin in social circles as well and was affectionately called "Franklinet" by some of their neighbors. Franklin tried to arrange a marriage between his grandson and one of the neighboring Brillons' daughters, but the Brillons replied that Temple belonged in America and they wanted a husband who would stay in France. He was fond of watching the women in Paris and, like his father and his grandfather, he fathered an illegitimate child. The mother, Blanchette Caillot, was a married neighbor in Passy, and the child, Thèodore, did not live to be a year old.

After the war Temple traveled to England to visit his father, who had moved there in 1782. He returned to America with Franklin in 1785 and, after unsuccessfully trying to obtain a political post, operated a 600-acre farm given to him by his father. It pleased Franklin that Temple had, in becoming a farmer, chosen "the most useful, the most independent, and therefore the noblest of employments." The farm was only 16 miles away from Franklin's home. In 1786 he was elected to the American Philosophical Society.

Along with Benjamin Franklin Bache, Temple was present in 1790 when Franklin passed away. Among the items his grandfather bequeathed to him were the right to 3,000 acres of land given to him by the state of Georgia, a Chinese gong, a timepiece, money, and most important, many of his papers. Temple took some of the papers to London to be printed, and others were left in America. Most of them eventually found their way to the American Philosophical Society.

In 1792 he gave up his farm and went to London, where his father encouraged him to marry and work on an edition of his grandfather's writings. Temple got around to neither marriage nor Franklin's works for many years. In 1798 he fathered another illegitimate child, Ellen, by the sister-in-law of William's wife. Ellen stayed with William, and Temple moved to Paris, estranged from his father.

He later married Hannah Collier, from England, and died in Paris in 1823.

Suggestions for further reading:
"To Richard Bache," June 2, 1779 (Labaree et al., vol. 29).
"To William Temple Franklin," June 13, 1775 (Labaree et al., vol. 22).
"To William Temple Franklin," September 19, 1776 (Labaree et al., vol. 22).
"To William Temple Franklin," September 22, 1776 (Labaree et al., vol. 22).

Franklin Stove

*I*n 1742 Franklin invented a stove designed to heat rooms more effectively and to save fuel. He gave the design of the stove to his friend Robert Grace, of the Junto, who began to manufacture them. The governor of Pennsylvania was impressed by the stove and offered to give Franklin an exclusive patent to sell them for ten years, but the inventor wished his stove to benefit as many people as possible. As he explained in his *Autobiography:* "I declined [the patent] from a principle which has ever weighed with me on such occasions, viz., that, as we enjoy great advantages from the inventions of others, we should be glad of an opportunity to serve others by any invention of ours; and this we should do freely and generously."

To publicize his stove, which he called the "Pennsylvania Fireplace," he wrote "An Account of the New-Invented Pennsylvanian Fire-Places" in 1744. It contained detailed explanations of why his stove worked better than existing ones, how it was constructed, how it heated rooms, and how to use it. He also answered some of the objections to his stove that were circulating among the colonists. He compared six different existing methods of heating. Some common problems with existing stoves, he said, were that they filled rooms with smoke and they needed to use a lot of wood to produce a little heat in a room. Wood often had to be obtained from sources at great distance, and the stoves then in use wasted a lot of it. Strong currents of frigid air that rush in through crevices in the house, which resulted from the draw of the fireplace, were also a problem.

He speculated that open fires and the cold currents that they caused to be drawn into the houses contributed to colds and other diseases, eye damage (caused by bright light), and excessive drying of the skin. He described some later stoves that remedied some of the problems, especially that of the cold air currents drawn into the room. But they, too, had their inconveniences, and most of them were not popularly used in the colonies.

His stove consisted of nine iron plates. The advantages of his model, he wrote, were that: the entire room was uniformly warm; the cold air drafts associated with other stoves were eliminated; rooms warmed by the stove were good for treating those who were ill, because it brought in a constant supply of fresh air; heat was directed into the room instead of up the chimney, a previous problem that required the use of a lot more wood; less wood meant less smoke and less soot; and it had an element that allowed the fire to be secured at night, which helped to prevent house fires.

The stove was popular in the colonies and apparently saved a great deal of wood. An inventor in England made some minor changes in the model, which Franklin said hurt its performance. The workmen in England, he said, did not "well comprehend the principles of that machine, [and] it was much disfigured in their imitations of it. . . . " Franklin later designed a stove that burned pit-coal (1771). He wrote a detailed description of it on his voyage from France to Philadelphia in 1785.

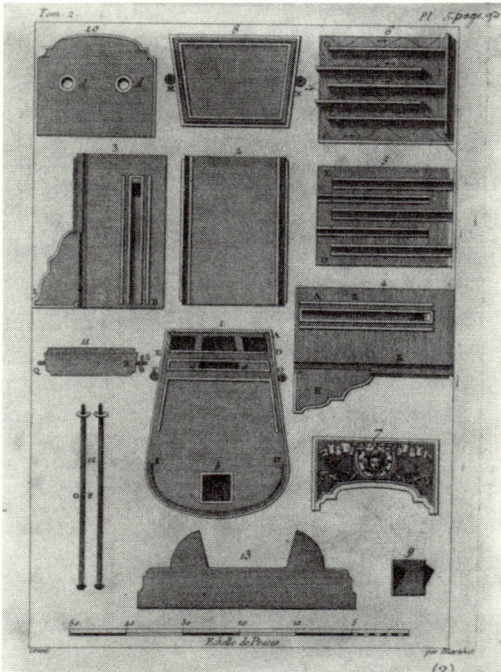

The Franklin Stove. Engraving by Martinet in Oeuvres de M. Franklin, 1773, volume II, plate 5.

He wrote in his *Autobiography* that a number of his inventions had been imitated, but he never contested the thefts because he disliked disputes and did not desire to profit from his inventions.

Related entry:
    Fire

Suggestions for further reading:
    "An Account of the New Invented Pennsylvanian Fire-Places," 1744 (Labaree et al., vol. 2).
    "Description of a New Stove for Burning of Pitcoal, and Consuming All Its Smoke," August 1785 (Smyth, vol. IX).
    Masur, Louis P., ed. 1993. *The Autobiography of Benjamin Franklin*. Boston: Bedford Books of St. Martin's Press.

Freemasonry

Many political and social leaders since the early 1700s have been Freemasons, and Franklin was not an exception. Although the original groups of masons in Europe were stoneworkers' guilds, they eventually evolved into social brotherhoods that gained political influence and worked for, they believed, the betterment of mankind. Modern Freemasonry is traditionally traced back to 1717, when the Grand Lodge of England formed by the union off our lodges. After 1717 lodges formed all over Europe and in the American colonies.

Masons did not necessarily adhere to any particular religion, but members generally believed in one God, advocated moral and virtuous behavior, and encouraged the betterment of humanity. Members sometimes held radical political ideas that called for reforming or overthrowing existing governments, as was the case in the French lodges in the later 1700s. For this reason, and because of the secrecy and mystery surrounding their religious beliefs and rituals, lodges were often persecuted by European governments.

The Freemasons already enjoyed a measure of influence in Europe, but the lodges were somewhat less influential in America during Franklin's lifetime. Nevertheless, many of the Founding Fathers were Freemasons, and debates over issues surrounding the Revolutionary War, the framing of the Constitution, and the Bill of Rights took place in lodges.

Franklin was involved with many different groups during his life that sought to further intellectual endeavors and influence political matters—the Junto, the American Philosophical Society, Royal Societies in Europe—some of which he was instrumental in forming. St. John's Lodge in Philadelphia was the first Freemason's lodge in the American colonies. Franklin became involved with this lodge early on in his and the lodge's life. He joined in 1731, about a year after St. John's was formed, and was involved with the Freemasons for the remainder of his life. His contemporaries Joseph Warren, George Washington, John Hancock, and Paul Revere were also Masons.

Franklin quickly climbed the ranks from member to warden to grand master of the lodge, a post to which he was elected in 1734. *The Constitutions of the Free-Masons* had been published by Franklin earlier that year. In subsequent years he served as the lodge's secretary, and in 1749 he became provincial grand master. Members of the lodge held their meetings in taverns until 1755, when a Masonic temple was completed.

Franklin's involvement with the Masons raised suspicion among both his family members and some fellow colonists. He was falsely implicated by a writer for the *American Weekly Mercury,* the rival of his *Pennsylvania Gazette,* as a participant in an incident that resulted in a man's death. Some Masons had concocted mock rituals to make a young man think that he was being initiated into Freemasonry, and a flaming bowl of rum that was used in part of the charade accidentally burned him to death. Franklin responded to the *Mercury*'s charges in his *Gazette,* explaining that he had not taken part in the running joke and had disapproved of it long before it culminated in the man's death. At least two of his acquaintances verified his statements.

His parents, too, were concerned about the beliefs he might have acquired as a result of his involvement with the Masons. He wrote a letter to them in 1738 to try to alleviate their fears. Addressing his mother, he said:

> As to the Freemasons, unless she will believe me when I assure her that they are in general a very harmless sort of people; and have no principles or practices that are inconsistent with religion or good manners, I know no way of giving my mother a better opinion of them than she seems to have at present (since it is not allowed that women should be admitted into that secret society). She has, I must confess, on that account, some reason to be displeased with it; but for any thing else, I must entreat her to suspend her judgment till she is better informed, and in the mean time exercise her charity.

St. John's was not the only lodge he became involved with. He met with Masons in Boston when his travels brought him there, but he became especially involved in France's Nine Sisters Lodge. The American Revolution and the ideas that influenced it were attractive to many French intellectuals who favored a constitution to limit the monarch's powers. As one of the driving forces behind the American Revolution, a fellow Mason, and a reputable philosopher, Franklin was welcomed by the Nine Sisters. The French philosopher Voltaire was initiated into the same lodge and met Franklin just before his (Voltaire's) death. Franklin was elected grand master in 1779.

In 1781 he published the *Book of Constitutions,* which contained the Articles of Confederation (which preceded the current U.S. Constitution) and the state constitutions of all the American colonies. The book was subsequently translated into French by one of the Nine Sisters Masons, the Duc de La Rochefoucauld, and given to ambassadors and others in Europe.

Related entry:
  Religious Beliefs

Suggestion for further reading:
  "To Josiah and Abiah Franklin," April 13, 1738 (Labaree et al., vol. 2).

French Academy of Sciences

Franklin was a member of several prestigious European academies, including the Royal Society in London and the French Academy of Sciences, to which he was elected in 1772. The Academy in Paris was formed in 1666 and had as its members the most prominent scientists in France as well as a handful of foreign members. It published its *Memoirs* as scientific journals. At the time that Franklin was elected, only eight foreign members were allowed into the Academy. He considered his election as a sort of victory over the Abbé Nollet, a member of the Academy who had vocally opposed Franklin's theories on electricity.

While he was in France from 1776 to 1785, Franklin attended the Academy's meetings in Paris. His friends from that society included Antoine-Laurent Lavoisier (1743–1794) and Jean-Baptiste Le Roy (1724–1800). Lavoisier, often called "the founder of modern chemistry," was instrumental in devising the modern system of chemical names. He was the first to prove that water was composed of hydrogen and oxygen. Franklin and Lavoisier, one of the Farmers-General who were in charge of gunpowder manufacturing for France, worked on the manufacture of the powder during the American Revolution. Lavoisier was later beheaded during the French Revolution. Le Roy, a physicist who studied electricity, took an early interest in Franklin's electrical experiments and had defended his theories against Abbé Nollet's attacks before Franklin was ever elected. In 1779 he read Franklin's paper on the aurora borealis before a pleased audience at the Academy. Both Lavoisier and Le Roy served with Franklin on the royal commission chosen to investigate the theories of Friedrich Anton Mesmer (1734–1815) in 1784. Mesmer claimed that he could heal people by manipulating a universal fluid he called "animal magnetism" and was seeking scientific approval for his methods in France. The commission found no support for his healings.

In 1779 members of the Academy, including Franklin, investigated the theories of the future French revolutionary Jean-Paul Marat (1743–1793), who designed a series of experiments using his *microscope solaire* to prove that an "igneous fluid" emanates from fire. Marat's theories went against established scientific beliefs—notably those of Lavoisier—about fire. Marat wrote to Franklin frequently in 1779 asking him to be present at the investigations of his experiments. He believed that the scientific community was working against him and hoped that Franklin's pres-

ence would add a more objective perspective. Franklin was interested in the new instrument that Marat had invented but seems not to have been convinced that his theories were valid.

The famous philosopher Voltaire (1694–1778) and Franklin met at a meeting of the Academy in 1778. A cynical John Adams, who was in France as an American representative to the French court, recounted the event in his diary. The two had first bowed and spoken to each other and then taken each other by the hand. The crowd was still not satisfied with the introduction, and, Adams wrote, "the two great actors upon this great theater of philosophy and frivolity then embraced each other, by hugging one another in their arms, and kissing each other's cheeks, and then the tumult subsided."

After Franklin died in 1790 the Marquis de Condorcet (1743–1794) read a eulogy for him at the Academy.

Related entries:
　Adams, John
　Electricity
　France
　French Revolution

Suggestions for further reading:
　"From Jean-Paul Marat," March 13, 1779 (Labaree et al., vol. 29).
　Masur, Louis P., ed. 1993. *The Autobiography of Benjamin Franklin*. Boston: Bedford Books of St. Martin's Press.
　"To Jean-Baptiste Le Roy," June 22, 1773 (Labaree et al., vol. 20).
　"To Jean-Baptiste Le Roy," March 30, 1773 (Labaree et al., vol. 20).

French and Indian War

The French and Indian War of 1754–1763 was the fourth in a series of wars between France and England over territory in North America, preceded by King George's War (1744–1748), Queen Anne's War (1702–1713), and King William's War (1689–1697). The war started in America over territory in the Ohio region. Hostilities erupted in Europe, where the war was called the Seven Years' War, and in India, where it was known as the Third Carnatic War.

At the end of King George's War, English traders had begun to move into the Ohio valley region and to cut into French trade with the Indians. Both countries claimed the territory. The French resolved to erect a series of forts along the Allegheny River in order to protect their interests in America. Construction of the forts began in 1753, and by the following year, the French had erected Fort Duquesne at what is now Pittsburgh, Pennsylvania. Alarmed by the French intrusion into English territory, Lieutenant Governor Robert Dinwiddie of Virginia sent George Washington to warn the French of their trespass. The French ignored the warning, and Dinwiddie sent Washington on a military expedition against Fort Duquesne. The French checked Washington and his men at the Battle of Fort Necessity on July 3–4, 1754. He returned to Virginia. Franklin was appointed as a delegate to the Albany Congress the same year, where he presented a plan of union for the colonies and insisted that some sort of colonial union was necessary for success in the looming war. Franklin's plan, however, was modified in the congress and rejected by both colonial assemblies and England.

The following year, England sent General Edward Braddock to America to take Fort Duquesne. Braddock arrived in Alexandria, Virginia, and then marched his troops to Frederictown, Maryland. The Pennsylvania Assembly, of which Franklin was a member, knew that Braddock disliked them because of their lack of success in raising money for the war (owing to long-standing disputes between the Assembly and the proprietaries, Thomas and Richard Penn, over the taxation of their estates). The Assembly sent Franklin to the general at Frederictown, officially as postmaster general to establish communication routes between Braddock and the colonial governors. Franklin's son William

accompanied him. When Braddock's efforts to find the wagons in Maryland and Virginia that he needed for his campaign produced only 25 of them, some of which were unusable, Franklin offered to obtain some in Pennsylvania. The frustrated general readily agreed, and he approved the terms Franklin drew up for them.

Franklin and his son printed advertisements declaring the need for wagons and outlining the terms on which they were to be taken. Wagon owners were to be advanced a sum of money, have their wagons and horses valued, and obtain guarantees for reimbursement if they did not come back. Some potential wagon donors protested because they did not know General Braddock, and therefore did not know if he was good for the reimbursements, so Franklin gave a bond for £20,000 and made himself personally responsible for all of them. Franklin obtained 150 wagons and 259 carrying horses for Braddock and his men, as well as supplies of food. All told, Franklin lent £1,300 of his own money for the campaign and made himself legally responsible for £20,000 more.

Franklin had warned Braddock about the Native American tactic of surprise attacks, and Braddock retorted that Indians might "be a formidable enemy to your raw American militia, but upon the King's regular and disciplined troops, sir, it is impossible they should make any impression." Braddock was ambushed by French and Indians on the way to the fort and mortally wounded; about 900 of his 1,200 men were either killed or wounded. George Washington, who was then Braddock's aide-de-camp, survived the attack and conducted the remaining men to safety. The wagons Franklin had procured were either destroyed or captured. "This whole transaction," Franklin wrote in his *Autobiography,* "gave us Americans the first suspicion that our exalted ideas of the prowess of British regulars had not been well founded." Franklin thought Braddock was "a brave man, and might probably have made a figure as a good officer in some European War. But he had too much self-confidence, too high an opinion of the validity of regular troops, and too mean a one of both Americans and Indians."

After the news of Braddock's defeat, Pennsylvania remained undefended and in a state of alarm. Indians had scalped frontier families, and the governor and the Assembly quarreled over bills to provide money for defense. For Franklin, Braddock's defeat was nearly a personal disaster. A few days before the battle, Braddock had luckily ordered Franklin repaid £1,000 of the money he had advanced, but he never saw the remaining £300. The owners of the horses and wagons demanded compensation for their losses, and some began to take legal action against him. However, General William Shirley (1694–1771), the governor of Massachusetts from 1741 to 1756 who led a failed expedition against Fort Niagara during the war, finally appointed commissioners to resolve and pay the claims of the former wagon owners.

In the emergency situation, the Assembly passed a bill appropriating £55,000, exempting the proprietary estates with a formal protest. Although the bill exempted the Penns' estates from taxation, public opinion scared them into adding £5,000 to whatever amount the Assembly appropriated. Franklin was one of seven appointed to spend the money. Franklin also authored a militia bill that passed in November 1755 and wrote "A Dialogue Between X, Y, and Z Concerning the Present State of Affairs in Pennsylvania" to promote the militia act. The same year, Franklin helped Josiah Quincy obtain money from the Assembly for a Massachusetts expedition to Crown Point.

Robert Hunter Morris, who was the commander in chief of Pennsylvania and the lieutenant governor, placed Franklin in charge of militia in Northampton County and allowed him to appoint officers. Franklin took charge of fortifying the northwestern frontier and raised troops. He had 560 men under his command. On January 15, 1756, Franklin started for Gnadenhutten—which had been burned by Indians, and its inhabi-

tants massacred—with 47 men. After marching through January rain and witnessing horrid scenes of massacred inhabitants, Franklin and his men reached Gnadenhutten and constructed Fort Allen. The Assembly called him back to Philadelphia in February.

Franklin declined but took a new commission as colonel of the Regiment of Philadelphia. However, news from England soon revoked all of the commissions, and Franklin's military career ended. In October 1756 Franklin participated in a treaty with the Delaware Indians in Easton. Pennsylvania's new governor, William Denny, laid projected expenses for the war before the Assembly. The Assembly passed another appropriations bill, which the governor rejected because it did not exempt the proprietary estates. The Assembly sent Franklin to England in 1757 to protest the proprietary demands for exemption.

Until 1758 the British fared poorly in the war. Britain paid its own troops better than American soldiers, creating tension. England's fortunes began to change for the better in 1757, when William Pitt rose to power and reorganized the war effort. He appointed competent commanders and began to treat American soldiers as equals. In 1758 English and American troops took the fort at Louisbourg. An English victory at Fort Frontenac on Lake Ontario cut French supply lines to the Ohio forts. Finally, the British captured Fort Duquesne. The following year, General James Wolfe defeated the French army at Quebec, and in 1760 the remaining French forces surrendered to General Jeffrey Amherst at Montreal. Franklin was by this time in England, and he wrote a pamphlet with Richard Jackson, "The Interest of Great Britain Considered" (1760), arguing that England should ask France for Canada at the upcoming treaty. The Treaty of Paris in 1763 ended the war and ceded all of France's territory in Canada to Britain.

The French and Indian War was important in shaping the American Revolution. England resorted to taxation of the American colonies to ease the debt it acquired during the war, and the colonists resented being taxed by a Parliament in which they had no representatives. When their grievances led to war, France, eager for revenge against England for the humiliating losses it suffered after the French and Indian War, was encouraged to support the Revolution.

Related entries:
Albany Plan of Union
Native Americans
Penn, Thomas
Pennsylvania Assembly
Quincy, Josiah, Sr. and Josiah, Jr.
Volunteer Militia
Washington, George

Suggestions for further reading:
Masur, Louis P., ed. 1993. *The Autobiography of Benjamin Franklin.* Boston: Bedford Books of St. Martin's Press.
Nolan, J. Bennett. 1936. *General Benjamin Franklin: The Military Career of a Philosopher.* Philadelphia: University of Pennsylvania Press.

French Revolution (1789–1799)

The French Revolution began just six years after the Treaty of Paris ended the American Revolutionary War and involved many of the people whom Franklin had befriended during his stay in France (1776–1785). The Revolution's most violent phases took place after Franklin's death, and he did not live to learn of the lost lives and ruined fortunes of his friends.

The events of the Revolution that Franklin knew about were those of its relatively moderate beginnings. The French treasury was nearly empty after the country's successive involvements in the French and Indian War and the American Revolution. In America, subjects of the British Crown had succeeded in throwing off the monarchy and establishing a republic. Many different political groups developed in France, all advocating different forms of new governments. During the first part of the Revolution, moderate advocates of a constitutional monarchy, including

Franklin's friend and American hero the Marquis de Lafayette, carried the most influence.

In 1788 national financial woes and popular pressure forced Louis XVI, who had been the king of France since 1774, to call an election of the Estates-General, which had not met since 1614. Three different Estates were represented—the clergy, the nobility, and the commoners. After an unsuccessful meeting at Versailles in May 1789, a caucus of commoners withdrew and proclaimed themselves the National Assembly. Among the principal leaders of this group was the Comte de Mirabeau, who on Franklin's suggestion had translated into French an American pamphlet criticizing the Society of the Cincinnati.

When the king took away the Assembly's meeting place, its members gathered on a tennis court and proclaimed that they would not dissolve until France had a new constitution. This famous event was known as the Tennis Court Oath. Members of the other two Estates also joined the National Assembly. On July 14, 1789, mobs of Parisians, angry at the concentration of royal army regiments in Paris and the king's dismissal of his minister, Jacques Necker, stormed the Bastille, the royal prison. The king recalled Necker, but mob violence continued. On August 12 the Assembly adopted the Declaration of the Rights of Man, which stressed rights to "liberty, equality, and fraternity." The Assembly drew up a new constitution that created a national legislature, which they called the Legislative Assembly, and outlined a constitutional monarchy. Titles and privileges of the nobility were abolished.

These were the events that Franklin had likely heard of when he wrote to his friend Benjamin Vaughan in November 1789, "The revolution in France is truly surprising. I sincerely wish it may end in establishing a good constitution for that country. The mischiefs and troubles it suffers in the operation, however, give me great concern." Thomas Jefferson visited Franklin just before his death in 1790 and updated him on events that followed. After Franklin's death, the Comte de

The storming of the Bastille, July 14, 1789. Engraving by Berthault.

Mirabeau read a eulogy before the French National Assembly, which voted to wear mourning for Franklin for three days. Many of Franklin's old acquaintances found themselves on opposite sides of the controversy. Edmund Burke, the English statesman and philosopher who had supported fair treatment of the American colonies before the war, condemned the French Revolution in *Reflections on the Revolution in France* (1790). Thomas Paine, who authored the famous pamphlet *Common Sense* (1776) urging independence of the American colonies from Britain, criticized Burke's perspective in *The Rights of Man* (1791–1792). Franklin's former political ally in Pennsylvania, Joseph Galloway, was a vocal critic of the Revolution.

Outside of the Assembly in France, tension mounted. On October 5–6, 1789, a mob of Parisians, mostly women, laid siege to the Royal Palace. The Marquis de Lafayette and the National Guard rescued the king and his family. Lafayette escorted them to Paris. In 1790 Louis XVI reluctantly approved the first draft of the constitution. The new reforms, however, were not sufficient for more radical groups like the Jacobins in Paris and the Cordeliers. They resented the fact that only the propertied class could vote.

Many noblemen had already fled the country, and Louis XVI tried to flee with his family in 1791. He was stopped and returned to Paris, and people began to suspect that he was conspiring with the nobles who had fled abroad. The year 1791 brought the downfall of the moderates and the rise of the radicals. Radicals gained influence in the new Legislative Assembly created by the constitution. Among these radicals was Jean-Paul Marat, who had earlier begged Franklin to observe his experiments while he was trying to prove that an "igneous fluid" emanated from fire. In 1792 war with Austria prompted the Assembly to adopt a stricter government. Further violence ensued, and the king was imprisoned. Radicals soon dominated the

Assembly, and it called for a National Convention to establish a new constitution. Louis XVI, who had been so generous toward the American cause, was guillotined for treason in 1793.

The radical factions gained the upper hand in the Assembly, and the famous Reign of Terror ensued. It began in April 1793, when the convention appointed a Committee of Safety that effectively ruled France. Strict rule was imposed on the country, and any suspected subversives were rounded up. An estimated 40,000 aristocrats, moderates, and other "enemies" of the radical government died either by execution or as an indirect result of arrest.

Many of the friends whose company Franklin had greatly enjoyed in France met with misfortune and death during the Terror. The Marquis de Condorcet, a member of the Nine Sisters Lodge with Franklin, was thrown into prison and poisoned. The chemist Antoine-Laurent Lavoisier lost his life on the guillotine in 1794. Louis-Guillaume Le Veillard was sent to the scaffold the same year. Ironically, the person who was most instrumental in the deaths of Franklin's friends was

Maximilien Robespierre (1758–1794), a member of the Committee of Safety. Robespierre had written to Franklin in 1783 commending him on his lightning rod, and he had enclosed a printed copy of the defense of Franklin's invention that he presented to the Council of Artois. Robespierre himself was eventually executed.

Moderates wrested control from the radicals, and France again received a new constitution in 1795, establishing a board of directors with executive powers and a two-house legislature. In 1799 Napoleon Bonaparte established himself as the emperor of France.

Related entries:
Burke, Edmund
France
French Academy of Sciences
Lafayette, Marquis de
Paine, Thomas

Suggestions for further reading:
"To David Hartley," December 4, 1789 (Smyth, vol. X).
"To M. Le Veillard," November 13, 1789 (Smyth, vol. X).

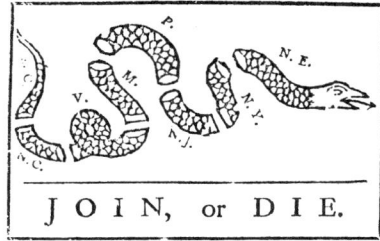

JOIN, or DIE.

G

Galloway, Joseph
(1731–1803)

Franklin worked closely with Joseph Galloway for 20 years from the time both were serving in the Pennsylvania Assembly until the beginning of the Revolutionary War. Galloway was a successful lawyer from a wealthy family, temperamental, and eloquent. He voiced ideas Franklin came up with. In the Assembly the two were allies in a long dispute with the proprietors of Pennsylvania, the sons of William Penn, who they believed were poor governors of the province. Galloway and Franklin objected to the long-standing exemption of proprietary lands from taxation, particularly when war required the colonists to raise more money than usual. In 1764 they worked together to persuade the Assembly to petition the king for royal government to replace the proprietorship.

One of Galloway's contributions to this dispute was a speech written in support of the petition and in response to a speech by John Dickinson, a vocal opponent of the petition. Franklin wrote a lengthy preface to the speech, which included a mock epitaph of Thomas and Richard Penn, who were the two surviving proprietors. In strong language, the epitaph accused the sons of abandoning their father's benevolent intentions, taking advantage of Pennsylvanians, refusing to approve measures necessary for their defense, and "daily endeavoring to reduce them to the most abject slavery."

Both Galloway and Franklin lost their seats in the Assembly in 1764, but Franklin was dispatched to England to present the petition anyway. Galloway regained his seat, and he and Franklin kept each other up-to-date on the political activity in Philadelphia and England, respectively, including the Stamp Act and the dispute with the proprietors. Franklin, his son William, and Galloway were all involved in the Grand Ohio Company, organized in 1769 to obtain American land from the Crown west of the existing colonies. Franklin kept him informed on their proposal's lethargic progress through the British bureaucracy.

Before the Revolutionary War began, Galloway authored an ill-fated plan of union for England and the colonies. The plan was defeated in the Continental Congress. Franklin, too, was skeptical about his trusted friend's plan: "[W]hen I consider the extreme corruption prevalent among all orders of men in this old rotten state, and the glorious public virtue so predominant in our rising country, I cannot but apprehend more mischief than benefit from a closer union."

After Franklin returned to Philadelphia in 1775 he tried to persuade both his son and Galloway to support the move for independence. Galloway sat in the First Continental Congress but refused to serve in the Second, despite Franklin's urging. Both refused, and the friendship between Galloway and Franklin later ended. Franklin left many of his papers with Galloway before he left for France, after he briefly indicated support for the colonial position, and they were subsequently lost. Galloway remained faithful to the Crown and became an administrator when the British occupied Philadelphia in 1777–1778. In 1778, he moved to England, where he testified for the loyalists in America before Parliament and denounced Franklin. After the war, he devoted his energies to criticizing the French Revolution.

Related entries:
Franklin, William
French Revolution
Grand Ohio Company
Pennsylvania Assembly

Suggestions for further reading:
Newcomb, Benjamin H. 1972. *Franklin and Galloway: A Political Partnership.* New Haven, Conn.: Yale University Press.
"Preface to Joseph Galloway's Speech," August 11, 1764 (Labaree et al., vol. 11).

The General Magazine and Historical Chronicle for All the British Plantations in America

Franklin founded *The General Magazine and Historical Chronicle for All the British Plantations in America* in Philadelphia in 1741. His short-lived magazine entered the local market sooner than he had wanted after the editor he planned to hire, John Webbe, betrayed him and informed his rival printer Andrew Bradford of the idea. Bradford, who published the *American Weekly Mercury*, announced his own plans to publish *The American Magazine.*

The Pennsylvania Gazette, Franklin's paper, announced *The General Magazine,* which would consist of "four sheets, of common-sized paper, in a small character" and would

be sold by the issue at "six pence sterling, or nine pence Pennsylvania money." Franklin accused Webbe of betraying the confidential plan to the *Mercury* and intending to "reap the advantage of it wholly to himself." In the *Mercury,* Webbe accused Franklin, who was the postmaster, of not allowing the *Mercury* to be delivered to its recipients. Franklin had in fact refused to deliver the papers. Bradford had been postmaster before Franklin and failed to turn in his accounts for more than five years. The deputy postmaster general, Colonel Alexander Spotswood, ordered Franklin not to deliver his papers unless Bradford paid the postage. In response to Webbe's accusation, Franklin printed the text of the order in the *Gazette.*

Bradford's magazine appeared a few days before Franklin's. Neither of them was successful or long-lived. Religious and philosophical questions, recent votes and political news, colonial paper currency, and other news were among *The General Magazine*'s topics. It lasted for only six months, but its failure was not a major setback for Franklin, whose *Pennsylvania Gazette* and *Poor Richard's Almanack* were by this time very successful.

Related entries:
Pennsylvania Gazette
Poor Richard's Almanack
Printing

Suggestion for further reading:
"The Life of Benjamin Franklin," pp. 166–170 (Smyth, vol. X).

George III (1738–1820)

Some of the harshest words to be found in Franklin's surviving writings were reserved for King George III (grandson of George II), who sat on the throne of England from 1760 to 1820. He was firm in his resolve to subdue his rebellious American subjects, often unreasonable, and prone to intermittent bouts of dementia (caused by porphyria, a metabolic disorder).

Franklin's first impressions of George III were dramatically different from the opinion he held of the king during the war. He was in London for the king's coronation in 1760, and three years later he reassured his apprehensive friend William Strahan, "I am of opinion that his virtue and the consciousness of sincere intentions to make his people happy will give him firmness and steadiness in his measures and in the support of the honest friends he has chosen to serve him. . . . " For a long time Franklin also believed that the king's rulership would be preferable to the proprietary governors of Pennsylvania. The Pennsylvania Assembly sent him to England in 1764 with a petition to the king to take over governing from the proprietors.

A curious controversy began in 1772, when the Board of Ordnance consulted Franklin, the inventor of the lightning rod, on protecting British powder magazines after lightning had struck one in Italy. The matter ended up being handled by a committee from the Royal Society of London. Franklin was on the committee, had visited the magazines in question, and drafted a report outlining the committee's reasons for recommending pointed lightning rods. There was one dissenter on the committee, Benjamin Wilson, who advocated instead the use of blunt rods and published arguments against the pointed rods. The pointed rods that Franklin preferred won out for the time being, but during the Revolutionary War, the king ordered the pointed rods on the powder magazine and his palace replaced with blunt ones. The king was adamant about the blunt rods, and his stubbornness was widely supposed to stem from his hatred of the American rebel Franklin. He tried to force Franklin's friend Sir John Pringle, who was then president of the Royal Society, to support the blunt rods. Pringle refused to support something he did not believe and subsequently lost his presidency and his position as queen's physician. At least one of Franklin's friends undertook the defense of the pointed rods, but he, for his part, declined to take part in the controversy.

The Declaration of Independence, signed in 1776, leveled all of its accusations not against Parliament but specifically against the king. Its signers believed him to be a tyrant "unfit to be the ruler of a free people." Franklin felt this sentiment perhaps even more strongly than most—he had not only seen the effects of restrictive British policies on the colonies but had also endured many years deeply entangled in English politics as an agent working on behalf of the colonies.

The king grew increasingly resentful of the belligerence and rebellion he perceived in his American subjects. He favored intensified restrictions on the colonies and force to subdue them if necessary. He had a supporter in the ministry of Lord North, and Franklin rightly understood royal designs behind the measures for which North pushed. The First Continental Congress sent the king a petition outlining its grievances, which he ignored. A subsequent petition from the Second Continental Congress, known as the "Olive Branch Petition," was also ignored. In 1775 the king declared that the colonies were in open rebellion.

George III's intelligence officers kept a close watch on Franklin while he was in France during the war. Franklin immediately suspected the intrigues of the king when a mysterious letter arrived at his home in Passy in 1778. The writer of the letter, who used the pseudonym "Charles de Weissenstein," offered to reward influential Americans like himself, John Adams, George Washington, and John Hancock for their aid in reconciling with Britain. Franklin was incensed and wrote a biting reply that was never delivered. In 1782 Franklin, still in France, produced and circulated a fictitious "Supplement to the Boston Independent Chronicle" as a propaganda piece brimming with accusations against England. One of the imaginary writers said, "[B]ut voluntary malice, mischief, and murder, are from hell; and this King will, therefore, stand foremost in the list of diabolical, bloody, and execrable tyrants."

George III. Painting from the studio of Alan Ramsey.

In the end, George III lost his colonies. He was stricken with a severe bout of dementia in 1788 and nearly forced to abdicate. By 1811 he was so ill that his son began acting as king. He died in 1820.

Related entries:
Adams, John
Continental Congresses
Declaration of Independence
Electricity
France
Revolutionary War
Revolutionary Writings
Stamp Act
Weissenstein, Charles de

Suggestions for further reading:
Aspinall, A., ed. 1962–1970. *The Later Correspondence of George III.* Cambridge, England: University Press.
Donne, W. Bodham. 1971. *The Correspondence of King George the Third with Lord North, 1768 to 1783.* New York: Da Capo Press.
Stevens, Richard B., ed. 1984. *The Declaration of Independence and the Constitution of the United States.* Washington, D.C.: Georgetown University Press.

Godfrey, Thomas (1704–1749)

One of Franklin's early acquaintances in Philadelphia was Thomas Godfrey, a glazier originally from Bristol, Pennsylvania. When Franklin and Hugh Meredith broke from Samuel Keimer to set up their own printing business, they took in Thomas Godfrey, along with his wife and children, to help pay for the new printing house. According to Franklin, he "worked little, being always absorbed in mathematics."

Godfrey was a skilled mathematician and one of the original members of the Junto, the discussion club that Franklin organized in 1727. "[H]e knew a little out of his way," Franklin said, "and was not a pleasing companion; as, like most great mathematicians I have met with, he expected universal precision in everything said, or was for ever denying or distinguishing upon trifles, to the disturbance of all conversation."

Troubles between Franklin and the Godfreys arose when Mrs. Godfrey tried to match Franklin with a daughter of one of her relatives. After a serious courtship, Franklin told Mrs. Godfrey that he expected a sum of money with his wife that was sufficient to pay off the debt of the printing house. The family said they could not provide a sum of money that large and did not think his printing profession was a promising one. They refused to allow the daughter to see Franklin anymore. Mrs. Godfrey later told Franklin that they had a better opinion of him, but he refused to have anything more to do with them. The Godfreys were offended and moved out of the house, after which Franklin and Meredith resolved not to rent to anyone else.

Franklin published Godfrey's almanacs annually from 1729 to 1731. Godfrey's major accomplishment was the invention of a quadrant, for which he was recognized by the Royal Society of London. In 1744 Godfrey joined the American Philosophical Society as an original member and the society's mathematician. He died in Philadelphia in 1749.

Related entries:
American Philosophical Society
The Junto
Printing
Royal Society of London

Suggestion for further reading:
Masur, Louis P., ed. 1993. *The Autobiography of Benjamin Franklin.* Boston: Bedford Books of St. Martin's Press.

Grand Ohio Company

When the Grand Ohio Company formed in 1769, Franklin had long thought that a British settlement in the western Ohio lands would prove beneficial to both England and the colonies. In 1756 he wrote a "Plan for Settling Two Western Colonies in North America," in which he outlined his belief that such new colonies would protect the existing ones from attacks, increase trade, encourage population growth, and prevent the French from uniting their Canadian settlements with those in Louisiana. A new opportunity for settlement arose in 1768, when a treaty signed with Indian nations at Fort Stanwix established new boundaries. Under the treaty, the Indians gave up land to repay traders who sustained damage at the hands of Indians. At the same time, additional lands were purchased for the British Crown. Before the 1768 treaty, the "Suffering Traders" Company had formed to prosecute the interests of traders who claimed damages by Indian raids.

Samuel Wharton, a Philadelphia merchant and one of the original Suffering Traders, was one of the driving forces behind a petition to Lord Hillsborough in 1769 for 2.4 million acres of land in that territory. Lord Hillsborough, who hoped to defeat the petition, rerouted it to the treasury and encouraged Wharton to ask for 20 million acres, believing that such a large request would undermine the project. Wharton and others reorganized the Indiana Company, which had emerged out of the Suffering Traders into the new Grand Ohio Company (also known as the Walpole Company, after one of its members, Thomas Walpole), of which Franklin and his son were members and which sought some of the additional land purchased for the Crown. Members included both Englishmen and Americans, many of them Franklin's friends—William Strahan, Joseph Galloway, Richard Jackson, and his partner at the post office, John Foxcroft. The new company made a formal offer to the treasury—it would pay more than £10,000 for 20 million acres, plus a regular quitrent after 20 years. The treasury added the stipulation that a colony also be established there. The company decided to name the potential settlement the Vandalia colony, after the Queen's Vandal heritage. But the battle was not over yet. Between Lord Hillsborough's objections, conflicting claims on the land from Virginia and that state's veterans of the French and Indian War, and a continuing series of other complications, the plan never worked out. By 1773 members of the company had all but an official document allowing them to proceed, but new conflicts with Virginia and the outbreak of the Revolution halted the plan permanently.

The company, however, did not disband until much later. Franklin withdrew early in 1774 but was reinstated the following year. In 1775, still expecting approval for the project, the Grand Ohio Company wanted to begin selling the part originally given to the traders before receiving the go-ahead from England. The Indiana Company held meetings in America on its own, and Franklin attended some of them in late 1775 and early 1776 as a representative for his son William, who himself had a stake in the company. In 1780 Wharton presented a memorial to Congress detailing the history of the company's claims.

Related entries:
Franklin, William
French and Indian War

Suggestions for further reading:
"From Franklin and Samuel Wharton: Memorial to Congress," February 26, 1780 (Labaree et al., vol. 31).
"A Plan for Settling Two Western Colonies," 1754 (Labaree et al., vol. 5).
"Settlement on the Ohio River," 1772 (Smyth, vol. V).

Great Awakening

A series of somewhat disconnected religious revivals, known collectively as the Great Awakening, swept through the American colonies in the 1700s. The revivals were, for the most part, spread out over time and distance. A number of American and European ministers, such as Jonathan Edwards, John Wesley, and George Whitefield, introduced new emphasis on individual conversion experiences and more charismatic styles of preaching.

The German minister Theodore J. Frelinghuysen spurred a revival among Dutch Reformed congregants in New Jersey during the 1720s. In the 1730s Edwards in Massachusetts delivered sermons in a dry and monotonous tone of voice, which was uncharacteristic of the others associated with the Great Awakening. However, the words of famous messages like "Sinners in the Hands of an Angry God" evoked crying, pangs of guilt, and other emotional outpourings beyond what Edwards himself intended. Wesley introduced Methodism, later a new denomination, to the colonies. Presbyterian revivals swept through Pennsylvania, New Jersey, New York, and other colonies, spurred by ministers such as Gilbert Tennent. One of the most extreme of the revivalists was the Congregationalist James Davenport, who delivered accusatory sermons in Connecticut, after which, on at least one occasion, his frenzied audience burned their idols and worldly possessions. Baptists and Lutherans were also represented in the Great Awakening.

The provocative words and deliveries of these men were not accepted by all colonists. Some held to Puritan beliefs in a sound understanding of scripture, piety, and temperance and deplored the emotional outbursts of the revivals. Within the sphere of the Great Awakening's pastors, stylistic and doctrinal differences divided the denominations that they represented, most notably the Presbyterians. Despite these differences, the revivals

George Whitefield (1714–1770), evangelistic preacher from England. Engraving.

changed the face of religion in the colonies and resulted in an explosion in the number of churches. Many of the newly formed Protestant churches regarded themselves as different "denominations" of the church rather than as exclusive representations of the church. In the public sphere, they spurred the establishment of charities, new colleges, and increased opposition to slavery in the colonies. The established church gradually began to move out of the affairs of the state.

Franklin crossed paths with the sweeping religious revivals in 1739, the year that George Whitefield arrived in Philadelphia. Whitefield, an Anglican minister from England as well a friend of Wesley's, toured the colonies on numerous occasions and delivered eloquent sermons. Franklin befriended the minister, and the friendship would last for the rest of Whitefield's life. In his *Autobiography,* Franklin recalled Whitefield's visit to Philadelphia:

[I]t was a matter of speculation to me . . . to observe the extraordinary influence of his oratory on his hearers, and how much they admired and respected him notwithstanding his common abuse of them by assuring them that they were naturally half beasts and half devils. It was wonderful to see the change soon made in the manners of our inhabitants. From being thoughtless or indifferent about religion, it seemed as if all the world were growing religious, so that one could not walk through the town in an evening without hearing psalms sung in different families of every street.

With his outspoken sermons and bold writing, Whitefield made enemies in Philadelphia and elsewhere. When other Philadelphia ministers forbade him to preach from their pulpits, he was forced to speak in open fields outdoors. Franklin, however, believed in tolerating all religion. A building was soon erected in Philadelphia to provide a platform for representatives of any religion. Franklin printed Whitefield's sermons and journals and invited him to stay in his house. Although he did not see eye to eye with him on religious matters, he believed the minister's sermons generally had a beneficial effect on the community.

Whitefield consulted Franklin on a charitable project he had in mind to alleviate the plight of poor children in Georgia. Franklin suggested that it would be better and cheaper to bring orphaned children to Philadelphia than send supplies to Georgia. Whitefield did not take his advice, and Franklin, who resolved during one of his sermons not to contribute to the fund for the Georgia project, nevertheless felt sufficiently moved by the end of the message to empty his pockets.

Franklin wrote to the minister in 1756 that he at times wished that Whitefield could join him in a plan to settle a colony in the Ohio region. Franklin, who many years later as a member of the Grand Ohio Company was still interested in settling western lands, believed that a sizable population of "religious and industrious" people would benefit England and the existing colonies in trade, population, and security. After Whitefield died in 1770, Franklin wrote of his friend: "I knew him upwards of 30 years. His integrity, disinterestedness, and indefatigable zeal in prosecuting every good work, I have never seen equaled, and I shall never see exceeded."

The Great Awakening as a whole was an important social and religious movement in Franklin's time, but it had little personal effect on him. He was from an early age an independent thinker who never allied himself with any denomination or sect of religious belief. His belief in the general goodness of Christian churches was based more on the beneficial effect they had on the character of people and society than acknowledgment of the truth of doctrines preached therein.

Related entries:
    Mather, Increase, Cotton, and Samuel
    Religious Beliefs

Suggestions for further reading:
    Masur, Louis P., ed. 1993. *The Autobiography of Benjamin Franklin*. Boston: Bedford Books of St. Martin's Press.
    "To George Whitefield," July 2, 1756 (Labaree et al., vol. 6).
    "To George Whitefield," June 19, 1764 (Labaree et al., vol. 11).

Great Britain

Aside from the early period that Franklin worked in London printing houses between 1724 and 1726, he lived in England during two other periods, from 1757 to 1762 and from 1764 to 1775. A mix of frustrating politics and private pleasantry marked these two stays in England.

The mission assigned to him by the Pennsylvania Assembly on his first voyage was to present a petition for the right to tax proprietary lands in Pennsylvania. After the Board of Trade allowed a tax to stand on the lands in 1758, Franklin remained in England as an agent for Pennsylvania. His political activity during this visit was related largely to the affairs of Pennsylvania, but as the quarrel between England and America blossomed after 1764, Franklin became an unofficial agent for the interests of all of the colonies during his second stay. The first major battle began with the passage of the Stamp Act, which the Assembly had instructed him to oppose. The act passed in 1765 and caused such an uproar in America that Franklin was soon immersed in working for its repeal. He was examined extensively before the House of Commons.

After the publication of the examination, other colonies began appointing him as their agent—Georgia, New Jersey, and Massachusetts. He worked in his agencies under the ministries of Sir George Grenville, the Marquess of Rockingham (Charles Watson-Wentworth), William Pitt (Earl of Chatham), the Duke of Grafton, and Lord Frederick North. Of them, only the short-lived Rockingham ministry and the weak, short-lived Chatham ministry showed any favorable disposition toward America. Grenville had introduced the Stamp Act. Lord North, prime minister from 1770 to 1782, acted according to the wishes of George III, who considered his subjects in America as lawless rebels.

The secretaries of American affairs gave no less trouble to Franklin. From 1766 to 1768, Lord Shelburne, who liked Franklin and supported policies favorable to America, held the post. His position passed to Lord Hillsborough in 1768. Of Hillsborough, Franklin wrote to Samuel Cooper in Boston: "His character is conceit, wrong-headedness, obstinacy, and passion.... I hope ... that our affairs will not much longer be perplexed and embarrassed by his perverse and senseless management" (1771). When the Massachusetts Assembly appointed Franklin as its agent in London, Lord Hillsborough obstinately refused to recognize his agency. After a brief exchange over the legality of agents appointed by colonial assemblies, Franklin, irritated, replied, "It is, I believe, of

no great importance whether the appointment is acknowledged or not, for I have not the least conception that an agent can at present be of any use to the colonies," and left. Lord Hillsborough also tried to obstruct the western land grant sought by the Grand Ohio Company, of which Franklin was part.

When Lord Dartmouth, who was at first thought to be more favorably disposed toward America, replaced Lord Hillsborough in 1772, Franklin briefly hoped for a better state of affairs. Just before he left England in 1775, however, he was as disgusted with Dartmouth, who began to side with advocates of restrictive policies toward America, as with Hillsborough. He wrote a sharply critical memorial to Dartmouth on behalf of the province of Massachusetts Bay, protesting an impending act of Parliament that would forbid Massachusetts fishers access to fisheries off Nova Scotia, Labrador, and the banks of Newfoundland. Thomas Walpole convinced him not to present the memorial. The members of Parliament who sympathized with American grievances and showed Franklin friendship—Lord Shelburne, Lord Chatham, Lord Camden, Edmund Burke, and others—held little influence before the Revolutionary War.

The ministries tried various subtle means of silencing Franklin, who, aside from his political agencies for the colonies, wrote popular pieces to British newspapers satirizing British policy toward America. It seized on an opportunity to humiliate him in 1774. He was summoned to the Cockpit, part of Whitehall, for the consideration of a petition from Massachusetts to remove the governor, Thomas Hutchinson. Franklin had mysteriously obtained and transmitted to Massachusetts letters written by Hutchinson, in which he recommended sending troops to Massachusetts and portrayed the province in a negative light. The Massachusetts Assembly wanted him removed and instructed its agents to present the petition. The agent for Hutchinson, Israel Manduit, retained as counsel the solicitor general, Alexander

Wedderburn. While many of the Lords in attendance applauded and laughed, Wedderburn denounced Franklin and Massachusetts for an hour at the hearing. A few days later, Franklin was fired from the post office.

By 1774 some of Franklin's friends began to fear for his safety in England. On October 12, 1774, he wrote to Joseph Galloway: "My situation here is thought by many to be a little hazardous; for that if by some accident, the troops and people of New England should come to blows, I should probably be taken up; the ministerial people affecting everywhere to represent me as the cause of all misunderstanding; and I have frequently been cautioned to secure my papers, and by some advised to withdraw." Soon afterward, he became involved in fruitless, unofficial, and secret negotiations aimed at averting war between England and America, and he dealt directly or indirectly with Lords Chatham, Stanhope, Camden, Dartmouth, Hyde, and Howe.

Aside from the increasingly frustrating political situation in which Franklin found himself, the rest of his life in England was generally pleasant. Almost as soon as he arrived in 1757, he rented rooms on Craven Street from Mrs. Margaret Stevenson, a widow who lived with her daughter, Mary (Polly). Mrs. Stevenson and Polly became two of his dearest friends, and Franklin lived on Craven Street during his entire residence in London after that year. Franklin's son William, and then William's illegitimate son, William Temple, lived with them at different times, as did a young English relative, Sally Franklin. Franklin's wife Deborah, who was frightened of the water and refused to cross it, stayed with their daughter in Philadelphia.

Franklin, who noted to Dr. Jan Ingenhousz in 1783 that America's geniuses all went to Europe, also found great enjoyment in the company of Britain's scientists and philosophers. He had previously corresponded with some of the people who became his closest friends—Peter Collinson, Dr. John Fothergill,

"The Colonies Reduced." Anti-British tax policy cartoon. Engraving in the **Political Register**, *1768.*

and William Strahan. He often dined with the Strahans and with Sir John Pringle, who became physician to the queen and president of the Royal Society of London. Other friends included Benjamin Vaughan, the entire family of Jonathan Shipley (the bishop of St. Asaph), Lord Kames (Henry Home), Dr. Joseph Priestley, Dr. Richard Price, and Sir Francis Dashwood (Lord Le Despencer). Acquaintances included David Hume, William Robertson, Edmund Burke, Adam Smith, and Lord Shelburne. Franklin met with the Honest Whigs, a philosophical discussion club, at a London coffeehouse every two weeks. Its occasional or regular members included James Boswell, Price, Priestley, Pringle, Fothergill, and Collinson. Franklin was a member of the Society of Arts and the prestigious Royal Society of London, and he received honorary degrees from the University of St. Andrews and Oxford University. While in England, Franklin also tried to procure books for the Library Company in Philadelphia as well as support for the Pennsylvania Hospital and Pennsylvania Academy. He encouraged interaction between the Royal Society of London and the American Philosophical Society in Philadelphia.

For health and for pleasure, Franklin traveled extensively. In 1760 Franklin and his son went to Banbury at Ectonshire, where Franklin's father had been born, and sought out information about their ancestors. The following year, both traveled with Richard Jackson to Belgium and Holland, during which Franklin visited the inventor of the Leyden jar, Pieter van Musschenbroek. In 1766 Franklin traveled with Pringle to Hanover, and both were elected to the Royal Academy of Sciences in Göttingen. Pringle and Franklin visited France in 1767, at which time they were presented to Louis XV. During a tour of Ireland and Scotland with Richard Jackson in 1771, Franklin attended the opening of the Irish Parliament.

The outbreak of the Revolutionary War interrupted all of his friendships from Britain. In most cases it was the post office more than differences over the war that caused interruptions in communication. Franklin saw, briefly, Vaughan and some of the Shipleys in Southampton before he returned from France to Philadelphia in 1785.

Related entries:
> Collinson, Peter
> Dashwood, Sir Francis (Lord Le Despencer)
> Fothergill, Dr. John
> George III
> Hewson, Mary (Polly) Stevenson
> Jackson, Richard
> Kames, Lord (Henry Home)
> Priestley, Dr. Joseph
> Pringle, Sir John
> Royal Society of London
> Stevenson, Mrs. Margaret
> Strahan, William

Suggestions for further reading:
> Currey, Cecil B. 1968. *Road to Revolution: Benjamin Franklin in England, 1765–1775.* Garden City, N.Y.: Anchor Books.
> Morgan, David T. 1996. *The Devious Dr. Franklin, Colonial Agent: Benjamin Franklin's Years in London.* Macon, Ga.: Mercer University Press.
> Nolan, J. Bennett. 1938. *Benjamin Franklin in Scotland and Ireland, 1759 and 1771.* Philadelphia: University of Pennsylvania Press.

Greene, Catharine Ray (1731–1794)

*T*he first of the younger women with whom Franklin is known to have corresponded on a regular basis was Catharine Ray. Franklin and Catharine met in Boston in 1755 and traveled together for part of his return journey to Philadelphia. He was nearly 50, and she was 23. The two talked "agreeably" the whole way and formed a friendship that would last until Franklin's death in 1790.

Their first letters were somewhat flirtatious. Franklin wrote to her after he returned to Philadelphia. Having watched her board an unsteady boat, he had been concerned about her getting home when they parted and was glad to hear that she had arrived safely. He was liberal with his compliments to her: "I write this during a northeast storm of snow, the greatest we have had this winter. Your favors come mixed with the snowy fleeces, which are pure as your virgin innocence, white as your lovely bosom, and—as cold. But let it warm towards some worthy young man, and may Heaven bless you both with every kind of happiness."

She sent the Franklins some turf and some English cheese, which both thought was very tasty. Deborah Franklin was aware of the correspondence and sent her regards with her husband's letters. She and Catharine later wrote to each other on their own. Franklin told Catharine that his wife was pleased that a young lady would have enough regard for her husband to send such a gift.

Franklin enjoyed the correspondence with "Katy," as he affectionately called her. "The small news, the domestic occurrences among our friends, the natural pictures you draw of persons, the sensible observations and reflections you make, and the easy, chatty manner in which you express every thing, all contribute to heighten the pleasure; and the more as they remind me of those hours and miles, that we talked away so agreeably, even in a winter journey, a wrong road, and a soaking shower," he wrote (1755).

As with some of the women much younger than himself with whom Franklin later became acquainted—Polly Hewson in England and Madame Brillon in France—he was at first something of a father figure to Catharine. Accordingly, he offered her fatherly advice in 1755. He admonished her to go to church faithfully until she found a husband, and then to stay home, nurse her children, and help with her husband's estate. In 1758 she married the "worthy young man" Franklin had wished for her—William Greene, who later became the governor of Rhode Island.

Franklin exchanged letters with her for the rest of his life but saw her infrequently. On a trip through the colonies in 1763 he and his daughter visited the Greenes. Franklin fell off his horse and was well taken care of at their home, and his daughter greatly enjoyed the visit. After he left them, he suffered another fall and was embarrassed to tell her that he had injured his shoulder. Franklin's sister, Jane Mecom, in danger from British attack, went to stay with the Greenes in Rhode Island in 1775. Franklin visited all of them there and took the Greenes' son Ray back to Philadelphia to attend school. Franklin continued to write to Catharine from Paris during the Revolutionary War and from Philadelphia after he returned to America.

Related entries:
Bache, Sarah Franklin
Brillon de Jouy, Anne-Louise Boivin d'Hardancourt
Franklin, Deborah Read Rogers
Hewson, Mary (Polly) Stevenson
Mecom, Jane Franklin

Suggestions for further reading:
Roelker, William Greene, ed. 1949. *Benjamin Franklin and Catharine Ray Greene: The Correspondence, 1755–1790*. Philadelphia: American Philosophical Society.
"To Catharine Ray," March 4, 1755 (Labaree et al., vol. 5).
"To Catharine Ray," October 16, 1755 (Labaree et al., vol. 6).
"To Catharine Ray," September 11, 1755 (Labaree et al., vol. 6).
"To Mrs. Catharine Greene," March 2, 1789 (Smyth, vol. X).

Gulf Stream

Franklin was one of the first people to study the Gulf Stream in detail. A warm ocean current that flows from Florida northeastward across the Atlantic Ocean, the Gulf Stream had a noticeable impact on the speed with which ships passed between the American colonies and England. On at least three separate voyages across the Atlantic, Franklin kept detailed records of the air temperature, water temperature, wind directions, weed content of the water, and the color of the water.

He first became interested in the Gulf Stream as a result of a complaint from the Boston board of customs to the London treasury that "packets [ships that traveled regular routes] between Falmouth and New York, were generally a fortnight longer in their passages than merchant-ships from London to Rhode Island, and proposing that for the future they should be ordered to Rhode Island instead of New York."

Franklin was consulted on the matter and learned from a relative, Timothy Folger, that the problem of the slow packets was likely due to the ship captains' lack of knowledge about the Gulf Stream. Folger, a whale hunter, had observed that whales swam next to the stream. While in pursuit of whales, he had crossed the stream and encountered the English ships sailing against the current. Folger said that the current flowed about three miles per hour against the ships, and on a day of little wind they actually lost distance.

His curiosity aroused, Franklin asked Folger to draw a diagram of the Gulf Stream. Once it was completed, Franklin had it engraved. He reported all of this information to Anthony Todd of the British post office in a letter dated October 29, 1769. The copies of Folger's chart, along with his instructions for avoiding the stream when sailing west toward the colonies, were given to mostly skeptical captains of the packets.

Franklin supposed that the stream was generated by accumulation of water on the east coast of America between the tropics, which was spurred by the area's trade winds. He first took daily air and water temperature readings on a voyage on the *Pennsylvania Packet* from London to Philadelphia in the spring of 1775. On two other journeys—from Philadelphia to France aboard the *Reprisal* in 1776, and again on a return voyage from Europe to America—he kept records of the same information.

He made several observations as a result of the records he kept on his voyages. First, he found that the water temperature in the Gulf Stream was much warmer than that of surrounding waters. Second, the higher temperature warmed the air above the stream's water, which caused both frequent waterspouts near the Gulf Stream and the heavy fog often found in cold Newfoundland. Third, he noticed that the Gulf Stream water was a different color and contained more weeds than the surrounding ocean water.

Related entries:
  Navigation
  Post Office

Suggestion for further reading:
  "To David Le Roy: Maritime Observations," August 1785 (Smyth, vol. IX).

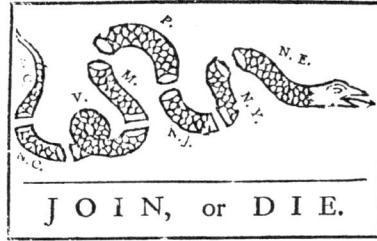

JOIN, or DIE.

H

Hall, David

See **Printing.**

Hare-Naylor, Georgiana Shipley

See **Shipley, Catherine and Georgiana (Hare-Naylor).**

Hartley, David

See ***Journal of the Negotiation for Peace with Great Britain;* Treaty of Paris, 1783.**

Helvétius, Anne-Catherine de Ligniville d'Autricourt (1719–1808)

"I see that statesmen, philosophers, historians, poets, and men of learning of all sorts are drawn around you, and seem as willing to attach themselves to you as straws about a fine piece of amber," Franklin wrote to Anne-Catherine Helvétius after meeting her. Madame Helvétius was the widow of the French philosopher Claude-Adrien Helvétius (1715–1771), the much-criticized author of *De l'esprit* (1758), and was renowned for her beauty in her youth. Her companions referred to her as "Notre Dame d'Auteuil." She lived near Paris in Auteuil, a neighboring village of Passy, where Franklin lived during the years of the American Revolution.

Franklin enjoyed the company of many women in Paris, but he had two favorites—Madame Brillon and Madame Helvétius. By the time he met the latter, she was almost 60 years old and had been widowed for more than 5 years. She was active and witty, and she lived on a small estate filled with a variety of plants, aviaries, and animals. Franklin dined with the Brillons on Wednesdays and Saturdays, and he spent Saturday afternoons with a regular circle of friends at Madame Helvétius's. Madame Brillon was a better and more frequent writer than her "amiable rival," as she called Madame Helvétius, but Franklin traded playful notes and letters with both of them.

The circle of intimates at Madame Helvétius's formed a small academy of sorts, and Franklin spent many hours in philosophical discussions with them. Among them were the Abbé Morellet (1727–1819) and the Abbé de La Roche, both of whom lived on her estate at least part of the time. Pierre-Jean-Georges Cabanis (1757–1808), a young physiologist and the future doctor of the

French revolutionary the Comte de Mirabeau (1749–1791), was practically adopted by Madame Helvétius and also lived with her. The French economist Anne-Robert-Jacques Turgot (1727–1781), who had proposed to Madame Helvétius twice and been rejected both times, had originally introduced Franklin to her.

Madame Helvétius surprised Abigail Adams with her open and expressive manner. Mrs. Adams recorded her perceptions of a dinner at which she, her husband, Franklin, and Madame Helvétius were present. Madame Helvétius sat between John Adams and Franklin. "She carried on the chief of the conversation at dinner, frequently locking her hands into the Doctor's [Franklin's], and sometimes spreading her arms upon the backs of both the gentlemen's chairs, then throwing her arm carelessly upon the Doctor's neck," Mrs. Adams observed. "I should have been greatly astonished at this conduct, if the good Doctor had not told me that in this lady I should see a genuine Frenchwoman, wholly free from affectation or stiffness of behavior, and one of the best women in the world." For her part, Mrs. Adams was disgusted with the behavior and hoped to meet French women whose manners were "more consistent with my ideas of decency, or I shall be a mere recluse."

Sometime around 1780, Franklin proposed to Madame Helvétius, though whether he intended it seriously or not is unknown. In any case, she declined the proposal, determined to remain single in memory of her late husband, and their relationship remained as friendly as ever. Franklin joked about the rejection in one of his bagatelles, which recounted an imaginary meeting between himself and M. Helvétius in the Elysian fields and began, "Vexed by your barbarous resolution, announced so positively last evening, to remain single all your life in respect to your dear husband, I went home, fell on my bed, and believing myself dead, found myself in the Elysian fields." Franklin wrote her another bagatelle from the perspective of the flies who lived in his house. The flies were thankful for Madame Helvétius's order to destroy the webs of their enemy spiders and had only one request: that she and Franklin form one household.

Franklin continued to visit with the little "academy" at Auteuil until he returned to Philadelphia in 1785. Madame Helvétius begged him to spend the rest of his life in France and even sent a last-minute note after him pleading for his return as he left. They wrote letters across the ocean, and Madame Helvétius sent gifts and other merchandise that Franklin had asked for from Paris to his daughter.

Related entries:
Bagatelles
Brillon de Jouy, Anne-Louise Boivin d'Hardancourt
France

Suggestions for further reading:
"The Elysian Fields," 1780 (Lemay 1987).
"The Flies," 1784 (Lemay 1987).
Lopez, Claude-Anne. 1966. *Mon Cher Papa: Franklin and the Ladies of Paris.* New Haven, Conn.: Yale University Press.
"To Madame Helvétius," April 23, 1788 (Smyth, vol. IX).

Hewson, Mary (Polly) Stevenson (1739–1795)

Franklin wrote some of his most interesting letters to Mary Stevenson, from whose widowed mother he rented four rooms during his two stays in England as an American agent. Polly, as Mary was called, lived with her mother at 7 Craven Street when Franklin moved in with them in 1757. Polly was intelligent, sensible, charming, and good-natured, and Franklin loved her almost as a daughter from the first. He was also fond of Polly's friends, including Dorothea Blount (Dolly), daughter of Sir Charles Blount. Polly was possibly the dearest to Franklin of the many younger women whom he befriended during his lifetime.

In 1759 Polly moved in with her aunt, Mrs. Tickell, at Wanstead in Essex, and the next year she proposed to her philosopher-friend that they correspond on matters of interest in natural philosophy. Franklin, 53, readily embraced the proposal from the inquisitive young woman then in her early twenties: "[N]ot only as it will occasion my hearing from her more frequently, but as it will lay under me a necessity of improving my own knowledge." To begin with, he suggested that she read some books he would recommend, and she could contribute questions and observations to the substance of their letters.

Polly continued corresponding with Franklin on many different subjects until her marriage to William Hewson in 1770. Among the earliest of their topics of discourse were the operation of barometers and the utility of insects, on which Franklin elaborated in a letter dated June 11, 1760. Polly asked him how air could affect a barometer when its opening was covered with wood. Franklin told her that there was a small opening, and that even an opening as small as a pinhole would allow the instrument to work properly. As for insects, Franklin wrote: "Superficial minds are apt to despise those who make that part of creation their study, as mere triflers; but certainly the world has been much obliged to them." Some people owed their livelihood to the silkworm, others owed their health to the Spanish fly, and still others their comfort and pleasure to the tasty honey of the bee or the scarlet dye cochineal, produced by an insect. At the same time, a more thorough understanding of insects might prove useful in preventing damage by mischievous insects. He concluded his letter with an account of a particular worm that had destroyed green lumber used for shipbuilding in Sweden. The king sent the famous Swedish botanist Carolus Linnaeus to find a solution to

the problem. Linnaeus's suggestion of submerging the lumber in water during the parent fly's brief egg-laying season in May was successful. Since the flies only laid eggs in the green lumber, the ships it was used to construct were unattractive to them when the wood had dried the next year. Franklin always sought to employ his knowledge in something useful and beneficial, and he advised his young student: "The knowledge of nature may be ornamental, and it may be useful; but if, to attain an eminence in that, we neglect the knowledge and practice of essential duties, we deserve reprehension."

In another letter, Polly asked him why water pumped at Bristol "though cold at the spring, becomes warm by pumping?" Franklin declined to answer the question until he saw proof of the phenomenon's veracity. He continued the letter with a lengthy and detailed explanation of water currents. "After writing 6 folio pages of philosophy to a young girl," he concluded, "is it necessary to finish such a letter with a compliment? Is not such a letter of itself a compliment? Does it not say, she has a mind thirsty for knowledge, and capable of receiving it; and that the most agreeable things one can write to her are those that tend to the improvement of her understanding? It does indeed say all this, but then it is still no compliment; it is no more than plain honest truth, which is not the character of a compliment."

In a subsequent letter, Polly gave him a satisfactory account of the water's being warmer after pumping at the Bristol well, and Franklin thought her explanation of it was "very ingenious and probable." She wrote to him her thoughts that the rising tide of rivers was not a direct effect of the Moon on river waters, but a later consequence of the Moon on ocean waters, with which Franklin agreed. He sent her a paper he had written on air and the evaporation of water and promised to show her some experiments "to explain the nature of the tides more fully" if he and her mother visited her the following week.

Their letters meandered through salt water and distillation to the color of clothing. Franklin told her that although distilled salt water contains no salt, it still has "disagreeable qualities." He repeated an idea that he had adopted from Cadwallader Colden in 1745—that skin has both pores that absorb and pores that discharge. The pores that absorb, he conjectured, might be fine enough to filter out salt when people swim in salt water. People at sea who run out of drinking water might benefit from soaking in a tub of salt water.

Franklin described an experiment he had conducted with different colors of cloth and proposed two others that Polly might try herself. In his experiment, he had laid pieces of different colored cloths on snow on a winter's morning. When he looked at them later, the snow under the black piece had melted so much that it had sunk beyond further reach of the Sun's rays. The white piece had not sunk at all, and the colors between them had sunk to varying depths, the darker the deeper. Franklin suggested that Polly walk in the sun with part of her dress showing white and part of it showing black. She could feel the difference in temperature with her hand. For a second experiment, he told her to hold a magnifying glass in the sun above a white sheet of paper. The black parts with ink or spots would ignite much more easily than the white portions. As always, Franklin's observations had practical applications. People who lived in warm areas or at sea should wear light clothing. Fruit walls lined with black might protect the fruit in a frost.

Franklin temporarily thought that Polly had abandoned her philosophical studies in March 1762 but wrote to her two weeks later: "I must retract the charge of idleness in your studies, when I find you have gone through the doubly difficult task of reading so big a book, on an abstruse subject, and in a foreign language." He also wrote to her about his particular area of expertise, electricity.

Franklin returned to Philadelphia that year, not knowing how much more he would see of Polly. On his return travels home, he bid her, "Adieu, my dearest child. I will call you so. Why should I not call you so, since I love you with all the tenderness, all the fondness of a father?"

The subject of their correspondence was not limited to philosophy. When Franklin traveled to Paris with Sir John Pringle in 1767, he sent Polly a detailed account of their journey and their experience at the court of Louis XV. He drew a diagram of the table of the royal family when they dined in public. The women of Paris wore circles of rouge on their cheeks, and Franklin thought that they did not "pretend to imitate nature in laying it on." In Paris and Versailles, he told Polly, were "a prodigious mixture of magnificence and negligence, with every kind of elegance except that of cleanliness, and what we call tidiness." The following year, Franklin and Polly exchanged letters written in a new phonetic alphabet that Franklin had produced.

Franklin had unsuccessfully tried to match his son William with Polly during his first stay at Craven Street. Another potential marriage was broken off around 1767 over financial matters, and Franklin was relieved that a young woman as valuable as Polly had not married the unworthy "mean-spirited mercenary fellow." Polly's life at her ill-tempered aunt's home was at times unpleasant, and Franklin tried to console her when she wrote to him complaining of the situation. In 1770 she married Dr. William Hewson (1739–1774), a surgeon, and the two moved back to Craven Street soon afterward. In 1772 Franklin and Mrs. Stevenson moved to another house on Craven Street, leaving the old one for the growing Hewson family. The Hewsons' first child, William Jr., was Franklin's godson, and Franklin thought he had, at nine months old, an "attentive, observing, sagacious look, as if he had a great deal of sense." The couple, with their sons William and Thomas, were happy until 1774, when Polly's husband accidentally infected himself during surgery and died. Polly was pregnant with their third child, Eliza, at the time of his death. Franklin mourned with her the loss of "an excellent young man, ingenious, industrious, useful, and beloved by all that knew him." Polly was able to live well and provide for her children with the large fortune her aunt left her.

The American Revolution soon placed limits on the communication between Franklin and Polly. He returned to Philadelphia in 1775 and sailed to France in 1776. His mail to England was opened and sometimes intercepted by spies, and he did not often come across a sound opportunity to write to Polly or any other of his English friends. In spite of these frustrations, the two were sometimes able to write. In 1777 he wrote to her, "I must contrive to get you to America. I want all my friends out of that wicked country." Franklin was pleased with her dedicated efforts to educate her children and sent books for them. "Instead of following the idle amusements, which both your fortune and the custom of the age might have led you into," he wrote, "your delight and your duty go together, by employing your time in the education of your offspring. This is following nature and reason, instead of fashion; than which nothing is more becoming the character of a woman of sense and virtue."

Polly's mother, Margaret Stevenson, died in 1783. Franklin begged her to bring her children and spend the winter of 1784–1785 with him at Passy: "Come, my dear friend, live with me while I stay here, and go with me, if I do go, to America." Polly complied with his first request and spent a happy winter in France. Franklin begged her to move to Philadelphia and thought she might sail with him when he returned. He thought her children would have better opportunities there, and that she could buy a large amount of land for a good price. Polly had still not made up her mind to go when Franklin sailed later that year, but Franklin never gave up asking.

By 1786 the 80-year-old Franklin had convinced her to come, and she moved to Philadelphia. Her sons attended college. Polly's presence, along with that of his daughter, Sally, comforted Franklin in his old age. He died in 1790 and left Polly and her children sundry items: a silver tankard for Polly, to be given to Eliza when she died; his new quarto Bible for William, to be used as his family Bible, as well as a description of plants in the emperor's garden in Vienna "in folio, with colored cuts"; and a set of *Spectators, Tatlers,* and *Guardians* "handsomely bound" for Thomas.

Related entries:
Craven Street Gazette
Stevenson, Mrs. Margaret

Suggestion for further reading:
Stifler, James Madison. 1927. *"My Dear Girl": The Correspondence of Benjamin Franklin with Polly Stevenson, Georgiana and Catherine Shipley.* New York: George H. Doran.

Hillsborough, Lord

See **Colonial Agent; Grand Ohio Company; Great Britain.**

Homes, Captain Robert and Mary Franklin (1694–1731)

*I*n his writings Franklin speaks little of his sister Mary, who married a captain of a trading vessel, Robert Homes (life dates not known). Homes and Franklin appear to have been on good terms. When circumstance brought Homes to Newcastle, near Philadelphia, where Franklin ended up after running away from home as a teenager, he wrote to Franklin expressing his Boston friends' concern for him and desire for his return. Franklin wrote back to him explaining his reasons for leaving Boston, apparently to Homes's satisfaction. Homes showed Franklin's letter to Sir Wil-liam Keith, then the governor of the province, who was impressed with the letter and encouraged him to set up business in Philadelphia. Homes later tried to convince Franklin's father to aid him in setting up the printing business, but his father refused.

Franklin's sister and Robert's wife, Mary, was apparently stricken with breast cancer around 1731, and Franklin wrote to another sister, Jane, about a potential cure he had heard of: "[W]e have here in town a kind of shell made of some wood, cut at a proper time, by some man of great skill (as they say), which has done wonders in that disease among us, being worn for some time on the breast." He had heard of spectacular successes with the shell and offered to obtain some for her. She died the same year.

Related entry:
  Printing

Suggestions for further reading:
  Masur, Louis P., ed. 1993. *The Autobiography of Benjamin Franklin*. Boston: Bedford Books of St. Martin's Press.
  "To Jane Mecom," June 19, 1731 (Labaree et al., vol. 1).

Home, Henry

See **Kames, Lord.**

Honest Whigs

Wherever he was living—America, England, or France—Franklin enjoyed getting together with the learned and discussing matters of philosophy and science. Sometimes he exercised his mind at the meetings of formal, scientific academies like the Royal Society of London or the French Academy of Sciences. But Franklin also liked to meet with less formal discussion clubs. One of his favorites was a group called the Honest Whigs, which he frequented at St. Paul's Coffeehouse, and later the London Coffeehouse, and about which little is known.

Members and guests, at least for a time, met for one night every other week at a coffeehouse. They smoked, drank, ate dinner, and discussed a wide variety of scientific and political topics. In general, the Honest Whigs disliked parliamentary restrictions on American colonies and sympathized with Franklin. Many of the members were Franklin's personal friends, and they came from diverse backgrounds. Peter Collinson was a Quaker botanist and merchant who had donated a Leyden jar to and sent books for the Library Company in Philadelphia. Dr. John Fothergill, also a Quaker, was a medical doctor, botanist, and political mediator. Sir John Pringle was also a widely respected medical doctor. Dr. Joseph Priestley was a chemist and clergyman. Jonathan Shipley was the Bishop of St. Asaph. Other members were scientists and writers, and many of them were also members of the Royal Society of London. John Canton (1718–1772) was interested in Franklin's electrical experiments and conducted his own. Franklin was fond of Dr. Richard Price (1723–1791), who in 1776 wrote a popular pro-American pamphlet entitled "Observations on the Nature of Civil Liberty, the Principles of Government, and the Justice of the War with America." The Scottish biographer of Samuel Johnson, James Boswell, attended a meeting of the Honest Whigs in 1769 and had previously dined with Franklin.

Franklin lamented his enforced absence from the club in a letter to Price in 1780: "Please to present my affectionate respects that honest, sensible, and intelligent society who did me so long the honor of admitting me to share in their instructive conversations. I never think of the hours I so happily spent in that company, without regretting that they are never to be repeated. . . . "

Related entries:
American Philosophical Society
Collinson, Peter
Fothergill, Dr. John
The Junto
Priestley, Dr. Joseph
Pringle, Sir John
Royal Society of London
Shipley, Jonathan

Suggestions for further reading:
Crane, Verner W. 1966. "The Club of Honest Whigs: Friends of Science and Liberty." *William and Mary Quarterly,* XXIII (3), pp. 211–233.
"To Richard Price," February 6, 1780 (Labaree, et al., vol. 31).

Hopkinson, Thomas (1709–1751) and Francis (1737–1791)

Thomas Hopkinson was an original member of the American Philosophical Society (its president) and took a keen interest in Franklin's electrical experiments. Franklin credited him with the discovery that points "throw off" electricity as well as draw it. Franklin and Hopkinson collaborated on political matters as well—notably the volunteer militia Franklin organized in 1747. Hopkinson had encouraged him to write against both of the warring political factions, the Quakers and the merchants, whose disagreements stalled efforts to organize a plan for the defense of the province. When Franklin communicated Hopkinson's electrical discovery to Peter Collinson, he described Hopkinson as a man "whose virtue and integrity, in every station of life, public and private, will ever make his memory dear to those who knew him, and knew how to value him."

Thomas's eldest son Francis, an accomplished lawyer, judge, writer, poet, and composer, was no less a friend to Franklin than his father. He served as a delegate to the Continental Congress from New Jersey and signed the Declaration of Independence.

While Franklin was in France, Francis borrowed his "electrical and pneumatic machines," some of which were damaged by the "Goths and the Vandals [Hessians]" during the war. Franklin thought Francis had inherited his father's "exactness in accounts and scrupulous fidelity in matters of trust," and he named Francis an executor of his will. He bequeathed all of his philosophical instruments in Philadelphia to his "ingenious friend, Francis Hopkinson." Francis died in 1791 and was buried in the Christ Church cemetery, where Franklin had been buried the year before.

Related entries:
American Philosophical Society
Continental Congresses
Declaration of Independence
Electricity
Last Will and Testament
Volunteer Militia

Suggestions for further reading:
Hastings, George Everett. 1926. *The Life and Works of Francis Hopkinson.* Chicago: University of Chicago Press.
"To Francis Hopkinson," June 4, 1779 (Labaree et al., vol. 29).

Hot-Air Balloons

Franklin was in Paris working out the details of a peace treaty with England when the first hot-air balloons in history took flight.

In 1782 two brothers, Jacques-Étienne and Joseph-Michel Montgolfier, kindled a fire and used it to inflate and lift a cloth bag in Annonay, France. They had earlier experimented with smoke-filled paper bags. The 1782 experiment was a success, and they put together another successful demonstration for the public in the summer of 1783. The linen bag in the second experiment was about 35 feet wide, and after it was inflated it soared for eight minutes and one and one-half miles.

Before Joseph Montgolfier lifted the first hot-air balloon passengers (a sheep, a duck,

Montgolfier balloon rising above a large crowd at Versailles, September 19, 1783. Engraving.

and a rooster) into the air in September 1783, Jacques-Alexandre-César Charles, a professor of experimental philosophy, oversaw another flight launched from Paris. This balloon was inflated not with heat from a fire as in the Montgolfiers' experiments, but with hydrogen formed by pouring oil of vitriol (concentrated sulfuric acid) over iron filings. The inflation of the oiled-silk balloon launched from the Champ-de-Mars took four days. The August 27 Paris launch was also successful, and it made an impression on Franklin. In a letter to Sir Joseph Banks of the Royal Society of London (to whom he dutifully reported on hot-air balloons), Franklin described "the new aerostatic experiment" he had witnessed:

It is supposed that not less than 50,000 people were assembled to see the experiment. The Champ de Mars being surrounded by multitudes, and vast numbers on the opposite side of the river.

At 5 o'clock notice was given to the spectators by the firing of two cannon, that the cord was about to be cut. And presently the globe was seen to rise, and that as fast as a body of 12 feet diameter with a force only of 39 pounds, could be supposed to move the resisting air out of its way. There was some wind, but not very strong. A little rain had wet it, so that it shone, and made an agreeable appearance. It diminished in apparent magnitude as it rose, till it entered the clouds, when it seemed to me scarce bigger than an orange, and soon after became invisible, the clouds concealing it.

The multitude separated, all well satisfied and much delighted with the success of the experiment, and amusing one another with discourses of the various uses it may possibly be applied to, among which many were very extravagant. But possibly it may pave the way to some discoveries in natural philosophy of which at present we have no conception.

Franklin was not present when Joseph Montgolfier floated the three animals into the air, but he was in the Passy crowd that watched the first balloon flight with human passengers. Pilâtre de Rozier and the Marquis François-Laurent d'Arlandes, the two passengers, burned straw as they flew at least 300 feet into the air, crossed the Seine, and landed safely in Paris. The flight lasted nearly half an hour.

The balloon experiments greatly interested Franklin, and he entertained ideas on their potential usefulness for travel and the military. He kept up with news of other balloon experiments of his lifetime, including the first balloon flight across the English Channel (1785).

Related entries:
France
Royal Society of London

Suggestions for further reading:
"To Sir Joseph Banks," August 30, 1783 (Smyth, vol. IX).
"To Sir Joseph Banks," December 1, 1783 (Smyth, vol. IX).
"To Sir Joseph Banks," November 21, 1783 (Smyth, vol. IX).
"To Sir Joseph Banks," October 8, 1783 (Smyth, vol. IX).

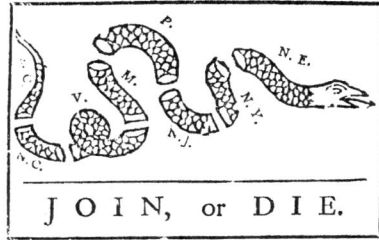

J O I N, or D I E.

Ingenhousz, Dr. Jan
(1730–1799)

Dr. Jan Ingenhousz, one of Franklin's correspondents, was a prominent Dutch physician interested in a variety of fields in natural philosophy. Ingenhousz was physician to the Austrian emperor and empress, Joseph II and Maria Theresa, and inoculated members of the royal family for smallpox. The correspondence between Franklin and Ingenhousz touched on politics and many scientific subjects, including electricity and disease.

Ingenhousz wrote a sympathetic letter to Franklin after Alexander Wedderburn denounced him before the Privy Council at the Cockpit (1774). In 1777 Ingenhousz wrote to Franklin disturbed at accounts of war and bloodshed in America that he heard in Europe, and of Franklin's involvement in it: "You told me more than once," Ingenhousz wrote, "that no more distinction should be made between a man residing in England and one residing in North America, than between the inhabitants of London and Sheffield. . . . " Franklin replied that England had burned American towns in the middle of winter and committed other atrocities on the populace. "It would therefore be deceiving you," Franklin said, "if I suffered you to remain in the supposition you have taken up, that I am come to Europe [France] to make peace. I am in fact ordered hither by the Congress

for a very different purpose; viz. to procure those aids from European powers, for enabling us to defend our freedom and independence. . . . " Ingenhousz translated some of Franklin's letters to him in Vienna, written for the purpose of feeling out and influencing sentiment toward America in Austria.

The same year, Franklin sent Ingenhousz "An Attempt to Explain the Effects of Lightning on the Vane of the Steeple of a Church in Cremona." Ingenhousz sent Franklin a description of an experiment he performed with wires, which pleased him and several of his acquaintances in France. The two exchanged accounts of accidentally shocking themselves while performing electrical experiments. Franklin had shocked himself while trying to electrocute a turkey and while experimenting with electricity on paralytics. "The stroke you received," he told Ingenhousz in 1785, "and its consequences, are much more curious. I communicated that part of your letter to an operator, encouraged by the government here to electrify epileptic and other poor patients, and advised his trying the practice on mad people according to your opinion."

In 1779 Ingenhousz published "Experiments on Vegetables," and the following year, Franklin told Francis Hopkinson that "the greatest discovery made in Europe for some time past is that of Dr. Ingenhousz's relating to the great use of trees in producing wholesome air." Franklin sent his correspondent his paper on the aurora borealis, an account

Illustration for "On the Causes and Cure of Smoky Chimneys" by Benjamin Franklin, c. 1787. Engraving.

of balloon experiments in Paris, and a brief description of an apparatus he conceived to test the gravitation of bodies during conjunctions of the Sun and Moon. If the force of gravity from the Sun and Moon could influence the tides, Franklin conjectured, "might we not expect, that an iron ball of a pound suspended by a fine spiral string, should, when the sun and the moon are together above it, be a little attracted upwards or rendered lighter, so as to be drawn up a little by the spring on which it depends, and the contrary when they are both below it?"

Ingenhousz did not share Franklin's reluctance to enter into public disputes. When George III ordered blunt lightning rods substituted for pointed rods (which Franklin favored) on his palace and the Purfleet powder magazines, Ingenhousz criticized the scientist, Benjamin Wilson, who had recommended blunt rods. Franklin, as was typical, remained silent during the controversy. Ingenhousz became involved in a public dispute with Dr. Joseph Priestley, another of Franklin's friends, and in 1782 Franklin advised Ingenhousz not to answer him: "The indiscretions of friends on both sides often

occasion such misunderstandings. When they produce public altercation, the ignorant are diverted at the expense of the learned. I hope, therefore, that you will omit the polemic piece in your French edition, and take no public notice of the improper behavior of your friend. . . ."

On his voyage home to Philadelphia from France in 1785, Franklin wrote his "On the Causes and Cure of Smoky Chimneys" and addressed it to Ingenhousz. In this piece he endeavored to answer the question, "What is it . . . which makes a smoky chimney; that is, a chimney which, instead of conveying up all the smoke, discharges a part of it into the room, offending the eyes and damaging the furniture?" Franklin described nine different causes of smoky chimneys and measures that people could take to remedy the problem.

The first cause was that, in newly built houses, there were no crevices or other openings to permit proper air circulation. People could best fix this problem by allowing air to come into the room near the ceiling. Another cause was too large an opening of the chimney in a room. Franklin asserted that chimneys had to be proportioned to the height of the funnel, and that shorter funnels needed smaller openings. "And there are some, I know," he complained, "so bigoted to the fancy of a large noble opening, that rather than change it, they would submit to have damaged furniture, sore eyes, and skins almost smoked to bacon." Thus, funnels that were too short, which was inevitable on low buildings, were a third cause of smoky chimneys. Franklin suggested building another story on the building and using a bigger funnel or building additional, adjoining funnels. A fourth cause was multiple chimneys, either in the same room or different rooms—the draw from one fire would overpower that of the other. Franklin would remedy this by ensuring that every room outside the room with the chimney had its own supply of air from outside.

When a house was situated in certain positions next to high buildings or hills, the wind could blow in such a way as to beat down the smoke into the house, a fifth cause of smoky chimneys. Franklin advised installing a turncap with a back that faced the wind or making the chimney higher. A sixth cause was the reverse of the fifth—a tall building or hill was farther away from the wind than the chimney commanded. To remedy this problem, the funnel had to be raised higher than the roof. The improper situation of a door was the seventh cause that Franklin listed. One could fix the problem by placing a screen around the fireplace or changing the hinges on the door so that it opened in another direction. A simple sliding plate that shut the funnel would remedy the eighth problem—smoke from a neighboring funnel that comes down a chimney when no fire is burning. Franklin did not have a certain remedy for the final cause, strong winds that drive smoke down the chimney. "For many years past," he told Ingenhousz, "I have rarely met with a case of a smoky chimney, which has not been solvable on those principles, and cured by these remedies, where people have been willing to apply them...."

Ingenhousz was elected to the American Philosophical Society in 1786 and continued corresponding with Franklin until the latter's death in 1790.

Related entries:
American Philosophical Society
Aurora Borealis
Electricity
Hot-Air Balloons
Oliver-Hutchinson Letters Affair
Priestley, Dr. Joseph

Suggestions for further reading:
"Franklin: Answers to Queries from Dr. Ingenhousz," 1780 (Labaree et al., vol. 32).
"From Jan Ingenhousz," June 28, 1777 (Labaree et al., vol. 24).
"To Jan Ingenhousz," January 16, 1784 (Smyth, vol. IX).
"To Jan Ingenhousz," March 18, 1774 (Labaree et al., vol. 21).
"To Jan Ingenhousz," October 2, 1781 (Smyth, vol. VIII).
"To Jan Ingenhousz," On the Causes and Cure of Smoky Chimneys, August 28, 1785 (Smyth, vol. IX).
"To Jan Ingenhousz," September 30, 1773 (Labaree et al., vol. 20).

Izard, Ralph (1742–1804)

Ralph Izard was a South Carolina delegate to the Continental Congress and later a U.S. Senator. The Congress appointed him commissioner to the court of the grand duke of Tuscany during the war, a duty that he was never able to fulfill because of the unwillingness of most European courts to recognize the United States as a nation. Izard instead spent the early years of the Revolutionary War in France, where he and Arthur Lee remained constant thorns in Franklin's side.

Izard became offended when the other commissioners from the United States (Franklin, Lee, and Silas Deane) did not consult him on portions of the Treaty of Alliance they negotiated with France in 1778. He related his complaints in one of his many angry letters to Franklin. Franklin's reply was no less rude than Izard's letter. He promised he would explain the commissioners' conduct as soon as he had an opportunity to meet with him, "but," he said, "I must submit to remain some days under the opinion you appear to have formed not only of my poor understanding in the general interests of America, but of my defects in sincerity, politeness, and attention to your instructions." Franklin offered him a piece of advice: "Always to suppose one's friends may be right till one finds them wrong; rather than to suppose them wrong till one finds them right."

Tension between Franklin and Izard also flared when Franklin refused to pay him for expenses out of congressional money. Franklin, who was daily pressed to pay America's military bills from dwindling and sometimes nonexistent funds, believed that he had disbursed enough money to Izard, who was wealthy, already. Izard had earlier been granted funds for expenses for a journey to Florence, but he had not been able to go and did not incur the expected expenses. Franklin thought Izard was wealthy enough to support himself until there was sufficient money, and he related the matter to Congress for its judgment.

Richard Bache, Franklin's son-in-law, wrote to Franklin in 1778 and told him that Izard and Arthur Lee had been writing letters critical of him to Congress. Among the objections to Franklin he thought Izard and Lee espoused was the employment of Temple Franklin as his secretary. Temple, Franklin's grandson, was the son of a loyalist, and some believed that he presented a security risk. Franklin, who was enormously popular in France, tried not to worry about the accusations and thought the "dark, uncomfortable passions of jealousy, anger, suspicion, envy, and malice" in the minds of the two men were punishment enough for them.

Franklin tried to steer clear of public arguments during the crucial years of the war and said that he made it a rule not to answer "angry, affronting, or abusive letters, of which I have received many, and long ones, from Mr. Lee and Mr. Izard." Both Izard and Lee left France in 1780, to which Franklin remarked, "no soul regrets their departure." Izard took leave of him civilly, as Franklin had not told him that he knew about Izard's critical letters to Congress. After the war Izard served as a U.S. Senator from South Carolina. Franklin wrote his "The Petition of the Letter Z" as a satire on Izard.

Related entries:
Adams, John
Continental Congresses
Lee, Dr. Arthur
Treaty of Alliance with France

Suggestions for further reading:
"To Ralph Izard," January 29, 1778 (Labaree et al., vol. 25).
"To Ralph Izard," March 30, 1778 (Labaree et al., vol. 26).

J O I N, or D I E.

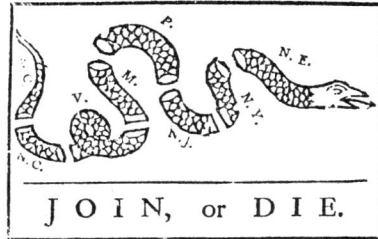

Jackson, Richard
(1721–1787)

Richard Jackson was an Irish lawyer and a member of the House of Commons in England. Jackson was known in England as "omniscient" and "the all-knowing" on account of his widespread knowledge, particularly of the law. Probably through their mutual friend Peter Collinson, Jackson and Franklin had corresponded before they began working together in 1757, when Franklin was sent to England to petition for the right to tax proprietary estates in Pennsylvania. Before he was elected to Parliament, Jackson anonymously authored *An Historical Review of the Constitution and Government of Pennsylvania,* a work that sharply criticized Pennsylvania's proprietary government. Franklin, who had long opposed the proprietary government, paid to publish the work; another of his friends, William Strahan, printed it.

Jackson became Pennsylvania's agent after Franklin returned to Philadelphia in 1762 and remained in that position until he resigned in 1770. In addition, he served as an agent for Connecticut and Massachusetts. He was interested in America and in agriculture, and he purchased a farm in Connecticut with the assistance of Franklin's and his correspondent Jared Eliot.

Franklin and Jackson were also traveling companions, through Belgium and Holland in 1761 and to Ireland in 1771. On the 1761 trip Franklin met the Dutch physicist Pieter van Musschenbroek, inventor of the Leyden jar, a central apparatus in his electrical experiments. It was possibly during their trip to Ireland that Franklin met his ardent admirer Sir Edward Newenham (1732–1814), a member of the Irish Parliament. Newenham was a vocal supporter of the American Revolution, wore mourning to Parliament after the Irish-American General Richard Montgomery was mortally wounded in battle, and sent an Irish jaunting car as a gift to Franklin in Philadelphia in 1787. Jackson and Franklin were guests at the Irish House of Commons, where they were warmly received.

After the defeat of the French in the French and Indian War, a debate emerged over whether to ask for Canada or the island of Guadeloupe at the treaty. Jackson and Franklin coauthored a pamphlet entitled "The Interest of Great Britain Considered," also known as the "Canada Pamphlet," arguing that Canada would benefit England more than the island. Both believed that having Canada under British control would prevent future attacks by the French, and they sought to expand the British Empire with the vast territory.

As a member of Parliament, Jackson generally acted in favor of American interests. In 1764 the Pennsylvania Assembly appointed Franklin a joint agent with Jackson for "representing, soliciting and transacting the affairs of this province for the ensuing year."

Jackson did not think that the Assembly's 1764 decision to petition for a change in Pennsylvania's government from the proprietorship to the Crown was a prudent one at the time. The natural course of action, he thought, would move toward government by the Crown anyway.

Larger issues, such as parliamentary taxation of the colonies, soon took precedence over the petition. Jackson opposed the Stamp Act from its conception in 1763 and believed that laying internal taxes in America would lead to disaster for England. He and Franklin became involved in efforts to repeal the act, as well as the Townshend Duties that followed. Another of Jackson's interests was the plan of the Grand Ohio Company, with which Franklin and his son William were involved, to purchase and settle lands west of the existing American colonies.

Franklin and Jackson lost contact during the Revolutionary War. In 1784 William Temple Franklin visited Jackson in England, after which he and Franklin exchanged cordial letters. Jackson died in 1787.

Related entries:
>   Bartram, John
>   Collinson, Peter
>   Eliot, Jared
>   Grand Ohio Company
>   Great Britain
>   Penn, Thomas
>   Pennsylvania Assembly
>   Stamp Act

Suggestions for further reading:
>   Nolan, J. Bennett. 1938. *Benjamin Franklin in Scotland and Ireland 1759 and 1771*. Philadelphia: University of Pennsylvania Press.
>   Van Doren, Carl. 1947. *Letters and Papers of Benjamin Franklin and Richard Jackson, 1753–1785*. Philadelphia: American Philosophical Society.

Jay, John (1745–1829)

Almost 40 years Franklin's junior, John Jay (with Franklin and John Adams) was one of the three commissioners who

John Jay. Engraving after a painting by Gilbert Stuart.

signed the Treaty of Paris in 1783, ending the war between the United States and England. Jay, like Franklin, was involved in many aspects of the Revolution. In 1774 he was elected to the First Continental Congress, and his home state of New York returned him as a delegate to the Second Continental Congress. He served with Franklin, Benjamin Harrison, Thomas Johnson, and John Dickinson on the Committee of Secret Correspondence, which was charged with communicating with agents friendly toward America in England and other countries. In 1778 Jay was elected president of the Continental Congress, and on September 27, 1779, Congress appointed Jay minister plenipotentiary to the court of Spain, the same position Franklin held in France.

Jay arrived in Madrid in April 1780. Franklin corresponded with him and with William Carmichael, the secretary for the Americans in Spain. Jay was much less successful in gaining any support from Spain than Franklin was with France. Franklin encouraged Jay to cultivate the friendship of the Marquis de Yranda, who thought Jay was too reserved toward him. Congress, expecting a loan from Spain, sent Jay bills that he could not pay, and they were frequently forwarded to Franklin in the more generous France.

In 1781 Congress instructed Franklin, Jay, Henry Laurens, and Thomas Jefferson to join Adams on a commission treat with Great Britain. Franklin wrote to Jay in Spain urging him to leave the stubborn country and assist him with the negotiations in France. Adams was in Holland and could not get away until August, Jefferson did not come, and Laurens had been captured at sea and imprisoned in the Tower of London. Jay arrived in France in June and spent several days with Franklin learning the state of the negotiations. The two called on the Count d'Aranda, the Spanish ambassador to France. Jay fell ill with the flu and was incapacitated until early August.

Jay distrusted both the Spanish and the French. "Mr. Jay likes Frenchman as little as Mr. Lee and Mr. Izard did. He says they are not a moral people; they know not what it is; the Marquis de Lafayette is clever, but he is a Frenchman," John Adams observed. He was particularly adamant that the commission of the British negotiators explicitly specify that they were to treat with the United States of America. While Jay did not share Franklin's trust in the French, he admired him and worked well with him as well as with Adams. During part of Jay's travels to England in 1783, his wife and daughter (Maria) lived with Franklin in Passy. Franklin particularly adored little Maria. "[S]ince I had the pleasure of their being with me in the same house," he later wrote to Jay, "I have ever felt a tender affection for them, equal I believe to that of most fathers."

Jay served as the U.S. secretary for foreign affairs from 1784 to 1789 and was appointed the first chief justice of the Supreme Court by George Washington in 1789. Franklin named him as one of the executors of his will.

Related entries:
Adams, John
Continental Congresses
France
Revolutionary War
Treaty of Paris, 1783

Suggestions for further reading:
"To John Jay," June 13, 1780 (Labaree et al., vol 32).
"To John Jay," September 19, 1785 (Smyth, vol. IX).
"To Mr. and Mrs. Jay," May 13, 1784 (Smyth, vol. IX).

Jefferson, Thomas (1743–1826)

A central figure in the American Revolution, Thomas Jefferson was a native of Virginia, a student of many aspects of natural philosophy, and a prominent statesman. Born to an aristocratic family in 1743, he devoted much of his time to studying history, law, philosophy, and science. He attended William and Mary College, where he studied under William Small, and studied law under George Wythe. He was admitted to the bar in 1767. Jefferson's political career began in 1769, when he was elected to the Virginia House of Burgesses. In his 1774 pamphlet, *Summary View of the Rights of British North America,* he attacked notions of British sovereignty over the colonies and won national acclaim. He served as a delegate to the Second Continental Congress in 1775 and 1776 and continued in the Virginia legislature from 1776 to 1779. For the next two years he served as Virginia's governor.

Jefferson first worked with Franklin when both served in the Second Continental Congress. In June 1776 Congress appointed Franklin, Jefferson, John Adams, Roger Sherman, and Robert R. Livingston to a committee to draft the Declaration of Independence. The committee chose Jefferson to write the document, and Jefferson later explained that Franklin was not chosen as its author because he could not have resisted writing a joke into the draft. Franklin seems to have been happy not to write it; while the draft was undergoing the tough scrutiny of Congress, Franklin explained to a frustrated Jefferson that he tried to avoid writing documents that were subject to public review.

Portrait of Thomas Jefferson.

In December 1776 Congress appointed Franklin and Jefferson commissioners to join Silas Deane in France. Unfortunately for Franklin, Jefferson turned down the appointment, and Arthur Lee (who gave Franklin and Deane an enormous amount of trouble) was chosen instead. Congress again commissioned Jefferson to join Franklin, Adams, Henry Laurens, and John Jay in negotiating a peace treaty with England after the war ended. Jefferson did not arrive in France until 1784, after which he, with Adams and Franklin, spent a few months negotiating treaties of amity and commerce. The most significant of these treaties was the agreement concluded with Prussia in 1785. Congress appointed Jefferson minister plenipotentiary to France on March 10, 1785, to replace Franklin, who had long wanted to return to Philadelphia. "The succession to Dr. Franklin at the court of France was an excellent school of humility," Jefferson later wrote. "On being presented to any one as the minister of America, the commonplace question in such cases was . . . 'It is you, sir, who replace Dr. Franklin?' I generally answered, 'No one can replace him, sir; I am only his successor.'"

Franklin and Jefferson worked harmoniously together during the few months that both were in France. Jefferson, who according to Franklin was "much esteemed and respected" in France, admired Franklin, whom he later described as "the greatest man and ornament of the age and country in which he lived." Franklin introduced him to his friends, including the Comtesse d'Houdetot. When Franklin left for Philadelphia Jefferson wrote to Congress: "Europe fixes an attentive eye on your reception of Doctor Franklin. He is infinitely esteemed. Do not neglect any mark of your approbation which you think proper. It will honor you here."

Franklin wrote the last known letter of his life to Jefferson nine days before his death. Jefferson visited him before he died and updated him on the events of the French Revolution, and Franklin gave him a portion of his *Autobiography*. A letter Jefferson wrote to William Smith on February 19, 1791, reflects the deep respect he had for Franklin: "We have reason to be thankful he was so long spared; that the most useful life should be the longest also; that it was protracted so far beyond the ordinary span allotted to man, as to avail us of his wisdom in the establishment of our own freedom, and to bless him with a view of its dawn in the east, where they seemed, till now, to have learned everything, but how to be free." Jefferson concluded, "These small offerings to the memory of our great and dear friend, whom time will be making greater while it is spunging us from its records, must be accepted by you, sir, in that spirit of love and veneration for him, in which they are made; and not according to their insignificance in the eyes of a world, who did not want this mite to fill up the measure of his worth."

After Franklin's death, Jefferson served as the third president of the American Philosophical Society (first conceived by Franklin in 1743), vice president of the United States under John Adams, and later the third president of the United States (1801–1809). The motto on one of Jefferson's seals, "Rebellion to Tyrants Is Obedience to God," was probably taken from Franklin, who used the same expression in his proposal for the U.S. seal.

Jefferson carried on an extensive correspondence with John Adams during his retirement at Monticello, and both of them died on July 4, 1826, exactly 50 years after Congress adopted the Declaration of Independence.

Related entries:
Continental Congresses
Declaration of Independence
France
Revolutionary War

Suggestions for further reading:
"To Thomas Jefferson," April 8, 1790 (Smyth, vol. X).
"To Thomas Jefferson," April 19, 1787 (Smyth, vol. IX).
"To Thomas Jefferson," March 20, 1786 (Smyth, vol. IX).

Jones, John Paul (1747–1792)

John Paul Jones was a successful American naval officer. Born John Paul in Scotland, he began his long career at sea at age 12. His first voyage sent him to Fredericksburg, Virginia. He lost favor with the British when he evaded imprisonment and a trial after executing the leader of a mutiny in the West Indies. Jones escaped to Fredericksburg and changed his name to John Paul Jones. In 1775 he traveled to Philadelphia to join the American navy. He was commissioned as a lieutenant and promoted to captain in 1776, when he was placed in command of the *Providence*. Jones led successful expeditions against British fisheries in Nova Scotia and captured 16 British prize ships. The following year, he took command of the *Ranger*. Jones and his men crossed the Atlantic, raided the coasts of England and Scotland, and captured a number of British prize ships.

Franklin was in charge of fitting American ships from France, exchanging prisoners of war (in which he worked with David Hartley in England), and handling prize ships—duties that troubled him on account of his minimal time, distance from the coast, and lack of expertise. Nevertheless, he remained on very friendly terms with Jones, who admired Franklin. Franklin wrote to congratulate him on his successes while he commanded the *Ranger* and told him in 1778, "It will always be a pleasure to me to contribute what may lie in my power towards your advancement, and that of the brave officers and men under your command." Five days later he told Jones of secret plans for him to take command of the *Indien,* a new ship that had been finished in Amsterdam. However, this scheme met with too many difficulties to be carried out.

In 1779 Jones was given command of the French 40-gun *Duras,* which he renamed the *Bonhomme Richard* (after Franklin's "Poor Richard," which had been translated into French and published in France). The United States and France planned (but never executed) a joint assault under Jones (at sea) and the Marquis de Lafayette (on land), and Franklin sent Jones instructions. He instructed Jones to keep watch on English prisoners and not to allow his crew (many of whom were recently escaped American prisoners of war) to exact revenge on them. "[A]lthough the English have wantonly burned many defenseless towns in America," Franklin instructed, "you are not to follow this example, unless where a reasonable ransom is refused; in which case, your own generous feelings, as well as this instruction, will induce you to give timely notice of your intention, that sick and ancient persons, women and children, may be first removed." Lafayette ended up not participating in the engagement, and Jones undertook a modified version of the plans without him. On September 23, 1779, Jones captured the British 44-gun *Serapis* and the 20-gun *Countess of Scarborough* after a bloody battle. Franklin wrote to Samuel Cooper in 1779: "Few actions at sea have demonstrated such steady, cool, determined bravery, as that of Jones in taking the *Serapis*."

After that engagement, however, a dispute arose between Jones and Captain Peter

Landais, who had recently been involved in a quarrel with his own officers and who, Jones charged, did not assist him in the battle as he should have. Landais's *Alliance* had inadvertently fired on the *Bonhomme Richard* and damaged it. At the request of the French minister of marine Gabriel de Sartine, Franklin ordered Landais to come to Paris and explain his conduct, and he asked Jones for his account of the action. Jones was to appoint a new commander for his ship or take it himself. Franklin, who did not think himself a qualified judge in military disputes, gave up trying to sort out the quarrel and turned the matter over to the Congress. However, his personal regard for Landais was much less than it was for Jones. He told Landais: "I think you, then, so imprudent, so litigious and quarrelsome a man, even with your best friends, that peace and good order and, consequently, the quiet and regular subordination so necessary to success, are, where you preside, impossible."

A false letter from Jones was the highlight of an edition of Franklin's "Supplement to the Boston Independent Chronicle," a fictitious newspaper intended as anti-British propaganda that he printed in Passy, where he lived during his stay in France. The letter was addressed "To Sir Joseph Yorke, Ambassador from the King of England to the States-General of the United Provinces." The British had (in reality) labeled Jones a pirate, and the fictitious letter from Jones answered this charge: "A pirate is defined to be *hostis humani generis* (an enemy to all mankind). It happens, sir, that I am an enemy to no part of mankind, except your nation, the English; which nation at the same time comes much more within the definition, being actually an enemy to, and at war with, one whole quarter of the world. . . . "

In 1781 Jones returned to the United States, where he oversaw the construction of the *America*. Congress awarded him a gold medal in 1787. In 1788 Catherine the Great offered Jones a position in the Russian navy, where he remained until his retirement to Paris two years later. He was appointed U.S. consul to Algiers in 1792 but died before he could go. In 1905 the United States brought Jones's remains from Paris.

Related entries:
Continental Congresses
France
Revolutionary War

Suggestions for further reading:
"From John Paul Jones," March 6, 1779 (Labaree et al., vol. 29).
"To Antoine-Raymond-Gualbert-Gabriel de Sartine," March 20, 1780 (Labaree et al., vol. 32).
"To John Paul Jones," June 10, 1778 (Labaree et al., vol. 26).
"To John Paul Jones," March 14, 1779 (Labaree et al., vol. 29).
"To John Paul Jones," May 27, 1778 (Labaree et al., vol. 26).
"To Landais," October 15, 1779 (Labaree et al., vol. 30).
"To the Eastern Navy Board," March 15, 1780 (Labaree et al., vol. 32).

Journal of the Negotiation for Peace with Great Britain

After the surrender of General Charles Cornwallis at Yorktown in 1781 and the fall of the North ministry in 1782, England sought peace with America. Franklin resolved to keep a journal of the ensuing peace talks. It began: "As, since the change of ministry in England, some serious professions have been made of their disposition to peace, and of their readiness to enter into a general treaty for that purpose; and as the concerns and claims of five nations are to be discussed in that treaty, which must therefore be interesting to the present age and to posterity, I am inclined to keep a journal of the proceedings. . . ." Congress had appointed five commissioners to negotiate a treaty—Franklin, John Adams, John Jay, Thomas Jefferson, and Henry Laurens. Adams was in Holland until October 1782, Jay was in Spain until June 1782, Laurens was ill and declined the appointment, and Jefferson never came to France during the negotiations. Until Jay arrived in France at the end of June 1782, the burden of negotiation fell entirely on Franklin.

Franklin wrote to Lord Shelburne on March 22, 1782, to laud him on the Whig victory in the House of Commons and said he hoped a general peace would follow. Shelburne and Charles James Fox (who belonged to an opposing faction of Whigs) became secretaries for the northern department and southern department, respectively. In these offices, Shelburne had authority to treat with America, and Fox with France. Shelburne, who had known, worked with, and liked Franklin for many years, sent Richard Oswald to France with letters of recommendation from himself and from Henry Laurens, the American who had been captured at sea on his way to Holland and imprisoned in the Tower of London. Oswald, who was a friend of Laurens, made a favorable impression on Franklin, and he maintained that the ministry wanted peace and was finally willing to recognize American independence.

Franklin, Oswald, and the Comte de Vergennes (the French foreign minister) met on April 18, 1782. England, which had been at war not only with America but also with Holland, France, and Spain, wanted from the start to deal with each power separately. Britain still entertained the possibility of concluding peace with America and continuing the war with France. During the meeting Franklin and Vergennes told Oswald that neither the United States nor France would conclude a peace unless the other did. In a later conversation with Oswald, he and Franklin discussed some suggestions for conversation that Franklin had written down, and Oswald prevailed on him to let him take them. Americans, Franklin told Oswald, were concerned about the dangers that British retention of Canada and Nova Scotia would have on the United States. Oswald showed Franklin's suggestions to Lord Shelburne.

Franklin requested specific instructions on Oswald's powers to treat from England, and Oswald returned. Oswald returned to France and announced that Fox was sending his own representative, Thomas Grenville (the son of Richard Grenville, the mastermind of the Stamp Act). Oswald said that England would agree to treat at Paris for a general peace, but neither Franklin nor Vergennes could get many particulars out of him. Grenville arrived shortly thereafter, and Franklin thought him "a sensible, judicious, intelligent, good-tempered, and well-instructed young man." Franklin introduced him to Vergennes, who had served with Grenville's uncle as an ambassador to Constantinople.

Congress had instructed the Marquis de Lafayette to assist the American commissioners in their work. Lafayette proposed to go to London and reside there during the negotiations to provide an easy means of communication between the court of France and England. Franklin liked Lafayette's proposal and encouraged him to ask the ministry, but the plan never materialized. Lafayette, Grenville, Oswald, and Franklin ate breakfast together on May 11, 1782.

Oswald returned to England shortly thereafter, and Franklin wrote to Shelburne to say that he was "really concerned at the thoughts of losing so good a man as Mr. Oswald." Henry Laurens wrote to Franklin to tell him that he had decided to decline Congress's commission on account of ill health and that he would not be coming to France. Franklin urged him to reconsider: "I regret your taking this resolution, principally because I am persuaded your assistance must have been of great service to our country. But I have besides some private or particular reasons, that relate to myself." Since Laurens was in England, Franklin asked him to update him on prevailing sentiments there and give him an idea of his own sentiments on what the United States should ask for in the treaty.

Grenville informed Franklin that he had received from England full powers to treat for peace with "France and her allies."

Surrender of Lord Cornwallis at Yorktown, Virginia, October 19, 1781. Lithograph by Currier and Ives, 1876.

Vergennes that said Grenville's instructions related only to France, and when Franklin read the instructions, he discovered that they in fact contained no mention of France's allies. Vergennes was offended by the omission and thought that England was trying to stall the negotiations. Grenville sent to England for more specific instructions.

Oswald returned with fresh instructions from Lord Shelburne indicating that Franklin and Oswald could choose commissioners to negotiate a treaty. Oswald left the decision up to Franklin, who preferred Oswald to Grenville. Franklin asked him if he would rather join a general commission to treat with the foreign powers (France, Spain, Holland, and America) or obtain a general commission for negotiating with America only. Oswald, who had lived in America, preferred the special commission. Of Oswald and Grenville, Franklin thought: "The truth is, [Oswald] appears so good and reasonable a man, that though I have no objection to Mr. Grenville, I should be loth to lose Mr. Oswald.

He seems to have nothing at heart but the good of mankind, and putting a stop to the mischief; the other, a young statesman, may be supposed to have naturally a little ambition of recommending himself as an able negotiator."

Grenville's revised commission authorized him to treat with the king of France or his ministers, or with the ministers of any other prince or state whom it might concern. Grenville said he was authorized to acknowledge the independence of America before the treaty began. Vergennes accepted the language, but Franklin still objected to Grenville's instructions, because Britain had always considered Americans to be "rebellious subjects" and not a state. The Enabling Act, a bill that would allow the king to negotiate a truce with America, was still pending in England's Parliament. John Jay finally arrived in France on June 23, 1782, much to Franklin's relief. England had by then gained some new military successes in the West Indies, and Franklin and Jay now feared that they might delay the negotiations on account of the news.

During all of this time, Franklin recorded peripheral events that were not directly related to the treaty in the *Journal*. He discharged Cornwallis from his parole, subject to the final approval of Congress. David Hartley, Franklin's friend and a member of Parliament, wrote Franklin many letters from England expressing his desire for peace. As Jay and Adams were not present during most of this period of the talks, Franklin wrote letters to them in Spain and Holland to keep them up-to-date. The last significant event recorded in Franklin's *Journal* is his and Jay's visit to the Spanish ambassador in France on June 29, 1782. The *Journal's* final entry is on July 1, 1782, and the entire record contains only the substance of unofficial discussions relating to a treaty. For the official treaty negotiations that followed shortly thereafter, *see* Treaty of Paris, 1783.

Related entries:
Adams, John
France
Jay, John
Treaty of Paris, 1783
Vergennes, Comte de (Charles Gravier)

Suggestion for further reading:
"Journal of the Negotiation for Peace with Great Britain," 1782 (Smyth, vol. VIII).

The Junto

As a curious 21-year-old in Philadelphia, Franklin "had formed most of my ingenious acquaintance into a club called the Junto; we met on Friday evenings." It was the first of many discussion clubs and academies of which he was a member during his life—the Honest Whigs, the American Philosophical Society, the Royal Society of London, the French Academy of Sciences, and others—and was first known as the "Leather Apron Club." Franklin's Junto limited itself to 12 members and met first in an alehouse, and its members kept the organization a secret to prevent unwanted applications for membership. Questions for discussion were presented a week ahead of time, enabling the members to read on the topics before they talked about them. A president directed the debates, which were to be conducted "in the sincere spirit of inquiry after truth, without fondness for dispute, or desire of victory."

In 1728 Franklin drew up 24 "Rules for a Club Established for Mutual Improvement," which governed the Junto's meetings. "The rules that I drew up required that every member, in his turn, should produce one or more queries on any point of morals, politics, or natural philosophy, to be discussed by the company," Franklin wrote in his *Autobiography*. At each meeting, members were asked to share stories of citizens who both failed and succeeded in their businesses, and how. They looked for promising young people or newcomers that had lately moved into the area and discussed encroachments on liberties of the populace. Question number one read: "Have you met with anything in the author you last read, remarkable, or suitable to be communicated to the Junto? Particularly in history, morality, poetry, physic, travels, mechanic arts, or other parts of knowledge." Number 11 was: "Do you think of anything at present, in which the Junto may be serviceable to mankind, to their country, to their friends, or to themselves?"

To join the Junto, a member had to declare love for mankind in general, regardless of any person's religion; declare oneself free from disrespect of any other member; uphold a belief in the right of all people to remain free from harm regardless of their beliefs; and declare a love of truth for truth's sake, promise to receive it impartially, and promise to share it with others. The Junto's first members were mostly tradesmen. Thomas Godfrey was a mathematician who lodged with his family at Franklin's printing shop for a short period. Franklin found his company very disagreeable and complained that he disrupted smooth conversation by arguing about trifles. Joseph Breintnal was a copier of deeds, good-natured, and loved poetry, and he was Franklin's partner in authoring the Busy-Body letters to Andrew Bradford's *American Weekly Mercury*. William Parsons was a shoemaker who had studied mathematics and who later became the surveyor-general of Pennsylvania. Nicholas Scull was a surveyor who loved to read. William Maugridge was a joiner and a mechanic, and Hugh Meredith was Franklin's printing partner. An Oxford scholar and another fellow printer, George Webb, betrayed Franklin's idea for a newspaper to his rival. He was, according to Franklin, "lively, witty, good-natured, and a pleasant companion, but idle, thoughtless, and imprudent to the last degree." A particular favorite of Franklin's was William Coleman, a merchant's clerk, "who had the coolest, clearest head, the best heart, and the exactest morals of almost any man [he] ever met with." Franklin described Robert Grace as generous and lively. Finally, Stephen Potts, who had worked with Franklin at Samuel Keimer's printing house, was a "great wit and humor, but a little idle."

The success of the original Junto created the desire for additional clubs. The Junto had agreed to limit its membership to 12, so Franklin proposed that each of the original members form a subordinate club. The members of the new clubs met under the same rules but were not to know of their connection to the Junto, and the Junto members reported back to the original group on their discussions. The five or six clubs that resulted, according to Franklin, used names like "the Band," "the Vine," and "the Union."

Franklin used the Junto and the subordinate clubs to influence public opinion and to promote public projects. The Junto was involved, in some form or another, in the formation of the town watch, the academy that Franklin founded (which later became the University of Pennsylvania), the fire company, the Library Company, and Franklin's pamphlet on the necessity of paper currency. Some of the issues were discussed at the club's meetings before the public heard of them. Franklin published pieces that he had originally written for the Junto in his *Pennsylvania Gazette*. The club lasted almost 40 years and was, Franklin thought, "the best school of philosophy, morality, and politics that then existed in the province."

Related entries:
American Philosophical Society
The Busy-Body
Education
Fire
French Academy of Sciences
Honest Whigs
Library Company of Philadelphia
Paper Currency
Pennsylvania Gazette
Printing
Royal Society of London

Suggestions for further reading:
"Standing Queries for the Junto," 1732 (Labaree et al., vol. 1).
"To Hugh Roberts," February 26, 1761 (Labaree et al., vol. 9).
"To Hugh Roberts," July 7, 1765 (Labaree et al., vol. 12).
"To Hugh Roberts," September 16, 1758 (Labaree et al., vol. 8).
"To William Parsons," December 5, 1755 (Labaree et al., vol. 6).

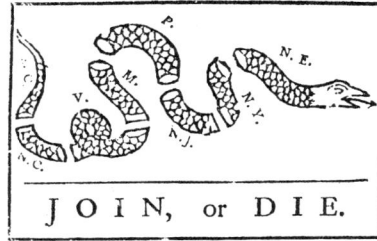

JOIN, or DIE.

K

Kames, Lord (Henry Home) (1696–1782)

When Franklin and his son William visited Scotland in 1759 he met the economist Adam Smith (1723–1790), author of *The Wealth of Nations;* William Robertson; the philosopher David Hume (1711–1776); Sir Alexander Dick, president of the College of Physicians at Prestonfeld; and Lord Kames (Henry Home), and he developed a particular friendship with Lord Kames. Lord Kames married Agatha Drummond, was a judge of the Court of Session in Edinburgh, and authored *Introduction to the Art of Thinking* (1761), *Elements of Criticism* (1762), and *Sketches of the History of Man* (1773). Of the first work, Franklin wrote to him in 1761: "[Y]ou sow thick in the young mind the seeds of good sense concerning moral conduct, which, as they grow and are transplanted into life, must greatly adorn the character and promote the happiness of the person. . . . " He added: "I think I never saw more solid, useful matter contained in so small a compass, and yet the method and expression so clear, that the brevity occasions no obscurity." After visiting Scotland, Franklin wrote to Kames: "[I] think the time we spent there, was six weeks of the densest happiness I have met with in any part of my life: and the agreeable and instructive society we found there in such plenty, has left so pleasing an impression on my memory, that did not strong connections draw me elsewhere, I believe Scotland would be the country I should choose to spend the remainder of my days in."

After Franklin left, the two kept up a correspondence on widely varied subjects. In 1760 Lord Kames offered Franklin a portrait of William Penn, which, if it genuinely resembled Penn, Franklin said he would have copied. However, he was skeptical because Quakers generally did not sit for portraits. Lord Kames took an interest in American affairs and asked Franklin for his writings. Franklin could not locate many of them while he was in London, but he sent Lord Kames his "Observations Concerning the Increase of Mankind" (1751) and his "An Account of the New-Invented Pennsylvania Fireplaces" (1744). In 1760 Franklin expressed his joy that Britain had defeated France in Canada, and he hoped that Britain would obtain the Canadian territory. One of his letters to Kames, in which he complained about an air of superiority that Britain took toward America, is thought to have been intercepted and given to the ministry. In any case, the original, written in 1767, never reached Kames, and Franklin sent him a copy almost two years later. "Every man in England," Franklin complained, "seems to consider himself as a piece of a sovereign over America; seems to jostle himself into the throne with the King, and talks of *our subjects in the colonies.*"

Franklin read Lord Kames's *Elements of Criticism* on his voyage home in 1762, and he told him in 1765 that it entertained him and that "there was much to admire and nothing to reprove." The only defect in the work, Franklin thought, was that he did not examine music more fully. Franklin continued the letter with an analysis of Scottish tunes. He alleged that "the pleasure which artists feel in hearing much of that composed in the modern taste, is not the natural pleasure arising from melody or harmony of sounds, but of the same kind with the pleasure we feel on seeing the surprising feats of tumblers and rope dancers, who execute difficult things." During contemporary musical performances, he had observed the faces in the audience during a great part of a piece of music, and there was no pleasure on the faces of its hearers. People did take pleasure, however, in a Scottish tune, Franklin asserted.

Franklin expanded on Lord Kames's assertion that "melody and harmony are separately agreeable, and in union delightful." He argued that Scotch tunes had been around for so long because they "are really compositions of melody and harmony united, or rather that their melody is harmony." Scottish tunes were originally composed for a harp, which had no mechanism to stop the vibration of a string after it was played. Consequently, "it was . . . necessary that the succeeding emphatic note should be a chord with the preceding, as their sounds must exist at the same time." This, Franklin thought, was the origin of the beauty of a Scottish tune. Their ancestors, listening to a song sung to a Scottish tune, must have "felt more real pleasure than is communicated by the generality of modern operas, exclusive of that arising from the scenery and dancing." Modern songs, he asserted, did not have natural harmony and resorted to artificial harmony provided by the bass or another instrument.

Always interested in ventilation, Franklin advised Lord Kames on his problem with smoky chimneys in 1768. The following year,

Lord Kames sent Franklin a paper on the use of oxen in agriculture, and Franklin observed that American farmers were more successful when they used cattle instead of horses, because horses required twice as much land to maintain them.

Franklin visited five days at Blair Drummond, near Stirling, with Lord Kames in 1771. In 1773 Lord Kames published Franklin's "A Parable against Persecution" in his *Sketches of the History of Man,* without his permission. The parable, which Franklin called "Genesis 51," was a lesson in toleration of differing religious viewpoints. The publication of the parable, which was similar to a parable in Jeremy Taylor's "Liberty of Prophesying," brought charges of plagiarism against Franklin. Franklin had circulated it among a few friends and said he never claimed the idea as his own. "The publishing of it by Lord Kames, without my consent," Franklin wrote to Benjamin Vaughan in 1789, "deprived me of a good deal of amusement, which I used to take in reading it by heart out of my Bible, and obtaining the remarks of scripturians on it, which were sometimes very diverting. . . . " However, he thought its moral was worth being made known.

Related entries:
Franklin, Peter
Strahan, William

Suggestions for further reading:
Nolan, J. Bennett. 1938. *Benjamin Franklin in Scotland and Ireland, 1759 and 1771.* Philadelphia: University of Pennsylvania Press.
"A Parable against Persecution" (Smyth, vol. VI).
"To Lord Kames," April 11, 1767 (Labaree et al., vol. 14).
"To Lord Kames," February 21, 1769 (Labaree et al., vol. 16).
"To Lord Kames," January 3, 1760 (Labaree et al., vol. 9).
"To Lord Kames," June 2, 1765 (Labaree et al., vol. 12).
"To Lord Kames," May 3, 1760 (Labaree et al., vol. 9).
"To Lord Kames," October 21, 1761 (Labaree et al., vol. 9).

Keimer, Samuel

See **Printing; Vegetarianism.**

Kinnersley, Ebenezer (1711–1778)

After Franklin observed electrical experiments performed by Dr. Adam Spencer in Boston, he became very interested in pursuing further studies in electricity himself. Many Philadelphians came to his house to watch the curious new experiments he performed. An "ingenious" neighbor, Ebenezer Kinnersley, was one of those most interested in the new wonders. Kinnersley was an eloquent, English-born Baptist minister and out of work after a heated controversy with the Baptist Church during the Great Awakening. He criticized the excessive fervor and emotion of the religious revivals. Franklin engaged him to show the electrical experiments to earn money. Franklin organized the experiments and designed two lectures for Kinnersley to present. Kinnersley was ready and very interested, and the arrangement worked out well. From 1749 to 1753 Kinnersley traveled through America presenting the experiments to other colonists. He was introduced in Boston, by Franklin's letter, to Franklin's correspondent James Bowdoin. The popular lectures attracted thousands of colonists. Kinnersley had the syllabus for the upcoming lectures printed in local papers beforehand. His show was entertaining as well as instructional.

Kinnersley and others like Thomas Hopkinson, president of the American Philosophical Society, exchanged ideas with Franklin and conducted new experiments. Franklin dutifully reported them to Peter Collinson in London. Among the many subjects concerning electricity that interested both Kinnersley and Franklin were the nature of the charge of clouds. The two tested lightning during many storms and concluded that the charge of clouds was rarely positive and almost always negative. (Scientists now believe that most thunderclouds are charged negatively at the base and positively on top.) In another experiment on conductivity, Franklin reported: "Mr. Kinnersley has found, by a very good experiment, that when the charge of a bottle hath an opportunity of passing two ways, i.e. straight through a trough of water . . . or round about through 20 feet of wire, it passes through the wire, and not through the water, though that is the shortest course; the wire being the better conductor." When the wire was taken away, the electricity traveled through the trough of water.

In 1753, with Franklin's assistance, Kinnersley was appointed Professor of English and Oratory at the Philadelphia Academy, where he remained until 1772. He continued to lecture on electricity as well and was elected to the American Philosophical Society in 1768.

Franklin's travels to London forced him to abandon many of his electrical experiments, but he and Kinnersley continued to write one another on the subject.

Related entries:
American Philosophical Society
Bowdoin, James II
Collinson, Peter
Education
Electricity
Meteorology

Suggestions for further reading:
Lemay, J. A. Leo. 1964. *Ebenezer Kinnersley, Franklin's Friend*. Philadelphia: University of Pennsylvania Press.
"To Ebenezer Kinnersley," March 2, 1752 (Labaree et al., vol. 4).
"To Ebenezer Kinnersley," March 16, 1752 (Labaree et al., vol. 4).
"To Ebenezer Kinnersley with Associated Papers," February 20, 1762 (Labaree et al., vol. 10).

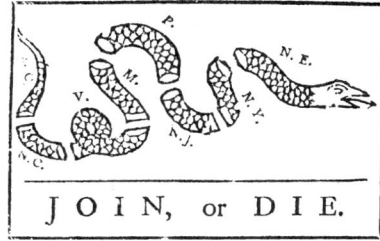

JOIN, or DIE.

L

Lafayette, Marquis de (1757–1834)

Marie Joseph Paul Yves Roch Gilbert du Motier, better known as the Marquis de Lafayette, was instrumental in securing the victory of the American colonies in the Revolutionary War and a friend and admirer of Franklin's. Following in the footsteps of a long family military tradition, he enrolled in the Versailles military academy as a youth. He served in the French army between 1771 and 1776. By age 16 he was a captain in the cavalry.

At the age of 19 Lafayette wanted to join the American army. He deeply admired the American colonies and their drive for independence. He obtained a recommendation from Silas Deane, an American representative in France. A personal recommendation from Franklin, who had met members of Lafayette's wife's family, to George Washington also preceded his arrival in the colonies. In July 1777 his ship landed in South Carolina. Lafayette traveled to Philadelphia, where he met and befriended Washington. By the end of the month Lafayette was a major general in the American army.

Lafayette's military contributions to the American cause helped the colonies win independence from Britain. During the war he divided his time between America and France. He was wounded in the Battle of Brandywine. In 1779 he traveled to Paris and planned a never-realized joint attack on the British coast with John Paul Jones, and continued to solicit assistance from France for the American cause. Congress presented him with a sword, which was delivered to him by William Temple Franklin. Upon his return to America he took part in the military campaign that culminated in the surrender of General Charles Cornwallis at Yorktown.

Franklin frequently wrote of his admiration and respect for Lafayette, who was an essential link between the Americans and the French government during the peace negotiations. He and Lafayette remained friends until Franklin's death in 1790. In a 1782 letter to Lafayette, Franklin congratulated him on the birth of his first daughter and humorously suggested that he name her after the first American state. He had already named a son after George Washington. When Franklin died in 1790, Lafayette was among those who mourned his loss at the French National Assembly.

After the war ended in the colonies, Lafayette returned to France, where he became involved in the storm of the French Revolution. He joined the French National Assembly and voted in favor of the "Declaration of the Rights of Man and of the Citizen," 17 articles of political freedom heavily influenced by the revolution of the American colonies. The assembly approved the declaration on August 26, 1789. Louis XVI

The Marquis de Lafayette leading troops into battle. Engraving by Godefroy.

signed the articles under pressure but did not support them.

Lafayette favored a constitutional monarchy in France, a position unpopular with the nobility. He became unpopular in his home country and in 1792, branded a traitor, had to flee the country. He was arrested in Flanders and did not return to France until eight years later, only to find that all of his money had been seized. In 1815 he won a spot in the Chamber of Deputies. He supported the abdication of Napoleon after he was defeated at Waterloo, and later worked against the Bourbon kings. He later supported the constitutional monarchy with Louis Philippe on the throne.

In 1790 Princeton College made Lafayette an honorary doctor of laws. He was in France at the time and did not officially receive his diploma until he returned to the United States for a visit in 1824. During that visit, which was at the invitation of President James Monroe and the Congress, Lafayette was greeted warmly everywhere he went. On his extensive tour of the United States he survived a shipwreck and was the frequent object of honor and pomp. He returned to France in 1825, served in the Chamber of Deputies, and died in 1834.

Related entries:
Adams, John
French Revolution
Jay, John
Journal of the Negotiation for Peace with Great Britain
Revolutionary War
Treaty of Paris, 1783
Washington, George

Suggestions for further reading:
"Journal of the Negotiation for Peace with Great Britain," 1782 (Smyth, vol. VIII).
"To the Marquis de Lafayette," April 17, 1787 (Smyth, vol. IX).

Last Will and Testament

Franklin drew up a will as early as 1750, but abandoned it and made others in 1788 and 1789. His son William inherited all of Franklin's land in Nova Scotia, all of the books and papers of his father's that he had in his possession, and was forgiven a debt that he owed Franklin. Franklin's bequests to him were relatively sparse because William had opposed him and remained loyal to England during the American Revolution. Richard and Sarah Bache, Franklin's daughter and son-in-law, received the largest share of Franklin's money and property, including seven houses, a printing office, several plots of land, other buildings, and all of Franklin's possessions from the house in which he lived that were not specifically left to someone else.

To Richard Bache, Franklin left all of his land near the Ohio River and some plots of land in Philadelphia that he had purchased from the state. He released him of a debt, requesting that he would free Richard's slave Bob in return, and authorized him to collect other debts owed to Franklin. Finally, he received all of Franklin's musical instruments. Sarah Bache inherited a picture of the king of France, "set with four hundred and eight diamonds . . . requesting, however, that she would not form any of those diamonds into ornaments either for herself or daughters, and thereby introduce or countenance the expensive, vain, and useless fashion of wearing jewels in this country. . . . " Franklin also left her half of his money that remained in a London bank. Franklin left a house to his youngest sister, Jane Mecom, along with an annual sum of £60 sterling from the dividends of Franklin's 12 shares in the Bank of North America. Upon her death, the money was to go to Richard and Sarah Bache.

William Temple Franklin, Franklin's grandson, received the right to 3,000 acres of land in Georgia that had been granted to Franklin, as well as his grandfather's papers. Upon his marriage, he was to be forgiven of a debt to Franklin; but if he died unmarried, the debt was to be recovered and divided among the children of Sarah Bache. He also received his grandfather's timepiece, a Chinese gong, and one-fourth of the money remaining in a London bank. Benjamin

Franklin Bache, another of Franklin's grandsons, received the right to collect a debt in Delaware, Franklin's types and printing materials, his share in the Library Company, some of his books, and one-fourth of the money left in a London bank.

Miscellaneous items that Franklin left included: a walking stick to George Washington; various items to the family of Mary Hewson, including his new Bible to her son William; one of his pictures to the Supreme Executive Council of Pennsylvania; 20 guineas to Dr. John Jones; a telescope to David Rittenhouse; a silver cream pot to Henry Hill; a French wayweiser ("a piece of clockwork in brass") to Edward Duffield; and his "philosophical instruments" to Francis Hopkinson.

Franklin left money and books to various other individuals and institutions. The American Philosophical Society received some of his books, as did his grandson William Bache and his cousin Jonathan Williams. The descendants of Franklin's brother Samuel were to divide £50 sterling among them, as were the descendants of his sisters Anne, Sarah, Lydia, and Jane, and of his brother James. To the Pennsylvania Hospital, Franklin left the right to collect a number of debts owed to him. Franklin left sums of money to benefit grammar schools in Boston and to aid young, married tradesmen in Boston and Philadelphia who had successfully completed apprenticeships and needed to borrow money to set up businesses. He envisioned the £1,000 sterling he left each increasing dramatically over a period of 200 years and asked that some of the excess be donated to public works. His money did not increase at the rate he had planned but was used in both cities.

As his executors, Franklin requested John Jay, Henry Hill, Edward Duffield, and Francis Hopkinson, who were to divide £60 sterling equally among them. He asked that he be buried with as little ceremony and expense as possible—a request that was not adhered to—and to be buried next to his wife. The epitaph he had written for himself early in his life was abandoned in favor of a more simple one bearing the names of him and his wife.

Related entries:
American Philosophical Society
Bache, Benjamin Franklin
Bache, Richard
Bache, Sarah Franklin
Childhood
Death
Franklin, William
Franklin, William Temple
Hewson, Mary (Polly) Stevenson
Hopkinson, Thomas and Francis
Jay, John
Mecom, Jane Franklin
Pennsylvania Hospital
Washington, George

Suggestions for further reading:
"Franklin's Last Will and Testament," 1788–1789 (Smyth, vol. X).
St. John, Gerard J. 1993. "Ben and I: After 200 Years and a Few Unforeseen Difficulties, Benjamin Franklin's Bequest to Philadelphia Is Found Practicable." Philadelphia: Philadelphia Bar Association.
"Will and Testament," 1750 (Van Doren 1945).

Lavoisier, Antoine-Laurent

See **French Academy of Sciences.**

Le Despencer, Lord

See **Dashwood, Sir Francis.**

Le Roy, Jean-Baptiste

See **French Academy of Sciences.**

Le Veillard, Louis-Guillaume

See **France; French Revolution.**

Lee, Dr. Arthur (1740–1792)

The tension-filled working relationship between Franklin and Arthur Lee began in London in the years immediately preceding the American Revolution. Lee, the youngest of ten children, had studied medicine and received his doctorate but later turned to law. When England began to impose a series of taxes and other restrictions on Americans, Lee and and some of his brothers became vocal critics of British policy. Franklin served as an agent for Massachusetts in the early 1770s, and that colony's Assembly appointed Lee to replace him in the event of his death or departure. The two worked together on the behalf of Massachusetts. Franklin expected for several years in a row to return to America, but events kept him in England. At this time the two men worked civilly together and with other agents of the colonies, but Lee, who wanted Franklin's position and resented him for extending his stay, wrote letters to Congress insinuating that Franklin was influenced by the British government.

When the Revolutionary War broke out, Congress voted to send several commissioners to represent the United States in France. Franklin, Silas Deane, and Thomas Jefferson were chosen, but Jefferson refused the appointment so that he could stay in America with his ailing wife. Arthur Lee was appointed instead—a choice that was unfortunate for Franklin and for Deane. Jefferson was an admirer of both Franklin and France, and his presence might have prevented many of the problems generated by the volatile Lee. Lee disliked the French and was a perpetual fount of trouble for Deane and Franklin.

Lee was zealous for the American cause, firm, suspicious, and ill-tempered. He arrived in France in December 1776. In 1777 he succeeded in obtaining a small amount of money from the Spanish government for American military supplies but was not permitted to come to the court at Madrid. Journeys to Berlin and Vienna were even less successful, as all of these countries refused to recognize the independence of the United States. In France, Lee quarreled with almost everyone. The most bitter argument he carried on was with Deane, whom he accused of stealing public money in Paris. Franklin, who tried to stay out of the dispute, drew Lee's suspicion with his seeming indifference and his respect for Deane. Lee believed that Franklin and Deane withheld vital information from him and were trying to destroy his reputation.

He wrote to the Congress suggesting that Deane be sent to Holland and Franklin to Vienna, while he remained in France, the country most important to the American Revolution. Merchants and politicians in France refused to deal with him. Lee feared a security risk with William Temple Franklin—grandson of Franklin but son of William Franklin, a loyalist—as Franklin's secretary and conveyed his objections to Congress. However, while Temple proved a faithful secretary to his grandfather, Lee's own secretary was a British spy. Lee suspected both Franklin and his nephew, Jonathan Williams, of improperly taking public money.

By 1778 letters between Franklin and Lee had grown contentious. Franklin politely rebuked him for the superior airs and suspicious insinuations characteristic of some of his letters. On April 2, 1778, Lee wrote to Franklin angry that he had not been consulted in the decision to appoint Conrad-Alexandre Gérard de Rayneval as minister to America and that he had not been informed of Gérard's and Deane's sailing to America, which would have provided another opportunity to write to Congress. He accused Franklin of trying to overthrow the authority of the joint commission and acting injuriously toward him and the public. Franklin's immediate reply (which he did not likely send) was, for him, uncharacteristically harsh:

> If I have often received and borne

Arthur Lee. Etching by H. B. Hall, 1869.

> your magisterial snubbings and rebukes without reply, ascribe it to the right causes, my concern for the honor and success of our mission, which would be hurt by our quarreling, my love of peace, my respect for your good qualities, and my pity for your sick mind, which is forever tormenting itself, with its jealousies, suspicions, and fancies that others mean you ill, wrong you, or fail in respect for you. If you do not cure yourself of this temper it will end in insanity, of which it is the symptomatic forerunner, as I have seen in several instances. God preserve you from so terrible an evil: and for His sake pray suffer me to live in quiet.

In another letter Franklin addressed Lee's specific objections, but he was not much less insulting to Lee. Franklin had not been consulted by the court in the decision either, and he had honored Deane's request to keep his departure secret. France had not been consulted in the choice of American commissioners sent to her country, and Americans should have had no reason to expect France to consult them in their choice of a minister. The charge about concealing an opportunity to write to Congress was also groundless, Franklin said, because ships that were leaving later would arrive sooner than Deane and Gérard's, and they had just written to Congress.

When John Adams arrived to replace Deane that same year, he was disturbed to hear from Franklin about the tension between the American commissioners. He resolved to keep himself out of the disputes. He liked Lee and thought him honest, but he soon found himself apologizing to others for the temper of his fellow countryman.

In 1779 Congress revoked the joint commission and appointed Franklin sole plenipotentiary to the court of France—a great relief to Adams and a big disappointment to Lee. Franklin wrote to both of them requesting the public papers pertinent to the commission. Adams readily complied with his request, but Lee accused Franklin of trying to obtain papers he needed in his perpetual quarrel with Deane. Franklin politely told Lee he would settle for copies of the necessary papers and had no intention of taking documents he needed. Lee asked Franklin for expenses to travel to Spain and said that he would return to America if the request was denied. Franklin, who saw no chance of Lee's being received in Madrid, would not give him the funds.

Franklin's friends and relations in America kept him informed of Lee's attempts to discredit him through letters to Congress and newspapers. William Carmichael sent him some of Lee's writings in 1780. Franklin responded: "[W]hen I consider him as the most malicious enemy I ever had (though without the smallest cause), that he shows so clear his abundant desire to accuse and defame me, and that all his charges are so frivolous, so ill founded, and amount to so little, I esteem them rather as panegyrics on me and satires against himself." Franklin warned Joseph Reed, president of the Supreme Executive Council of Pennsylvania, in Philadelphia: "I caution you to beware of him; for in sowing suspicions and jealousies, in creating misun-

derstandings and quarrels among friends, in malice, subtlety, and indefatigable industry, he has I think no equal."

After returning to America Lee served in the Virginia Assembly in 1781 and in the Continental Congress from 1782 to 1785. He helped negotiate a treaty with the Six Nations at Fort Stanwix in 1784. Lee was the brother of William Lee, appointed by Congress as a commissioner to Berlin and Vienna; of Richard Henry Lee (1732–1794), who introduced the original motion for independence in the Continental Congress; and of Francis Lee (1734–1797), also a delegate to the Continental Congress.

Related entries:
 Adams, John
 Continental Congresses
 Izard, Ralph
 Revolutionary War

Suggestions for further reading:
 "From Arthur Lee," April 2, 1778 (Labaree et al., vol. 26).
 "To Arthur Lee," April 1, 1778 (Labaree et al., vol. 26).
 "To Arthur Lee," April 3, 1778 (Labaree et al., vol. 26).
 "To Arthur Lee," April 4, 1778 (Labaree et al., vol. 26).
 "To Arthur Lee," March 17, 1778 (Labaree et al., vol. 26).
 Middlekauff, Robert. 1996. *Benjamin Franklin and His Enemies.* Berkeley: University of California Press.

Library Company of Philadelphia

"At the time I established myself in Pennsylvania, there was not a good bookseller's shop in any of the colonies to the southward of Boston. . . . Those who loved reading were obliged to send for their books from England," Franklin wrote in his *Autobiography*. There were no public libraries in America either. The first library in

Franklin opening the first subscription library in Philadelphia. Painting by Charles E. Mills, c. 1914.

the colonies was established at Harvard College in 1638, but no library made books accessible to the general public until Franklin founded the Library Company of Philadelphia in 1731. In 1730 he proposed to the members of the Junto, a club he had recently formed for discussion and "mutual Improvement" in Philadelphia, that they gather their books into a collection. Housing the books at a central location, Franklin hoped, would give each member the benefit of access to the rest of his fellows' books. In addition members could easily consult them during the discussions at their meetings.

The fledgling library was successful at first, but members soon began to complain about the deteriorating condition of the books. Franklin next suggested a subscription library. The idea met with enthusiasm among the club members, and Franklin enlisted the scrivener Charles Brockden to draw up Articles of Agreement. In 1732 Junto members compiled a list of books they wanted to acquire. That same year, the Library Company took in enough money to order a small set of books through Peter Collinson, a Quaker merchant in London. Among the earliest works on the shelves were Daniel Defoe's *Complete English Tradesman;* Sir Isaac Newton's *Principia;* Homer's *Iliad* and *Odyssey;* and Pierre Bayle's *Historical and Critical Dictionary.*

Franklin donated a *Magna Carta* and a copy of Michel Eyquem de Montaigne's *Essays.*

The original library had 50 subscribers. Initially, many of Philadelphia's residents were either not interested or could not afford to subscribe. Those who did each paid an initial fee of 40 shillings and agreed to an additional annual fee of 10 shillings. The library's first home was at the Junto headquarters, and it was open for borrowing only for a few hours each week. Louis Timothée, who later published the *South Carolina Gazette* as Franklin's partner, served as the first librarian. Only subscribers could borrow books free of charge, though other people of the town were permitted to read the books in-house. Those who failed to return materials were obliged to pay double the lost book's value. The books were moved to houses owned by Junto members Robert Grace and William Parsons. In April 1740 they were relocated to a room in the State House. By 1742 the number of subscribers had doubled and the library housed more than 300 books on theology, science, history, literature, and other subjects. Some non-subscribers borrowed books for a small fee.

Encouraged by the success of the Library Company of Philadelphia, other towns in the colonies established subscription libraries. Rival libraries also sprang up in Philadelphia, but all had been absorbed by the Library

Company by 1769. Franklin continued to support it throughout his life, acquiring books during his travels to London. He believed that the library inspired public interest in reading and contributed to an overall rise in education among the colonial populace. The new availability of books benefited him personally as well: "This library afforded me the means of improvement by constant study, for which I set apart an hour or two each day; and thus repaired in some degree the loss of the learned education my father once intended for me."

Before he died, Franklin wrote an inscription for a stone at the library's new building:

Be it remembered
In Honour of the Philadelphian Youth
(then chiefly Artificers)
That in MDCCXXXII
They chearfully, at the Instance of one
of their Number,
Instituted the Philadelphia Library
Which tho' small at first
Is become highly Valuable
and extensively useful
And which the Walls of this Edifice
Are now destined to Contain and
Preserve
The First Stone of whose Foundation
was here placed
the 31st Day of August
MDCCLXXXIX

When he died, he left a portion of his books to the library that had blossomed throughout his life. He still owned a portion of the Library Company, which he bequeathed to his grandson Benjamin Franklin Bache. The library still exists in Philadelphia and contains some of the original books.

Related entries:
  Collinson, Peter
  The Junto

Suggestions for further reading:
  Korty, Margaret Barton. 1965. *Benjamin Franklin and Eighteenth-Century American*

Libraries. Philadelphia: American Philosophical Society.
Masur, Louis P., ed. 1993. *The Autobiography of Benjamin Franklin.* Boston: Bedford Books of St. Martin's Press.

The Long Arm

Franklin was 80 years old when he wrote out a "Description of an Instrument for Taking Down Books from High Shelves" (1786). Old men, he said, find it difficult to climb ladders in their libraries because they suffer from giddiness in the head and unsteady joints. They also found it difficult to move ladders around their libraries. Franklin designed the "Long Arm" to remedy this problem.

The Long Arm was made from a stick of pine 8 feet long and 1 inch square. At the end of the arm were attached a "thumb" and "finger" made of ash lath. They were 1 1/2 inches wide and attached to the arm with wooden screws, with the finger extending 1/2 inch beyond the thumb. The outside of the finger and thumb were tapered to be thin enough that they could slide between books easily. A piece of sinew was strung through two holes in the finger and thumb, with a knot tied at the end on the other side of the finger to stop the string. The other end of the string was looped, and a series of knots 3 to 4 inches apart were tied down the string.

One used the instrument first by holding the loop with one hand and pulling the string down the side of the arm. The finger was slid in next to the book to be pulled down. One then adjusted the width of the finger and thumb and slid the thumb on the other side of the book. The instrument was pushed until the back of the book touched the string. Using the loop, the string was pulled tight until the book was securely in the instrument's grip. The book was then pulled down and turned sideways as soon as it left the shelf so that it lay flat on either the finger or the thumb. The instrument could also be used to place books back on high shelves. "All new tools," Franklin wrote, "require some practice before we can become expert in the use of them. This requires very little."

Related entry:
Bowdoin, James II

Suggestions for further reading:
"Description of an Instrument for Taking Down Books from High Shelves," 1786 (Smyth, vol. IX).
"To Jonathan Williams," February 12, 1786 (Smyth, vol. IX).

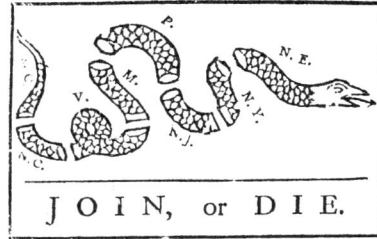

J O I N, or D I E.

M

Magic Squares/ Magic Circles

Franklin first began to compose magic squares as a youth, and later composed them while he was bored as a clerk in the Pennsylvania Assembly. His first squares were simple compositions in which the numbers of each diagonal, vertical, and horizontal row all produced the same sum. He grew bored with these squares, which he found he could compose very easily, and invented squares that had more peculiar properties.

While he was visiting the home of James Logan, his host brought down from his shelves a book full of magic squares composed by Bernard Frénicle de Bessy (1605–1675). Franklin perused the book and told Logan that he had composed magic squares himself in his youth, and he later brought him an 8-by-8 square that he had saved. Logan showed Franklin a 16-by-16 square composed by Michael Stifelius, and, "not willing to be outdone by Mr. Stifelius," Franklin composed in a single evening a complex square that had many more properties than Stifelius's.

Franklin included an 8-by-8 magic square in a letter to Peter Collinson sometime around 1750. The properties of the square, Franklin noted, are as follows (see illustration in next column): all of the horizontal and vertical rows add up to 260; half of each horizontal and vertical row adds up to 130,

half of 260; bent diagonal rows add up to 260; the eight numbers touching either side of the corner numbers (14 and 61, 36 and 19, 32 and 47, and 50 and 1) add up to 260; the four middle numbers (54, 43, 23, and 10), combined with the four corner numbers (52, 45, 17, and 16), add up to 260; bent rows add up to 260. Franklin later composed a 16-by-16 square that has all the properties of this square except that the sums total 2,056 instead of 260; in addition, the numbers within any 4-by-4 square within the larger square add up to 2,056.

An interest in magic circles accompanied his interest in magic squares. He wrote to Collinson: "I did not, however, end with squares, but composed also a magic circle,

52	61	4	13	20	29	36	45
14	3	62	51	46	35	30	19
53	60	5	12	21	28	37	44
11	6	59	54	43	38	27	22
55	58	7	10	23	26	39	42
9	8	57	56	41	40	25	24
50	63	2	15	18	31	34	47
16	1	64	49	48	33	32	17

Franklin's 8-by-8 magic square.

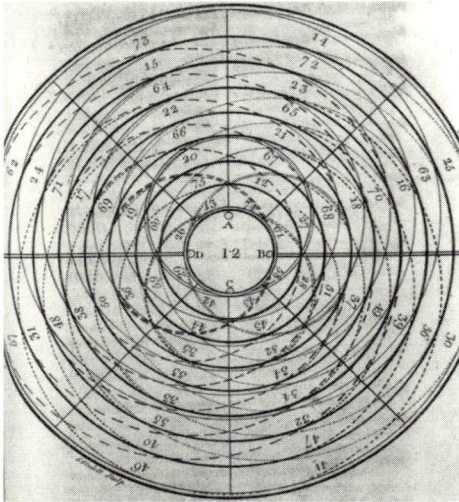

"A magic circle of circles" and "a magic square of squares." Engravings by J. Hulett in **Benjamin Franklin: Experiments and Observations on Electricity, 1774, plates V and IV.**

consisting of 8 concentric circles, and 8 radial rows, filled with a series of numbers, from 12 to 75, inclusive, so disposed as that the numbers of each circle, or each radial row, being added to the central number 12, they made exactly 360, the number of degrees in a circle; and this circle had, moreover, all the properties of the square of 8." (Excentric circles are circles that do not have a common center; concentric circles share a common center. Franklin's circles are marked on the diagram with various dotted and dashed lines and are, as he explained, difficult to read and discern without becoming confused.)

Franklin's circle has many other characteristics as well. All of the following combinations produce a sum of 180, the number of degrees in a semicircle: half of the number in any radial row, along with half the center number; half of the number in any of the concentric circles, above or below the double horizontal line, plus half of the center number; and any four adjoining numbers that almost form a square added to half of the central number.

"There are, moreover," he continued, "included four other sets of circular spaces, excentric with respect to the first, each of these sets containing five spaces. The centers of the circles that bound them, are at A, B, C, and D. . . . These sets of excentric circular spaces intersect those of the concentric, and each other." There are 20 excentric spaces, and the numbers in each of them combined with the central number add up to 360, as do the eight numbers in each of the concentric circles combined with the center number. The halves of the circles drawn from centers A and C above or below the double horizontal line, and the halves of those drawn from centers B and D either to the right or the left of the vertical line, add up to 180. Finally, Franklin told Collinson, each number belongs to at least 2 of the 28 total circular spaces, but none of them ever breaks the number 360. By 1765 Franklin had improved the circle and sent it to John Canton, and his circles and squares had sparked the curiosity of intellectuals in Europe. Dr. Jacques Barbeu-Dubourg found two mistakes in the 16-by-16 square.

Related entries:
Barbeu-Dubourg, Dr. Jacques
Collinson, Peter

Suggestions for further reading:
"To Peter Collinson, 1752" (Labaree et al., vol. 4).

Mather, Increase (1639–1723), Cotton (1663–1728), and Samuel (1706–1785)

In 1635 Richard Mather (1596–1669), an ordained minister in the Church of England who had been suspended for nonconformity, moved from England to Boston. He served as the pastor of the church at Dorchester until his death, and he left a line of descendants who preached after him. Franklin, who spent his childhood in Boston, knew three generations of Mathers. He remembered hearing Increase Mather preach at the Old South Church when he was young, and his characterization of "that wicked old persecutor of God's people, Lewis XIV" stuck in his mind.

The writers for James Franklin's *New England Courant* (where Franklin was working as an apprentice under his brother) verbally persecuted Increase's son Cotton for his tireless support of smallpox inoculations. Cotton thought the paper was, for the anti-inoculation articles and its other irreverent pieces, "full freighted with nonsense, unmanliness, profaneness, immorality, arrogance, calumnies, lies, contradictions, and what not. . . . " Increase wondered what answer James would give before the judgment seat of God for "printing things so vile and abominable."

Franklin remembered being in Increase's house when he was "old and feeble," but he remembered Cotton "in the full vigor of his preaching and usefulness." Cotton was a prolific writer on diverse subjects and had written his *Magna Christi Americana,* a church history of New England, in 1702. In this text he made "honorable mention" of Franklin's grandfather, Peter Folger of Nantucket. He was the first American-born person elected to the Royal Society of London, on account of his work in promoting smallpox inoculations and other scientific writings. Franklin read a ragged copy of his *Essays to Do Good* as a youth. At age 78 he told Cotton's son Samuel that the book had given him "such a turn of thinking, as to have an influence on my conduct through life; for I have always set a greater value on the character of a doer of good, than on any other kind of reputation; and if I have been, as you seem to think, a useful citizen, the public owes the advantage of it to that book."

Franklin last saw Cotton Mather in 1724 at Mather's house. He had received the young Franklin in his library, and when Franklin got ready to leave, Mather led him down a narrow passage with a beam that reached across the top of it. As they approached the beam, Franklin turned toward Mather, who warned him to "Stoop! Stoop!" Franklin neither understood was he was talking about nor saw the beam, and he hit his head on it. "He was a man that never missed any occasion of giving instruction," Franklin said, "and upon this he said to me 'You are young, and have the world before you; stoop as you go through it, and you will miss many hard thumps.' This advice, thus beat into my head, has frequently been of use to me; and I often think of it, when I see pride mortified, and misfortunes brought upon people by their carrying their heads too high."

Much later in Franklin's life, he exchanged friendly letters and pamphlets with Samuel Mather, Cotton's son, who preached in his father's church and who was alarmed at the restrictions that England placed on the American colonies. "I perused your tracts with pleasure," Franklin told him. "I see you inherit the various learning of your famous ancestors, Cotton and Increase Mather." Samuel had tried to convince Franklin that America was known to Europeans more ancient than Columbus, and Franklin forwarded him a pamphlet by a Swede who believed his countrymen had known of the continent.

Related entries:
  Great Awakening
  Religious Beliefs

Suggestions for further reading:
"To Samuel Mather," July 7, 1773 (Labaree et al., vol. 20).

"To Samuel Mather," May 12, 1784 (Smyth, vol. IX).

Mecom, Benjamin

See **Mecom, Jane Franklin.**

Mecom, Jane Franklin (1712–1794)

"I always judged by your behavior when a child," Franklin wrote to his sister in 1727, "that you would make a good, agreeable woman, and you know you were ever my peculiar favorite." Although Franklin was concerned with the welfare of all of his relatives, he always supported and favored his youngest sister Jane the most. They corresponded regularly throughout his life, in large part about family matters. Jane was Franklin's regular link to news about their other siblings, some of whom he kept in touch with more than others. In 1727 Franklin sent her a spinning wheel, which he thought a practical gift for a future housewife. She married a saddler who had little money, Edward Mecom, on July 27 of that year, and the couple lived in their native Boston. To provide extra money for a growing family, the Mecoms took in boarders. Jane's proximity to her parents enabled her to take care of them in their old age.

Franklin tried to reassure his pious and devout sister that he was not a religious heretic in 1743. "I am so far from thinking that God is not to be worshiped, that I have composed and wrote a whole book of devotions for my own use; and I imagine there are few if any in the world so weak as to imagine that the little good we can do here can merit so vast a reward hereafter," he wrote. He further explained that he disagreed with some of the common doctrines taught in New

England, but that he did not mean to discourage her from her beliefs.

If Jane was Franklin's favorite sister, her third son Benjamin was one of his least favorite nephews. Franklin set up several partners in printing houses throughout the colonies, commonly paying one-third of the expenses and taking one-third of the profits to start out with. On this scheme, he sent Benjamin Mecom to Antigua in 1752. Benjamin was to replace Franklin's former partner, Thomas Smith, who had died the same year. Thinking he would ease the financial burden on his nephew, he abandoned the first agreement and proposed that Benjamin send a small annual sum to aid his parents with a house payment, along with rum and sugar for Franklin's family. Benjamin was not pleased with the agreement and resented the control placed on him by his uncle.

Benjamin ran up a debt with William Strahan, Franklin's printer friend in London. Franklin seems to have understood where his nephew was headed early on. Despite polite assurances of Benjamin's character and potential to Jane, Franklin urged Strahan not to be too generous to him, fearing that he might dig himself too deeply into debt. By 1755 he had reason for his wariness. He wrote to Strahan, "I do not at all approve of B. Mecom's being so much in your debt, and shall write to him about it." The following year, Benjamin decided to quit the printing venture in Antigua altogether and move back to Boston. He purchased the business from his uncle and set up a printing house in Boston.

By 1763 Benjamin had failed at other printing efforts. Franklin told Strahan that he seemed "so dejected and spiritless that I fear little will be got of him. He has dropped his paper on which he built his last hopes." Benjamin gave up all of his printing materials to his creditors, and a sympathetic James Parker gave him a small printing house in New Haven. He later moved to Philadelphia. Franklin asked his wife in 1768 not to be generous to him. "I cannot comprehend how so very sluggish a creature as Ben. Mecom is grown, can maintain in Philadelphia so large a family," he told her. Around 1775, Benjamin went mad and was confined in Burlington, New Jersey. He disappeared in 1776 and was never heard from again.

The Revolutionary War brought pressure on Jane. She inevitably heard some of the critical portrayals of her prominent brother circulated by his political enemies in England, and though Franklin refused to answer them in public, he reassured her they were all false. Her mail to him, as well as his other correspondence, was opened in London. She was forced to move temporarily to the home of Franklin's and her friend Catharine (Ray) Greene in Warwick, Rhode Island, when Boston was under siege in 1775. Franklin visited both of them there in the middle of his many duties as a delegate to the Second Continental Congress, and Jane went the following year to Philadelphia. Letters made it to France from time to time after Franklin relocated there in 1776.

Jane's life was marked by poverty and disappointment—she outlived her husband, all of her 16 siblings, and all of her 12 children except one, Jane Mecom Collas, a melancholy woman married to an unsuccessful husband. Two of her sons, Peter and Benjamin, suffered from insanity. Her long and happy correspondence with her brother contrasted sharply with the chain of tragedies she endured.

Franklin took special care of Jane in their old age and encouraged her to ask for anything she needed. He paid for her winter firewood each year and provided her with an annual sum of £60 sterling in his will. Jane was the only one of Franklin's siblings to outlive him. She died in 1794.

Related entries:
    Parker, James
    Printing

Suggestions for further reading:
    "To Jane Franklin," January 6, 1726/1727 (Labaree et al., vol. 1).
    "To Jane Mecom," July 28, 1743 (Labaree et al., vol. 2).

"To Jane Mecom," June 19, 1731 (Labaree et al., vol. 1).
Van Doren, Carl. 1950. *Jane Mecom, the Favorite Sister of Benjamin Franklin: Her Life Here First Fully Narrated from Their Entire Surviving Correspondence.* New York: Viking Press.

Medicine

Health—his and that of others—was on Franklin's mind throughout his life. Although he is not credited with major advances in medicine, he corresponded regularly with prominent European and American physicians and others who were interested. Some of his correspondents and acquaintances were: in England, Dr. Thomas Percival, Sir John Pringle, and Dr. John Fothergill; in America, Dr. Thomas Bond and Dr. Benjamin Rush; and in France, Dr. Jacques Barbeu-Dubourg. Franklin was elected to the Royal Medical Society of Paris in 1777 and as an honorary member of the Medical Society of London in 1787. His papers were read at the Royal Society of London, to which he was elected in 1756.

His interest in ailments was not confined simply to thinking about them. In his description of the Franklin Stove that he invented in 1742, he said that one of the stove's advantages was that the continual supply of fresh air it brought into the room made it ideal for caring for the sick. In 1751 he helped to found the Pennsylvania Hospital. The following year, he designed a flexible catheter for his ailing brother, had it constructed, and sent it to him. The Earl of Buchan credited Franklin with saving his life in 1759, after he had followed Franklin's advice to cure his fever.

Franklin thought and wrote extensively about the common cold in 1773. At a time when comparatively little was known about the spread of diseases, Franklin believed that colds and influenza were probably contagious, and that they were often transmitted between people who sat next to one another or were confined in the same room together. Among his suppositions in his "Preparatory Notes and Hints for Writing a Paper Concerning What is Called Catching a Cold" was that colds were probably spread "by particular effluvia in the air, from some unknown cause." That cause, we know today, is a transmittable virus. Another contributing factor, he thought, was the English lifestyle of "too full living with too little exercise."

A potential relationship between perspiration and colds also interested him. He believed that the perspiration that collects on old books, clothes that had been worn and sitting around for a long time, and beds that had not been slept on for a while contributed to the spread of colds. The consumption of animals that do not perspire, such as oysters and pork, could also be a factor. In March 1773 he described an experiment undertaken with a young doctor to compare his perspiration when he was clothed with his perspiration when he was unclothed. The doctor found that he sweated twice as much when he was unclothed. For good health, Franklin thought, people should allow themselves plenty of fresh air and free perspiration. Although it is now known that colds are spread by viruses, it has also been established that harmful toxins are eliminated from the body through perspiration.

Contrary to the prevailing wisdom of the time, he did not believe that cold or moist air necessarily contributed to colds. Franklin questioned the notion that colds were caused by spending time in cold weather or water, and he eventually came to believe that moist air had a beneficial effect on people's health rather than a detrimental one. He wrote to Barbeu-Dubourg, "I shall not attempt to explain why damp clothes occasion colds, rather than wet ones, because I doubt the fact; I imagine that neither one nor the other contribute to this effect, and that the causes of colds are totally independent of wet and even of cold."

John Adams recorded an account in which he and Franklin were forced to spend the night in a tiny room in an overcrowded inn. When they were ready to go to sleep, Adams started to shut the window for fear of becoming sick from the night air. Franklin insisted that it was healthier to leave it open, and the two men fell asleep while Franklin explained his beliefs on the spread of colds.

Other diseases interested Franklin, too. In a letter to John Perkins he wrote about the successes of smallpox vaccinations. He reported that in five smallpox epidemics, 800 people had been vaccinated, and only 4 had died. He was interested in reports of pokeweed as a cure for cancer. With Cadwallader Colden he discussed, among many other subjects, perspiration and the nature of the heart and circulatory system. Colden suggested that pores on the body perspire and absorb at the same time, and Franklin was pleased with this hypothesis. He outlined an experiment to test one particular point he doubted—that the direction of a small vessel where it joined to a larger one sufficed to produce absorption and perspiration. He also suggested to Colden that the heart did not merely cause blood to circulate by forcing it through the arteries, as was hypothesized by the anatomists he knew. He thought that "the ventricles of the heart, like syringes, *draw* when they dilate, as well as use force when they contract."

Around the time of his electrical experiments in Philadelphia, paralytics who had heard reports from Europe of electric shocks restoring feeling and movement came to him seeking treatment. His "method was, to place the patient first in a chair on an electric stool, and draw a number of large strong sparks from all parts of the affected limb or side. Then I fully charged two six gallon glass jars, each of which had about three square feet of surface coated and I sent the united shock of these through the affected limb or limbs, repeating the stroke commonly three times each day."

The experiments at first seemed to have an effect on a patient. In the short term, some reported increased warmth in their limbs, prickling sensations at night, and increased ability to move voluntarily. The immediate successes following treatment, however, turned out to be temporary. The patients quickly grew weary from the shocks, became discouraged, and relapsed to their former paralysis. Franklin said that he had never witnessed any improvement at all after the fifth day of treatment, but he left room for the possibility of successes with different methods of application.

Through various observations and experiences, he came to believe that lead was harmful. After setting his types in front of a fire to dry and working with them while they were warm, he sometimes felt pain in his hands. An acquaintance told him that others had almost lost their hands from this practice. Franklin believed that the accidental consumption of lead caused "dry belly ache," or "colica pictonum." He recounted to Benjamin Vaughan in 1786 a story he had heard about a European family that suffered from the dry belly ache. The family's water supply came from rainwater that dripped off a lead roof. They drank it without suffering harm for several years, but when a newly planted tree shed leaves on the roof, it was believed, an acid corroded the lead, and small particles of it entered the water supply, causing the dry belly ache.

In 1784 Franklin, along with several others, was chosen as an investigator into the controversial theories of the Austrian Friedrich Anton Mesmer (1734–1815), who believed that a universal magnetic fluid flowed throughout bodies. Mesmer, who had attracted a following in France, attempted to cure diseases by altering the flow of "animal magnetism" in his patients, which he claimed to accomplish in group séancelike treatment sessions. Several tests conducted by one of his disciples were carried out at Franklin's living quarters in Passy, near Paris. Franklin, who had been skeptical to begin with, agreed with his fellow investigators that there was no proof for Mesmer's theories. Mesmer soon fell into disrepute.

Franklin's intentions were less than serious when he published this illustrated chart showing the influences that certain planets and stars have on different parts of the body in **Poor Richard's Almanack.**

Franklin kept notes on his own health in France. Two particular health problems afflicted him—the gout and a bladder stone. During a spell of gout in France, he wrote his "Dialogue between Franklin and the Gout" (1780), in which "the gout," personified, used Franklin's own beliefs about health to explain to him why he was sick. "What have I done to merit these cruel sufferings?" Franklin asked. The gout replied, "Many things; you have ate and drank too freely, and too much indulged those legs of yours in their indolence." Franklin refused to have surgery for his bladder stone, and during one bout in 1784, he told John Jay: "You may judge that my disease is not very grievous, since I am more afraid of the medicines than the malady."

Meteorology

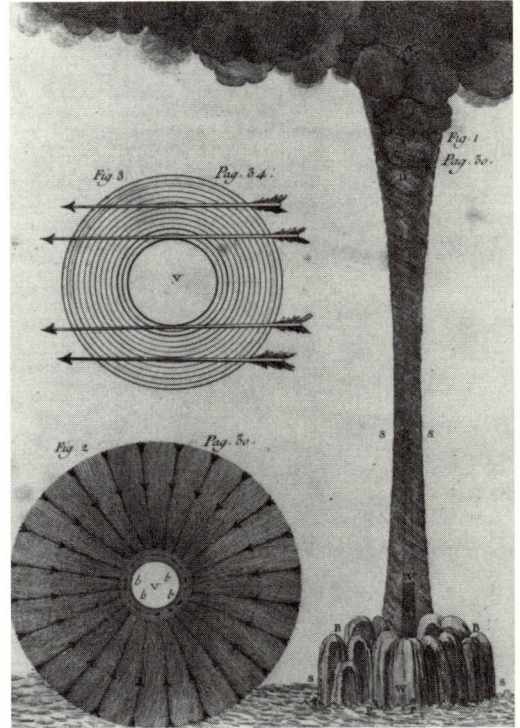

Waterspout, illustrating Benjamin Franklin's discussion of terrors at sea, c. 1753. Engraving by Martinet in Oeuvres de M. Franklin, *1773. Vol IX, plate 4.*

Weather was one of the many scientific subjects that interested Franklin. He wrote papers and letters on the formation of clouds, air temperature, evaporation, humidity, storms, lightning, whirlwinds (tornadoes), waterspouts, and hurricanes, many of which were sent to his philosophical and scientific acquaintances and read at the Royal Society of London.

Franklin lived during a time when advances in meteorology were made as a result of the development of improved atmospheric measuring instruments. Galileo had invented the first thermometer in 1593. It was not very accurate and was followed by an improved alcohol thermometer in 1641. The mercury thermometer was not introduced until Franklin's lifetime (1714, by Gabriel Fahrenheit). A barometer, used to measure air pressure, was invented in 1643.

Franklin's extensive travels enabled him to observe weather conditions in many different places. One area of his curiosity was the origin of the violent, lengthy storms in the northeastern United States, which he came to believe originated in the Southwest. He began to think about the storms after he had tried to watch a lunar eclipse at nine o'clock one night, and a nasty storm spoiled his plans. He later read an account of the eclipse in Boston, where people had seen it clearly. If the storm had come from the northeast, it would have been in Boston before it arrived in Philadelphia and would have obscured the celestial event.

After writing to his brother in Boston and obtaining accounts of the storm from other colonists, he was able to form an idea of the general path it had taken. He estimated that it had traveled about 100 miles per hour in a northeasterly direction. He did not believe that all storms in Philadelphia had their origins in the Southwest—Franklin proposed a different and detailed explanation for the "thunder-gusts," or short thunder-and-lightning storms, in a letter to John Mitchell.

Franklin also spent some time trying to unravel the mysteries of waterspouts and whirlwinds (tornadoes). He supposed them to be similar. On one occasion he had the opportunity to follow a developing whirlwind. While traveling through Maryland, he and his companions saw a small whirlwind developing in front of them. Franklin began to follow it. He tried to break it up by flinging his whip through it and found that repeated swings had no effect. It swirled the dust under it, and it grew progressively larger and whirled very rapidly, sucking up leaves as it entered the woods. Franklin noted that a person could follow its progression on foot, but it spun much more rapidly. He deduced by observing the leaves that the current of air that drove them moved "upwards in a spiral line."

In his "Physical and Meteorological Observations, Conjectures, and Suppositions," Franklin wrote out a number of his scientific speculations on weather. He said that air and water attract one another, and that water dissolves in air. When all of the air particles become overwhelmed with too many water particles, precipitation—or rain—results. Franklin observed that "very warm air, clear though supporting a very great quantity of moisture, will grow turbid and cloudy on the mixture of a colder air: as foggy, turbid air will grow clear by warming. . . . Thus the sun, shining on a morning fog, dissipates it; clouds are seen to waste in a sunshiny day."

He also believed that the part of the Earth closest to the surface is heated the most by the Sun's rays because, in addition to receiving direct sunlight, rays are reflected there. The higher regions of the Earth were colder because they received neither the warmth from the Earth nor the reflected rays at the surface, and this accounted for both snowy mountaintops and hail in summer weather.

In 1784, while in Passy, France, pursuing thoughts that he had much earlier, he wrote about his belief that raindrops and hailstones became gradually enlarged as they fell to Earth. "In descending," he wrote, "both the drop of water and the grain of ice are augmented by particles of the vapor they pass through in falling, and which they condense by their coldness, and attach to themselves."

Related entries:
Astronomy
Electricity

Suggestions for further reading:
"To Cadwallader Colden," December 6, 1753 (Labaree et al., vol. 5).
"To John Mitchell," 1749 (Labaree et al., vol. 3).
"To Peter Collinson," August 25, 1755 (Labaree et al., vol. 6).

Music

See **Armonica; Franklin, Peter; Kames, Lord (Henry Home).**

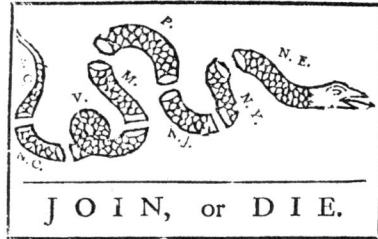

JOIN, or DIE.

Native Americans

The native inhabitants of Franklin's developing nation interested him throughout his life. As a philosopher, he studied their manners, customs, and ways. As a politician, he negotiated with and sought means to purchase new territory from them. Living in Philadelphia, the Indians with whom Franklin was chiefly concerned were the Six Nations, a confederacy originating in the New York area of six North American tribes. The confederacy began as the Five Nations in the 1500s—a league of the Seneca, Cayuga, Mohawk, Oneida, and Onondaga Indians. In the early 1700s the Tuscaroras joined, establishing the influential League of Six Nations. These tribes were all of the Iroquoian language family, and although they totaled less than 25,000 in number at their peak, they were politically influential during the years preceding the American Revolution. Franklin read with great interest *History of the Five Indian Nations* (1727), a book written by Cadwallader Colden, one of his correspondents and a future lieutenant governor of New York.

The relationship between the Six Nations and the European settlers varied. In general these tribes chose to side with the British—first against the French in the French and Indian War, and then against the Americans during the Revolutionary War. However, the Six Nations generally resented the continuing encroachment of English traders and settlers on their territories, and they were not always loyal allies. In Franklin's 1747 pamphlet "Plain Truth," he warned that "The French know the power and importance of the Six Nations, and spare no artifice, pains or expense, to gain them their interest." In 1756 he wrote to Thomas Pownall (1722–1805), a future governor of Massachusetts, with skepticism regarding a treaty that had recently been negotiated at Easton. "For my own part," he wrote, "I make no doubt but the Six Nations have privily encouraged [other] Indians to fall on us. They have taken no step to defend us, as their allies, nor to prevent the mischief done us."

In 1753 Franklin, Richard Peters, and Isaac Norris (then speaker of the Pennsylvania Assembly) negotiated a treaty at Carlisle with prominent members of the Six Nations and other Indians. After wading through the required ceremonies, which had already been held up because of the delayed arrival of the necessary goods, the negotiators got down to business. The enemy of the colonists on the horizon at that time was not England but France. The Indians represented here were alarmed at French advances toward the Ohio Valley, as were the English. But the Indians also resented the incursion of Pennsylvania traders into their territory. They insisted on allowing only three trading posts. After the negotiations Franklin wrote to James

The defeat of General Braddock in the French and Indian War in Virginia in 1755. Wood engraving by J. Andrew in **Ballou's Pictorial,** *July 7, 1855.*

Bowdoin that the Indians "complained much of the abuses they suffer from our traders, and earnestly requested us to put the trade under some regulation." In the years preceding the French and Indian War, he believed that the English should sell goods to the Indians as cheaply and as fairly as possible, thereby securing their loyalty and underselling the French.

At the end of the negotiations, some of the Indians, who had not been allowed to consume rum during the talks, drank too much of it and grew violent toward one another. No harm was done to the others present, who ignored them, but the scene made an impression on Franklin. Franklin had always believed in moderation when it came to alcohol and had lost friends and partnerships to drunkenness. He was aware of the devastating effect that rum had on the Indians. He wrote many years later in his *Autobiography* that rum had "already annihilated all the tribes who formerly inhabited the sea coast."

The Albany Congress, where Franklin presented his "Plan of Union" for the colo-

nies, met in 1754 to discuss the looming war with the French. Franklin was one of the most ardent supporters of a union and believed that official unity would give the English more credibility with their Indian allies and present a bigger threat to their French and Indian enemies. His plan was unsuccessful in the end. Negotiators also concluded a treaty with the Six Nations that essentially tricked them into giving up more land than they were willing to part with. This use of deception was a poor decision, for its unfairness and for the resentment it generated among the Indians the English needed as their allies. The French and Indian War began the same year.

The year 1755 brought the disastrous defeat of the English General Edward Braddock, who perished shortly after a surprise Indian and French attack on his way to Fort Duquesne. Franklin had earlier warned him of this common Indian war tactic, but the confident general had "smiled at my ignorance, and replied, 'These savages may, indeed, be a formidable enemy to your raw American militia, but upon the king's regular and disciplined troops, sir, it is impossible they should make any impression.'" (For a fuller account of Franklin's involvement in the French and Indian War, *see* French and Indian War.

The Treaty of Paris in 1763 ended the war between the French and the British. However, brutal warfare between the English and enemy Indians continued on both sides and reached into western Pennsylvania. Frontier settlers fled east. These conflicts spurred widespread resentment toward Indians in Pennsylvania. Accusations against both Quakers and Indians flew. Enemies of the Quakers, who on religious principle refused to fight, spread rumors that Quakers were giving gifts to hostile Indians and provoking them to attack other white settlers. A flustered Franklin wrote to his friend Dr. John Fothergill (a Quaker in England), "Would you think it possible that thousands even here should be made to believe this, and many hundreds of them be raised in arms, not only to kill some converted Indians, supposed to be under the Quakers' protection, but to punish the Quakers that were supposed to give that protection?"

Violence erupted when a group of armed settlers from the Donegal and Paxton Townships, known as the Paxton Boys, brutally massacred a small band of peaceful Conestoga Indians in two separate attacks. Franklin was outraged not only by the unprovoked murders of the men, women, and children but also by the support of many of his fellow townspeople for the violent action. He wrote and printed a pamphlet entitled "A Narrative of the Late Massacres in Lancaster County" (1764), in which he vividly recounted the events and brutality of the murders and compared the high regard for strangers held by other cultures around the world to the baseness of the "Christian white savages" who committed the murders. It began:

These Indians were the remains of a tribe of the Six Nations, settled at Conestogoe, and thence called Conestogoe Indians. On the first arrival of the English in Pennsylvania, messengers from this tribe came to welcome them, with presents of venison, corn, and skins; and the whole tribe entered into a treaty of friendship with the first proprietor, William Penn, which was to last "as long as the sun should shine, or the waters run in the rivers."

Franklin strongly criticized those who would punish all people of one race for the actions of a few.

When the Paxton Boys, now enlarged in number, threatened another group of peaceful Indians, who were Moravian converts living under government protection in Philadelphia, Franklin organized a voluntary association of hundreds of people for their defense. Governor John Penn (one of Franklin's chief political enemies) took refuge in his house for two days. Franklin and three others rode out to meet the gang, and they succeeded in averting the conflict by convincing them that the Indians were well defended. This action, to which there was vocal opposition, cost Franklin his seat and speakership in the Pennsylvania Assembly. Governor Penn was embarrassed by the event and had long resented Franklin's opposition to the proprietors, and he used his power to discredit Franklin. Many years later, Franklin heard word in France that some of the same Moravian Indians had been murdered and were again under threat of violence. Franklin assured his friend James Hutton in 1782, "I shall not fail to write the government of America, urging that effectual care may be taken to protect and save the remainder of those unhappy people."

A peace treaty concluded at Niagara in 1764 ended the war with all Indians who had been at war with the British. Franklin thought that the terms were too easy on the Indians and might leave the door open for another war. Another treaty with the Six Nations at Fort Stanwix in 1768 expanded English territory and opened a new opportunity for settlements on the western lands, which Franklin had long been interested in.

He and his son William became involved in the Grand Ohio Company, which wanted to purchase some of the western land from the Crown and establish English settlements, "with the approbation of the Indians." Some members of Parliament embraced the idea of expanding the British Empire into these territories. Among them was William Petty, the Earl of Shelburne, who asked Franklin to critique a "Plan for Regulating Indian Affairs" in 1767.

Others in England were reluctant to approve the proposal. Franklin wrote in 1768 to the Committee of Correspondence in Pennsylvania: "Government here begins to grow tired of the enormous expense of Indian affairs, and of maintaining posts in the Indian country." He hoped that Pennsylvania would deal fairly with Indians, because the British were not about to send help if renewed conflicts broke out. Colonial resistance to the Stamp Act (1765) had stirred up resentment toward America in the English government, and Franklin feared that a disgruntled government could use an Indian attack to chastise the colonists and prove that America depended on England for protection.

Franklin believed that English frontier traders, "the most vicious and abandoned wretches of our nation," were coming dangerously close to provoking another war. In 1766 he had written to Sir William Johnson (1715–1774), the British-appointed superintendent of affairs with the Six Nations, "It grieves me to hear that our frontier people are yet greater barbarians than the Indians, and continue to murder them in time of peace." He hoped that negotiations would avert another war and prevent such future "horrid outrages."

The Revolutionary War brought new problems. The Six Nations, for the most part, sided with the British against the colonists. Britain paid Indians to scalp rebel colonists who rebelled against its authority, a practice that brought unanimous outrage in America and harsh words in the Declaration of Independence. Franklin sharply criticized the English-instigated scalpings from his press in Passy, France. In 1782 he printed a fictitious "Supplement to the Boston Independent Chronicle," which he designed to look like a genuine Boston newspaper. It contained a graphic and detailed account of American scalps that had been ordered by the British. A fictitious letter read, in part: "At the request of the Seneca chiefs, I send herewith to your excellency, under the care of James Boyd, eight packs of scalps, cured, dried, hooped, and painted, with all the Indian triumphal marks...." It described the scalps in detail, including some that had been "ripped out of their mothers' bellies." Franklin sent copies to Charles W. F. Dumas in Holland, explaining that the form of the account was fictitious, but not the substance of it.

The war had a disastrous effect on the population and territory of the Six Nations. In 1779 war with the Americans pushed some of them north into Ontario. They were forced to surrender land to the new country after the war, and their dwindling numbers now came to fewer than 8,000. Two treaties were negotiated and signed between the Six Nations and the United States during the remainder of Franklin's life—one in 1784 and the other in 1789. (One of the negotiators at the 1784 treaty was Franklin's constant political critic, Arthur Lee.) In the 1784 treaty the United States of America agreed to terms of peace and boundaries with the Six Nations. The treaty in 1789 essentially renewed the terms of the 1784 treaty, with the exception of the Mohawks, who chose not to participate.

After the war, Scotosh, son of the half-king of the Wyandot Nation, visited Franklin en route to New York to speak to Congress. He acquainted Franklin, who was then president of the Supreme Executive Council of Pennsylvania, with concerns that his people had about Americans measuring new territory. Franklin communicated the message to the Council and delivered its reply to Scotosh. Pennsylvania, it said, did not measure any land

THE
TREATY
HELD WITH THE
INDIANS
OF THE
SIX NATIONS,
AT
PHILADELPHIA,
In JULY, 1742.

PHILADELPHIA:
Printed and Sold by B. FRANKLIN, at the New-Printing-Office, near the Market. M,DCC,XLIII.

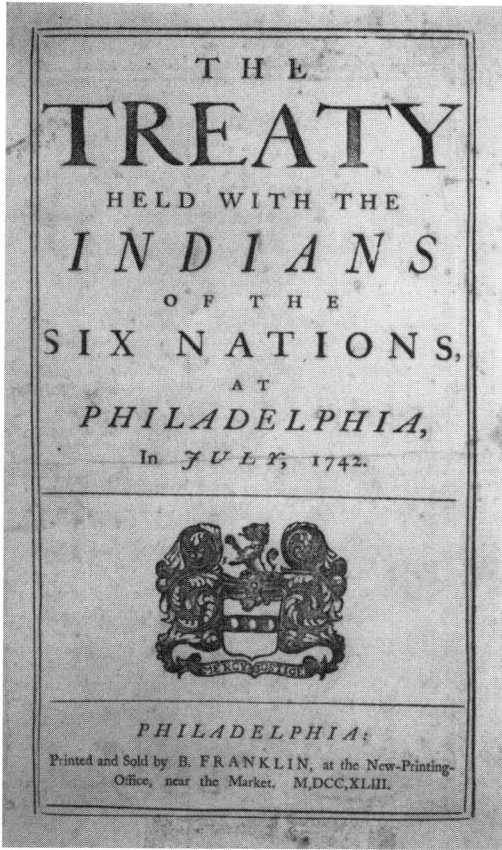

Title page of "The Treaty Held with the Indians of the Six Nations at Philadelphia in July 1742." Woodcut by Benjamin Franklin, 1743.

that had not been fairly bought from the Six Nations. The territory of which Scotosh spoke was being measured by Congress, to which he should relate the concerns. Franklin wrote a letter of introduction for him to Charles Thomson.

In 1787 Georgia had been involved in a war with the Creek Indians. Lamenting the conflict, Franklin wrote to the governor of that state: "During the course of a long life in which I have made observations on public affairs, it has appeared to me that almost every war between the Indians and whites has been occasioned by some injustice of the latter towards the former." He thought it was fruitless to engage in territorial disputes with Indians, who were often willing to sell land at good prices. To defend towns against In-

dian attacks, Franklin thought the New England mode of settling land was ideal. Land was granted in townships six miles square for 60 families, and houses were organized so that attackers from any direction could be seen by others. A stockaded school in the center of the town served as a protective fortress in times of need.

Franklin was also interested in Indian culture and languages. As a printer, he had published Indian treaties. He was fascinated by the differences that he saw between Indians and Europeans. "They are not deficient in natural understanding," he wrote to Richard Jackson in 1753, "and yet they have never shown any inclination to change their manner of life for ours, or to learn any of our arts." He explained characteristics of Indian languages to his European friends. In 1787 he sent the Marquis de Lafayette a vocabulary of Delaware and Shawnee words that he had obtained for him from an acquaintance. He wrote "Remarks Concerning the Savages of North America" ("Savages, we call them, because their manners differ from ours, which we think the perfection of civility; they think the same of theirs.") for his curious French friends sometime around 1784. He described for them differences in English and Indian customs and civilities. Franklin argued that all peoples are rude in some manner, including the English. As an example, he compared the treatment of strangers entering English and Indian towns. The Indians, he said, hid behind bushes to catch a glimpse of the curious visitors without offending them. The English, in contrast, rudely descended on visitors and stared at them.

On the whole, Franklin respected Native Americans and believed in treating them fairly, but he thought they were different from his own people. He respected the differences and studied them with interest. He supported war against some of them when he thought it was necessary to defend his own people, and he sought to protect other Native Americans against the abuses of members of his own nation.

Suggestions for further reading:
    Historical Society of Pennsylvania. 1938.
    Indian Treaties Printed by Benjamin Franklin.
    Philadelphia: Historical Society of Penn-
    sylvania.
    Johansen, Bruce E. 1982. *Forgotten Founders:*
    Benjamin Franklin, the Iroquois, and the Rationale
    for the American Revolution. Ipswich, Mass.:
    Gambit.
    "A Narrative of the Late Massacres," 1764
    (Labaree et al., vol. 13).
    "Remarks on the Plan for Regulating the
    Indian Trade," 1767 (Labaree et al., vol. 13).

Navigation

During Franklin's eight transatlantic voyages, he carefully observed the Gulf Stream, air and water temperatures, the efficiency of ships, wind speed, and many other matters related to navigation. He wrote two significant pieces related to navigation, his *Journal of a Voyage from London to Philadelphia* (1726) and *Maritime Observations* (1785). He filled the first, written when he was 20 years old, with general observations on day-to-day life at sea, curious creatures they encountered, and interesting meteorological and celestial events he witnessed. The second, written when he was 79, was a much more technical piece.

He kept the *Journal* during his second voyage, which began in England and ended in Philadelphia. A hard west wind kept them around the Isle of Wight for several days. He visited a harbor at Portsmouth and collected stories from its inhabitants about the harshness of a former lieutenant governor, Sir John Gibson (1637–1717). Franklin visited Carisbrooke Castle, where Charles I was confined. At Yarmouth, Franklin and three oth-

ers ventured inland and were forced to cross a stream at night to return. The local ferry boy preferred to sleep rather than to carry them across, so, with a great deal of trouble, Franklin and his companions succeeded in loosing his boat. The three started rowing, but the tide had risen so high on the banks that they could not see where they were rowing. About halfway across, they hit a mud bank and broke one of their oars. Finally, two of the three got out of the boat and pulled it to deeper water. "With much ado," they reached the shore.

Monotony soon set in after the voyage got under way. The ship's "court of justice" punished one of the crew members for marking cards. "I rise in the morning and read for an hour or two," Franklin recorded on August 25, "perhaps, and then reading grows tiresome. Want of exercise occasions want of appetite, so that eating and drinking afford but little pleasure. I tire myself with playing at draughts [checkers], then I go to cards; nay, there is no play so trifling or childish, but we fly to it for entertainment."

Franklin recorded sundry natural curiosities. On August 30 he saw a night rainbow, "The first time I ever saw a rainbow in the night, caused by the moon." On several days the crew caught dolphins. On September 14 they witnessed a partial solar eclipse: "At least ten parts of twelve of [the Sun] were hid from our eyes, and we were apprehensive [it] would have been totally darkened." On September 21 a shark began following the ship, and it had gone by the next day. Franklin stayed up to watch a partial lunar eclipse on September 30.

The vessel met other ships during the voyage, which delighted the crew. "There is really something strangely cheering to the spirits in the meeting of a ship at sea, containing a society of creatures of the same species and in the same circumstances with ourselves, after we had been long separated and excommunicated as it were from the rest of mankind," Franklin noted on September 23 upon meeting a ship bound for New York from Dublin.

On September 28 Franklin found peculiar "vegetable animals" in some gulf weed they had taken into the ship. "[I]t had a leaf about three quarters of an inch long, indented like a saw, and a small yellow berry, filled with nothing but the wind; besides which it bore fruit of the animal kind, very surprising to see. It was a small shell-fish like a heart, the stalk by which it proceeded from the branch being partly of a grisly kind." Franklin spotted a more mature crab crawling on the branch and thought the others must be younger versions of the mature one. He resolved to keep the branch and crabs in salt water until they came ashore. Franklin found another crab the next day, but the rest of the small ones died. He found more crabs in a fresh batch of gulf weed he took in on September 30, and he put one of them in a glass vial with salt water to preserve it. The crew, anxious to hit land, passed Newcastle and reached Chester on October 11.

On Franklin's eighth and final voyage, he wrote "Maritime Observations" for Julien-David Le Roy (1724–1803), a brother of his friend Jean-Baptiste Le Roy, who was himself interested in navigation. He dedicated the first part of the essay to his thoughts on ships, sails, and nautical technology. "Those mathematicians who have endeavored to improve the swiftness of vessels by calculating to find the form of least resistance," Franklin thought, "seem to have considered a ship as a body moving through one fluid only, the water; and to have given little attention to the circumstance of her moving through another fluid, the air." He proposed means of reducing air resistance without diminishing the power of the wind on the sails: dividing one large sail into four smaller ones. With an experiment using two playing cards, one cut and the other uncut, he found that "the sum of the resistances to the pieces of the cut card is not equal to the resistance of the whole one." Based on the success of this experiment and another one that tested air resistance, he suggested testing the idea on a larger scale.

Franklin also tried to explain why leaky ships found abandoned at sea sometimes remained afloat. He asserted that the water gushed in more rapidly at first, and, once it reached a certain level, it slowed. Pumps that could not keep up with incoming water at first might be able to do so later, when the rate of its entry into the ship slowed, and the ships' crews often deserted them prematurely. Other factors that might contribute to keeping a leaky ship afloat included empty casks and barrels that float when immersed in water, and incoming water dissolving heavy cargoes like salt and sugar, rendering the boat lighter. Franklin suggested implementing the Chinese practice of dividing the hold of ships into separate compartments, so that if one compartment sprung a leak, water would not gush into the entire hold.

Next Franklin proposed remedies for other sea catastrophes: "1. Oversetting by sudden flaws of wind, or by carrying sail beyond the bearing. 2. Fire by accident or carelessness. 3. A heavy stroke of lightning, making a breach in the ship, or firing the powder. 4. Meeting and shocking other ships in the night. 5. Meeting in the night with islands of ice." He offered alterations in ship design to guard against oversetting. To prevent the mischiefs of fires, Franklin thought, "It is high time to make it a general rule, that all the ship's store of spirits should be carried in bottles." Lightning rods would protect ships from being struck. A lookout-before and bells or drums could help prevent night accidents; a lookout-before could also spot blocks of ice.

Franklin offered observations on the Gulf Stream and on ships' motion and design as well as suggestions for surviving shipwrecks. He was interested in a new windmill-type propulsion apparatus that he had seen exhibited on the Seine River and thought that a similar one might be employed to move water instead of air. He attempted to explain why greasing the bottom of ships sped up the vessel. To stop a ship during a storm and prevent it from going off course, Franklin suggested and described a "swimming anchor." Shipwrecked seafarers, he suggested, could make an emergency compass by floating a magnetized needle on a cup of water. It would generally point north. A person who could swim could save energy by floating on his or her back and raising in the air a handkerchief formed into a kite.

Passengers, Franklin suggested, should not let their friends in on their travel plans too far in advance. Friends would only trouble them with visits and interrupt their preparations. Passengers should consider bringing their own provisions, as those on the ship were generally poor. Turkeys and chickens occasioned too much trouble; sheep and hogs provided better meat at sea. Passengers with extra provisions should share with poorer ones to boost morale, prevent sickness, and so forth. A remedy for the notoriously poor ship cooks was to do a little of their own cooking with a spirit-lamp and blaze pan. Cider best quenched the thirst occasioned by salt meat and fish, Franklin asserted. To prevent spilling and scalding from a large pot of soup, Franklin suggested that "potters and pewterers" design a set of small bowls united together, so that if a sudden motion of the ship caused it to tip, the soup stayed in the bowls.

Franklin ended his essay with his opinions on the utility of navigation and commerce. It was useful, he conceded, in alleviating the terrible consequences of famine. However, overseas trade promoted human misery in the transportation of slaves and superfluities, such as tobacco and sugar. He agreed with "an eminent French moralist" who said "that when he considers the wars we excite in Africa to obtain slaves, the numbers necessarily slain in those wars, the many prisoners who perish at sea by sickness, bad provisions, foul air . . . in the transportation, and how many afterwards die from the hardships of slavery, he cannot look upon a piece of sugar without conceiving it stained with spots of human blood!" If he factored in the European wars over the sugar islands, and those who perish in them, "he might have seen his sugar not merely spotted, but thoroughly dyed scarlet in grain."

Appended to the essay were "Remarks upon the Navigation from Newfoundland to New York, in Order to Avoid the Gulf Stream on One Hand, and, on the Other, the Shoals That Lie to the Southward of Nantucket and of St. George's Banks" and the records of the air temperature, water temperature, and other daily observations from his final voyage. The letter to Le Roy was translated into French and printed in Paris in 1787.

Related entries:
  Astronomy
  Gulf Stream
  Oil

Suggestions for further reading:
  "Journal of a Voyage," 1726 (Labaree et al., vol. 1).
  "To David Le Roy: Maritime Observations," 1785 (Smyth, vol. IX).

New England Courant

See **Franklin, James.**

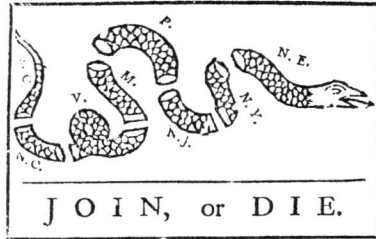

oil

Sometime in his youth, Franklin read an account in Pliny's writings of pouring oil on rough seawater during a storm to calm it. He first took a real interest in the effects of oil on water in 1757, when he noticed, on board a ship in a fleet of 96, that the water around 2 other ships was more tranquil than the water around the others. He asked the captain why this was so, and the captain replied that the cooks might have dumped greasy water, which greased the sides of the ships. Franklin doubted his explanation but, remembering Pliny's account, resolved to experiment with oil and water himself.

In 1762 he "first observed the wonderful quietness of oil on agitated water" aboard a ship bound for Philadelphia. In a lamp he made to use on the boat, he noticed that the oil on top of the water was tranquil, but the water underneath the oil was "in great commotion." The following morning, all of the oil had burned, and the water under it was still. When oil was put on top of the water again at night, the water resumed its state of agitation. When Franklin arrived home, he conducted an experiment with a tumbler of water. He swung it through the air with only water in it. The water kept its position. But when he added an equal amount of oil, the water became agitated underneath, and the oil remained calm as he swung the tumbler. Franklin could not explain the phenomenon, nor could he find anyone else who could. He sent a description of these observations to Dr. John Pringle in London.

Franklin first tried to calm water with oil on a pond in Clapham. The experiment failed on the first try—because he poured it in the wrong direction, and the wind blew it back to shore—but the second try was a success: "I then went to the windward side where [the waves] began to form; and there the oil, though not more than a tea spoonful, produced an instant calm over a space several yards square, which spread amazingly, and extended itself gradually till it reached the lee side, making all that quarter of the pond, perhaps half an acre, as smooth as a looking-glass." After this experiment, he began carrying a small amount of oil in an upper hollow joint in his bamboo cane whenever he traveled to the country. Franklin was also interested in the rapid spreading of a drop of oil when it hit water, which he thought was caused by repulsion between oil and water particles.

During a visit with Pringle to northern England, they stayed with the chemist and physician Dr. William Brownrigg (1711–1800), and Franklin calmed the rough waves of a lake with his oil. Pringle and Franklin subsequently visited the civil engineer John Smeaton (1724–1792) near Leeds, and Franklin performed his experiment there. He repeated the experiment at Wycombe in 1772 in the company of the Earl of Shelburne, the Abbé Morellet (with whom Franklin would later spend a significant amount of time in France), and others. Morellet described the incident: "A fresh breeze was ruffling the water. Franklin ascended a couple of hundred paces from the place where we stood, and, simulating the grimaces of a sorcerer, he shook three times upon the stream a cane [with his oil in the upper hollow joint] which he carried in his hand. Directly the waves diminished, and soon the surface was smooth as a mirror."

Over the years, Franklin gathered accounts of oil used to calm water. Fishermen in Bermuda calmed water with oil so that they could see the fish. Fishermen in Lisbon emptied oil into the water when they were ready to reenter the river. Mediterranean divers let small amounts of oil out of their mouths from time to time; the oil floated to the surface and smoothed it, enabling them to have the undisturbed light they needed. From a letter written to Count Bentnick in Holland, he learned of a Dutch ship that had been saved during a storm by calming waves with olive oil.

Franklin conducted another experiment with the assistance of the count's son, Captain Bentnick. He had read accounts of circumnavigators who wanted to land on islands during their voyages but were prevented from doing so by rough waves around the shore. He thought that oil poured continuously at a distance from the leeward shore might calm the surf enough for them to land. The younger Bentnick invited Franklin to Portsmouth to test his idea. In the experiment, the oil calmed the water for a stretch, but the waves remained violent at the shore. Franklin thought that they might have had more success if they had poured oil farther out from the shore, as the continual motion of waves that had already been raised needed a considerable distance to subside, or if they had used more oil.

Franklin's experiments were eagerly imitated by others. He related the history of his interest in oil and water in a lengthy letter to Brownrigg in 1773, and it was read before the Royal Society of London the following year.

Related entries:
France
Helvétius, Anne-Catherine de Ligniville d'Autricourt
Pringle, Sir John
Royal Society of London

Suggestions for further reading:
"To John Pringle," December 1, 1762 (Labaree et al., vol. 10).
"To William Brownrigg," November 7, 1773 (Labaree et al., vol. 20).

Oliver-Hutchinson Letters Affair

*I*n 1772, in an effort to prove to a skeptical Franklin that the coercive measures taken toward Massachusetts did not originate with the British ministry, an unidentified "gentleman of character and distinction" in England gave him a bundle of letters. Most of the letters were written by the royal governor of Massachusetts, Thomas Hutchinson, and the lieutenant governor, Andrew Oliver, and pertained to events that took place in Massachusetts between 1767 and 1769. At the time of their writing, Hutchinson was lieutenant governor and chief justice, and Oliver was secretary. The letters portrayed Massachusetts in a negative light and recommended that England send troops to that province—which England had already done by the time Franklin saw the letters. One of the letters suggested that "there must be an abridgement of what are called English liberties." Although the addresses on the letters had been removed when the unidentified source gave them to Franklin, they were supposed to have been written to Thomas Whately, a deceased member of Parliament.

It appeared to Franklin, as an agent of the province of Massachusetts, that it was his "duty to give my constituents an intelligence of such importance to their affairs. . . ." His source authorized him to send them to Boston on the conditions that they not be copied or printed, that they be returned, and that only a few notable people see them. Franklin, still hopeful of a reconciliation between England and the colonies, said he hoped that the letters would pacify resentment toward England and direct the blame to those who merited it. He sent them to Thomas Cushing in the Massachusetts Assembly, who showed them to others. The Committee of Correspondence read them, and they were later read to the entire Assembly. The Assembly's ensuing outrage at the governor's conduct prompted a series of resolves condemning Hutchinson and Oliver and a petition to the king to have them removed. The letters were published in a pamphlet, and they landed in England at about the same time as the Assembly's petition.

The publication of the letters sparked an unexpected near-tragedy. As people in England speculated on their source, a public quarrel erupted between William Whately, brother of the alleged original recipient of the letters, and John Temple, a former governor of New Hampshire, whom Whately accused of stealing them from his brother's papers. Some accused Whately, while Whately maintained that Temple was the only person who had been given access to the papers. Temple did not get the public apology he demanded from Whately and challenged him to a duel. The South Carolinian Ralph Izard, who later became a thorn in Franklin's side in France, delivered the challenge. At the duel, neither of them suffered injury from the gunfire, but Temple severely wounded Whately in the ensuing sword fight. Franklin, who did not know about the duel until afterward, had remained silent during the quarrel in the hope that it would die out, so as not to have to reveal sources. However, when newspapers reported that Whately was ready for a second duel when he recovered, Franklin wrote to the *Public Advertiser* claiming responsibility for sending the letters to Boston: "Finding that two gentlemen have been unfortunately engaged in a duel, about a transaction and its circumstances, of which both of them are totally ignorant and innocent; I think it incumbent upon me to declare (for the prevention of farther mischief . . .) that I alone am the person that obtained and transmitted to Boston the letters in question." Franklin further stated that the letters had never been in the possession of either Temple or Whately, and he signed it "B. Franklin, Agent for the House of Representatives of Massachusetts Bay."

Franklin's troubles were only beginning. Whately filed a chancery suit against Franklin, falsely accusing him of planning to publish his brother's letters and failing to return them when he had been asked to. Newspapers denounced him as an enemy to England. The Lords of the Committee for Plantation Affairs summoned him to the Cockpit, part of Whitehall, on January 11, 1774, at noon, for a hearing on the Massachusetts petition to remove Hutchinson and Oliver. They had also summoned William Bollan, another agent for Massachusetts, and the two men agreed that Bollan should speak in favor of the petition. They did not see the need for counsel and did not retain any. However, Franklin was informed the day before the hearing that Israel Mauduit, agent for Hutchinson and Oliver, had been granted permission to be heard by counsel—Alexander Wedderburn, the solicitor general.

When Franklin was called on to support the petition, he tried to defer to Bollan, but Bollan was refused the opportunity to speak. After Franklin offered the Assembly's resolutions, Wedderburn began asking him about his conduct in obtaining the letters. Franklin objected that he had not brought counsel because he had not thought he needed to, and he wanted to be heard with counsel. He was given three weeks and in the meantime retained John Dunning and John Lee, who assured Franklin that he was not legally required to answer questions about his conduct.

At the hearing at the Cockpit on January 29, 36 members of the Privy Council were present. Franklin had friends and sympathizers in attendance—Edmund Burke, Jeremy Bentham, Lord Shelburne (William Petty), Lord Le Despencer (Sir Francis Dashwood), and Joseph Priestley. But the day belonged to Wedderburn, who for an hour mercilessly condemned Massachusetts, its Assembly, and Franklin. Wedderburn, whose tirade was accompanied by laughter and applause from "their lordships," alleged that Franklin could not have obtained the letters honestly. He criticized Franklin for remaining silent before the Whately-Temple duel. According to Dr. Edward Bancroft (a future spy), Franklin held his composure, stood perfectly still, and showed no signs of emotion. Lord Shelburne was outraged at Wedderburn's conduct, as were Burke and Priestley. The following Monday, Franklin was fired from his position at the post office.

This event left an emotional scar on Franklin and further alienated him from England. After the examination, Franklin wrote a "Tract Relative to the Affair of Hutchinson's Letters" in which he explained his conduct, but it was never published during his lifetime. Whately's chancery suit was still pending when Franklin returned to America in 1775, and it was never heard. In 1778 Franklin wore the same Manchester velvet cloak he had worn at the Cockpit to the signing of the treaty of alliance with France "to give it its revenge."

Related entries:
Burke, Edmund
Dashwood, Sir Francis (Lord Le Despencer)
Great Britain
Post Office
Priestley, Dr. Joseph
Treaty of Alliance with France

Suggestion for further reading:
"Tract Relative to the Affair of Hutchinson's Letters," 1774 (Labaree et al., vol. 21).

"On the Causes and Cure of Smoky Chimneys"

See **Ingenhousz, Dr. Jan.**

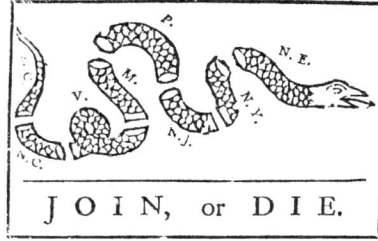

JOIN, or DIE.

P

Paine, Thomas
(1737–1809)

homas Paine was an acquaintance of Franklin's and was one of the most prominent voices in the colonies for independence from Britain. He was born in England and moved to Philadelphia in 1774, after Franklin recommended that he do so. Franklin sent with him letters of introduction. Although he was a native of England, his political sympathies were with the American colonists. In 1776 he wrote his famous *Common Sense,* which presented bold and somewhat inflammatory arguments in favor of independence from Britain. He reportedly sent the first copy of the pamphlet to Franklin.

Paine's pamphlet was extremely popular in the colonies and influenced the opinions of many Americans. Independence from England was inevitable, and the time was now, he insisted. He attacked England's constitution and hereditary monarchies: "[I]f we will suffer ourselves to examine the component parts of the English constitution, we shall find them to be the base remains of two ancient tyrannies, compounded with some new republican materials. First—The remains of monarchical tyranny in the person of the king. Secondly—The remains of aristocratical tyranny in the persons of the peers. Thirdly—The new republican materials, in the per-

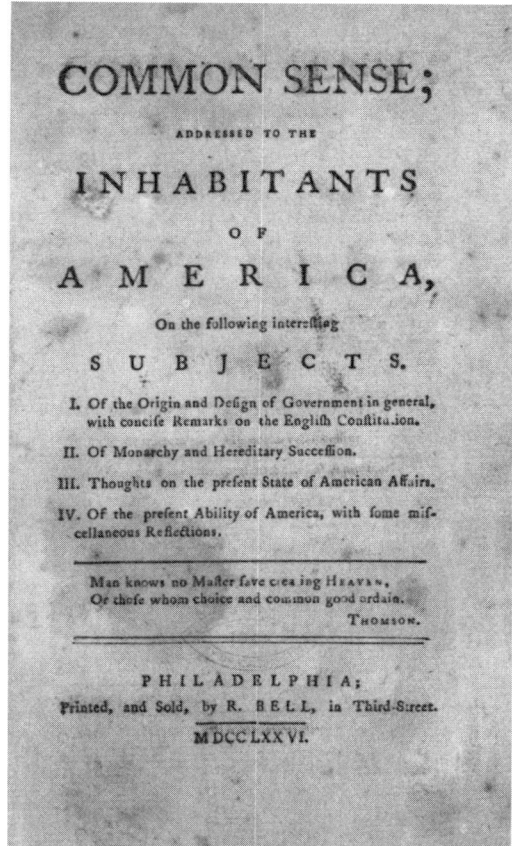

COMMON SENSE;

ADDRESSED TO THE

INHABITANTS

OF

AMERICA,

On the following interesting

SUBJECTS.

I. Of the Origin and Design of Government in general, with concise Remarks on the English Constitution.

II. Of Monarchy and Hereditary Succession.

III. Thoughts on the present State of American Affairs.

IV. Of the present Ability of America, with some miscellaneous Reflections.

Man knows no Master save creating HEAVEN, Or those whom choice and common good ordain.
THOMSON.

PHILADELPHIA;
Printed, and Sold, by R. BELL, in Third-Street.
MDCCLXXVI.

Title page of Thomas Paine's **Common Sense,** *printed in Philadelphia 1776.*

sons of the commons, on whose virtue depends the freedom of England. . . ." He also believed that America was capable of raising a military sufficient for the task of fighting against Britain.

During the Revolutionary War, he wrote his *American Crisis* papers. He served in the revolutionary army, served as secretary to the Congressional Committee on Foreign Affairs, and served as the clerk of the Pennsylvania Assembly for brief periods. He returned to Europe in 1787 and later became involved in the French Revolution. During this period, he wrote *The Rights of Man,* a critical response to Edmund Burke's *Reflections on the Revolution in France* (1790), an attack on the French Revolution. In France he became a member of the National Convention but was removed from it and arrested during the Terror under Maximilien Robespierre. He remained in a French prison for more than ten months, until James Madison obtained his release.

Though Paine said he believed in one God, he was attacked as an atheist and became very unpopular in the United States after his *Age of Reason* was published. Nevertheless, he returned to America at Thomas Jefferson's invitation in 1802. His life in the United States until his death was unpleasant, suffering as he did from poor health and the disrespect that accompanied *Age of Reason*.

Related entries:
  Burke, Edmund
  Declaration of Independence
  French Revolution
  Jefferson, Thomas
  Lafayette, Marquis de
  Revolutionary War

Suggestion for further reading:
  Paine, Thomas. 1976. *Common Sense*, edited by Isaac Kramnick. Harmondsworth, England: Penguin.

Paper Currency

*I*n 1723, the year that Franklin moved to Philadelphia, the Pennsylvania Assembly issued £15,000 in paper currency, to circulate for eight years. The balance of trade between the colonies and England leaned so far in England's favor that the colo-

nies held little gold or silver and had limited supplies of money with which to conduct internal commerce. Encouraged by the favorable response of the economy, people began to demand more paper currency. Franklin and his fellow members in the Junto discussed the issue of introducing more money to the colonies in 1728 and 1729. Franklin favored the idea, and to promote it, he wrote and published a pamphlet entitled "A Modest Inquiry into the Nature and Necessity of a Paper Currency" (1729).

He argued that "[t]here is a certain proportionate quantity of money requisite to carry on the trade of a country freely and currently; more than which would be of no advantage in trade, and less, if much less, exceedingly detrimental to it." He believed that an inadequate supply of money gave rise to high interest and usury, which were detrimental to the economy. Without enough money in circulation, people would not buy land when they could make more money by lending at high interest rates, and they would keep their money rather than risking it in trade. Money in short supply would occasion many other disadvantages: a diminished demand for goods, a proportionally higher rate of consumption of European goods, and a province unattractive to laborers and craftsmen—"[N]othing makes more bad paymasters than a general scarcity of money." Plentiful money would encourage trade, Franklin believed, and augment the demand for produce, which would in turn elevate the value of land required for the produce.

Franklin believed that a short money supply unnecessarily increased the cost of goods to consumers. In a country with no money, exchanges would have to be direct trades in goods. "Now, if it takes one fourth part of the time and labor of a country," he conjectured, "to exchange or get their commodities exchanged; then, in computing their value, that labor of exchanging must be added to the labor of manufacturing those commodities." Time and labor could be saved by introducing enough money, ensuring that goods could change hands at the value it cost to make them. People could use the additional time and labor to make one-fourth more goods. Franklin also objected to gold and silver as media of exchange: "But as silver itself is of no certain permanent value, being worth more or less according to its scarcity or plenty, therefore it seems requisite to fix upon something else, more proper to be made a measure of values, and this I take to be labor." Pennsylvania, he thought, could secure paper money with land instead of gold and silver.

Franklin thought moneylenders, lawyers (whose work benefited from indebtedness), people who were wealthy and disposed toward purchasing land, and people who owed their jobs to any of them would oppose the introduction of paper currency. Honest people who wanted to see trade expand and manufactures increase would support it.

The House passed a measure that provided for more paper currency, and Franklin acquired the lucrative job of printing it. Working under Samuel Keimer, he had already printed currency for New Jersey: "I contrived a copperplate press for it, the first that had been seen in the country; I cut several ornaments and checks for the bills." By the time he printed the Pennsylvania currency, he had set up his own shop with Hugh Meredith. Later he also printed money for Newcastle.

Other colonies issued their own paper currencies with varying degrees of success. In 1764 England passed the Currency Act, which placed restrictions on colonial paper money. Coupled with the Stamp Act, passed the next year, it generated resentment in the colonies. The Pennsylvania Assembly had sent Franklin to England to petition the Crown to take the government of Pennsylvania from the proprietors. He quickly found himself working for the repeal of the Stamp Act and the Currency Act; the Stamp Act was repealed in 1766, but the Currency Act remained on the books and was amended in 1773.

During the American Revolution the paper currency became a critical issue. Rather than raise taxes, Congress issued paper money to finance the war, and Franklin served on a committee that oversaw its printing. As a result of an overabundance of money (further aggravated by the issue of counterfeit currency issued into circulation by the British), the American currency depreciated to the point of crisis. Franklin said he had first advised that the bills bear interest, and later that no more bills be issued, and that Congress borrow on interest those that had already been issued. "This was not then approved of," he told Samuel Cooper in 1779, "and more bills were issued. When, from the too great quantity, they began to depreciate, we agreed to borrow on interest; and I proposed that in order to fix the value of the principal, the interest should be promised in hard dollars." Nevertheless, Franklin thought, "This currency, as we manage it, is a wonderful machine. It performs its office when we issue it; it pays and clothes troops, and provides victuals and ammunition; and when we are obliged to issue a quantity excessive, it pays itself off by depreciation."

Related entries:
Printing
Revolutionary War

Suggestions for further reading:
Carey, Lewis J. 1928. *Franklin's Economic Views.* Garden City, N.Y.: Doubleday, Doran & Co.
"The Nature and Necessity of a Paper Currency," 1729 (Labaree et al., vol. 1).
"Of the Paper Money of the United States of America," 1784 (Smyth, vol. IX).
"Remarks and Facts Relative to American Paper Money," March 11, 1767 (Labaree et al., vol. 14).

Parker, James (1714–1770)

*I*n 1742 Franklin entered into a printing partnership with James Parker, a former apprentice of William Bradford originally from New Jersey. The terms of the partnership were similar to those Franklin used in his other partnerships. He provided Parker with materials to set up in New York, paid one-third of the operating expenses, and received one-third of the profits. The partnership was one of Franklin's most successful ventures. In spite of his pessimism, Parker was a talented printer and "a very honest, punctual man." He ran the *New York Gazette,* later established the *Connecticut Gazette* and other colonial papers, and handled printing for the colonies of New York and New Jersey, and for Yale College. Benjamin Mecom, Franklin's nephew, served as his apprentice before his uncle set him up in a printing house in Antigua.

Parker and Franklin also traded thoughts on political and philosophical matters, such as a plan for uniting the colonies and electricity. In 1752 Parker published a controversial religious article in the *New York Gazette.* "I cannot conceive how he was prevailed on to do it," Franklin wrote to Cadwallader Colden, "as I know him to be a thorough believer himself, and averse to everything that is commonly called freethinking. He is now much in his penitentials. . . . " Parker published a response to complaints in the *Gazette,* saying: "[T]hough that piece is not at all agreeable to [the printer's] religious principles, yet he is willing to give the adversaries to Christianity a fair hearing, and such can only conduce to make it shine brighter. . . . "

Parker became controller of the post office in North America in 1757 and later became a judge.

Related entries:
Mecom, Jane Franklin
Post Office
Printing

Suggestion for further reading:
"Artices of Agreement with James Parker," February 20, 1741/1742 (Labaree et al., vol. 2).

Penn, Richard

See **Penn, Thomas.**

Penn, Thomas (1702–1775)

Before he became embroiled in controversies surrounding the American Revolution, Franklin played a prominent part in a lengthy political dispute with the proprietors of Pennsylvania and their supporters. The first proprietor of the Pennsylvania land was William Penn (1644–1718), a Quaker to whom the king had granted a land charter in 1681. He named the province in honor of his father. The Penns, who spent much of their time in England, had controlled Pennsylvania since, and their estates included millions of acres of land. Upon William's death, proprietorship passed to his three sons, John, Thomas, and Richard. After the death of John, the eldest, in 1746, Thomas controlled three-fourths of the original land, and Richard controlled the rest. Thomas was most involved in the province's affairs, and in time he and Franklin developed a deep and mutual animosity toward one another.

Franklin played a key role in long disputes between the Pennsylvania Assembly, to which he was elected in 1751, and the Penn sons. Government under them was set up with a deputy governor, appointed and carefully instructed by the proprietors, and an Assembly made up of representatives from the area that paid the deputy governor's salary. Disputes arose when the proprietors refused to pay taxes on their property, especially in times when extra money was needed to defend Pennsylvania. Franklin and many others believed that proprietary lands should be taxed along with everyone else's, and later that "government and property of a province should not be in the same family. 'Tis too much weight on one scale." The Assembly and the proprietary interests also wrangled over the issue of paper currency, and underneath this ongoing dispute was a conflict in the understanding of the boundaries between the Assembly's power and the proprietors'.

Thomas's suspicions of Franklin began when the latter organized an extra governmental voluntary militia to defend the province from French and Spanish privateers in 1747. Franklin had acted after the Assembly (of which he was not yet a member) and the governor remained deadlocked in a needed effort to organize some sort of defense against the looming threat. Penn, however, viewed the militia as an encroachment on governmental authority and feared it might set a dangerous precedent. After Franklin was elected to the Assembly in 1751, he began to push for the right to tax the Penns' estates. Thomas's trusted correspondents, including Secretary Richard Peters and William Smith (a former friend of Franklin's who had obtained his post as provost of the Philadelphia Academy with Franklin's assistance), sent frequent reports of Franklin's intrigues to him in England.

During Franklin's years in the Assembly, the debate over taxing the proprietary lands became most heated when the colonists were threatened with attacks during the French and Indian War. Franklin wrote in his *Autobiography:* "These public quarrels were all at bottom owing to the proprietaries, our hereditary governors, who, when any expense was to be incurred for the defense of their province, with incredible meanness instructed their deputies to pass no act for levying the necessary taxes, unless their vast estates in the same act were expressly excused."

After the defeat of General Edward Braddock in the midst of the French and Indian War, the threatened province desperately needed a plan for defense. The Penns gave in to criticism and donated £5,000, still refusing to pay taxes. In the emergency situation, the Assembly passed a £55,000 appropriations bill, as well as a militia bill Franklin had drawn up. The same quarrel erupted again, and in 1757 the Assembly dispatched Franklin to England to petition the king to allow them to tax the proprietary lands.

With the advice and help of his friend Dr. John Fothergill, Franklin negotiated first with the proprietors. Franklin found Thomas even more disagreeable in person than he had imagined. Penn asked Franklin for written complaints, which Franklin delivered to him. After a long delay, Penn maintained that the complaints were groundless. During this period, Franklin's friend Richard Jackson, later an agent for Pennsylvania, anonymously authored *An Historical Review of the Constitution and Government of Pennsylvania,* which sharply criticized the proprietary government. Penn erroneously believed Franklin had written it, and their dislike for one another continued to grow.

Meanwhile, Governor William Denny in Pennsylvania had disobeyed the Penns' instructions and allowed a tax to stand on their land in the Assembly's Supply Act (1759). The outraged Penns brought their objections to the act before the Privy Council, which had under its consideration a number of Pennsylvania's statutes. When the case ended its course through various hearings, the Supply Act remained on the books, and the Penns agreed to limited taxation of their lands. Franklin returned to Philadelphia in 1762.

In 1763 a gang of men known as the Paxton Boys brutally murdered 6 Indians who had lived peacefully among the settlers for many years. Governor John Penn (who was Richard Penn's son) ordered that offenders be found and punished, and he had the 14 remaining Indians brought into the town for protection. The men found them and murdered them as brutally as they had done before. The Paxton Boys threatened to murder yet another band of peaceful Indians, who had taken refuge in the town, and Governor Penn fled to Franklin's house. Franklin and others formed a voluntary militia to defend the Indians, negotiated with the Paxton Boys, and succeeded in averting the potential crisis. However, in the aftermath of the incident, which marked a temporary cooperation between proprietary and antiproprietary interests, war between the two reached new levels of intensity.

A majority in the Pennsylvania Assembly grew increasingly dissatisfied with the proprietors, but they could not act without a fight from vocal supporters of the proprietors, led by John Dickinson. The Assembly adopted a petition Franklin drafted asking the king to take over rulership of the province from the proprietors. It complained, "The government of this province by proprietaries has by long experience been found inconvenient, attended with many difficulties and obstructions to your Majesty's service, arising from the intervention of proprietary private interests in public affairs and disputes concerning those interests."

Franklin wrote profusely during this controversy in support of the petition, including "Cool Thoughts on the Present Situation of Our Public Affairs" and a lengthy preface to his eloquent ally Joseph Galloway's speech in favor of royal rule in Pennsylvania. Franklin's preface included a scathing mock epitaph for Thomas and Richard Penn. He was elected speaker of the Assembly when the previous speaker, Isaac Norris, a powerful Quaker, resigned.

In the midst of this dispute, Franklin and his enemies traded scathing attacks on one another. One of the most vicious and personal attacks on Franklin, "What Is Sauce for a Goose Is Sauce for a Gander," was written anonymously and alleged that William Franklin's mother was one of Franklin's maidservants, Barbara, whom he had overworked, underpaid, and starved. Franklin, along with Galloway, lost his Assembly seat in the next election by a narrow margin. The new Assembly, still dominated by antiproprietary sentiment, voted not only to present the petition but to return Franklin to England again as its agent. The opposition protested the appointment, and Franklin replied with "Remarks on a Late Protest."

In 1765 Franklin presented the petition, but it was ignored, and he found little support for the change in government in England. The proprietors were never ousted from their positions while the colonies remained under British rule. The Stamp Act and other intrusions of Parliament into the internal affairs of America began to occupy most of Franklin's time. Much later in his life, Franklin wrote to Jan Ingenhousz: "William Penn, the first proprietor, father of Thomas, was a wise and good man . . . but the said Thomas was a miserable churl." Thomas died in 1775, during the early stages of the American Revolution.

Related entries:
    French and Indian War
    Galloway, Joseph
    Jackson, Richard
    Pennsylvania Assembly
    Volunteer Militia

Suggestions for further reading:
    "Cool Thoughts on the Present Situation of Our Public Affairs," April 12, 1764 (Labaree et al., vol. 11).
    Middlekauff, Robert. 1996. *Benjamin Franklin and His Enemies.* Berkeley: University of California Press.
    "A Narrative of the Late Massacres," 1764 (Labaree et al., vol. 11).
    "Petition of the Pennsylvania Freeholders and Inhabitants" 1764 (Labaree et al., vol. 11).
    "Preface to Joseph Galloway's Speech," August 11, 1764 (Labaree et al., vol. 11).
    "Remarks on a Late Protest," November 5, 1764 (Labaree et al., vol. 11).

Penn, William

See **Penn, Thomas.**

Pennsylvania Assembly

The single-house Assembly in Pennsylvania was composed of representatives of the people living in Pennsylvania, and the laws it passed were subject to the approval of the governor. Under the system of government that existed before the American Revolution, the Assembly remained perpetually at odds with the governor. The proprietors of the province—Thomas and Richard Penn during most of Franklin's service in the Assembly—appointed the governor, and the Assembly paid the governor's salary. Within the Assembly itself there was little harmony either. Quakers dominated, but strong factions of merchants and other interests also existed. "My being many years in the Assembly," Franklin wrote, "the majority of which were constantly Quakers, gave me frequent opportunities of seeing the embarrassment given them by their principle against war, whenever application was made to them, by order of the crown, to grant aids for military purposes."

Franklin's political career began in the Pennsylvania Assembly in 1736, when he was chosen as its clerk. The position as clerk benefited his printing business, as it gained him work printing laws, votes, and paper money. However, he could not participate in discussions or take part in making laws, and he sometimes eased his boredom by composing magic squares and circles. The governor appointed him to the commission of the peace; the corporation of Philadelphia appointed him to the common council and later made him an alderman. In 1751 Franklin was elected to the Assembly, and he "conceived [his] becoming a member would enlarge [his] power of doing good." His son William was chosen as the clerk in his stead. A few months before his election, Franklin had already convinced the Assembly to donate £2,000 for the Pennsylvania Hospital, provided that private contributions amounting to an equal sum could be raised. The hospital was founded the same year.

Franklin found himself involved in many issues. He was frequently employed to answer the governor's speeches. About Governor Robert Hunter Morris, he wrote in his *Autobiography:* "Our answers, as well as his messages, were often tart, and sometimes indecently abusive; and, as he knew I wrote for the Assembly, one might have imagined that, when we met, we could hardly avoid cutting throats; but he was so good-natured a man that no personal difference between him and me was occasioned by the contest, and we often dined together." In 1754 Franklin was

appointed to a committee on Indian trade and sent by the governor as a delegate to the Albany Congress. He was involved in considering a petition of bakers, a bill to regulate dogs, paper currency, boundaries, building a bridge over the Schuylkill River, and other routine business. Franklin served on the committees of correspondence and of aggrievances and was charged with revising the minutes.

The Assembly chose Franklin to assist General Edward Braddock during the French and Indian War. "Our Assembly apprehending, from some information, that he had conceived violent prejudices against them, as averse to the service, wished me to wait upon him, not as from them, but as postmaster-general," Franklin wrote. He and his son procured wagons for Braddock's ill-fated expedition to Fort Duquesne, after which the Assembly gave him a vote of thanks for his successful efforts. In 1755 Franklin helped Josiah Quincy obtain money from the Assembly for Massachusetts to fund an expedition to Crown Point. The same year, he pushed a much-needed militia bill, which he had drawn up, through the Assembly. In 1756 Franklin was sent to help negotiate a treaty with the Delaware Indians at Easton.

Franklin's lengthy dispute with the Penns was one of the main issues of his Pennsylvania political career. The Assembly refused to appropriate money for defense or needed projects unless the Penns paid taxes on their vast estates, and the Penns steadfastly refused to pay them. The governor was under strict orders from the Penns to veto any bill that levied taxes on their estates.

In 1756 the Assembly implemented Franklin's scheme for reforming the town watch (which he had proposed in a paper to the Junto many years earlier) and a modified version of a bill he had drafted for paving the city streets. In 1757 Franklin drew up a "Report of the Committee of Aggrievances of the Assembly of Pennsylvania," which for the most part amounted to a denunciation of the proprietors. The committee asserted that the proprietors had "so abridged and restricted their late and present governor's discretion in matters of legislation, by their illegal, impracticable, and unconstitutional instructions and prohibitions" that it was impossible to pass a bill to appropriate money for the king that would meet with their approval. They believed that William Penn's sons had violated the intentions of their father. Among the other grievances listed in the report were the enlistment of peoples' servants without any compensation and exorbitant taxes. The same year, the Assembly elected Franklin as an agent for the province to travel to England and petition for the right to tax proprietary lands.

While he was in England the Assembly prevailed upon Governor William Denny to disobey the proprietors' instructions and approve a bill taxing their estates. After a political fight with the Penns in England, the tax remained. Richard Jackson authored *An Historical Review of the Constitution of Pennsylvania,* which criticized the proprietary government and which Franklin paid to have printed. Franklin stayed in England until 1762 and was reelected to the Assembly every year in his absence. Upon his return to Philadelphia that year, he was again thrust into heated dispute with the supporters of the proprietors.

In the Assembly, Joseph Galloway and John Dickinson debated over the issue of proprietary government. A move began to petition the king to assume the government from the Penns. Franklin and Galloway favored the change, while Dickinson served as the voice for proprietary government. Galloway spoke in favor of royal government, and Franklin wrote in favor of it: "Cool Thoughts on the Present Situation of Our Public Affairs" (1764), and "Preface to the Speech of Joseph Galloway, Esq." (1764). The latter was written in response to the long preface of a speech by Dickinson against changing the government, which had been printed in pamphlet form. Dickinson's preface contained a complimentary memorial to William Penn, and

Franklin responded with a memorial that sharply criticized Thomas and Richard Penn.

When the Assembly speaker, Isaac Norris, resigned in 1764, Franklin obtained his position. His tenure was short-lived, however. The Penns actively tried to remove Franklin from the Assembly. In the bitter 1764 election, Franklin and Galloway, representing the "old ticket," lost their seats by a narrow margin to the candidates representing the "new ticket." The majority of the Assembly, however, supported a change to royal government, and it sent Franklin to England again to petition for the change. John Dickinson vocally opposed the appointment, and his fellow dissenters wrote an official protest. Franklin responded with "Remarks on a Late Protest," in which he attacked the practice of minorities in the House entering protests into the minutes and defended his appointment as the Assembly's agent. He sailed for England in 1764.

In 1766 Franklin asked the Assembly to relieve him of his duty as its agent and allow him to come home. However, the Assembly voted him agent again, and he ended up remaining in England until 1775. The affairs of Pennsylvania were soon the least of his troubles. Other colonies appointed him as their agent—New Jersey, Georgia, and Massachusetts—and the growing tension between England and the colonies began to absorb most of Franklin's time and energy. The king never took the government of Pennsylvania from the Penns.

The day after Franklin's return to America in 1775, the Assembly chose him as a delegate to the Second Continental Congress. After the American Revolution, Pennsylvania had a new government.

Related entries:
Albany Plan of Union
French and Indian War
Galloway, Joseph
Jackson, Richard
The Junto
Penn, Thomas
Pennsylvania Hospital

Quincy, Josiah, Sr. and Josiah, Jr.
Volunteer Militia

Suggestions for further reading:
"B. Franklin's Services in the General
Assembly" (Smyth, vol. X).
Hanna, William S. 1964. *Benjamin Franklin and
Pennsylvania Politics.* Stanford, Calif.: Stanford
University Press.
Jennings, Francis. 1996. *Benjamin Franklin:
Politician.* New York: W. W. Norton.
Newcomb, Benjamin H. 1972. *Franklin and
Galloway: A Political Partnership.* New Haven,
Conn.: Yale University Press.
"Papers from the Election Campaign," 1764
(Labaree et al., vol. 11).
"Pennsylvania Assembly Committees: Report
on Grievances," February 22, 1757 (Labaree et
al., vol. 7).
"Petition of the Pennsylvania Freeholders and
Inhabitants to the King," March 29, 1764
(Labaree et al., vol. 11).
"Preface to Joseph Galloway's Speech," August
11, 1764 (Labaree et al., vol. 11).
"Remarks on a Late Protest" November 5,
1764 (Labaree et al., vol. 11).

Pennsylvania Gazette

In 1729 Franklin and Hugh Meredith purchased *The Universal Instructor in All Arts and Sciences and Pennsylvania Gazette* "for a trifle" from their former boss, Samuel Keimer. Franklin had planned his own newspaper, but a friend betrayed his secret to Keimer, who started one before Franklin could. Keimer's paper was unsuccessful, however, and he was forced to sell it within a year. When Franklin and Meredith began to print it in October 1729, they shortened its name to the *Pennsylvania Gazette*. Franklin published the *Gazette* successfully from 1729 to 1757 (from October 1729 to May 1732 the paper was published by Franklin and Meredith, but the work was largely Franklin's). "Our first papers," Franklin wrote in his *Autobiography*, "made a quite different appearance from any before in the province; a better type, and better printed; but some spirited remarks of my writing, on the dispute then going on between Governor Burnet and the Massachusetts Assembly, struck the principal people, occasioned the paper and the manager of it to be much talked of, and in a few weeks brought them all to be our subscribers."

Along with his *Poor Richard's Almanack,* Franklin used his newspaper "as another means of communicating instruction." He printed essays that he wrote for the Junto and extracts from the *Spectator*. "In the conduct of my newspaper," he said, "I carefully excluded all libeling and personal abuse, which is of late years become so disgraceful to our country." The pages of the *Gazette* were filled with advertisements, philosophical pieces, political essays, news, and letters, often penned by Franklin. One of the early philosophical pieces that Franklin published, "A Dialogue between Philocles and Horatio, Meeting Accidentally in the Fields, Concerning Virtue and Pleasure" (1730), featured a conversation between a philosopher (Philocles) and a pleasure-seeker (Horatio). A follow-up dialog between the two appeared in a subsequent edition.

Franklin advertised goods he sold in his shop and published lost-and-found notices for his family. On June 30, 1737, the *Gazette* carried an admonition for the person who stole his wife's prayer book from the church pew: "The person who took it is desired to open it, and read the eighth commandment, and afterwards return it into the same pew again; upon which no further notice will be taken." Using pseudonyms such as "Anthony Afterwit," "Celia Single," and "Alice Addertongue," Franklin wrote letters to the paper and answered them himself. An account of Franklin's electrical kite experiment appeared in the paper in 1752.

Franklin promoted public and political projects in the *Gazette*. Writing as "A.A.," he offered his advice on protecting towns from fire in 1734. He used the *Gazette* to help Dr. Thomas Bond solicit subscriptions for the Pennsylvania Hospital in 1751. He wrote "A Dialogue between X, Y, and Z Concerning the Present State of Affairs in Pennsylvania" to promote his militia act in 1755. In

"Exporting of Felons to the Colonies" (1751), Franklin humorously attacked the British practice of shipping convicts to America for "the well peopling of the colonies." He advised: "Such a tender parental concern in our mother country for the welfare of her children, calls for the highest returns of gratitude and duty." Rattlesnakes, he suggested, were unfairly persecuted in America, and their mischievous personalities might benefit from a change of climate. "In the spring of the year," he continued, "when they first creep out of their holes, they are feeble, heavy, slow, and easily taken; and if a small bounty were allowed per head, some thousands might be collected annually, and transported to Britain." The rattlesnakes were to be deposited in St. James Park, in the spring gardens, and "particularly in the gardens of the prime ministers, the Lords of Trade, and members of Parliament; for to them we are most particularly obliged." Franklin concluded that "rattlesnakes seem the most suitable returns for the human serpents sent us by our mother country" and signed his piece "Americanus." On May 9, 1754, Franklin printed his famous "Join or Die" cartoon, depicting the colonies as broken segments of a rattlesnake, to promote the idea of a union for the colonies. Although he promoted his own agendas with the paper, he did not deny a platform to dissenting opinions.

The pages of the *Gazette* never lacked humor, even when they were intended to instruct and admonish. Franklin's "Drinker's Dictionary" listed euphemisms for drunkards for each letter of the alphabet. Drunkenness, Franklin wrote, was "a very unfortunate vice; in this respect it bears no kind of similitude with any sort of virtue, from which it might possibly borrow a name; and is therefore reduced to the wretched necessity of being expressed by round about phrases, and of perpetually varying those phrases as often as they come to be well understood plainly to signify that a man is drunk." Under the letter "M" were: "He sees two moons; He's merry; He's middling; He's muddled; He's moon-eyed; He's maudlin; He's mountainous; He's muddy; He's mellow; He's seen a flock of moons; He's raised his monuments."

Encouraged by the success of the *Gazette* in Philadelphia, Franklin bought or established papers as partnerships. In 1732 he sent Thomas Whitemarsh to South Carolina as his partner, and Whitemarsh established the *South Carolina Gazette*. Another partner, Thomas Smith, published the *Antigua Gazette*, which was later printed for a short period by Franklin's nephew, Benjamin Mecom. Franklin and James Parker entered into a partnership in 1742 to operate the *New York Gazette*, which Parker ran successfully for many years. With William Smith, Franklin established the *Freeport Gazette* in Dominica. James Franklin printed the *Rhode Island Gazette* for about a year.

Andrew Bradford's *American Weekly Mercury* was the *Gazette*'s only significant competition. Bradford, who was the postmaster, used his position to keep Franklin's paper out of the mail, and Franklin bribed carriers to deliver it. When Franklin took Bradford's position at the post office, his carriers delivered Bradford's *Mercury* until 1739, when Colonel Alexander Spotswood, the deputy postmaster general for the colonies, ordered him not to carry it because Bradford was delinquent in turning in his accounts. After Franklin obtained Bradford's job at the post office, the *Gazette*'s subscriptions rose, and the *Mercury*'s declined. Franklin gave up actively running the paper in 1748, but it was still operating when he died in 1790.

Related entries:
Mecom, Jane Franklin
Parker, James
Pennsylvania Assembly
Pennsylvania Hospital
Post Office
Printing
Volunteer Militia

Suggestions for further reading:
"Alice Addertongue," September 12, 1732 (Labaree et al., vol. 1).
"An Apology for Printers," June 10, 1731 (Labaree et al., vol. 1).

Pennsylvania Hospital, c. 1800. Lithograph.

"The Drinker's Dictionary," January 13, 1737 (Labaree et al., vol. 2).

Masur, Louis P., ed. 1993. *The Autobiography of Benjamin Franklin.* Boston: Bedford Books of St. Martin's Press.

Oswald, John Clyde. 1917. *Benjamin Franklin: Printer.* Garden City, N.Y.: Doubleday, Page & Company.

"A Witch Trial at Mount Holly," October 22, 1730 (Labaree et al., vol. 1).

Pennsylvania Hospital

Until the mid-1750s Pennsylvania had no hospital for its sick, for the mentally ill, and for people who needed surgery. The mentally ill in Philadelphia were kept in the jail for want of adequate facilities. Patients who required the constant postsurgical care of a nurse had to hire one privately, at considerable expense. The poor of the province could not afford necessary medical care. When Dr. Thomas Bond (1712–1784) came to Franklin with a practical plan to alleviate these problems by establishing a hospital, Franklin was eager to help.

Bond, originally from Maryland, studied medicine in Paris and established his medical practice in Philadelphia. He was an original member of the American Philosophical Society. In 1751 he began to seek and collect subscriptions to build a hospital in Philadelphia. Meeting with little success in spite of his earnest efforts, he approached Franklin for his help in raising money and generating public support for the project. By this time, Franklin had founded or helped to found the American Philosophical Society, the Library Company of Philadelphia, the Junto, the Philadelphia Academy, a volunteer militia for the defense of the province, and a fire-fighting organization. He was both innovative and successful in generating support and executing public projects. Bond told Franklin: "I am often asked by those to whom I propose subscribing: Have you consulted Franklin about this business? And what does he think of it? And when I tell them I have not (supposing it rather out of your line), they do not subscribe, but they say they will consider of it."

Franklin organized a meeting to discuss the plan for the hospital. He donated £25, encouraged new subscriptions, promoted the hospital in the *Pennsylvania Gazette,* and petitioned the Pennsylvania Assembly for money. The reluctant Assembly agreed to donate £2,000, if private subscribers could match the sum. Rural members opposed the project, maintaining that a hospital would benefit only people who lived in town, and they thought that residents of Philadelphia should pay for it. The Assembly doubted that Franklin and Bond could raise the sum; however, Franklin wrote, representatives who had opposed the bill voted for it because their "charitable" vote would enhance their images without having to appropriate money. Franklin used the Assembly's conditional gift as motivation for the private subscriptions, and he and others succeeded in raising more than the necessary £2,000. The Assembly granted the gift.

The hospital was founded in 1751 and admitted its first patient the following year. Franklin was a member of the hospital's board of managers, its first secretary, and later its president. He wrote and printed "Some Account of the Pennsylvania Hospital" in 1754 and composed an inscription on the hospital's cornerstone. Construction of the original building was completed in 1755. The hospital employed Bond and Franklin's friend Dr. Benjamin Rush, who worked tirelessly during an epidemic of yellow fever in 1793, founded a free dispensary, and devoted much of his time to establishing humane treatments for the mentally ill. In his *Autobiography* Franklin wrote of this public project: "I do not remember any of my political maneuvers, the success of which gave me at the time more pleasure, or wherein, after thinking of it, I more easily excused myself for having made some use of cunning."

Franklin left some of his uncollected debts to the hospital in his will, but it was able to collect very little. Two more sections were added to the building after his death. The Pennsylvania Hospital was the first incorporated hospital in the United States and still exists in Philadelphia.

Related entries:
American Philosophical Society
Education
Fire
The Junto
Library Company of Philadelphia
Pennsylvania Assembly
Rush, Dr. Benjamin
Volunteer Militia

Suggestions for further reading:
"Appeal for the Hospital," August 8, 1751 (Labaree et al., vol. 4).
Franklin, Benjamin. 1954. *Some Account of the Pennsylvania Hospital.* Baltimore: Johns Hopkins University Press.
Masur, Louis P., ed. 1993. *The Autobiography of Benjamin Franklin.* Boston: Bedford Books of St. Martin's Press.

Pitt, William, Earl of Chatham

See *An Account of Negotiations in London for Effecting a Reconciliation between Great Britain and the American Colonies;* Colonial Agent; Stamp Act.

Poor Richard's Almanack

Franklin began publishing his *Poor Richard's Almanack,* famous for its homespun humor, down-to-earth adages, and practical advice, in 1732. "I endeavored to make it both entertaining and useful," he wrote in his *Autobiography,* "and it accordingly came to be in such demand, that I reaped considerable profit from it, vending annually near ten thousand." *Poor Richard's* and other colonial almanacs contained weather forecasts, tides, and information on astronomical events. As with the *Pennsylvania Gazette,* Franklin viewed the *Almanack* as a vehicle for instructing the public: "I . . . filled all the little spaces that occurred between the remarkable days in the calendar with proverbial sentences, chiefly such as inculcated industry and frugality, as the means of procuring wealth, and thereby securing virtue; it being more difficult for a man in want, to act always honestly, as, to use here one of those proverbs, 'it is hard for an empty sack to stand upright.'"

The alias Franklin used in the almanac was "Richard Saunders," who with muffled humor characterized himself in the first year as an impoverished stargazer, married to a proud wife who disapproved of his indolence. The following year, profits from the almanac had improved their circumstances to the point where she could afford a few luxuries, and the reduced tension in their relationship enabled him to sleep better. The first volumes joked about the death of Titan Leeds (who was still alive), the author of a rival almanac, and featured ongoing disagreements between Richard and his wife, Bridget. "Mistress Saunders" wrote the preface to the 1738 edition, and she purported to have crossed her husband's preface out and substituted her own. "Upon looking over the months," Mistress Saunders wrote, "I see he has put in abundance of foul weather this year; and therefore I have scattered here and there, where I could find room, some fair, pleasant, sunshiny, &c. for the good women to dry their clothes in."

Beginning with the 1748 edition, Franklin added more material to the almanacs and retitled them *Poor Richard Improved.* The 1751 almanac featured a piece designed to demonstrate the absurdity of noble blood. Poor Richard calculated that a nobleman living in that time, figuring only 21 generations back (to approximately the time of the Norman Conquest), should have 1,048,576 noble ancestors in order to have pure noble blood. If one calculated to 300 years before that, "the

Poor Richard, 1743.

A N

Almanack

For the Year of Chriſt

1 7 4 3,

Being the Third after LEAP YEAR.

And makes ſince the Creation Years
By the Account of the Eaſtern *Greeks* 7251
By the Latin Church, when ☉ ent. ♈ 6942
By the Computation of *W. W.* 5752
By the *Roman* Chronology 5692
By the *Jewiſh* Rabbies 5504

Wherein is contained,

The Lunations, Eclipſes, Judgment of the Weather, Spring Tides, Planets Motions & mutual Aſpects, Sun and Moon's Riſing and Setting, Length of Days, Time of High Water, Fairs, Courts, and obſervable Days. Fitted to the Latitude of Forty Degrees, and a Meridian of Five Hours Weſt from *London,* but may without ſenſible Error, ſerve all the adjacent Places, even from *Newfoundland* to *South-Carolina.*

By *RICHARD SAUNDERS,* Philom.

PHILADELPHIA:
Printed and ſold by *B. FRANKLIN,* at the New Printing-Office near the Market.

Frontispiece of **Poor Richard's Almanack,** *1743.*

number amounts to above 500 millions; which are more than exist at any one time upon earth, and shows the impossibility of preserving blood free from such mixtures, and that the pretension of such purity of blood in ancient families is a mere joke." The 1756 edition featured a colonial "Plan for Saving One Hundred Thousand Pounds," based on frugal living: "Remember a patch on your coat, and money in your pocket, is better and more creditable, than a writ on your back, and no money to take it off," Poor Richard advised. In the 1757 edition, Richard provided humorous instructions for making a sundial "by which not only a man's own family, but all his neighbors for ten miles round, may know what a clock is, when the sun shines, without seeing the dial." The sundial, as constructed, would direct sunlight through carefully placed glasses to fire guns, one gun at one o'clock, two guns at two o'clock, and so forth. Other topics covered in Poor Richard's almanacs were astrology, instructions for making wine, instructions for protecting one's house from lightning, rules for maintaining one's health, the uses of microscopes, and a history of mankind's use of calendars in honor of England's change from the Julian to the Gregorian calendar in 1752.

Poor Richard's is best remembered for the many adages that Franklin put in the almanacs. Some were taken directly from other authors, some were modified versions of existing maxims, and some were Franklin's own sayings. Among them were: "Would you live with ease, Do what you ought, and not what you please"; "Many dishes many diseases, Many medicines few cures"; "Where carcasses are, eagles will gather, And where good laws are, much people flock thither"; "Blame-all and praise-all are two blockheads"; "No man e'er was glorious, who was not laborious"; "Take this remark from Richard poor and lame, Whatever's begun in anger ends in shame"; "Fools multiply folly"; "If you would be revenged of your enemy, govern your self"; "A learned blockhead is a greater blockhead than an ignorant one"; "Great talkers, little doers"; "A rich rogue, is like a fat hog, who never does good 'til as dead as a log"; "To lengthen thy life, lessen thy meals"; "He's the best physician that knows the worthlessness of the most medicines"; "Cheese and salt meat, should be sparingly eat"; "Presumption first blinds a man, then sets him a running"; "Most of the learning in use, is of no great use"; "Keep conscience clear, then never fear"; "There are lazy minds as well as lazy bodies"; "Today is yesterday's pupil"; "The proud hate pride—in others"; "Many a man thinks he is buying pleasure, when he is really selling himself a slave to it"; "If man could have half his wishes, he would double his troubles"; "Haste makes waste"; "He that best understands the world, least likes it"; "If you would be loved, love and be loveable"; "The

doors of wisdom are never shut"; "Diligence overcomes difficulties, sloth makes them"; "Love your neighbor; yet don't pull down your hedge"; "Love your enemies, for they tell you your faults"; "Plough deep, while sluggards sleep; and you shall have corn, to sell and to keep"; "Work as if you were to live 100 Years, pray as if you were to die tomorrow"; "The borrower is a slave to the lender; the security to both"; "Silence is not always a sign of wisdom, but babbling is ever a mark of folly"; "Half the truth is often a great lie"; "Diligence is the mother of good luck"; "He that speaks much, is much mistaken"; "Creditors have better memories than debtors"; "Let thy discontents be secrets"; and "No gains without pains."

The most famous of the prefaces to the almanacs is "Father Abraham's Speech," at the beginning of the final edition for 1758. It was reprinted as "The Way to Wealth" in many European countries and was a collection of Poor Richard's sayings "formed into a connected discourse . . . as the harangue of a wise old man to the people attending an auction. The bringing all these scattered counsels thus into a focus enabled them to make greater impression."

Franklin's almanac was not the only one that circulated in the colonies, nor even the first, but it proved to be the most popular at home and abroad. "The Way to Wealth" was published as "La Science du Bonhomme Richard" in France and became popular during the Revolutionary War. Over the 25 years that Franklin published the almanac from 1732 to 1757, Americans bought more than 250,000 copies.

Related entries:
Pennsylvania Gazette
Printing

Suggestions for further reading:
Lemay, J. A. Leo, ed. 1987. "Poor Richard's Almanack." In *Benjamin Franklin: Writings*. New York: Literary Classics of the United States.
Masur, Louis P., ed. 1993. *The Autobiography of Benjamin Franklin*. Boston: Bedford Books of St. Martin's Press.

Population

Throughout his life, Franklin envisioned the expansion of the English people in North America. Before the American Revolution, he pictured a vast British Empire that could be strengthened by an increase in the number of English people in North America. He believed that populations grew according to a country's means of subsistence, and that the potential for population growth in America was enormous. The character of the population was just as important to him as its number. He thought that agriculture and workers who were industrious and frugal formed the backbone of a successful nation.

Franklin wrote one of his earliest essays on population in response to proposed British restrictions on the manufacture of iron in Pennsylvania. In "Observations Concerning the Increase of Mankind, Peopling of Countries, Etc." (1751), Franklin outlined his vision of the growth of North America's population. He believed the number of people living in the colonies would necessarily increase at a faster rate than the population of Europe. He argued that people married earlier in the colonies because it was easier to support a family, and people were less hesitant to marry. People who married young had more children. "If it is reckoned there," Franklin wrote, "that there is but one marriage per annum among 100 persons, perhaps we may reckon two; and if in Europe, they have but 4 births to a marriage (many of their marriages being late), we may here reckon 8, of which if one half grow up, and our marriages are made, reckoning one with another at 20 years of age, our people must at least be doubled every 20 years."

Franklin did not favor the stream of immigrants from other European countries, largely because he believed that English culture should dominate in the colonies: "I pray God to preserve long to Great Britain the English law, manners, liberties, and religion," he wrote in 1753. The number and wealth of German immigrants grew steadily in Pennsylvania, and Franklin feared that their numbers would one day overtake the British population there. Nevertheless, he saw no reason to try to exclude German settlers and instead suggested that they be encouraged to spread out to other colonies and intermix with the English. "I say, I am not against the admission of Germans in general," Franklin wrote, "for they have their virtues. Their industry and frugality are exemplary. They are excellent husbandmen; and contribute greatly to the improvement of a country."

The English had their drawbacks in Franklin's estimation. Franklin observed that the productivity of English laborers who received better pay in America declined, while better pay did not encourage idleness in German laborers. "When I consider, that the English are the offspring of the Germans, that the climate they live in is much of the same temperature," he said, "and when I see nothing in nature that should create this difference, I am tempted to suspect it must arise from our constitution; and I have sometimes doubted whether the laws peculiar to England, which compel the rich to maintain the poor, have not given the latter a dependence, that very much lessens the care of providing against the wants of old age."

If the Germans might pose a threat in the future, the French already threatened English settlements. France had settlements in Canada and in Louisiana, and in 1753 it began constructing forts from Lake Erie to the forks of the Ohio River. If the Canadian settlement joined with the one in Louisiana, English settlers would face a powerful French presence to their west. Franklin was long interested in acquiring western land and settling colonies on it. He feared that if the English delayed settling the western areas, their population would soon become limited, and the French would increase. In 1756 he wrote a "Plan for Settling Two Western Colonies in North America, with Reasons for the Plan."

After Britain's triumph in the French and Indian War, a dispute arose over what terms to ask for in a treaty. Some suggested asking for the sugar island of Guadeloupe, and others believed that Britain should try to obtain France's territory in Canada. Franklin favored the vast Canadian territory and believed that it would provide valuable additional room for English expansion. With Jackson he authored "The Interest of Great Britain Considered, with Regard to Her Colonies and the Acquisitions of Canada and Guadeloupe" and tried to dispel the belief that acquiring Canada would drain the population of England. "The annual increment alone of our present colonies," they argued, "without diminishing their numbers, or requiring a man from hence, is sufficient in ten years to fill Canada and double the number of English, that it now has of French inhabitants." England would benefit from an increased demand in North America for British manufactures, which would create better means of livelihood in England and spur enough increase in the population to replace people lost by emigration.

When Franklin was in London in 1774 he criticized an act that was rumored to be introduced into Parliament for restricting emigration to America. He wrote "A Proposed Act of Parliament for Preventing Emigration" (1774), published in the *Public Advertiser.* He maintained that it was as natural for people to flow from one country to another as it was for water to flow from one part of the globe to another. Franklin thought that any law to restrict emigration would actually encourage people to move, as they would resent the restriction on their liberties and become more resolved to remove. "God has given to the beasts of the forest, and to the birds of the air," he wrote, "a right, when their subsistence fails in one country, to migrate to another, where they can get a more comfortable living; and shall man be denied a privilege enjoyed by brutes, merely to gratify a few avaricious landlords?"

When the American Revolution began, Franklin abandoned his idea of an extensive British Empire, but he was no less enthusiastic about the expansion of the American population. After the war he wrote "Information to Those Who Would Remove to America" in France to inform potential European emigrants to America. He tried to dispel some of the romantic notions that people had about obtaining easy riches, offices, and titles. Franklin wrote that "a general happy mediocrity prevails" instead of the extreme riches and poverty found in Europe. The type of people who should move to America, he said, were agricultural laborers, artisans, and people with moderate fortunes who wished to bring their children up to be industrious and to leave them inheritances.

Related entries:
French and Indian War
Jackson, Richard
Revolutionary War

Suggestions for further reading:
"Information to Those Who Would Remove to America," 1784 (Smyth, vol. VIII).
"The Internal State of America, Being a True Description of the Interest and Policy of That Vast Continent," (Smyth, vol. X).
"Observations Concerning the Increase of Mankind," 1751 (Labaree et al., vol. 4).

Post Office

Franklin's nearly 40 years of working in both British and American post offices began in 1737, when Colonel Alexander Spotswood, deputy postmaster general for America, appointed him postmaster of Philadelphia. Franklin replaced his rival printer and newspaper publisher, Andrew Bradford, who lacked management skills and failed to turn in his accounts for a number of years. At first he ran the post office out of his printing office, but he later relocated it to a house he purchased on Market Street.

Franklin obtained many positions in the post office for members of his family. Franklin was promoted to controller, leaving his former position to his son William. When William was promoted to controller by his father, Joseph Read, a relative of Franklin's wife, took his position, and it later passed to Franklin's brother Peter. Another brother, John Franklin, served as postmaster in Boston from 1754 until his death in 1756, after which his widow took the job.

In 1753 Franklin and William Hunter (a printer and the postmaster of Williamsburg, Virginia) obtained appointments from England as joint deputy postmasters general for America. Upon hearing of the poor health of Elliot Benger, then deputy postmaster general for America, Franklin had written to Peter Collinson in 1751 asking for his help in obtaining the post. The chief justice of Pennsylvania, William Allen, also helped Franklin obtain the appointment. "We were to have six hundred pounds between us, if we could make that sum out of the profits of the office," Franklin wrote in his *Autobiography*. "To do this, a variety of improvements were necessary; some of these were inevitably at first expensive, so that in the first four years the office became above nine hundred pounds in debt to us. But it soon began to repay us; and before I was displaced by a freak of the ministers . . . we had brought it to yield three times as much clear revenue to the crown as the post office of Ireland."

Franklin inspected all of the post offices in the northern colonies and as far south as Virginia between 1754 and 1756. In 1757 he and his son traveled to England, leaving his printing partner, James Parker, in New York as controller. Among the improvements Franklin implemented with Hunter, and later with John Foxcroft, were an improved accounting system, new routes, shorter and more frequent delivery times between Philadelphia and New York, and nighttime riders. Newspaper publishers no longer had the privilege of sending their papers for free, and

Franklin encouraged newspapers to print the names of people who had letters waiting for them. Franklin created the penny post in Philadelphia, by which letters that had not been picked up the day they arrived were delivered for an additional charge, and established the Dead Letter Office, which held letters that had not been picked up after three months. In 1761 the colonial post office could for the first time in history report a profit to the British postmaster general. Upon Hunter's death the same year, Foxcroft was appointed in his place. In the spring of 1763 Franklin and Foxcroft embarked on a 1,600-mile tour of the northern colonies to "inspect and regulate" their post offices.

Franklin, in England from 1764 to 1775, began to fear that he would lose his position after the furor over the Stamp Act. Lord Sandwich, an ardent enemy of Franklin and of America, became postmaster general in England in 1768. He tried to have Franklin dismissed on the basis of his living in England, away from the postal affairs in America. Franklin believed that the real reason was his "being too much of an American." The Oliver-Hutchinson letters affair finally forced Franklin from his position in the post office in London in January 1774.

After Franklin's dismissal, the American printer William Goddard established an intercolonial mail service funded by subscription. By the time the Second Continental Congress met in 1775, 30 colonial post offices were operating in Goddard's system. Franklin had barely returned from England to sit in the Congress when it appointed him to a committee to organize a postal system. Franklin drew up a plan, which reorganized Goddard's system, and the committee appointed him postmaster general for the colonies. His son-in-law, Richard Bache, served as controller, and Goddard as surveyor. Franklin served in his position until he sailed for France at the end of 1776. This post office was the beginning of the modern postal system in the United States. By 1789, the year before Franklin's death, the postal service had 75 offices nationwide.

Price, Dr. Richard

See **Honest Whigs.**

Priestley, Dr. Joseph (1733–1804)

Franklin met Dr. Joseph Priestley, a chemist and minister, in London in 1766 and kept up correspondence with him for the rest of his life. Priestley and Franklin were members of the Royal Society of London and of the London club Honest Whigs. When Franklin's residence in America and in France separated them, they kept up a correspondence covering a variety of philosophical subjects.

Priestley conducted many important experiments in chemistry and was particularly interested in gases. He was elected to the French Academy of Sciences in 1772, and the Royal Society awarded him the Sir Godfrey Copley medal in 1773, an honor Franklin received 20 years earlier. In 1774

he discovered oxygen, which he called "dephlogisticated air." Other gases that he isolated include nitrous oxide, carbon monoxide, ammonia, and sulfur dioxide. Priestley was an adherent of the now-discredited phlogiston theory, which postulated that every flammable substance contained a substance called phlogiston that was lost during combustion. Priestley disagreed with the theories of another of Franklin's friends, the French chemist Antoine-Laurent Lavoisier, who was the first to disprove the phlogiston theory and to name oxygen.

Franklin spurred Priestley's interest in electricity and provided him with advice and books for his *History of Electricity* (1767). Priestley conducted his own electrical experiments, one in which he discovered that charcoal conducts electricity. He and Franklin exchanged ideas on many other subjects, and Franklin told him in 1786, "I know of no philosopher who starts so much good game for the hunters after knowledge as you do."

Franklin took an interest in Priestley's ideas about vegetation and the purification of air, and Priestley published some of Franklin's observations in his *Experiments on Air*. During a visit with Priestley, Franklin noticed that mint growing in the area prospered in the polluted air, and he thought that the plants took harmful substances out of the air. "That the vegetable creation should restore the air which is spoiled by the animal part of it," Franklin thought, "looks like a rational system. . . . We knew before, that putrid animal substances were converted into sweet vegetables, when mixed with the earth, and applied as manure; and now it seems that the same putrid substances, mixed with the air, have a similar effect." Franklin hoped that these observations would "give some check to the rage of destroying trees that grow near houses, which has accompanied our late improvements in gardening from an opinion of their being unwholesome."

Priestley tutored at the Academy at Warrington and later became a minister at Leeds. In 1772 the Earl of Shelburne (William Petty) hired him at £300 per year to keep his library. Franklin hoped that the appointment would secure his subsistence and give him leisure to write and conduct his experiments. When Priestley sought advice from Franklin on whether or not to take the position, Franklin declined to advise him on what to do and instead suggested he try a decision-making process that he himself used to arrive at a conclusion. Franklin called this process "moral or prudential algebra." It involved making two columns on a piece of paper, one for "pro" and the other for "con." He listed reasons in the appropriate column and then assigned importance to each reason. After he had written every pro and con, he began to cross them out. A pro and a con of equal importance would cancel one another out. If two cons equaled one pro in importance, he crossed all three of them out. He made a decision on the basis of what was left at the end. Priestley broke amicably with Shelburne in 1780 over religious differences, and he again sought Franklin's advice before the separation.

The American Revolution had no ill effect on their friendship, as Priestley supported it. Priestley had been present at the Cockpit in 1774, when Alexander Wedderburn criticized and humiliated Franklin over his role in the Oliver-Hutchinson letters affair, and he opposed the stringent measures the British government placed on the colonies. Franklin spent his last day in England with Priestley, very disturbed about the prospect of war. The two continued to write throughout the Revolution.

After the fighting ceased, Franklin told Priestley that he believed men were "a sort of beings very badly constructed," as they were more apt to provoke one another than reconcile, and more inclined to kill with war than to reproduce. "[I]n your zeal for their welfare, you are taking a great deal of pains to save their souls," Franklin wrote to him. "Perhaps as you grow older, you may look upon this as a hopeless project, or an idle amusement, repent of having murdered in

Dr. Joseph Priestley. Halftone reproduction of a painting.

mephitic air so many honest, harmless mice, and wish that to prevent mischief, you had used boys and girls instead of them."

Although Priestley had been educated as a minister for the dissenting church, his theology developed toward Unitarian thought. His radical religious views stirred up heated controversy, and copies of his *History of the Corruptions of Christianity* (1782) were burned in 1785. Franklin, who usually distanced himself from theological arguments, thought Priestley an "honest heretic," which he meant as a compliment: "I do not call him honest by way of distinction; for I think all the heretics I have known have been virtuous men."

After Franklin's death, a mob angry with Priestley's support of the French Revolution burned his home. Three years later, he emigrated to the United States, where he lived until his death in 1804.

Related entries:
French Academy of Sciences
Honest Whigs
Ingenhousz, Dr. Jan
Oliver-Hutchinson Letters Affair
Royal Society of London

Suggestions for further reading:
"To Joseph Priestley," April 10, 1774 (Labaree et al., vol. 21).
"To Joseph Priestley," February 8, 1780 (Labaree et al., vol. 31).

"To Joseph Priestley," July 7, 1775 (Labaree et al., vol. 22).

"To Joseph Priestley," June 7, 1782 (Smyth, vol. VIII).

"To Joseph Priestley," May 4, 1772 (Labaree et al., vol. 19).

"To Joseph Priestley," September 19, 1772 (Labaree et al., vol. 19).

Pringle, Sir John (1707–1782)

Sir John Pringle was a prominent Scottish physician whom Franklin met during the years he spent in London. Like Franklin's other friends, Pringle was interested in a variety of philosophical subjects and, according to Franklin, liked "his theology as well as his philosophy." Pringle was a student of Hermann Boerhaave and physician to the queen, and he effected improvements in sanitation and military medicine and authored *Observations on the Diseases of the Army*. As a doctor, he was interested in Franklin's experiments with paralytics and electricity.

Franklin and Pringle were traveling companions in journeys through Scotland, Germany, Switzerland, Holland, and France. The two set out on the first trip on Pringle's desire to drink the waters, for his health, at Pyrmont in Hanover. They met the German soldier Baron von Münchhausen (1720–1797), famed for his exaggerated stories of his military adventures, and both Pringle and Franklin were elected to the Royal Society of Sciences. Franklin brought back from Germany a pulse-glass, a sealed tube with water inside of it that boiled from the heat of a person's hand.

During their first trip to France, Pringle visited a hospital known for curing the "dry belly ache" and obtained a list of cured patients and their professions. Franklin noted that all of the sufferers worked with lead in some way. Franklin sent a description of their trip to Polly Stevenson, including details of their presentation before the king and a diagram of the royal dinner table. On their travels to France, the two men observed that tremors were more common in that country than anywhere else, and they attributed the malady to the use of snuff. Franklin never used tobacco, but Pringle's own tremors disappeared when he stopped using snuff.

Pringle became the president of the Royal Society in 1772, a position he retained until the king forced him out of it during the American Revolution. George III had asked Pringle to offer scientific proof in support of one of Franklin's scientific opponents, who argued that blunt lightning rods provided better protection than pointed rods. Pringle maintained that "the laws of nature were not changeable at royal pleasure" and was subsequently forced to resign his presidency as well as his position as queen's physician.

In addition to topics in medicine, Franklin wrote to Pringle about the strata of the Earth, agitated water in the bottom of oil lamps, and the effect of the depth of water on the speed of boats. Franklin was characteristically positive in his assessment of the convulsions that most scientists believed occurred on the Earth. The convulsions, he surmised to Pringle, provided mankind with minerals and other materials that would never have been accessible had they remained buried: "So what has been usually looked upon as a ruin suffered by this part of the universe, was, in reality, only a preparation, or means of rendering the earth more fit for use, more capable of being to mankind a convenient and comfortable habitation."

Franklin devised an experiment to test a phenomenon the two men had observed on one of their journeys. In Holland they had been told that boats traveled more slowly when the water in a canal was shallow. Franklin thought this was an important principle to investigate to improve knowledge in building canals. He constructed a trough 14 feet long, six inches wide, and six inches deep and used a weight to pull a miniature boat down the length of it. When he varied the depth of the water, he found that the boat did indeed move more slowly in shallow water. "Whether this difference is of consequence enough to justify a greater expense in deepening canals, is a matter of calculation, which our ingenious engineers in that way will readily determine," Franklin concluded in his description for Pringle.

Franklin recommended Pringle to the American Philosophical Society, but he was never elected. He died in 1782.

Related entries:
Electricity
France
Great Britain
Hewson, Mary (Polly) Stevenson
Medicine
Royal Society of London
Rush, Dr. Benjamin

Suggestions for further reading:
"To John Pringle," December 1, 1762 (Labaree et al., vol. 10).
"To John Pringle," December 21, 1757 (Labaree et al., vol. 7).
"To John Pringle," January 6, 1758 (Labaree et al., vol. 7).
"To Mary Stevenson," September 14, 1767 (Labaree et al., vol. 7).
"To Sir John Pringle," May 10, 1768 (Labaree et al., vol. 15).

Printing

Franklin's career as a printer began when he was 12 years old. His father, observing that the boy disliked his own tallow-chandling trade, feared that Franklin would run away, as had his other son Josiah, if he did not find a more acceptable profession for his son. He at last settled on printing, and Franklin was apprenticed to his brother James, who had set up a printing house in Boston in 1717. Franklin was supposed to remain until he reached the age of 21. He liked his new trade and acquired proficiency at it.

The sharpness, talent, and wit of Franklin's pen blossomed at an early age, and it led him into trouble on occasion. His first published

The printer as a young man at work on the press c. 1720. Engraving by Gilbert and Gihon in **The Pictorial History of Benjamin Franklin.**

writings were poems, which he printed and sold. One of them, "The Lighthouse Tragedy," which recounted the 1718 drowning of Captain George Worthilake and his family in verse, sold well. In 1721 James began to publish the *New England Courant.* The following year, Franklin, without his brother's knowledge of his authorship, contributed 14 witty letters to the *Courant* using the pseudonym "Mrs. Silence Dogood." Franklin also put his pen to use when James was jailed for offending members of the Assembly. Franklin ran the paper for the month that James spent behind bars and lampooned the politicians who had put him there. James was released from jail under order not to publish the *Courant,* so it was published for a few months under Franklin's name instead.

Troubles began to brew between the brothers, however. James treated Franklin harshly, and the independent-minded Franklin resented the unfair treatment. Their quarrels sometimes grew violent and ended with James beating his younger brother. The two had dissolved the indentures Franklin signed and secretly drawn up new ones as a formality to allow them to print the *Courant* under Franklin's name, and Franklin took advantage of the dissolution to declare himself free from James. James took care to persuade

The printing press used by Franklin, 1725–1726.
Smithsonian Institution.

the other printers in town not to allow him to work for them, so, at age 17 and almost penniless, Franklin resolved to run away to New York.

When he arrived, he found only one printer, William Bradford. Bradford had been Pennsylvania's first printer, but he had moved to New York after he had run into trouble with the governor. He sent Franklin to look for employment under his son Andrew in Philadelphia. Franklin visited him upon arriving in Philadelphia, but Bradford could not use him and sent him to a new printer in town, Samuel Keimer. Bradford did, however, offer to let Franklin lodge at his home. William Bradford, who had arrived in Philadelphia, took Franklin to Keimer's. He did not let Keimer know that he was the father of his main rival and listened to Keimer explain some of his business plans. "I," Franklin wrote, "who stood by and heard all, saw immediately that one of them was a crafty old

sophister, and the other a mere novice. Bradford left me with Keimer, who was greatly surprised when I told him who the old man was."

Andrew Bradford and Keimer were, Franklin thought, poor printers: "Bradford had not been bred to it, and was very illiterate; and Keimer, though something of a scholar, was a mere compositor, knowing nothing of press work." Franklin began to work with Keimer and lived temporarily with Bradford. Keimer, however, unhappy with Franklin's living with his rival, moved him to the house of John Read's family, the family of his future wife Deborah. His brother-in-law, Robert Homes, happened to be near Philadelphia and heard that Franklin had been living there, and he urged Franklin to return to his friends in Boston. Franklin wrote him a letter explaining his reasons for running away. The letter impressed his brother-in-law, who showed it to Governor William Keith.

Keith was impressed that a young man of Franklin's age could have written it and called on him at Keimer's printing house. "I was not a little surprised," Franklin said, "and Keimer stared like a pig poisoned." He encouraged Franklin to set up a printing business in Philadelphia and sent him home to his father with letters of commendation. Franklin's father believed he was too young to set up his own business and would not assist him. Keith promised to help him set up and to send Franklin to England with letters of credit and introduction to buy types. When Franklin arrived in England, however, he found no letters and realized that Keith's promises had all been hollow. He was forced to seek employment. He found work at Samuel Palmer's, where he stayed for almost a year, and impressed Palmer with his pamphlet "A Dissertation on Liberty and Necessity, Pleasure and Pain" (although Palmer disagreed with him). Franklin then obtained work at John Watts's, a larger printer, where he found that his coworkers "were great guzzlers of beer." A merchant, Thomas Denham, who had sailed to England with Franklin, persuaded him to return to Philadelphia in 1726 so that they could both go into business. Only a few months after they set up, Franklin suffered a severe attack of pleurisy and Denham fell ill. The latter never recovered from his illness, and Franklin was forced to return to Keimer's.

Keimer's printing house had improved from its shoddy beginnings since Franklin left it. He made Franklin the manager and paid him relatively high wages, while the rest of the hands received little money. Franklin understood that Keimer wanted him to teach the others. At first Franklin worked efficiently and well with Keimer and the rest of the workers, but Keimer began to grow more demanding and wanted to reduce Franklin's wages. Franklin's employment under Keimer ended temporarily when he peeked out of a window one day to look at a disturbance outside, and Keimer yelled at him in front of a large crowd. After a loud argument, Franklin quit.

In 1728 he set up his own printing house with Hugh Meredith, who had also worked at Keimer's, as his partner. Meredith's father financed the venture. Before the materials to set up arrived, however, Keimer sent a cordial note to Franklin and asked him to help him with a new job he had acquired printing money for New Jersey. Meredith prevailed upon Franklin to do the work. Franklin helped print the money, to the satisfaction of many in New Jersey, and he soon acquired the friendship of some of its people. Franklin and Meredith left Keimer, who did not know of their intention to set up a competitive business, on civil terms.

The same year, he resolved to publish a newspaper to compete with Bradford's *American Weekly Mercury*. Keimer, who resented his former employees' competition, found out about Franklin's plans through George Webb, a journeyman who had come to Franklin and Meredith for work, and launched his own paper, *The Universal Instructor in All Arts and Sciences and Pennsylvania Gazette*. Keimer printed less than a year's worth of his new paper, and Franklin contributed his "Busy-Body" letters to Bradford's *Mercury* to draw readership away from Keimer's paper.

Keimer eventually went bankrupt, sold his printing business, and moved to Barbados. By October 1729 Franklin and Meredith had bought the *Gazette* from Keimer, and the paper began its long and successful run. Bradford handled the government printings, but when Franklin and Meredith sent a much nicer edition of a speech to the House, its members voted them their printers for the following year. Meredith, however, proved to be an incapable partner and was often drunk. To make matters worse, a creditor of Meredith's father threatened to sue all of them. Two different people, William Coleman and Robert Grace, both members of the Junto, came to Franklin and lent him enough money to get him out of the mess, and the partnership with Meredith dissolved amicably in 1730.

Franklin was again engaged to print paper money in 1730, this time for Pennsylvania and under his own business. He had written a pamphlet entitled "On the Nature and Necessity of a Paper Currency" that he believed had so influenced the town that a measure favoring the currency passed in the House. Grateful to Franklin, the House hired him to print the money. He soon after acquired the job of printing money in Newcastle, and then of printing the laws and votes of the government. He opened a small stationer's shop. Combining the success with which he met with frugal living, he began to work off all of his debts. A rival business sprang up under David Harry, a former apprentice of Keimer's, but he too soon went bankrupt and moved to Barbados.

An "Apology for Printers," written by Franklin, appeared in the *Gazette* in June 1731. "Being frequently censured and condemned by different persons for printing things which they say ought not to be printed," it began, "I have sometimes thought it might be necessary to make a standing

Franklin outside the door of the printing shop. Painting by Jean Leon Gerome, June 14, 1910.

apology for myself, and publish it once a year, to be read on all occasions of that nature." Franklin asked his disgruntled readers to consider that "the opinions of men are almost as various as their faces," and that the printing business has to do with those opinions. Printers, he said, have the peculiar problem of having to do work that will inevitably offend someone. Franklin had always tried to make his newspaper a forum for different opinions and believed that "when truth and error have their fair play, the former is always an overmatch for the latter." It is unreasonable, he said, to think that printers approve of everything they print, just as it is unreasonable to think that printers should refuse to print everything they do not like.

Franklin further asserted that when printers sometimes produce ridiculous and worthless reading, they bow to the demands of people who do not want quality reading. "I myself have constantly refused to print anything that might countenance vice, or promote immorality," he said. To a particular complaint he had received about printing an advertisement that had at the bottom "N.B. no sea hens nor black gowns will be admitted on any terms," Franklin replied that he was unfamiliar with the term "sea hens" and did not think that the reference to the black gowns (the clergy of the Church of England) should offend.

Another of Franklin's printing successes was *Poor Richard's Almanack,* which he began in 1732 and continued until 1757. Each printing sold thousands of copies throughout the colonies. The same year, Franklin introduced the first German newspaper in the colonies, the *Philadelphische Zeitung,* which was an unsuccessful project. In 1736 Franklin became the clerk of the Pennsylvania Assembly. With the new position came the business of the Assembly's printing needs. In time, he also acquired the printing of the official documents of surrounding colonies. He was called on again to print New Jersey paper money, and he introduced an anticounterfeiting image onto the currency.

With Keimer out of business, Bradford remained his only rival. Bradford had a better reputation for advertising, and furthermore, he worked at the post office and was thought to have better access to news. He used his office to impede the distribution of Franklin's *Gazette.* In the end, however, Franklin beat Bradford at both. When Colonel Alexander Spotswood, the postmaster general for the colonies, fired Bradford in 1737 for failing to turn in his accounts, Franklin acquired his position as deputy postmaster general for Philadelphia. Franklin therefore gained the advantages that Bradford had formerly enjoyed. In 1741 Franklin began to print *The General Magazine and Historical Chronicle,* a short-lived magazine that Bradford tried to outdo with his equally unsuccessful *American Magazine.* Bradford's *Mercury* eventually failed.

In 1748 Franklin took David Hall into partnership with himself. Hall ran the business and the *Gazette* for the most part, and Franklin received half of the profits. "He is obliging, discreet, industrious, and honest," Franklin told William Strahan upon first meeting him in 1744, "and where those qualities meet, things seldom go amiss." Hall was a Scot and was Strahan's friend in London. He and Franklin worked amicably and successfully together for 18 years.

Franklin was always more than a printer. He often authored what he printed. To the *Gazette* he contributed articles and letters he believed would benefit and instruct the public. He printed pamphlets expressing his views on political and social issues that arose from time to time. He tried to maintain a level of dignity in the *Gazette:* "In the conduct of my newspaper, I carefully excluded all libeling and personal abuse, which is of late years become so disgraceful to our country."

Grateful for the aid he had been given when he wanted to set up a business and desirous of increasing his own profits, he tried to aid young journeymen who wanted to do the same. He would commonly set them up by providing materials, paying one-third of the costs, and taking one-third of the profits for a six-year term. At the end of the term, some of the successful journeymen bought their new businesses. His first was Thomas Whitemarsh, who founded the *South Carolina Gazette* in 1731. Other partnerships under similar terms were established with Louis Timothée, who took over Whitemarsh's enterprise; James Parker, who set up in New York; and Thomas Smith in Antigua.

Franklin dutifully assisted his relations who wanted to go into printing. In 1752 he sent his nephew Benjamin Mecom (son of his youngest sister, Jane) to Antigua. The venture, however, did not work out. Rather than deal with his nephew on the typical terms he required of journeymen, Franklin asked him to pay his parents a small sum toward the rent on their new house and to send rum and sugar for Franklin's family, and keep the rest of the profits. Franklin had intended to give him the printing house altogether after a few years of experience. Young Mecom, however, resented the demands placed on him and gave up the printing house. More successful was Franklin's grandson Benjamin Franklin Bache. He had learned some of the trade while he was with Franklin in France during the Revolutionary War, and he returned to Philadelphia with his grandfather in 1785. Franklin set him up in a printing house under his direction. Bache inherited all of Franklin's types and printing materials when he died in 1790.

Printing never left Franklin throughout his life. He communicated with prominent printers of his day about new techniques and other aspects of the business. Correspondence with one of his closest friends, William Strahan, lasted for more than 40 years. Strahan was a successful London printer and became King's printer in 1769. Cadwallader Colden, his friend in New York, sent Franklin a description of a new printing technique he had designed (stereotyping) and asked for his opinion. Franklin wrote to the printer John Baskerville (1706–1775) and defended him when one of his rivals took to criticizing his printing. Franklin secretly substituted the work of another printer for the perusal of Baskerville's critic, who proceeded to describe all of the minute faults he could find with it. The work was not Baskerville's but that of the printer William Caslon (1692–1766), whose work the critic had claimed to admire.

In France in 1780, Franklin visited François-Ambroise Didot (1730–1804), son of François Didot and a member of the famous French Didot printing family. Didot instructed Franklin's grandson, Benjamin Franklin Bache, for six months. Franklin was impressed with his work and wrote to Strahan in 1781: "The utmost care is taken of his press work; his ink is black, and his paper fine and white. . . . Didot . . . improves every day, and by his zeal and indefatigable application bids fair to carry the art to a high pitch of perfection." Types in France, he found, were "very good, cheaper than in England, and of harder metal."

In 1783 the London printer John Walter (1739–1812), who had become interested in a new printing technique, logography, wrote to Franklin to ask his opinion of it. This correspondence, however, was a mistake for Walter. When the king's librarian learned that he had contacted the American revolutionary Franklin, he began to ignore Walter even though he had previously shown enthusiasm for the new printing method.

In Passy, France, where Franklin lived during his service as an American diplomat during the Revolutionary War, he set up his printing press, which was of great aid to him in circulating anti-British propaganda in Europe during the war. One of the pieces he printed was a fictitious *Supplement to the Boston Chronicle,* which he composed to look like an actual colonial newspaper. The *Chronicle* contained a stinging satire of the British practice of paying Indians for rebel colonists' scalps. He also used the press at Passy to print "bagatelles" for the entertainment of his French friends.

By the end of Franklin's life, new styles in printing and language began to replace the ones he had been used to. He complained to Benjamin Vaughan in 1785, "One can scarce see a new book, without the excessive artifices made use of to puff up a paper of verses into a pamphlet, a pamphlet into an octavo, and an octavo into a quarto, with scabboardings, white lines, sparse titles of chapters, and exorbitant margins, to such a degree, that the selling of paper seems now the object, and printing on it only the pretense." Franklin also objected to new language and styles being employed, and he related some of his complaints to Noah Webster in 1789. Among his objections were the use of a small "s" instead of the long "S," the lowercasing of substantive nouns, the elimination of italic types for emphasis, and new usages of variations of nouns as verbs—for example, the noun "advocate" took on verb forms as "advocates" and "advocated."

Printing helped Franklin to succeed in his public endeavors. He had learned to live frugally while he worked his way toward owning his business. When he became involved in political controversies, he had access to a public voice for his opinions. When he needed to publicize an idea or an invention, he had a ready means. With his press at Passy, he helped spread propaganda through Europe about his country's enemy in the war.

Related entries:
Bache, Benjamin Franklin
"A Dissertation on Liberty and Necessity, Pleasure and Pain"
Franklin, James
Mecom, Jane Franklin
Parker, James
Pennsylvania Gazette
Poor Richard's Almanack
Strahan, William
Webster, Noah

Suggestions for further reading:
"Advice to a Young Tradesman," July 21, 1748 (Labaree et al., vol. 3).
"Apology for Printers," 1731 (Labaree et al., vol. 9).
Oswald, John Clyde. 1917. *Benjamin Franklin: Printer.* Garden City, N.Y.: Doubleday, Page & Company.
"To Edward and Jane Mecom," November 14, 1752 (Smyth, vol. III).
"To John Baskerville," 1760 (Labaree et al., vol. 9).
"To Mrs. Jane Mecom," June 28, 1756 (Smyth, vol. III).
"To Noah Webster," December 26, 1789 (Smyth, vol. X).
"To Richard Bache," June 2, 1779 (Labaree et al., vol. 29).

JOIN, or DIE.

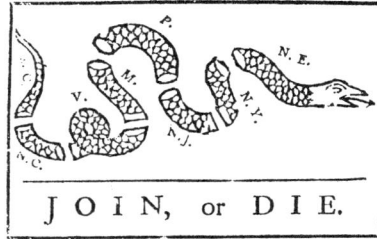

Quincy, Josiah, Sr. (1710–1784) and Josiah, Jr. (1744–1775)

The friendship between the wealthy Josiah Quincy and Franklin began during the French and Indian War and lasted through the American Revolution. In 1755 the governor of Massachusetts sent Quincy to Pennsylvania to seek assistance for an expedition to Crown Point. Quincy visited Franklin, who was a member of the Pennsylvania Assembly and a fellow native of Massachusetts, and sought his assistance. Franklin read an address that Quincy had written to the Assembly, which voted £10,000 for provisions. The governor had refused to allow a previous appropriations bill unless proprietary estates were specifically exempted from any necessary taxation. To get around the governor, Franklin suggested drawing orders on the trustees of the loan office. The orders would be payable in one year with 5 percent interest. The plan was a success, Franklin said in his *Autobiography,* and "Mr. Quincy returned thanks to the Assembly in a handsome memorial, went home highly pleased with the success of his embassy, and ever after bore me the most cordial and affectionate friendship."

Franklin especially liked Quincy's son, Josiah Quincy Jr., an ardent supporter of the American cause before the Revolution. He wrote frequently to Boston newspapers denouncing the Stamp Act and other British restrictive policies. In 1775 Franklin wrote to Quincy Sr. to thank him for sending his son to England but was concerned for his health: "His coming over has been of great service to our cause and would have been much greater, if his constitution would have borne the fatigues of being more frequently in company." He wrote to James Bowdoin: "I am much pleased with Mr. Quincy. It is thousand pities his strength of body is not equal to his strength of mind. His zeal for the public, like that of David for God's house, will, I fear, eat him up." The younger Quincy took notes on the pro-American speeches given by Lords Chatham and Camden to the House of Lords on January 20, 1775. Franklin's concerns for his health had been valid—Josiah Quincy Jr. died on his voyage home to America the same year.

The elder Quincy was no less a supporter of American independence. He and Franklin traded news and opinions about the war while Franklin was in France. Franklin encouraged him to push Americans to give up consuming unnecessary items, such as tea, for the duration of the war in order to free up additional money for needed provisions. After the war ended, Franklin's reputation came under fire in Boston. Quincy thought it his duty to relate to his friend the rumors circulating about him, for which Franklin thanked

him. Quincy died in 1784, the year before
Franklin returned from France to America.

Related entries:
French and Indian War
Revolutionary War

Suggestions for further reading:
"To Josiah Quincy, Sr.," April 15, 1776
(Labaree et al., vol. 22).
"To Josiah Quincy, Sr.," April 22, 1779
(Labaree et al., vol. 29).
"To Josiah Quincy, Sr.," February 26, 1775
(Labaree et al., vol. 21).

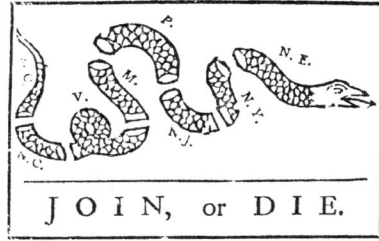

JOIN, or DIE.

R

Religious Beliefs

As a devout Boston Presbyterian, Josiah Franklin brought up his children to go to church on Sundays, and Franklin frequently read the Bible in his youth. His father entertained thoughts of devoting him to the service of the church. As a teenager, however, Franklin began to doubt some of the church doctrines that his father had tried to instill in him. "[W]hen I was scarce fifteen, when, after doubting by turns of several points, as I found them disputed in the different books I read, I began to doubt of revelation itself," he reported in his *Autobiography*. Franklin read books aimed at refuting the arguments of the deists, and it turned out that he found the deists' arguments stronger than their refutations. Franklin soon became a "thorough deist." Deists of the seventeenth and eighteenth centuries did not believe in the miracles of the Bible and believed instead in "natural religion" based on reason.

When he went to London in 1724, he wrote a pamphlet entitled "A Dissertation on Liberty and Necessity, Pleasure and Pain," in which he argued that no evil could exist in a world ruled by an all-wise, all-powerful, and all-good God. Anything that seemed evil ultimately worked for the good. However, Franklin began to believe that he had erred in writing the pamphlet and "grew convinced that truth, sincerity, and integrity between man and man were of the utmost importance to the felicity of life...." Morality and virtue in human behavior became the cornerstone of Franklin's religious ideals; he never took an interest in speculating on the mystical or understanding the doctrines of a particular sect. Although he had abandoned his belief in revelation, he thought that commandments and prohibitions existed because of the positive effect that resulted from obedience to them. Franklin acknowledged that this belief brought him through his youth, keeping him from "any willful gross immorality or injustice, that might have been expected from my want of religion."

"I never doubted . . . the existence of the Deity," Franklin wrote, "that He made the world, and governed it by His providence; that the most acceptable service of God was the doing good to man; that our souls are immortal; and that all crime will be punished, and virtue rewarded, either here or hereafter. These I esteemed the essentials of every religion." Particular sects that insisted on adherence to their doctrines divided people and created resentment, instead of encouraging moral behavior. Although Franklin disliked organized religion and rarely attended church himself, he thought public worship was generally beneficial to people and society. In Philadelphia, the local Presbyterian minister visited him from time to time, urging him to come to his church.

Franklin complied with his requests from time to time, but, although he thought the man a good preacher, "his discourses were chiefly either polemic arguments, or explications of the peculiar doctrines of our sect, and were all to me very dry, uninteresting, unedifying, since not a single moral principle was inculcated or enforced, their aim seeming to be rather to make us Presbyterians than good citizens." Nevertheless, he regularly paid his subscription to the Christ Church.

In 1728 Franklin composed his own declaration of belief and personal liturgy, "Articles of Belief and Acts of Religion, in Two Parts." Franklin said that he believed in one supreme God, that there existed beings both inferior and superior to humans elsewhere in the universe, and that a lesser, created God presided over each solar system. It was to the wise and good God of our solar system that Franklin directed his worship, as he thought it vain to assume that "the Supremely Perfect does in the least regard such an inconsiderable nothing as man."

Franklin's liturgy proceeded through declarations of praise to the Deity to either the reading of books like John Ray's *Wisdom of God Manifested in the Works of Creation,* Sir Richard Blackmore on the Creation, or the Archbishop of Cambray's *Demonstration of the Being and Attributes of God,* or to silent meditation on those topics. Next he sang John Milton's "Hymn to the Creator," and then he read a book that examined moral virtue. His subsequent "petition" asked the Deity to help him eschew vice and embrace virtue, in many forms, and he concluded with "Thanks" to the Deity for the comforts and blessings of the existence he provided. Three years later, his brief "Doctrine to Be Preached" seemed to abandon the polytheistic ideas of the articles. Franklin purposely avoided discoursing on particulars "that might tend to lessen the good opinion another might have of his own religion." He maintained close friendships with people who held widely divergent views.

In 1735 Franklin became involved in a controversy between the Reverend Samuel Hemphill, a Presbyterian who came under fire for his unorthodox beliefs, and the more orthodox Presbyterian Reverend Jedediah Andrews. Franklin liked Hemphill's sermons, which stressed the value of moral behavior. Andrews charged Hemphill with unorthodoxy before the synod, and Franklin put his pen and press to work in Hemphill's defense. Hemphill, however, lost out to the orthodox persuasion and left town. Franklin always wished that faith was "more productive of good works, than I have generally seen it: I mean real good works, works of kindness, charity, mercy, and public spirit; not holiday-keeping, sermon-reading, or hearing; performing church ceremonies, or making long prayers, filled with flatteries and compliments, despised even by wise men, and much less capable of pleasing the Deity." In 1733 he decided to undertake the "bold and arduous" task of attaining moral perfection. After identifying and describing 13 ideal virtues, he developed a system by which he graded himself on his adherence to them. Many years after he came up with the virtues, he believed his attempts to attain them, which were not always successful, nevertheless had a positive effect on his behavior.

Franklin wrote no serious declarations or descriptions of his religious beliefs after these compositions of his youth. In 1784 Franklin told Joseph Priestley that he believed there were portions of the Old Testament that could not have been divinely inspired, for example, the account in Judges, chapter 4, of the "abominably wicked and detestable action" of Jael. "If the rest of the book were like that, I should rather suppose it given inspiration by another quarter, and renounce the whole," he said.

Nevertheless, Franklin never thought of himself as an enemy of Christianity. He believed that churches had a positive influence in shaping the general morality of his countrymen and frequently donated money to them. When the Anglican Reverend George Whitefield came to Philadelphia and was refused a pulpit, Franklin helped in constructing a building that would guarantee any minister from any sect a place to speak. He befriended Whitefield and printed his sermons. Franklin's thorough knowledge of the Bible, whether he believed it or not, runs through all of his writings. He summed up his views in response to an inquiry from Ezra Stiles in 1790, written about a month before he died:

> As to Jesus of Nazareth, my opinion of whom you particularly desire, I think the system of morals and his religion, as he left them to us, the best the world ever saw or is likely to see; but I apprehend it has received various corrupting changes, and I have, with most of the present dissenters in England, some doubts as to his divinity; though it is a question I do not dogmatize upon, and think it needless to busy myself with it now, when I expect soon an opportunity of knowing the truth with less trouble. I see no harm, however, in its being believed, if that belief has the good consequence, as probably it has, of making his doctrines more respected and better observed. . . .

Related entries:
The Art of Virtue
"A Dissertation on Liberty and Necessity, Pleasure and Pain"
Great Awakening
Mather, Increase, Cotton, and Samuel
Priestley, Dr. Joseph

Suggestions for further reading:
"Articles of Belief and Acts of Religion," November 20, 1728 (Labaree et al., vol. 1).
Stifler, James Madison. 1925. *The Religion of Benjamin Franklin.* New York: D. Appleton and Company.
"To Ezra Stiles," March 9, 1790 (Smyth, vol. X).
"To Jane Mecom," July 28, 1743 (Labaree et al., vol. 2).
"To Joseph Huey," June 6, 1753 (Labaree et al., vol. 4).
"To Joseph Priestley," August 21, 1784 (Smyth, vol. IX).

Revolutionary War

Serious troubles between England and the American colonies began in the 1760s, around the time Parliament passed the Navigation Acts. Many American colonists saw themselves as British subjects who had their own "parliaments" in their colonial assemblies. Parliament should concern itself with British internal affairs; the assemblies should concern themselves with colonial internal affairs. Britain, however, had a different understanding of its colonies—it envisioned them as subservient domains that would, among other things, serve as a source for raw materials for manufacturing in England. It was a perfectly natural assumption to many members of Parliament that it had the right to tax Americans. Americans, who had no representatives in Parliament, vehemently objected to "taxation without representation." In the 1760s the British Parliament began to impose taxes on the colonies to replenish the British treasury, which the French and Indian War had drained. Americans maintained that their assemblies had always complied with the king's requests for money and resented the encroachment of Parliament on their authority.

One major seed of discontent was sown with the Stamp Act, passed in 1765. The act required Americans to purchase stamps for documents, cards, pamphlets, newspapers, and other items. Colonists were almost universally outraged. Franklin played a prominent role in this and nearly every other step in the American Revolutionary period. He had just crossed the Atlantic as agent for Pennsylvania to petition the king to assume the government of that state from the proprietors, and he soon found himself in the middle of the Stamp Act controversy. He had objected to the act, but once it passed he had recommended an agent to collect the tax. Enemies at home falsely accused him of helping to pass it. He soon became involved in working for its repeal. Franklin pleaded the American

Washington and Lafayette at Valley Forge. Engraving by H. B. Hall after the painting by Alonzo Chappel.

cause before the House of Commons in 1766. Colonial assemblies denounced the act, boycotts of British goods ensued, and nine states sent delegates to a Stamp Act Congress in New York. The Congress produced the Stamp Act Resolves and formally petitioned the king and Parliament to repeal the act. Although the Stamp Act was repealed, Parliament stubbornly reserved its right to tax the colonies.

In 1767 Parliament passed the Townshend Acts (named for Charles Townshend, who had initiated them), which imposed taxes on lead, paint, tea, glass, and paper that Americans imported from England. The acts also created an American Board of Customs Commissioners to enforce the augmented taxes created by amendments to the Navigation Acts. American colonists were once again outraged, and further boycotts and protests ensued. Massachusetts bore the brunt of British fury at American resistance to the acts. The Massachusetts Assembly sent a circular

letter to other colonies that condemned the acts and called for resistance against them. Many assemblies signed the letter after British officials dissolved the Massachusetts Court. In 1770 Massachusetts appointed Franklin as its agent in England, and he corresponded regularly with members of its Assembly.

In England Franklin set his pen to work lampooning British government policies in London newspapers. In 1768 he wrote "Causes of the American Discontents before 1768," which was printed in the *London Chronicle.* Satires such as "Rules by Which a Great Empire May Be Reduced to a Small One" (1773) and "An Edict by the King of Prussia" mocked British treatment of the colonies.

British customs officials began to seize American merchant ships, including John Hancock's *Liberty* in Boston (1768). Outraged Bostonians rioted and forced the customs officials out of town. Britain sent troops to Boston. In 1770 British troops fired on rioting Bostonians and killed five of them, a tragic event that became known as the Boston Massacre. That same year, Parliament repealed all of the Townshend Duties except the tea tax, which it kept as an example of its right to tax the colonies. In 1773 Parliament passed the Tea Act, which reduced the tea tax and in effect gave traders from the near-bankrupt British East India Company the exclusive right to sell tea in America. After three ships loaded with the tea arrived in Boston, a group of citizens dressed as Mohawk Indians dumped the tea into Boston Harbor.

This act of colonial resistance prompted Parliament to pass what the colonists came to call the "Intolerable Acts" in 1774. The Intolerable Acts included the Boston Port Act, which closed that city's port; the Quartering Act, which allowed British soldiers to stay in uninhabited colonial buildings; the Massachusetts Government Act, in which Parliament took the unprecedented step of altering a colonial constitution; and the Impartial Administration of Justice Act, which allowed British soldiers and royal officials charged with capital crimes to be tried in England. Lieutenant General Thomas Gage, commander of British forces in North America, was appointed governor of Massachusetts.

Delegates from all colonies except Georgia attended the First Continental Congress, which met in Philadelphia in 1774. Franklin was in London at that time and, along with a half dozen other American agents, charged with the task of presenting the Congress's "Declaration of Rights and Grievances" to the king. Americans became more adamant in their resistance to the punitive legislation, and Congress resolved that the colonies should not trade with Britain until the Intolerable Acts were repealed. The delegates adjourned, agreeing to convene again in 1775.

At the end of 1774 and the beginning of 1775, Franklin was involved in secret and informal negotiations with British government officials in an attempt to avert war. Among those with whom he communicated either directly or indirectly were William Pitt, Earl of Chatham; Richard Howe; the Earl of Camden; the Earl of Dartmouth; the Earl of Stanhope; and Lord Hyde. The American colonies had a few friends in Parliament, such as William Pitt and Edmund Burke, who feared that Britain would lose the colonies if it continued its course of action. However, the willingness of a few to make amends for the restrictions on the colonies was not the dominant political spirit in Parliament. Franklin became disgusted with the fruitless negotiations and, also pressed by the desire to return home after his wife's death, he sailed for America in the spring of 1775.

Armed combat between America and Britain broke out in April 1775. Under order to take American munitions and arrest Samuel Adams and John Hancock, Gage moved his men toward Concord. April 18 was the night of Paul Revere's famed "Midnight Ride." Revere and William Dawes warned Adams and Hancock at Lexington that the British were on their way. British and American troops exchanged fire the following morning. Eight Americans were killed, and the British marched on toward Concord. American militias repulsed the British, who retreated to Boston.

The Second Continental Congress met in May 1775. George Washington was chosen as the commander in chief of the Continental army, which was, to begin with, made up of the troops engaged in laying siege to British-occupied Boston. The Congress sent its "Olive Branch Petition" to King George III, reaffirming at the same time American loyalty to the king and their objections to Parliament's policies. The king refused to receive it. The Congress and Pennsylvania bestowed many important responsibilities on Franklin. He was chairman of Pennsylvania's Committee of Safety, which was charged with preparing the colony for defense. It became necessary to establish a colonial post office independent of British authority; Franklin reorganized the one begun by William Goddard and served as postmaster general.

Benjamin Franklin reading the draft of the Declaration of Independence, with John Adams and Thomas Jefferson. Painting by J. L. G. Ferris, 1921.

Other committees on which he sat were charged with printing colonial money; seeking out saltpeter; dealing with Indian affairs; protecting American trade; and seeking out assistance from foreign countries. Franklin presented a plan of union for the colonies in 1775, but it was not his that was eventually adopted. In September of that year, he went to Massachusetts to consult with Washington on methods of supplying and raising the new Continental army. He served on the Committee of Secret Correspondence, which was to seek out friends of America in foreign countries. It employed Silas Deane as an agent in France.

At the Battle of Bunker Hill in June 1775, American forces led by Colonel William Prescott clashed with British troops led by Major General William Howe. Although the British technically won the battle, their losses were twice those of the Americans. American forces led by Colonel Benedict Arnold and Colonel Ethan Allen had captured Fort Ticonderoga. Both Parliament and the king declared that the colonies were in rebellion. In November, General Richard Montgomery and his American forces captured Montreal, but after uniting with Arnold, they were subsequently defeated in Quebec. Montgomery lost his life. Colonel Henry Knox and his men began to move the heavy artillery that had been captured at Fort Ticonderoga to Boston for Washington.

Thomas Paine, who had met Franklin in London and come to America with letters of introduction written by him, published his famous pamphlet *Common Sense* in January 1776. Cries for independence grew in the colonies. On March 4 Washington forced General Howe, his men, and many loyalists to evacuate Boston and remove to Nova Scotia. Franklin traveled to Canada with two other commissioners (Samuel Chase and Charles Carroll) on a futile mission to try to obtain Canadian support for the American cause. He returned to Philadelphia in June, when he was promptly placed on a committee to draft a declaration of independence.

General Howe returned to Sandy Hook, New Jersey, with a force of British troops and German mercenaries. On July 4, 1776, delegates of the Congress approved the Declaration of Independence.

The same month, Richard Howe, with whom Franklin had negotiated in England, along with his brother, General William Howe, had been invested with powers by England to negotiate a reconciliation with the colonies. After his fleet landed in New York, a brief and futile correspondence ensued between Franklin and Lord Howe. In August, General Howe made a long-awaited move at Gravesend Bay, New York. Washington and his men were camped on Long Island and Manhattan Island. American troops, most of whom were poorly trained, suffered defeat and were driven back. The British occupied New York. After this clash (the Battle of Long Island), Lord Howe asked to negotiate with members of Congress. Franklin, Adams, and Edward Rutledge went to Staten Island to speak with him. Congress had instructed them to find out if Lord Howe had any authority to deal with the Congress, which England considered an illegal body. Again, the talks were futile. The only authority Lord Howe appeared to have was to grant pardons and declare that any or all of the colonies were once again in peaceful submission to the king.

In September 1776 Franklin's friend Dr. Jacques Barbeu-Dubourg wrote from France to encourage Congress to send commissioners to France. Deane, who was already in France, was chosen along with Franklin and Arthur Lee. (Thomas Jefferson had originally been chosen instead of Lee, but he stayed home to be with his ailing wife.) Franklin set sail across the Atlantic with his two grandsons, William Temple Franklin and Benjamin Franklin Bache, and soon settled in Passy outside of Paris. The commissioners dealt chiefly with the Comte de Vergennes, the French foreign minister.

The Battle of White Plains took place on October 28, with no clear winner. In November the British captured two American forts that had been constructed to block British access to the Hudson River. Washington retreated through New Jersey to Pennsylvania. General Howe, thinking the Americans would consider submitting to the Crown, held back from attacking again. He had miscalculated, however. Washington led his battered force in a successful surprise attack against the Hessian mercenaries at Trenton, New Jersey, on a snowy Christmas night in 1776. On January 3, 1777, Washington defeated the British at the Battle of Princeton. Washington had forced the British out of New Jersey, and they retreated to New York. These two successes rejuvenated hopes that the American cause would succeed and inspired much-needed men to enlist.

Franklin was actively involved in all aspects of financing the Revolution and accomplished more toward that end than any other American could have. His invention of the lightning rod had made him famous in France years before the Revolution, and now he was a noted philosopher championing the cause of independence from England, France's worst enemy. If Franklin had many fans, he also had enemies. English spies kept a close watch on Franklin and intercepted his mail. French police were ordered to keep a close watch on him for his protection.

Franklin's previous acquaintances with influential people in France assisted his efforts as well. He negotiated a treaty with the Farmers-General, a group of financiers, in France (one of whom was his friend from the French Academy of Sciences, the chemist Antoine-Laurent Lavoisier) that facilitated trade of southern tobacco and French saltpeter between the two countries. Franklin's nephew Jonathan Williams sold American goods in France and invested profits in French manufactured goods. Unlike John Adams and Arthur Lee, Franklin liked the French and got along well with France's government. His repeated requests for French loans and money from the Comte de Vergennes and the king were usually complied with.

From America, George Washington kept Franklin informed of the needs of the American army, and Franklin tried to accommodate them as well as he could. Adventurous European army officers visited Franklin constantly for recommendations to bring to America. Franklin grew weary of the requests, and Washington and Congress grew weary of receiving more officers than there were places for. Among those whom Franklin did recommend, however, was the Marquis de Lafayette, who played a valuable role in the Revolution and became a close friend of Washington. Franklin also employed his pen in political propaganda aimed at ruining British credit and turning popular opinion against the war. Among the pieces he wrote to this end were "A Catechism Relative to the English National Debt," and "Comparison of Great Britain and the United States in Regard to the Basis of Credit in the Two Countries."

In 1777 the British adopted a military strategy in which they intended to separate the New England colonies from the southern colonies. Major General John Burgoyne, Colonel Barry St. Leger, and General Howe were involved in the northern campaign. General Burgoyne's troops began to march down from Canada, and they recaptured Fort Ticonderoga from the Americans. Burgoyne, however, suffered successive defeats at the hands of Vermont and New Hampshire militia and the Continental army. He was forced to surrender to the American Major General Horatio Gates at Saratoga in October 1777. Howe moved his troops toward Philadelphia. Washington tried to stop him at Brandywine Creek and suffered defeat. The British occupied Philadelphia in September 1777, forcing the Continental Congress to flee to York, and then to Baltimore. Washington attacked Howe at Germantown on October 4 but was defeated.

Burgoyne's defeat was received with universal joy in France, and the American victory softened the minds of French officials who had been reluctant to enter into an alliance with America. (Madame Brillon composed "March of the Insurgents" for Franklin in honor of the American victory.) Franklin drafted a treaty outlining an alliance of America, France, and Spain. A final treaty was signed in February 1778 and made public a few weeks later. France formally recognized America as an independent country.

In England, members of Parliament made speeches against continuing the campaign in America. Lord Shelburne (William Petty) delivered a speech on March 6, 1778, urging the end of the war and the withdrawal of British troops in America, but "no independence alluded to." Lord North, the prime minister, introduced conciliatory bills. However, the king was adamant about continuing the war, and those who shared his opinion prevailed.

The American Congress became dissatisfied with Deane's work in France and recalled him in 1778, replacing him with John Adams. But the joint commission proved to be inconvenient, and the commissioners requested that Congress appoint a sole plenipotentiary. Arthur Lee and Deane had become bitter enemies, and Lee disliked Franklin. There was also tension between Adams and Franklin. The honor went to France's preference—Franklin—who was appointed sole minister plenipotentiary in October 1778. Lee had wanted the position himself and was angry at the appointment. Franklin was more at ease when the others had left, but he was constantly in the difficult position of asking the French for more money. Congress sent him bills to be paid, and he had nothing to pay them with.

In America, Washington and his men spent the winter at Valley Forge, Pennsylvania, where they were joined by the Prussian army officer Baron Friedrich Wilhelm von Steuben. Baron von Steuben brought much-needed discipline and professionalism to the Continental army. France sent a naval fleet commanded by the Comte d'Estaing. General Sir Henry Clinton, who had replaced General Howe as commander of British troops in Philadelphia, evacuated that city. Washington pursued them as they marched toward New York. They clashed at Monmouth, New Jersey; the British were victorious, but not without facing fierce resistance.

Operations became increasingly difficult for the British. They needed access to the sea in order to receive supplies and could not remain inland. France had joined the war against them. Troubles were brewing in Europe, and they were forced to distribute their manpower. Faced with mixed successes in the north, the British turned their attention to the south. They now aimed to defeat the southern colonies one by one.

On December 29, 1778, the British took Savannah. After defeats at Savannah and Charleston, the American Major General Benjamin Lincoln was forced to surrender, and d'Estaing sailed back to France. Lieutenant General Charles Cornwallis took control of the British southern campaign in 1780. Americans, meanwhile, had taken control of the Ohio Valley and other western regions. Cornwallis moved through the Carolinas in 1780 and 1781 with mixed success. British troops were defeated at the Battle of Kings Mountain and at Cowpens in 1780. They clashed with Americans under General Nathanael Greene in a battle at the Guilford Courthouse in North Carolina. After heavy losses on both sides, there was no decisive victor, and Cornwallis marched to Wilmington, then moved north to Yorktown, Virginia.

Throughout the fighting, Franklin kept Washington informed of events in France and England. There had been growing opposition in Parliament to continuing the war. Washington, spurred by the knowledge of growing dissatisfaction in England, wanted to deal a decisive blow to British armies that might induce the British to sue for peace. He wanted to trap the British between French naval forces off the coast and American interior forces. Franklin was instrumental in selling this idea to the French government.

French troops under the Comte de Rochambeau arrived at Newport, Rhode Island, in 1780. Meanwhile, Benedict Arnold had treasonably planned to surrender a key fortress at West Point to the British, but he fled after learning his intentions had been made known to Washington. Washington and Rochambeau marched south and surrounded Yorktown. With a French fleet under the Comte de Grasse off the Virginia coast, Cornwallis was trapped and forced to surrender in 1781.

There were no major battles after Yorktown. Negotiations for peace began in Paris, with Franklin as one of the negotiators, and a final treaty was signed in 1783.

Related entries:

Suggestions for further reading:
Lemay, J. A. Leo, ed. 1976. *The Oldest Revolutionary: Essays on Benjamin Franklin.* Philadelphia: University of Pennsylvania Press.
"The Life of Benjamin Franklin," pp. 290–388 (Smyth, vol. X).

Revolutionary Writings

*I*n the years immediately preceding the American Revolution, Franklin lived in England; during and immediately after the war, he lived in France. From these two countries, he actively tried to prejudice public opinion in Europe against England and the restrictive policy it practiced toward America.

One of Franklin's most popular pieces was his 1773 "An Edict by the King of Prussia," a satire on England's claim of sovereignty over the American colonies. In the fictitious edict, the king of Prussia laid claim to England's dominions as England laid claim to the American colonies. The first German settlements in Britain were colonies of people subject to the dukes of Prussia, he reasoned, and they had never been emancipated from the rule of "our August house." "[A]nd whereas it is just and expedient that a revenue should be raised from the said colonies in Britain," the edict continued, "towards our indemnification, and that those who are descendants of our ancient subjects, and thence still owe us due obedience, should contribute to the replenishing of our royal coffers as they must have done, had their ancestors remained in the territories now to us appertaining. . . ." The king declared a tax on all goods, wares, merchandise, grain, and produce exported from England, ordered that all ships pass through Königsberg before they arrive in England, and forbade the construction of any new mines. All raw iron was to be transported to Prussia for manufacturing, but shipping wool from Britain to Prussia was prohibited; "Nevertheless, our loving subjects there are hereby permitted (if they think proper) to use all their wool as manure for the improvement of their lands." The manufacture of hats was severely restricted, so as not to compete with the mother country's hat industry. Finally, Prussia would empty her prisons out into England "for the better peopling of that country." The penalty for disobeying the edict was an offense of high treason. Franklin intended the Prussian king's orders to place the similar and real measures England pursued in America in a negative light. The edict appeared in *The Gentleman's Magazine* in October 1773.

The same year, Franklin wrote another satire, "Rules by Which a Great Empire May Be Reduced to a Small One," the point of which was to show that England's current restrictive measures in America would lead to the loss of its colonies. Rule number one was to treat the provinces like a cake, "most easily diminished at the edges." Following the analogy, the empire should endeavor to rid itself of its most remote provinces first. To begin with, the mother country should govern remote provinces with stricter laws than at home. "If they should happen to be zealous Whigs, friends of liberty, nurtured in revolution principles, remember all that to their prejudice, and resolve to punish it," Franklin suggested. Rulers should also nurse suspicions of the colonies, even if they have been loyal, and quarter troops among them to provoke them. "By this means, like the husband who uses his wife ill from suspicion, you may in time convert your suspicions into realities," Franklin said. Wise and just men were poor governors unless an empire wanted to retain its provinces: "If you can find prodigals, who have ruined their fortunes, broken gamesters or stockjobbers, these may do well as governors; for they will probably be rapacious, and provoke the people by their extortions. Wrangling proctors and pettifogging lawyers, too, are not amiss. . . . "

All complaints from subjects in the colonies were to be delayed or accompanied with enormous expense, and judgment should always fall against their grievances. Corrupt governors who rendered themselves so odious to the colonists as to fear for their lives should be recalled and rewarded with pensions. Preference was to be given to taxes forcibly taken from the colonial subjects instead of voluntary grants, and he suggested sending tax collectors of the "most indiscreet, ill-bred, and insolent you can find. Let these have large salaries out of the extorted revenue, and live in open, grating luxury upon the sweat and blood of the industrious." Rulers seeking to reduce a great empire should endeavor to use unfair taxes for purposes other than what they intended them for and suppose all complaints from remote colonists "to be invented and promoted by a few factious demagogues, whom if you could catch and hang, all would be quiet." The government should send armies to the provinces under the pretense of protecting them, destroy the frontier forts, and move the soldiers into the heartland. "This will seem to proceed from your ill will or your ignorance, and contribute farther to produce and strengthen an opinion among them, that you are no longer fit to govern them," Franklin said. This popular piece, signed with the pseudonym "Q. E. D.," also appeared in *The Gentleman's Magazine*.

In 1774 Franklin sent a letter to the *Public Advertiser* signed "A well-wisher to the King and all his dominions," examining the history of grievances between the American colonies and England. The trouble had started with the Stamp Act, Franklin argued, when Parliament imposed a tax to raise revenue that colonial assemblies would have been willing to grant. One year after the repeal of the Stamp Act, another act laid duties on the export of American manufactured goods. Franklin's letter also related the American complaints that their assemblies had been dissolved unjustly and their petitions rejected in England.

In a different letter, Franklin responded to "Britannicus" in defense of his own character. Franklin's son had been appointed governor of New Jersey; he had been appointed deputy postmaster general of America and

Benjamin Franklin in his study, 1780. Mezzotint by Edward Fisher after the painting by Mason Chamberlin.

offered a position in the Salt Office, if he would abandon his zeal for the interests of America. "As it is a settled point in government here, that every man has his price, 'tis plain they are bunglers in their business, and have not given him enough," Franklin joked. He mused in another letter to the *Public Ledger,* "Surely the great commerce of this nation with the Americans is of too much importance to be risked in a quarrel, which has no foundation but ministerial pique and obstinacy!"

In 1775 Franklin wrote "A Dialogue between Britain, France, Spain, Holland, Saxony, and America," which portrayed Britain as a desperate country that would have no European allies in her conquest of America. Spain still remembered Britain's aid to rebel Spanish subjects in the low country, and France remembered Britain's aid to rebel French Huguenots. Holland thought her accounts were balanced with Britain and did not want an altercation. The dialogue then erupted into an exchange of harsh accusations between England and America. America asked Britain: "Do you run about begging all Europe not to supply those poor people [Americans] with a little powder and shot? Do you mean, then, to fall upon them naked and unarmed, and butcher them in cold blood? Is this your courage? Is this your magnanimity?" Britain responded: "Oh! you wicked—Whig—Presbyterian—Serpent! Have you the impudence to appear before me after all your disobedience? Surrender immediately all your liberties and properties into my hands, or I will cut you to pieces." Britain asserted that she was the mother country and demanded obedience, to which Saxony replied: "Mother country! Hah, hah, he! What respect have you the front to claim as a mother country? You know that *I* am *your* mother country, and yet you pay me none." Saxony warned Britain that she was on the road to making herself the contempt of Europe.

Franklin set his pen to work to tarnish England's credit when he reached France in late 1776. His "Comparison of Great Britain and the United States in Regard to the Basis of Credit in the Two Countries" (1777) was written with the purpose of helping the United States to obtain European loans to support its bid for independence. Franklin outlined seven particulars that established a person's good credit: repayment of former loans; industry in business; frugality in expenses; solidity of funds; prospects of greater future ability; prudence in managing general affairs; and known virtue and honest character. "The same circumstances, that give a private man credit," Franklin argued, "ought to have, and will have, their weight with lenders of money to public bodies or to nations." With regard to each of his seven particulars, Franklin tried to demonstrate to foreign powers that it was safer to lend money to America than to England. "On the whole," Franklin concluded, "it appears, that, from the general industry, frugality, ability, prudence, and virtue of America, she is a much safer debtor than Britain: To say nothing of the satisfaction generous minds must have in reflecting, that by loans to America they are opposing tyranny, and aiding the cause of liberty, which is the cause of all mankind." This piece was translated into many languages and circulated around Europe.

In "A Catechism Relating to the English National Debt" (1777), Franklin used a question-and-answer format to ridicule the size of England's debt. The answerer informed the questioner that it would take a person 148 years, 109 days, and 22 hours to count England's national debt in shillings; that the debt's weight in shillings would amount to 61,752,476 Troy pounds; that 314 ships or 31,452 carts would be required to carry it; that the shillings, laid in a straight line, would stretch for 61,552 miles, or 9,572 miles more than twice the circumference of the Earth; that the interest on the debt amounted to 6,770,000 pounds; that England paid the interest by taxing those who lent the principal and other people; and that England would never be able to pay the debt.

Another piece commonly attributed to Franklin, "The Sale of the Hessians," followed General George Washington's defeat of the Hessian soldiers at Trenton, New Jersey. It demonstrated the widespread American resentment of George III's hiring of German mercenaries (Hessians) to fight in America. In a fictitious letter, supposedly from the Count de Schaumbergh to the Baron Hohendorf, the former rejoiced that 345 of 1,950 Hessians escaped. "There were just 1,605 men killed, and I cannot sufficiently commend your prudence in sending an exact list of the dead to my minister in London," the Count de Schaumbergh wrote. It had been necessary to send the list, because the English ministry had underestimated the number of Hessian deaths and would have paid less for them, cutting into Schaumbergh's profit. The greedy count was to "insinuate to the surgeons with entire propriety that a crippled man is a reproach to their profession, and that there is no wiser course than to let every one of them die when he ceases to be fit to fight."

One of Franklin's final wartime writings aimed at discrediting England was a fictitious "Supplement to the Boston Independent Chronicle" (1782), designed to look like a genuine Boston newspaper and circulated in Europe. The first edition contained gruesome descriptions of American scalps for which England had paid Seneca Indians and was intended as an attack on "English barbarities." The inventory of scalps was presented in a fictitious letter from James Crauford to Colonel Haldimand, governor of Canada. "The form," he told Charles W. F. Dumas, "may perhaps not be genuine, but the substance is truth." A second edition contained a fictitious letter from Captain John Paul Jones to Sir Joseph York, in which Jones defended himself against England's charges that he was a pirate. "A pirate makes war for the sake of rapine. This is not the kind of war I am engaged in against England," Jones said. The American war was a war in defense of liberty, and England's was "a war of rapine; of course, a piratical war; and those who approve of it, and are engaged in it, more justly deserve the name of pirates, which you bestow on me."

Writing always played a prominent role in Franklin's activities, whether he was raising money to build a hospital or representing his country's interest against England. In addition to his popular published articles, he wrote letters to well-connected friends in Europe with hopes of influencing foreign opinion in favor of America.

Related entry:
Revolutionary War

Suggestions for further reading:
"A Catechism Relating to the English National Debt," 1777 (Labaree et al., vol. 24).
"Comparison of Great Britain and as to Credit," 1777 (Labaree et al., vol. 24).
"An Edict by the King of Prussia," September 22, 1773 (Labaree et al., vol. 20).
"Rules by Which a Great Empire May Be Reduced to a Small One," September 11, 1773 (Labaree et al., vol. 20).
"Supplement to the Boston Independent Chronicle," 1782 (Smyth, vol. VIII).

Rogers, Deborah Read

See **Franklin, Deborah Read Rogers.**

Royal Society of London

The Royal Society of London, which still exists, was formed in 1660 and given a royal charter two years later under King Charles II (1630–1685). Its members are generally accomplished in one or more areas in the natural sciences. It promotes scientific research and offers advice to the British government and others on scientific matters. A president and a council govern the society, and it prints new research and discoveries in its *Philosophical Transactions.*

Franklin's friend and member of the Royal Society Peter Collinson had Franklin's first papers on electricity read before the society. They met with indifference and laughter and were not deemed worthy enough to print in the *Philosophical Transactions.* Collinson's friend Dr. John Fothergill thought they should be printed, and Collinson found a printer and had them printed as a pamphlet. Franklin's papers were translated into French, and some of his experiments were performed before Louis XV, including the experiment "to draw lightning from the clouds." Franklin's name became known in France, and his theories on electricity were generally accepted by French scientists.

An English physician who was visiting France wrote to a friend in the Royal Society about the general regard for Franklin's theories in that country. The society then began to reconsider Franklin's papers. William Watson (1715–1787) summarized the original papers and new ones that Franklin had written since the rejection of the first set. Watson's summary was printed in the *Philosophical Transactions,* and members of the society successfully repeated some of Franklin's experiments. In 1753 they awarded him the Sir Godfrey Copley medal, which was sent to Governor William Denny in Pennsylvania and presented to Franklin. The society elected Franklin as a member in 1756, excused him of membership payments, and gave him their *Philosophical Transactions* free of charge. Franklin's papers on electricity as well as on other subjects were often read at the society.

Franklin was active in the Royal Society while he was in England—most of the years between 1757 and 1775. He regularly sent its *Philosophical Transactions* to the American Philosophical Society at home. His friends in the society included Peter Collinson, Dr. Joseph Priestley, and Sir John Pringle. In 1767 it was discovered that the clerk of the Royal Society had embezzled almost £1,300 over a period of four years. Franklin was on the governing council that year and was one of the people charged with investigating the clerk's accounts. While he was investigating the clerk, he looked through the society's old books and found comments relating to his own admission into the society. He told his son that he had had the rare honor of being elected without applying.

In 1771 a committee from the Royal Society, including Franklin, was asked to provide advice for protecting British powder magazines from lightning. Franklin and most of the committee recommended pointed lightning rods, but one dissenter pushed for blunt rods. The pointed rods were chosen for the powder magazines and for the Royal Palace. After the American Revolution began, the king had the pointed rods on the palaces replaced with blunt ones. The war made communication with Franklin's friends in England difficult, but he began to correspond with them regularly after the war. From France he kept the Royal Society informed of the first hot-air balloon launches with a series of letters to its president, Sir Joseph Banks.

Related entries:
Collinson, Peter
Electricity
Fothergill, Dr. John
George III
Hot-Air Balloons
Pringle, Sir John

Suggestions for further reading:
"Report of the Purfleet Committee to the

Royal Society," 1772 (Labaree et al., vol. 19). "To William Franklin," December 19, 1767 (Labaree et al., vol. 14).

Dr. Benjamin Rush. Stipple engraving by St. Memin, 1802.

Rush, Dr. Benjamin (1746–1813)

As one of the most prominent early American doctors, Benjamin Rush practiced medicine, was a member of the American Philosophical Society, and served as a surgeon general for the American armies in the Revolutionary War. In the political and social realm, Rush was a delegate to the Second Continental Congress, a signer of the Declaration of Independence, a vocal opponent of slavery, and later the treasurer of the United States beginning in the administration of John Adams. In many of these areas of interest—medical ailments, the abolition of slavery, and the independence of the colonies—he shared interests and friendship with Franklin.

Rush was a native of Pennsylvania and one of seven children brought up chiefly by their mother. He was an exceptional student at the school he attended in Maryland, and later at the College of New Jersey (now Princeton University), from which he graduated at age 15. After his graduation, he decided to study medicine and became apprenticed to Dr. John Redmond in Philadelphia. He later went to Edinburgh, Scotland, where he earned his M.D. degree after two years of study. After obtaining his degree, he spent a year in London, where he communicated with Franklin, and in Paris. Upon returning to America, he became a chemistry professor and set up a private medical practice. He married Julia Stockton in 1776, and the couple had 13 children.

During the period preceding the American Revolution, Rush became a staunch advocate of independence. He encouraged Thomas Paine to write his famous pamphlet *Common Sense.* He and Franklin both served as delegates from Pennsylvania to the Continental Congress and signed the Declaration of Independence. During the war he became a surgeon general for the army and treated wounded soldiers. Frustrated with an administration he felt was not doing enough to improve poor hospital conditions, he resigned his post as surgeon general.

In his diary Rush recorded conversations he had with Franklin about tobacco, quacks in the medical profession, the plague in Turkey, and climates. Franklin told Rush that he had never used tobacco in his life and that he believed excessive use of snuff was responsible for the frequent tremors he noticed among his acquaintances in France. Rush, who was a respected medical doctor, recorded Franklin's belief that only a few good doctors make money in their profession; quacks made most of the money. Reports of the plague in Turkey, Franklin thought, were exaggerated, and he related a story from a Dr. MacKensie who lived in Constantinople. MacKensie counted the corpses being carried from the city every day and found only one-tenth of the number widely reported (Smyth 1907).

Franklin related to Rush in 1773 his beliefs about common colds—that they were contagious and could be caused by corrupted air as well as by "too full living, with too little exercise." In 1786 Rush wrote "On the Influence of Physical Causes on the Moral Faculty," which he dedicated to Franklin. The original inscription was too elaborate for Franklin's taste, and he begged him to "suppress that most extravagant encomium on your friend Franklin" from his "ingenious discourse." In accordance with Franklin's request, Rush simplified the dedication before it was published.

After the war Rush had returned to teaching and medicine. He was instrumental in forming the Pennsylvania Society for the Abolition of Slavery, of which Franklin was president during the last years of his life. He was involved in projects to aid the poor and improve educational opportunities for women. He worked at the Pennsylvania Hospital, which Franklin had helped to found, treating victims of yellow fever during an epidemic in 1793 and trying to estab-

lish more humane treatment for the mentally ill. In 1812 he wrote *Medical Inquiries and Observations upon the Diseases of the Mind,* the first book on psychiatry in the United States. The last years of his life were spent as a doctor and as the treasurer of the U.S. mint.

Related entries:
American Philosophical Society
Continental Congresses
Declaration of Independence
Medicine
Revolutionary War
Slavery

Suggestions for further reading:
"To Benjamin Rush," March 1786 (Smyth, vol. IX).
Rush, Benjamin. *Letters.* 1951. Edited by L.H. Butterfield. Princeton University Press.
————. 1947. *The Selected Writings of Benjamin Rush.* New York: Philosophical Library. Edited by Dagobert D. Runes.

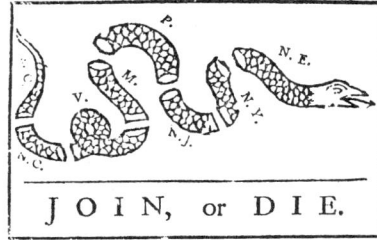

JOIN, or DIE.

Scott, Lydia Franklin (1708–1758)

Lydia Franklin Scott, Franklin's younger sister, was the next child after her famous brother and married Robert Scott, a shipmaster, in 1731. Franklin did not keep in close touch with her but inquired for news about her occasionally from their sister Jane (Mecom). About a month before he died, Franklin asked Jane if she knew the fate or whereabouts of Lydia's daughter. When he died, he left £50 sterling to be divided among her descendants.

Related entry:
Mecom, Jane Franklin

Suggestion for further reading:
"To Mrs. Jane Mecom," March 24, 1790 (Smyth, vol. X).

Shelburne, Earl of (William Petty)

See **Journal of the Negotiation for Peace with Great Britain; Native Americans; Treaty of Paris, 1783.**

Shipley, Catherine (1759–1840) and Georgiana (Hare-Naylor) (1756–1806)

Franklin spent some of his time pleasantly in England with the family of Jonathan Shipley, the bishop of St. Asaph, who had five daughters, Anna Maria, Amelia, Elizabeth, Georgiana, and Catherine. Franklin's frequent role as a father figure to young women applied to the Shipley daughters as well as to many others. He took a particular liking to the youngest two, Georgiana and Catherine.

Catherine (Kitty) was only 11 years old when she rode with Franklin to London, where she went to school, in 1771. During their journey she and Franklin discussed what kind of men she and her sisters should marry. Many years later (1785), as he prepared to sail for the United States, Catherine came with her parents to Southampton to meet him. She wrote to him to wish him a happy voyage that was long enough for him to finish his *Autobiography*. A few months later she sent him a purse with 13 stars and stripes she had made for him. Franklin soon after sent her a bagatelle, "The Art of Procuring Pleasant Dreams," which he had written at Catherine's request. She wrote back to thank him for taking the time to write it, but she could not find a Bible passage that described Franklin's assertion that Methuselah slept in the open air. Catherine wrote to Franklin in 1788 to tell him of her father's death. Ironically, Kitty never married.

Georgiana, Catherine's older sister, was multitalented, intelligent, attractive, and interested in natural philosophy. Franklin sent her one of his books in 1771, "as a small mark of [his] regard for her philosophic genius." In 1781 she recalled the "happy hours we once passed in [Franklin's] society when we were never amused without learning some useful truth. . . ." Against her father's advice, Georgiana hazarded a letter to Franklin in France during the American Revolution, assuring Franklin of her regard for him and asking if he had read Adam Smith's *Wealth of Nations*. They continued to trade letters during the war. Georgiana studied Latin and sent Franklin her translations of some of Horace's (65–8 B.C.) poems. In a subsequent letter she asked Franklin about cold nights in the desert, a phenomenon with which he was unfamiliar and about which he wanted more details. In his response he added, "I like to see that you retain a taste for philosophical enquiries." Franklin thanked her for some verses she had sent and remarked, "How many talents you possess! painting, poetry, languages, etc., etc. All valuable, but your good heart is worth the whole." Franklin begged her to do portraits of her family and send them to him. He sent Georgiana two of his bagatelles from Passy, "The Handsome and Deformed Leg" (1780) and "Dialogue between Franklin and the Gout" (1780).

While Franklin was in England, his wife, Deborah, sent a large, gray squirrel overseas that quickly endeared itself to the Shipleys. The squirrel, whom they named Mungo, was roaming outside of its cage when it had a fatal meeting with a dog in 1772. Franklin wrote an epitaph for Mungo for Georgiana, and it was placed on a monument over the squirrel's burial place in the garden. A special squirrel like Mungo, Franklin told her, deserved an epitaph. "Few squirrels were better accomplished," he wrote, "for he had a good education, had traveled far, and seen much of the world." The epitaph began:

Alas! poor Mungo!
Happy wert thou, hadst thou known
Thy own felicity.
Remote from the fierce bald eagle,
Tyrant of thy native woods,
Thou hadst nought to fear from his
piercing talons,
Nor from the murdering gun
Of the thoughtless sportsman. . . .

Franklin thought this epitaph was preferable to:

Here Skugg
Lies snug
As a bug
In a rug.

Mrs. Franklin sent her another squirrel in 1773; Georgiana reported that it was still alive in 1779.

Against her parents' wishes, Georgiana married the author and playwright Francis Hare-Naylor (1753–1815) in 1783 and asked Franklin questions about a potential move to America in 1784. The Hare-Naylors moved to Italy and had four sons. When Hare-Naylor's father died they moved to England, where Georgiana painted and her husband wrote. Georgiana lost her sight in her mid-forties, and the family fortune steadily declined. In 1804 they moved to Weimar, and Georgiana died two years later.

Related entries:
Bagatelles
Shipley, Jonathan

Suggestion for further reading:
Stifler, James Madison. 1927. *"My Dear Girl": The Correspondence of Benjamin Franklin with Polly Stevenson, Georgiana and Catherine Shipley.* New York: George H. Doran.

Shipley, Jonathan (1714–1788)

Jonathan Shipley was the bishop of St. Asaph, Wales, where he had a small cathedral and spent little time, and one of a handful of Franklin's closest friends during the years he spent in England. The Shipleys had a son, William, and five daughters—Anna Maria, Amelia, Elizabeth, Georgiana, and Catherine—and Franklin was particularly fond of the two youngest, Georgiana and Catherine. In the bishop Franklin found one of the strongest friends of America, and in his entire family he found pleasant company. Shipley and Franklin were members of the Honest Whigs, a philosophical discussion club that met in a London coffeehouse. Shipley's brother, William, had asked Franklin to become a member of the Society of Arts in London in 1756.

Franklin liked to pass time with the Shipleys. He spent a week at the bishop's country seat at Twyford in June 1771, and he returned in July for a three-week stay. During this second stay, he began his famous *Autobiography*, which the Shipleys and others never stopped urging him to finish. Catherine Shipley wrote to Franklin after seeing him before he returned to America in 1785: "We never walk in the garden without seeing Dr. Franklin's room and thinking of the work that was begun in it. I have sincerely wished you a good voyage but since the completion of that work depends on its length I cannot wish it may be short."

Shipley, a member of the House of Lords, was strongly pro-American during the controversies that erupted before the war—an unpopular position among his fellow bishops. In 1773 he delivered a sermon for the Society for Propagating the Gospel, which was subsequently published. Franklin thought it contained "such liberal and generous sentiments, relating to the conduct of government here towards America, that Sir J[ohn] P[ringle] says it was written in compliment to me. But from the intimacy of friendship in which I live with the author, I know he has expressed nothing but what he thinks and feels. . . . " In his 1774 "Speech Intended to Have Been Spoken," Shipley criticized the harsh measures that Parliament took toward Boston and a plan to alter the Massachusetts constitution, and Franklin thought it had a positive effect in shaping the sentiments of people in England on America.

Although the war interrupted their correspondence, it had no negative effect on their friendship. The bishop, his wife, and their youngest daughter, Catherine, came to Southampton in 1785 (along with Benjamin Vaughan and William Franklin) to see Franklin one last time before his ship set sail for America. After he arrived he kept Shipley updated on political affairs in America. When Catherine wrote to Franklin in 1788 to inform him of her father's death, Franklin had already heard the news. He responded in 1789: "That excellent man has then left us! His departure is a loss, not to his family and friends only, but to his nation, and to the world; for he was intent on doing good, had wisdom to devise the means, and talents to promote them."

Related entries:
Honest Whigs
Shipley, Catherine and Georgiana (Hare-Naylor)

Suggestions for further reading:
"To Jonathan Shipley," February 24, 1786 (Smyth, vol. VIII).
"To Jonathan Shipley," June 10, 1782 (Smyth, vol. IX).
"To Jonathan Shipley," June 24, 1771 (Labaree et al., vol. 18).
"To Jonathan Shipley," March 17, 1783 (Smyth, vol. IX).
"To Miss Catherine Louisa Shipley," April 27, 1789 (Smyth, vol. X).

Slavery

The issue of slavery was long a divisive one in the American colonies.

"To be sold . . . a cargo of 170 prime young likely healthy Guinea Slaves." Broadside, Savannah, Georgia, July 25, 1774.

British merchants began importing slaves from Africa in the 1500s. When he was younger, Franklin sold slaves and indentured servants on a small scale, and he and his wife kept some from time to time. As he grew older, however, his disapproval of slavery blossomed, and he became actively involved in trying to stop a practice he considered abhorrent and inhumane.

In 1770, when tension was running high between the American colonies and Britain, and talk of liberty was rampant, Franklin contributed "A Conversation on Slavery" to the *Public Advertiser* in England. The piece presented a fictional conversation between an Englishman, an American, and a Scotsman. Although his disdain for slavery was evident in the letter, his primary aim with this particular writing was to defend his fellow Americans against English charges that they were hypocritical in demanding freedoms while continuing to keep slaves.

In the conversation the American spoke eloquently and at length, while the Scotsman hardly spoke at all. To the Englishman's charge that Americans were tyrants because they kept slaves, the American responded that another form of slavery existed in England in the working class, which was forced to work under miserable conditions. Still another kind of slavery was practiced in Scotland's coal mines. The American also objected to generalized criticism of slavery in America, as many of his countrymen detested the practice and only a relative few (one in 100 families, he estimated) of them owned slaves. Further, he argued, many slaves were treated very well, and they were in the colonies in the first place because British merchants had brought them there (Lemay 1987).

Franklin's opposition to slavery grew stronger in his writings of subsequent years. In a letter to the abolitionist Anthony Benezet (1713–1784) in 1772 Franklin wrote, "I am glad to hear that the disposition against keeping negroes grows more general in North America. Several pieces have been lately printed here [England] against the practice, and I hope in time it will be taken into consideration and suppressed by the legislature." That same year, he wrote a stinging letter to the *London Chronicle* in response to the freeing of a slave in England. He blamed England for the continuing slave traffic, which he said amounted to the importation of 100,000 people every year, one-third of whom died of disease. He called the slave trade "a constant butchery of the human species by this pestilential detestable traffic in the bodies and souls of men" (Lemay 1987). Franklin made no objection to Thomas Jefferson's scathing denunciation of the slave trade in the Declaration of Independence in 1776; however, that paragraph was deleted to appease delegates from the South in Congress.

After the Revolutionary War and during the last few years of his life, Franklin was involved with the Quaker-formed Pennsylvania Society for Promoting the Abolition of Slavery, and he served as the society's president for a time. In 1789 the society released

"An Address to the Public," which was signed by its president, B. Franklin, and stressed the necessity of taking proper care of emancipated slaves. Franklin penned another release from the society, a "Plan for Improving the Condition of the Free Blacks." The plan called for the establishment of a 24-person committee to be made up of elected members and broken into subcommittees. Each subcommittee would take responsibility of a particular area of need among free blacks. The first committee was responsible for providing moral guidance and instruction. The second was to seek apprenticeships for young blacks; the third to facilitate educational opportunity; and the fourth to locate employment opportunities. Where need overlapped, the committees were to cooperate with one another. The society's efforts were to be financed by donations and subscriptions.

One of the last pieces Franklin wrote (March 1790) was a biting satire of a speech made by Georgia Congressman James Jackson, who had delivered a defense of the slave trade. The letter, printed in the *Federal Gazette,* mocked the prevailing defenses of slavery in America—that abolishing slavery would create confusion and chaos, would be an unjust theft of property from the people who owned them, and that slaves were needed to perform work. Franklin, then 84 and writing under the pseudonym "Historicus," parodied Jackson's speech with a fictitious one delivered by a member of the Algerian Divan, Sidi Mehemet Ibrahim, "against granting the petition of the sect called Erika, or Purists, who prayed for the abolition of piracy and slavery as being unjust."

Related entries:
  Declaration of Independence
  Rush, Dr. Benjamin

Suggestions for further reading:
  "An Address to the Public, from the Pennsylvania Society for Promoting the Abolition of Slavery, and the Relief of Free Negroes Unlawfully Held in Bondage," November 9, 1789 (Lemay 1987).

"On the Slave-Trade," March 23, 1790 (Smyth, vol. X).
"Plan for Improving the Condition of Free Blacks," (Smyth, vol. X).
"The Sommersett Case and the Slave Trade," June 18–20, 1772 (Labaree et al., vol. 19).
"To Anthony Benezet," August 22, 1772 (Labaree et al., vol. 19).

Society of the Cincinnati

After the Revolutionary War, former officers of the American army formed the Society of the Cincinnati. The society conferred hereditary honors on the eldest sons of its members. Franklin, who had long opposed hereditary titles, had called into question the concept of noble blood in his 1751 edition of *Poor Richard Improved*. He disapproved of the society and outlined his objections in a long letter to his daughter in 1784.

"[H]onor, worthily obtained (as for example that of our officers), is in its nature a personal thing, and incommunicable to any but those who had some share in obtaining it," Franklin maintained. In lieu of descending honors, he suggested ascending honors. In Chinese tradition, parents received honor when their children achieved something, because people assumed that their parents had instructed them well. Franklin thought that ascending honors encouraged parents to instruct their children properly, while descending honors encouraged pride and laziness in the children. He suggested that the Cincinnati direct parents to wear badges of honor instead of the children, which would amount to a sort of obedience to the Fourth Commandment to honor one's father and mother.

Franklin also undertook to prove to his daughter that "the absurdity of descending honors is not a mere matter of philosophical opinion; it is capable of mathematical demonstration." A man's son has only half of his father's traits, and his grandson only a fourth. The great-grandson has only an eighth, and his son a sixteenth. In nine generations, the son has only 1/512 of the original father's makeup. Franklin further calculated that it would take 1,022 people to contribute to the formation of the son of the ninth generation. If there were to be a thousand members of the society, 1,022,000 men and women would be involved in creating them. Franklin struck out 22,000 to account for any that might be involved in creating more than one. "Let us strike off then the 22,000, on the supposition of this double employ, and then consider whether, after a reasonable estimation of the number of rogues, and fools, and royalists and scoundrels and prostitutes, that are mixed with, and help to make up necessarily their million of predecessors, posterity will have much reason to boast of noble blood," he said.

Before he left France, he read with approval a pamphlet against the society written by Ædanus Burke of South Carolina, translated and enlarged by the future orator of the French Revolution, the Comte de Mirabeau. Despite his ridicule of the Cincinnati, Franklin accepted an honorary membership.

Related entries:
    Bache, Sarah Franklin
    France
    Poor Richard's Almanack
    Revolutionary War

Suggestions for further reading:
    "To Benjamin Vaughan," September 8, 1784 (Smyth, vol. IX).
    "To George Whatley," May 23, 1785 (Smyth, vol. IX).
    "To Mrs. Sarah Bache," January 26, 1784 (Smyth, vol. IX).

Stamp Act

Deep tension between Great Britain and the American colonies began with the introduction of the Stamp Act in 1765. Prime Minister George Grenville first proposed the act in 1763 to raise money from Americans after the French and Indian War. American colonists resented being taxed by Parliament, in which they had no representatives, and maintained that their colonial assemblies would freely grant money to the Crown when they were asked.

In 1763 and early 1764 Grenville summoned agents from the American colonies and informed them of his intention to introduce a measure in the next session of Parliament that would levy a stamp tax on the American colonies. Franklin was in Philadelphia when notice of the proposed act came to the Pennsylvania Assembly. The Assembly resented the threat of taxation by an act of Parliament and declared that they would grant money to the Crown "in the usual constitutional manner," by their own legislation. Franklin, whom the Assembly sent to England in 1764 to petition the king to assume the government of Pennsylvania from the proprietaries, took with him the Assembly's resolution against the Stamp Act to present to Grenville. "I am sure he would have obtained more money from the colonies by their voluntary grants," Franklin wrote in 1778. "But he chose compulsion rather than persuasion, and would not receive from their good will what he thought he could obtain without it."

In 1765 the Stamp Act passed in both the House of Commons and the House of Lords, with the king's approval. It placed duties on legal documents, newspapers, licenses, contracts, playing cards, and pamphlets and would particularly affect Franklin's own profession, printing. Americans were almost universally outraged at the act. Colonial assemblies denounced the measures, and Americans refused to buy British imports. Franklin, who from the beginning thought the act was "the mother of mischief," complied with the ministry's desire to appoint stamp agents from America rather than England and did not foresee the intensity and extent of the opposition in America. When Grenville's secretary called the American agents to recommend stamp distributors, Franklin suggested a friend, John Hughes. As soon as news of Franklin's recommendation hit Pennsylvania, Hughes was denounced, threatened, hung in effigy, and forced to resign. Accusations circulated that Franklin had promoted the act, and angry Pennsylvanians threatened his house, where his wife and daughter lived. Relatives of the family came to the Franklin house to stay with Mrs. Franklin, and they "turned one room into a magazine." Franklin wrote to Joseph Galloway in November 1766: "But what can console the writers and promoters of such infinitely false accusations, if they should ever come themselves to a sense of that malice of their hearts, and that stupidity of their heads, which by these papers they have manifested and exposed to all the world."

In 1765, on the initiative of the Massachusetts Assembly, the Stamp Act Congress convened in New York to consider a colonial response to the act. The congress, consisting of delegates from nine colonies, produced a set of resolves that declared their loyalty to the Crown and expressed their opposition to being taxed without representation. In addition to opposition in America, British merchants who found their orders from the colonies diminished also favored a repeal of the act.

Franklin worked tirelessly for the repeal of the Stamp Act during the following months, although he was not optimistic about the success of his efforts. He wrote critical letters to the *Public Advertiser* and other papers using pseudonyms such as "Homespun," "Pacificus," "Pacificus Secundus," and "N. N." "Pacificus" wrote a biting mock proposal for vicious armed enforcement of the act and concluded, "No man in his wits, after such terrible military execution, will refuse to purchase stamped paper. If any one should hesitate, five or six hundred lashes in a cold frosty morning would soon bring him to reason." "Pacificus Secundus" agreed and thought no less a force than 50,000 English troops would suffice to compel the colonists to adhere to the act. Franklin also spent time consulting with members of Parliament.

On January 14, 1766, William Pitt delivered a speech against the Stamp Act, and Franklin sent an account of the speech to the *London Chronicle*. He reported that Pitt spoke for a long time before he made his opinion of the act known, "till he finally declared in express terms that the British Parliament had in his opinion no right to raise internal taxes in America, though it had to regulate their commerce, and even restrain their manufactures." The following month, Franklin was examined extensively before the House of Commons and answered questions related to America's ability and willingness to comply with the act. Franklin stated more than once that Americans would never submit to the Stamp Act, even if it were moderated, and impressed many with his thorough knowledge of American affairs. The questions, presented to him by both political allies and enemies, and his answers were published and widely read in Europe.

The Stamp Act was repealed shortly after Franklin's testimony in 1766. Franklin's tarnished reputation was quickly restored in Philadelphia, where he was heralded as a hero. However, Parliament continued to assert its right to tax Americans, and the opposition to this principle that contributed to the American Revolution only grew stronger in subsequent years.

Related entries:
  Declaration of Independence
  Revolutionary War

Suggestions for further reading:
  "Examination before the Committee of the Whole of the House of Commons," 1766 (Labaree et al., vol. 13).
  "Letters Concerning the Stamp Act," 1766 (Smyth, vol. IV).

Steamboat

Before Franklin left France in 1785 he had observed the first successful hot-air balloon launches and speculated with interest on the potential of aerial navigation. He had always been interested in new inventions and was met with another significant advance after he returned to Philadelphia. John Fitch (1743–1798) had sought financial assistance from Congress to build his new invention, the steamboat. After Congress denied his request, he sought private financing. He came to Franklin in 1787 to ask him to subscribe to a company he was forming to finance the boat. For whatever reason, Franklin did not subscribe to Fitch's company, and he was not well enough to see the test run of a 45-foot boat that Fitch exhibited on the Delaware River that same year.

Franklin joined the Rumseian Society, formed around Fitch's rival James Rumsey (1743–1792) and his ideas for using steam to run boats, mills, and pumps. He was inactive in the society and seems to have been only mildly curious about the steamboat. He wrote to Jean-Baptiste Le Roy in 1788: "We have no philosophical news here at present, except that a large boat rowed by the force of steam is now exercised upon our river, stems the current, and seems to promise being useful when the machinery can be more simplified and the expense reduced." However, Franklin never took a deep interest in the steamboat and died (1790) before it came into general use.

Related entries:
French Academy of Sciences
Hot-Air Balloons

Suggestions for further reading:
"To Jean-Baptiste Le Roy," October 25, 1788 (Smyth, vol. IX).

Stevenson, Mary (Polly)

See **Hewson, Mary (Polly) Stevenson.**

Stevenson, Mrs. Margaret (c. 1706–1783)

Franklin rented rooms on Craven Street from Mrs. Margaret Stevenson during his stays in London from 1757 to 1762 and 1764 to 1775. Mrs. Stevenson was a widow who lived with her daughter Mary (Polly), and the kind woman, who was around Franklin's age, was much less a landlady than a family member to him. He moved into the Craven Street house soon after he arrived in England in 1757. During the bouts of fever and severe cold he suffered that year, Franklin told his wife, Mrs. Stevenson "nursed [him] kindly." Mrs. Stevenson and her daughter were almost a substitute family for Franklin, who had left his wife and daughter in Philadelphia because his wife refused to sail. Mrs. Stevenson sent gifts to Deborah and Sally in Philadelphia and helped Franklin choose the gifts he sent. Franklin wrote to his wife in 1758 that "she is indeed very obliging, takes great care of my health, and is very diligent when I am in any way indisposed," but he wished Deborah would come to England.

Mrs. Stevenson generously accommodated all of Franklin's circumstances. His son William lived with them during the first few years, and Mrs. Stevenson took William's illegitimate son, William Temple, into her house some time after his birth in 1760. When Franklin's English cousin, Sally Franklin, came to town with her father to visit, Mrs. Stevenson asked him to leave her under her care for "some schooling and improvement." She was very fond of the young girl. Mrs. Stevenson loved to hear accounts from Franklin's wife of the Franklins' new grandson in Philadelphia, Benjamin Franklin Bache.

Franklin delighted in Polly, who moved to her aunt's home in 1759 and corresponded with him about natural philosophy. He wrote letters to her for Mrs. Stevenson, who did not like to write. Franklin's enjoyable and harmonious life on Craven Street contrasted sharply with the political troubles with which he was frequently engaged. When Mrs. Stevenson took Sally to Rochester with her in 1770, Franklin wrote the *Craven Street Gazette,* a humorous mock newspaper-journal of daily events at the house. By that time Polly had married and moved back to Craven Street with her husband.

After Franklin left England in 1775, he never saw Mrs. Stevenson again. He took some of her money to invest in America, but he returned it, as war loomed and its fate in any investment was uncertain. She should, he advised, invest it in a mortgage on land and try to avoid stocks. She sent him a long journal of events that had taken place in the month after his departure. Franklin continued to write to her as he could, but the war with England rendered it difficult to get letters to his friends who lived there. In 1779 he wrote warmly to her from France: "It is always with great pleasure, when I think of our long continued friendship, which had not the least interruption in the course of twenty years (some of the happiest of my life), that I spent under your roof and in your company."

Franklin learned of Mrs. Stevenson's death in 1783 and wrote to Polly from France: "The departure of my dearest friend, which I learn from your last letter, greatly affects me. To meet with her once more in this life was one of the principal motives of my proposing to visit England again, before my return to America."

Related entries:
Craven Street Gazette
Franklin, Sarah (Sally)
Franklin, William
Franklin, William Temple
Hewson, Mary (Polly) Stevenson

Suggestions for further reading:
"To Margaret Stevenson," January 25, 1779 (Labaree et al., vol. 28).
"To Margaret Stevenson," July 17, 1775 (Labaree et al., vol. 22).
"To Mrs. Mary Hewson," January 27, 1783 (Smyth, vol. IX).
"To Mrs. Stevenson and Mrs. Hewson," April 19, 1782 (Smyth, vol. VIII).

Strahan, William (1715–1785)

William Strahan, a successful London printer, was one of Franklin's closest friends and began corresponding with him while the latter was a printer in Philadelphia. Strahan printed writings of David Hume (1711–1776), to whom he later introduced Franklin, Adam Smith (1723–1790), Edward Gibbon (1737–1794), and Sir William Blackstone (1723–1780), and he became King's printer in 1769. Early letters between him and Franklin were chiefly business-related. Franklin ordered books from Strahan in England for himself and to sell in his shop, and he sent Strahan books to sell in England. If he needed printing materials, he ordered them from England through Strahan. Franklin asked Peter Collinson, who purchased books in England for the Library Company of Philadelphia, to buy them from Strahan.

The two men helped with each other's businesses. Strahan recommended David Hall, a journeyman printer who he thought deserved a better position, to Franklin in 1743. Franklin asked Strahan to send Hall to America, where they could discuss the management of a printing house. If Hall did not like Franklin's offer, Franklin said he would give him enough work to pay his passage back to England. Franklin liked Hall immediately, and they entered into a successful 18-year partnership in 1748. Strahan's recommendation to Franklin worked out better than some of the people Franklin asked Strahan to help. Among them was his nephew Benjamin Mecom, whom Franklin sent to Antigua to manage a printing house. Mecom, James Read, and James Parker ran up debts with Strahan, much to Franklin's frustration.

Letters between Franklin and Strahan gradually took on a more familiar tone. They joked about marrying Franklin's daughter Sally to Strahan's eldest son William (which later turned into a serious but unsuccessful proposal). In 1750 Franklin asked him to enter his son, William, into the Inns of Court as a student of law, and William would finish the last year or two of his studies in England.

When he lived in Philadelphia, Franklin relied on his correspondents in England for English political news. "We have seldom any news on our side of the globe that can be entertaining to you or yours," Franklin wrote to Strahan in 1744. "All our affairs are petit. They have a miniature resemblance only, of the grand things of Europe." He heard political news from newspapers, from Collinson, and from Dr. John Fothergill, but he most enjoyed accounts penned by Strahan. "The characters of your speakers and actors are so admirably sketched," he later wrote to him, "and their views so plainly opened, that we see and know everybody. . . . If you do not commence author [sic] for the benefit of mankind, you will certainly be found guilty hereafter of burying your talent. It is true that it will puzzle the devil himself to find anything else to accuse you of, but remember he may make a great deal of that." In 1764 Franklin wrote to him: "Your political letters are oracles here. I beseech you to continue them."

In 1757 the Pennsylvania Assembly sent Franklin to England to petition for the Assembly's right to tax proprietary lands. Franklin would finally get to meet Strahan and wrote to him: "Our Assembly talk of sending me to England speedily. Then look out sharp, and if a fat old fellow should come to your printing-house and request a little smouting, depend on it, 'tis your affectionate friend and humble servant, B. Franklin." Franklin did sail for England that year and met Strahan, who took an instant liking to him. Franklin and the Stevensons sometimes dined with the Strahans. Franklin later sent his grandson William Temple to a school kept by Strahan's brother-in-law. Strahan schemed endlessly to get Franklin to move to England permanently and was so convincing that Franklin had half made up his mind to make the move—"if I can, as I hope I can, prevail with Mrs. F[ranklin] to accompany me, es-

pecially if we have a peace." No amount of urging from the Strahans ever convinced Deborah, who was terrified of the water, to move to England, but Franklin ended up spending most of the years between 1757 and 1775 in Britain anyway.

In England, Strahan printed pieces that Franklin wrote or wanted published from time to time, some of which appeared in his *London Chronicle* (edited by George Griffith). Among the pieces were Richard Jackson's *An Historical Review of the Constitution and Government of Pennsylvania* (1759), and Franklin's report on William Pitt's speech against the Stamp Act (1766), "Causes of American Discontents before 1768" (1768), and "Edict by the King of Prussia" (1773). Strahan and his son Andrew were also involved in the Grand Ohio Company, which wanted to settle western lands in America, with Franklin and his son.

The two men did not always see eye to eye in politics, and their differences over the Revolutionary War strained their long friendship. In 1763 Franklin had predicted to his apprehensive friend that George III was a worthy king who would have a happy and prosperous reign. Franklin's sentiments were dramatically different ten years later. To Franklin's frustration, Strahan, who was a member of Parliament, believed some of the negative and false reports of American cowardice and ineptitude that circulated in England before the war.

In 1769 Strahan asked Franklin to provide answers to some questions about the problems in America. "As I know your singular knowledge of the subject in question, and am as fully convinced of your cordial attachment to his Majesty, and your sincere desire to promote the happiness equally of all of his subjects, I beg you would, in your own clear, brief, explicit manner, send me an answer to the following questions," he said. Strahan asked Franklin if the repeal of all of the duties, except the tea duty, would satisfy the colonists. Franklin said it would not satisfy them, and that the colonists objected to the principle of the tea duty rather than the amount. Strahan asked him if the only way to remedy the differences between America and England was to return things to the way they were before the Stamp Act. Franklin thought so. Strahan asked if any other measures would repair the differences, and Franklin did not believe anything else would. Other methods had been tried and rejected. Parliament had threatened to punish Americans for treason, troops had been sent among them, and colonial assemblies had been arbitrarily dissolved. Franklin maintained that Americans objected to the authority Parliament claimed to tax them: "We are free subjects of the King, and . . . fellow subjects of one part of his dominions are not sovereigns over fellow subjects in any other part."

Franklin concluded his answers to Strahan's questions with a bleak view of coming trouble. Given the temperament of the ministry, England was not likely to appease the American colonists, and tension would only grow worse. He hoped his sentiments would prove to be "false prophecy." Franklin returned to Philadelphia in 1775 and penned an angry letter to him (which he never sent) on July 5: "You are a member of Parliament and one of that majority which has doomed my country to destruction. You have begun to burn our towns, and murder our people. Look upon your hands! They are stained with the blood of your relations! You and I were long friends: you are now my enemy, and I am yours."

Franklin and Strahan continued to write intermittently but civilly during the war, but Franklin was disappointed with Strahan's support for measures against America. In 1783 Franklin had "a regard for Mr. Strahan in remembrance of our ancient friendship, though he has as a member of Parliament dipped his hands in our blood." Franklin thought his friend had never understood America and wrote to him in 1784: "You 'fairly acknowledge, that the late war terminated quite contrary to your expectation.' Your expectation was ill founded; for you would not believe your old friend, who told you repeatedly, that by those measures England would lose her colonies, as Epictetus warned in vain his master that he would break his leg." Strahan died the following year.

Related entries:
    Great Britain
    Printing
    Revolutionary War

Suggestions for further reading:
    Cochrane, James Aikman. 1964. *Dr. Johnson's Printer: The Life of William Strahan.* Cambridge, Mass.: Harvard University Press.
    "From William Strahan," November 21–22, 1769 (Labaree et al., vol. 16).
    "To William Strahan," April 29, 1749 (Labaree et al., vol. 3).
    "To William Strahan," August 19, 1784 (Smyth, vol. IX).
    "To William Strahan," February 6, 1784 (Smyth, vol. IX).
    "To William Strahan," July 4, 1744 (Labaree et al., vol. 2).
    "To William Strahan," June 2, 1750 (Labaree et al., vol. 3).

Supreme Executive Council of Pennsylvania

On October 11, 1785, the Assembly elected the 79-year-old Franklin to the Supreme Executive Council of Pennsylvania (which was Pennsylvania's plural executive branch), and on October 18 the Council chose him as president. "They have engrossed the prime of my life," Franklin complained. "They have eaten my flesh, and seem now resolved to pick my bones." Pennsylvania's constitution, which had been formed in 1776 at a convention at which Franklin served as president, allowed a president, who was elected annually, to remain in office for three years. Franklin was reelected for all three years, during which he had only four votes cast against him, three of which were his own. However, he was much less active in his final political office than he had been in others. Illness prevented him from attending many of the Council's meetings, and for the most part, he was absent more often than not. As he did not believe in salaried presidents, he donated much of his own salary to churches, schools, and colleges. Two parties had formed in the Assembly, the constitutionalists and the anticonstitutionalists. Although both parties had voted unanimously for him as president, hoping his skill in reconciliation could bring them together, Franklin generally sided with the anticonstitutionalists.

The Assembly had passed a test act after Franklin sailed to France in 1776. The act prohibited people from voting or holding office unless they took an oath of allegiance to Pennsylvania's constitution—a provision intended to preserve loyalty during the American Revolution. However, many in Pennsylvania, including the Quakers, did not take oaths for religious reasons, and others disliked the constitution altogether. During Franklin's administration the Assembly rewrote the controversial act in March 1786. The new version required voters to renounce loyalty to the king of England, swear that they had not assisted British forces since the congressional delegates approved the Declaration of Independence, and declare themselves loyal to Pennsylvania.

Among the other prominent issues that arose during his administration were the restoration of the charter of the Bank of North America, the revision of the penal code, and a long-standing territorial dispute with Connecticut. The Bank of North America (a state bank) had been established in 1782 and its charter revoked in 1785. Franklin supported the bank and purchased 12 shares in it, and his son-in-law, Richard Bache, served as one of its directors for a time. (Franklin bequeathed the shares to his daughter and Bache.) The anticonstitutionalists in the Assembly supported a restoration of the bank's charter, which was reinstituted in 1787.

The revised penal code, instituted in 1786, eliminated hanging as a penalty for rape, arson, robbery, manslaughter, and all other crimes except intentional murder and treason. Branding, whipping, the pillory, and ear cropping were eliminated as punishments. Franklin had long objected to punishing lesser crimes with death. He had written to Benjamin Vaughan in 1785: "If I think it right, that the crime of murder should be punished with death ... does it follow that I must approve of afflicting the same punishment for a little invasion on my property by theft? If I am not myself so barbarous, so bloody-minded and revengeful, as to kill a fellow creature for stealing from me 14/3, how can I approve a law that does it?"

By the time Franklin was elected president, settlers in the territory under question in the boundary dispute, which was known as the Wyoming Territory and which Congress had given to Pennsylvania, talked of creating a new state. Although the territory was now Pennsylvania's, some members of the government had tried to dispossess the Connecticut settlers in the area of their farms. This action naturally stirred resentment, and John Franklin (no relation to Franklin) led the Connecticut settlers in a small rebellion in 1783. The Assembly in Pennsylvania restored the lands to the Connecticut settlers temporarily, but some of the settlers were still suspicious. Members of the Susquehannah Company had already organized a small militia before the law restoring the settlers' lands passed, and Ethan Allen, who owned land in the territory, was poised to fight against Pennsylvania. "Intelligence has been received here," Franklin wrote to Governor George Clinton of New York in 1786, "that Ethan Allen from Vermont, and one Solomon Strong of your state have lately been among the settlers at Wyoming, persuading them to join in erecting a new state to be composed of those settlements, those on the west branch of the Susquehannah, and a part of the state of New York. . . . " John Franklin appealed to the Council for a reconciliation of the matter, and the Assembly soon passed a plan that formed the Wyoming settlements into Luzerne County and returned land to Connecticut settlers. Pennsylvania settlers who had staked claims on their land were compensated with other land. Some Connecticut settlers were still not satisfied, and John Franklin led another small rebellion in September 1787. He was arrested, imprisoned, and indicted for treason. He was pardoned in 1792 and became sheriff of the new county.

In 1789, after he had left office, Franklin wrote "Queries and Remarks Respecting Alterations in the Constitution of Pennsylvania" in response to some "Hints for the Members of the Convention" that appeared in the *Federal Gazette*. Franklin criticized the author's suggestions, including reducing the plural executive to a single executive and dividing the legislature into two houses—two points he had unsuccessfully opposed in the formation of the U.S. Constitution. Franklin also objected to the author's notion that one chamber should represent property holders: "[W]hy should the upper house, chosen by a minority, have equal power with the lower chosen by a majority? Is it supposed that wisdom is the necessary concomitant of riches, and that one man worth a thousand pounds must have as much wisdom as twenty who have each only 999? . . . " Franklin retired from public service during the last three years of his life. When he died, he left £2,000 of the salary still due him from the government of Pennsylvania to benefit promising young tradesmen in Boston and Philadelphia.

Related entries:
Bache, Richard
Bache, Sarah Franklin
Last Will and Testament

Suggestions for further reading:
"Queries and Remarks Respecting Alterations in the Constitution of Pennsylvania," 1789 (Smyth, vol. X).
"To George Clinton," January 1, 1786 (Smyth, vol. IX).
"To Thomas Paine," September 27, 1785 (Smyth, vol. IX).

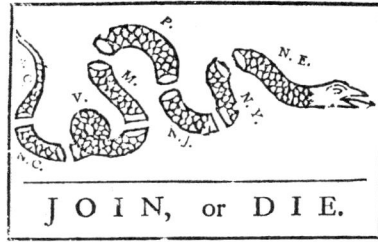

JOIN, or DIE.

Treaties of Amity and Commerce

"Since our trade is laid open, and no longer a monopoly to England, all Europe seems desirous of sharing in it, and for that purpose to cultivate our friendship," Franklin wrote to Robert R. Livingston, president of Congress, in 1783. Until the previous year, France had been the only European nation to conclude a treaty of amity and commerce with the colonies and formally recognize the United States as an independent nation. After the defeat of Cornwallis and England's apparent willingness to acknowledge America's independence, European nations began to enter into treaties of amity and commerce with the United States.

In 1784 Congress officially empowered Franklin, along with John Adams and Thomas Jefferson, to negotiate such treaties. Negotiations with other countries involving Franklin, John Jay, Adams, and Thomas Jefferson took place before these specific instructions, however. The least complicated treaty, with Sweden, was negotiated by Franklin in 1782. He received permission from Congress to treat with Sweden, and Sweden's ambassador, the Count de Creutz, received permission from his country. They negotiated with very little conflict, and Congress ratified the agreement in 1783. This treaty became a model for proposals to other nations.

Denmark was a more complicated matter. In 1783 Franklin wrote to Rosencrone, the minister of foreign affairs in Copenhagen, to acknowledge Denmark's intent to establish "connections of friendship and commerce with the United States of America." Franklin told him that he expected that the Congress would soon send a commission. In the meantime, he made it known that the United States expected reparations for American prize ships that had been seized by an order of Rosencrone's predecessor and turned over to the British.

Denmark offered £10,000 sterling for the ships, but Franklin refused the offer because he believed the amount was less than one-fifth of their estimated value. The ambassador from Denmark thought the estimate was excessive, and Franklin wrote to London to find out exactly how much the ships were worth. A treaty with Denmark stalled when Congress delayed sending proper instructions. On June 14, 1784, they still had not arrived, and Franklin told Charles Thomson that the Danish minister was "astonished, that the Congress are so long without taking any notice of the proposed treaty." By 1785 he thought the treaties with Denmark and Portugal "to be rather going backward." Franklin went home the same year, leaving the matter to the other American negotiators.

Franklin also proposed a plan to the Portuguese ambassador, who had given him very favorable overtures. It was modeled on the treaty with Sweden, and the ambassador took it to Portugal to be presented at the court. As with the Danish treaty, Congress delayed sending instructions, and the negotiations stalled until after Franklin left.

In 1784 Franklin found that European attitudes toward the United States were changing for the worse. He blamed the change in demeanor on the British reports of political chaos and dire financial circumstances in America. To combat these prejudices in Europe, Franklin had the Duc de La Rochefoucauld translate the American constitutions into French and sent two copies to every foreign minister, one for the minister, and one for each's king. "It has been well taken, and has afforded matter of surprise to many, who had conceived mean ideas of the state of civilization in America, and could not have expected so much political knowledge and sagacity had existed in our wildernesses," he thought. Franklin believed that the constitutions would help foreign countries understand more about America and heighten their respect for a country that most knew little about.

A treaty with Spain was difficult because of the interests that the Spanish had in America (the Floridas). John Jay, who served as an American envoy to Spain during the war, reported that the Spanish court began to grow more favorable toward America in 1782. On June 29 Franklin and Jay visited the Count d'Aranda, the Spanish ambassador in France. Jay and d'Aranda discussed the possibility of a treaty and held further talks. On August 12 Franklin thought, "[M]y conjecture of that court's design to coop us up within the Allegheny Mountains is now manifested." He hoped that the Congress would demand the Mississippi River as the western boundary, as well as free navigation of the river (a right that was obtained by the Treaty of Paris in 1783). In 1786 Franklin, who had by then returned to Philadelphia, advised Charles Petit, a member of Congress, to stall the negotiations and wait for a new king on the Spanish throne. Extra time, he thought, would also allow the United States

to grow stronger and add more weight to its claims.

Dr. Jan Ingenhousz, Franklin's physician friend at the Austrian court, indicated that Austria desired to enter into a treaty with the United States. In June 1784 Franklin wrote to the Comte d'Argenteau, the Austrian ambassador at Versailles, that American commissioners had received permission from Congress to enter into a treaty of amity and commerce with Austria. Nothing came of the proposal during his remaining months in France. Adams handled most of the negotiations with the Netherlands, with which a treaty was concluded in 1782.

Jefferson, Adams, and Franklin negotiated the most significant and idealistic treaty, with Prussia, in 1785. The philosopher-diplomats discouraged privateering, which Franklin had always personally disliked, and established rules of neutrality and fair treatment. The treaty abolished between the two countries "the ancient and barbarous right to wrecks of the sea . . . with respect to the subjects or citizens of the two contracting parties." Article 20 prohibited each of the two countries from accepting privateering commissions to act against the other from a power with which the other was at war (a provision also made by the treaty with Sweden). Franklin, Jefferson, Adams, and the Prussian envoy, Baron Frederick William de Thulemeier, signed the treaty three days before Franklin departed from France.

Related entries:
Adams, John
Continental Congresses
Jay, John
Jefferson, Thomas
Treaty of Alliance with France
Treaty of Paris, 1783
Vergennes, Comte de (Charles Gravier)

Suggestions for further reading:
"To Comte de Mercy Argenteau," June 30, 1784 (Smyth, vol. IX).
"To John Jay," September 19, 1785 (Smyth, vol. IX).
"To M. Rosencrone," April 15, 1783 (Smyth, vol. IX).

"To Robert R. Livingston," April 15, 1783
(Smyth, vol. IX).
"To Robert R. Livingston," July 22, 1783
(Smyth, vol. IX).
"To Robert R. Livingston," June 12, 1783
(Smyth, vol. IX).

Treaty of Alliance with France

One of Franklin's most important roles during the American Revolution was helping to secure the treaty of alliance with France in 1778. There were many obstacles to overcome before the French would venture into an alliance with the colonies. The French, ardent enemies of England, knew that to enter into an alliance with Britain's rebellious colonies would force an expensive war between the two countries. Before they would ally themselves with the United States they wanted to be sure that there was some prospect of success.

The principal negotiators for the United States were Franklin, Silas Deane, and Arthur Lee. When Franklin and Lee arrived in France at the end of 1776 (Deane was already there), they sent a note to the French foreign minister, the Comte de Vergennes: "We beg leave to acquaint your excellency that we are appointed and fully empowered by the Congress of the United States of America, to propose and negotiate a treaty of amity and commerce between France and the said states."

Vergennes and the French moved cautiously in 1776 and 1777. Vergennes favored an alliance, but the king and some of the nobles were reluctant. When the commissioners were allowed to see him, they offered him specific terms for a treaty of amity and commerce. Vergennes would do little more than assure them of France's goodwill, and he asked them to submit their proposal to Conrad-Alexandre Gérard de Rayneval, the secretary of the Foreign Office. France immediately began giving the United States aid, although secretly. In January 1777 the French loaned the United States 2 million livres. Pierre-Augustin Caron de Beaumarchais enthusias-tically smuggled military supplies to the American army against the orders of the government, which outwardly tried to calm British suspicion while it decided on a definite course of action.

In his "A Dialogue between Britain, France, Spain, Holland, Saxony, and America" (1775), Franklin had portrayed Britain as a base and desperate nation that had forfeited her respect in Europe and would be unable to keep her many European enemies from aiding the United States. At the end, Britain exclaimed, "O Lord! Where are my friends?" The other European countries replied in unison: "Believe us, you have none, nor ever will have any, 'till you mend your manners." He employed his pen in other anti-British propaganda pieces, such as "A Catechism Relating to the English National Debt." Privately, prominent people he had known in England wrote to Franklin and tried to dissuade him from seeking an American alliance with France. Their requests fell on deaf ears.

In September 1777 the commissioners began to press the French for more decisive and open help. Franklin's presence was essential in gaining the cooperation of the French. Franklin was universally famous in France and used his enormous popularity for the benefit of the American mission. French caution began to ease when American armies defeated Major General John Burgoyne at Saratoga in October 1777. The news reached France in early December. Americans had more leverage with which to persuade the French, who were now more eager, into an alliance. At first the French resolved to enter into an alliance only if Spain would join them. Gérard asked the Americans to renew their request for an alliance and presented the commissioners with questions at Deane's lodgings. Gérard asked them what France would have to do to prevent the Americans from entertaining any thoughts of reunion with England. The commissioners replied that they would like to see the conclusion of the long-sought treaty of amity and commerce with France.

The United States signed a treaty of amity and commerce and a treaty of alliance with France on February 6, 1778 (Spain had refused to join the alliance, but France had decided to go ahead). At the signing Franklin wore the blue coat that he had worn during the verbal abuse heaped upon him by Alexander Wedderburn at the Cockpit in 1774. The American commissioners were officially received at the court of France on March 20, and Congress ratified the treaties on May 4. Full recognition of American independence and diplomatic relations were established between the United States and France. The treaties stipulated that France help the United States attain independence from England, that neither of them could sign a peace treaty without the other's consent, and that the United States stand by France in war against England. Both countries were to enjoy most-favored-nation trading status from the other.

Gérard was chosen to represent France in America and stayed there for a year, until he was replaced by the Count de la Luzerne. The French alliance, which the British, through the intelligence of their spies, had known was looming, made waves in England. Lord North introduced conciliatory measures to Parliament, and Lord Shelburne and other members of Parliament called for an end to the war in America. They hoped to placate the colonies without granting them independence and sent commissioners to the United States with copies of North's bills, which offered essentially everything the Americans had demanded before the war broke out. However, the United States had already concluded the treaty with France, and the Congress chose to ratify the treaties rather than deal with the British commission, especially after one of the commissioners tried to bribe members of Congress. French military aid to the colonies soon followed.

Related entries:
Continental Congresses
France
Lee, Dr. Arthur

Revolutionary War
Vergennes, Comte de (Charles Gravier)

Suggestions for further reading:
Aldridge, Alfred Owen. 1957. *Franklin and His French Contemporaries.* New York: New York University Press.
Dull, Jonathan R. 1982. *Franklin the Diplomat: The French Mission.* Philadelphia: American Philosophical Society.
Hale, Edward, and Edward E. Hale, Jr. 1969. *Franklin in France: From Original Documents, Most of Which Are Now Published for the First Time.* New York: Burt Franklin.
Schoenbrun, David. 1976. *Triumph in Paris: The Exploits of Benjamin Franklin.* New York: Harper & Row.

Treaty of Paris, 1783

Official negotiation of the Treaty of Paris of 1783, which ended the war between England and the United States, began in late 1782. Franklin kept a journal of negotiations with England from March 21, 1782, to July 1, 1782, in which he chronicled the majority of the unofficial talks that preceded official negotiation. (*See Journal of the Negotiation for Peace with Great Britain* for the details of the unofficial talks.) On the day that Franklin's *Journal* entries ceased, July 1, 1782, the Marquess of Rockingham died, spurring a rearrangement of the ministry in England. Lord Shelburne held complete control of the ministry when Charles James Fox resigned. Thomas Grenville, who had been Fox's choice as a commissioner to negotiate with France, was recalled to England and replaced with Alleyne Fitzherbert. John Jay, the only other American commissioner then in France, caught the flu and could not participate in talks for the month of July.

Richard Oswald, who had remained Franklin's and Lord Shelburne's choice as a negotiator for England, expected soon to receive a commission to treat with the United States. Franklin presented preliminary points for his consideration. The four "necessary" points stipulated that England withdraw all

The signing of the treaty between France and the United States. Painting by Charles E. Mills, c. 1920.

troops from the United States and recognize its independence; proposed boundary settlements for the states and for Canada; and affirmed the right of Americans to fish off of the banks of Newfoundland. His "advisable" points included reparations for American towns that the British had burned; an admission of Parliament of the error of its oppressive behavior toward the colonies; the cession of Canada; and trading privileges. Lord Shelburne was pleased with the "necessary" points, but not the "advisable" points, and he hoped the treaty could proceed on the basis of the former.

In August 1782 Oswald received his commission from England to negotiate with America. Jay objected to the language in Oswald's instructions, which empowered him to negotiate with the "colonies and plantations." Jay insisted on acknowledgment of the independence of the United States in clear terms before the treaty negotiations commence, and Adams (who was still in Holland) agreed. Without consulting Franklin, Jay sent Benjamin Vaughan (a good friend of Franklin's and at that time an agent of Lord Shelburne) to Lord Shelburne to ask for a more explicit commission for Oswald.

Jay and Adams distrusted the Spanish and the French, who they believed had designs of depriving the United States of the Mississippi River as the western boundary and impeding its bid for independence. Franklin shared their suspicions of Spain's intentions, but he trusted the Comte de Vergennes and France. American and British negotiators finally exchanged commissions, and by the beginning of October the Americans had a first draft of a treaty. Caleb Whitefoord, an old friend of Franklin's and his former next-door neighbor on Craven Street in England, served as secretary to the British commission; Franklin's grandson, William Temple Franklin, served—over Adams's objections—as the secretary to the American commission.

Franklin's original "necessary" stipulations were included in the preliminary draft, along with an additional stipulation that both nations were to be allowed to navigate and conduct commercial activity on the Mississippi River. Added to the demand for Newfoundland fishing rights was a stipulation that Americans could dry fish on the shore. Lord Shelburne, after viewing the draft, sent Henry Strachey to join Oswald in the negotiations. Oswald had been unsuccessful in gaining reparations for loyalists, and Shelburne was under heavy political pressure to do something on their behalf. Adams finally arrived in France on October 26, 1782, and he, Jay, and Franklin agreed to negotiate with England without consulting Vergennes—a violation of their instructions from Congress that offended Vergennes. The chief items under dispute were the details surrounding Newfoundland fisheries and the compensation of loyalists. Franklin steadfastly objected to the latter (his son, William, had been a loyalist leader in New York). Finally, to pacify Lord Shelburne, an ornamental stipulation was added that Congress should recommend to the states restitution for confiscated loyalist estates. Franklin added a last-minute article in response that instructed George III to recommend to Parliament that it compensate Americans for goods, towns, slaves, and farms that had been ravaged or plundered by the British. Henry Laurens, who originally had been appointed a commissioner by Congress but had declined on account of ill health, had also arrived for the last day of discussions. The provisional articles contained a secret clause that gave Florida to England, and the commissioners signed them on November 30, 1782. The provisional articles were subject to the conclusion of the treaty between England and France. John Adams noted in his diary that day that Franklin had "gone on with us in entire harmony and unanimity throughout, and has been able and useful, both by his sagacity and his reputation, in the whole negotiation."

During the interim between the signing of the provisional articles and the final treaty, David Hartley, a member of Parliament and a friend of Franklin's, was sent to Paris to try to negotiate favorable terms of commerce, but the talks failed. Franklin wrote, "We had many conferences, and received long memorials from Mr. Hartley on the subject, but his zeal for systems friendly to us constantly exceeded his authority to concert and agree to them." The final treaty was the same as the provisional treaty, with the exception of the secret clause, as Britain had given Florida to Spain in a separate treaty.

The first article in the treaty was an acknowledgment of the independence of the United States, and the second established boundaries. Article three established fishing rights for the United States off the shores of Newfoundland and provided that Americans could dry their fish on uninhabited bays, creeks, and harbors of Nova Scotia, the Magdalen Islands, and Labrador. The fourth article mandated that both English and American creditors be permitted to collect their debts. The fifth article instructed Congress to recommend to the states the restoration of confiscated loyalist estates. Future confiscations of anyone's property on the basis of which side they took in the war were forbidden by article six. Article seven declared a "firm and perpetual peace" between England and the United States, and it required England to withdraw all troops from America without destroying or taking anything. All prisoners of war were to be freed. The free navigation of the entire Mississippi River for England and the United States was established by article eight, and article nine provided for the restoration of any territory that might have been conquered in the United States before the arrival of the provisional articles. The final article stated that both countries were to ratify the treaty within six months. Franklin, Adams, Jay, and Hartley signed the final document on September 3, 1783, at David Hartley's apartments at the Hôtel de York in Paris. France concluded a separate treaty with England on the same day.

Related entries:
Adams, John
Continental Congresses
Jay, John
Journal of the Negotiation for Peace with Great Britain
Revolutionary War
Treaty of Alliance with France
Vaughan, Benjamin
Vergennes, Comte de (Charles Gravier)

Suggestions for further reading:
Adams, John. 1850. *The Works of John Adams, Second President of the United States.* Boston: Little, Brown.
"Journal of the Negotiation for Peace with Great Britain," 1782 (Smyth, vol. VIII).

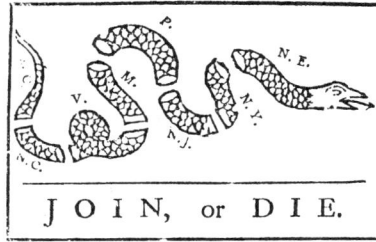

JOIN, or DIE.

U.S. Seal and Emblem

The Second Continental Congress appointed a committee of men (1776) including Franklin, John Adams, and Thomas Jefferson to design a seal for the United States. The men came up with their own designs and then chose one to submit to the whole Congress. Jefferson's and Franklin's appeared to be similar. Franklin's design, as recorded in the *Journals of the Continental Congress,* was: "Moses standing on the shore and extending his hand over the sea, causing the same to overwhelm Pharaoh, who is sitting in an open chariot, a crown on his head and sword in his hand. Rays from a pillar of fire in the clouds reaching to Moses, to express how he acts by command of the Deity. Motto, 'rebellion to tyrants is obedience to God.'"

Adams proposed "Hercules . . . resting on his club. Virtue pointing to her ragged mountain on one hand, and persuading him to ascend sloth, glancing at her flowery paths of pleasure, wantonly reclining on the mound, displaying the charms of both her eloquence and person to seduce him into vice." The committee submitted an entirely different design, which the Congress further altered. The seal, still used today, bearing the eagle and shield was not adopted until 1782.

Franklin did not like the choice of the bald eagle as the emblem of the United States. He complained that the bird has "bad moral character" and "does not get his living honestly." Further, he said, the bald eagle does not fish for itself but instead steals the catch of another bird. The much smaller king bird drives the cowardly eagle away when it wants to. He suggested that the turkey, despite its vanity and silliness, was a much nobler bird that would bravely attack a grenadier of red-coated British Guards that invaded its farmyard.

Related entries:
Adams, John
Continental Congresses
Jefferson, Thomas

Suggestions for further reading:
Ford, Worthington Chauncy, ed. 1904–1937. *Journals of the Continental Congress, 1774–1789,* vol. V. Washington, D.C.: U.S. Government Printing Office.
"To Mrs. Sarah Bache," January 26, 1784 (Smyth, vol. IX).

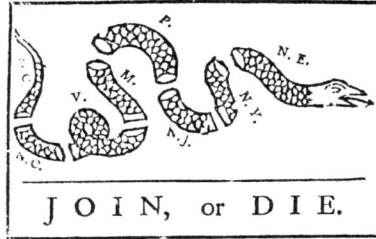

JOIN, or DIE.

Vaughan, Benjamin (1751–1835)

Benjamin Vaughan, who lived in England, was one of Franklin's most earnest friends and admirers. He was the son of a West Indian planter, well connected, and secretary to the Earl of Shelburne (William Petty). The American Revolution did not make the slightest dent in Vaughan's enthusiastic admiration for Franklin. He rounded up many of Franklin's writings and published an edition of his works in 1779, in England in the midst of the war, entitled "Political, Miscellaneous and Philosophical Pieces; Written by Benj. Franklin LL.D. and F.R.S., Now First Collected, with Explanatory Plates, Notes, and an Index to the Whole." Vaughan wrote of Franklin in the preface to the edition: "Reader, whoever you are and how much soever you think you hate him, know that this great man loves you enough to wish to do you good: His country's friend, but more of humankind."

Vaughan dutifully kept Franklin updated on political sentiment in England during the Revolution. He criticized even the moderate politicians in England who sought an end to the war in America. He complained of Lord Shelburne and described the Rockinghams as "warm and weak men who all hang together." In 1778 Vaughan sent Franklin a copy of minutes of Lord Shelburne's speech to Parliament urging an end to the war in America, without conceding independence. He reported on the testimony before Parliament of Joseph Galloway, Franklin's former political ally in Pennsylvania who had become a loyalist. In 1781 Vaughan informed Franklin that Henry Laurens, the American diplomat captured at sea and imprisoned in the Tower of London, lacked basic necessities in his confinement.

In 1782 Franklin sent a copy of the *Autobiography* he had begun at Bishop Jonathan Shipley's home in 1771, and from that point on, Vaughan never ceased begging Franklin to finish it. He wrote a long letter to Franklin in January 1783 (which Franklin inserted into the *Autobiography*) outlining the reasons he should complete the work. "Your history is so remarkable," Vaughan wrote, "that if you do not give it, somebody else will certainly give it; and perhaps so as nearly to do as much harm, as your own management of the thing might do good." He thought that Franklin's history would paint a much sought-after picture of American life that would encourage virtuous minds to settle there. "All that has happened to you is also connected with the detail of the manners and situation of a rising people," Vaughan continued, "and in this respect I do not think that the writings of Caesar and Tacitus can be more interesting to a true judge of human nature and society." Vaughan also encouraged him to write his never-realized project, *The Art of Virtue*.

In 1789 Franklin sent an unfinished copy of the *Autobiography* to Vaughan and Dr. Richard Price for their comments.

In a lengthy letter to Vaughan in 1784, Franklin commented on the fledgling U.S. economy. Vaughan had asked Franklin about reports of excessive luxury in America, and if he had a remedy for luxury. Franklin thought reports of excessive luxury were exaggerated. Strangers, he argued, were well treated as guests and did not see how families lived when they had no company. He believed that "[t]he first elements of wealth are obtained by labor, from the earth and the waters," and he thought Americans would remain industrious while there were still vast tracts of forested land to clear. "Look around the world and see millions employed in doing nothing, or in something that amounts to nothing, when the necessaries and conveniences of life are in question," Franklin wrote. "What is the bulk of commerce, for which we fight and destroy each other, but the toil of millions for superfluities, to the great hazard and loss of many lives by the constant dangers of the sea?" Franklin thought that industry and prudence were stronger forces than idleness and folly, so America would not suffer ruin on account of the luxury of a few merchants on the coast. He concluded, "[T]he eyes of other people are the eyes that ruin us. If all but myself were blind, I should want neither fine clothes, fine houses, nor fine furniture."

In 1785 Franklin sent Vaughan a piece entitled "On the Criminal Laws and the Practice of Privateering," written in response to "Thoughts on Executive Justice," by Dr. Martin Madan (1726–1790). Franklin criticized the application of the death penalty as punishment for lesser crimes. "Superfluous property is the creature of society," Franklin argued. "Simple and mild laws were sufficient to guard the property that was merely necessary." Franklin also denounced England's promotion of privateering: "Is there probably any one of those privateering merchants of London, who were so ready to rob the merchants of Amsterdam, that would not readily plunder another London merchant of the next street, if he could do it with impunity?" Franklin argued that a nation like England, which had commissioned "no less than 700 gangs of robbers," had no right to hang individuals for theft.

Vaughan came to Southampton to see Franklin off to the United States in 1785, and the two talked about lead poisoning, a subject on which Franklin elaborated by letter to him the following year. In 1786 Vaughan was elected to the American Philosophical Society. He and Franklin corresponded until Franklin's death in 1790.

Related entries:
> *Autobiography*
> France
> Medicine
> Revolutionary War
> Supreme Executive Council of Pennsylvania

Suggestions for further reading:
> "To Benjamin Vaughan," July 26, 1784 (Smyth, vol. IX).
> "To Benjamin Vaughan," July 31, 1786 (Smyth, vol. IX).
> "To Benjamin Vaughan," March 5, 1784 (Smyth, vol. IX).
> "To Benjamin Vaughan," November 9, 1779 (Labaree et al., vol 31).
> "To Benjamin Vaughan," November 2, 1789 (Smyth, vol. X).
> "To Benjamin Vaughan, On the Criminal Laws and the Practice of Privateering," March 14, 1785 (Smyth, vol. IX).

Vegetarianism

Franklin was a vegetarian for a short time during his teens. At age 16 he read *The Way to Health, Long Life, and Happiness, or a Discourse on Temperance,* by Dr. Thomas Tryon (1634–1703). Tryon advocated adhering to a strict vegetable diet. At the time, Franklin was apprenticed to his brother James as a printer, and both of them boarded with a local family. "My refusing to eat flesh occasioned an inconveniency, and I was frequently chid for my singularity," Franklin wrote in his *Autobiography*. He taught himself how to cook some of Tryon's vegetarian dishes.

Besides the added mental clarity Franklin believed he gained from the diet, there were other advantages. He offered to pay for his own boarding if James would give him half the money he paid for it every week. James agreed to the deal, and Franklin was able to save half of everything his brother gave him. He spent the additional money on books, and he studied during the additional time he gained by not eating with everyone else.

Franklin abandoned his vegetarian diet on his passage from Boston to New York. Some of his fellows fished for cod off of Block Island. Franklin said, "I considered, with my master Tryon, the taking of every fish as a kind of unprovoked murder, since none of them had, or ever could do us any injury that might justify the slaughter. . . . But I had formerly been a great lover of fish, and, when this came hot out of the frying-pan, it smelled admirably well." Franklin debated whether or not to eat the fish, and after he saw a smaller fish inside the stomach of a larger one that had been opened, he reasoned that, if fish ate one another, humans could eat fish.

Franklin abandoned vegetarianism on a permanent basis, but he returned to meatless cuisine for short periods of time. Not only did his abstention from animal flesh save him money, but also he believed that it had mental and physical health benefits. In Philadelphia, while Franklin worked in Samuel Keimer's printing house, he convinced his reluctant boss to try a vegetarian diet. "He was usually a great glutton," Franklin said, "and I promised myself some diversion in half starving him." Both of them stuck to the diet for three months, but Keimer, longing for his meat, broke down and ordered a roast pig. He invited Franklin and two women to join him, but he had eaten all of it by the time they got there.

"Cheese and salt meat, should be sparingly eat" was one of Poor Richard's adages. Franklin always believed that it was best not to eat too much meat, but he enjoyed it too much to give it up permanently. He did, however, abandon meat during some Lent seasons.

Related entries:
Franklin, James
Poor Richard's Almanack
Printing

Suggestion for further reading:
Masur, Louis P., ed. 1993. *The Autobiography of Benjamin Franklin*. Boston: Bedford Books of St. Martin's Press.

Vergennes, Comte de (Charles Gravier) (1719–1787)

As the French minister of foreign affairs during the American Revolution, Charles Gravier, the Comte de Vergennes, was the chief agent of the French government with whom Franklin and the American commissioners (Silas Deane, Arthur Lee, John Adams, Thomas Jefferson, John Jay, and Henry Laurens, at various times) worked during the war. Vergennes was artful and able, and he was favorably disposed to America as far as America would serve France's ends against Great Britain. Anxious to deal a blow to the British Empire, he had already sent an agent to Congress in 1775, before Thomas Jefferson drafted the Declaration of Independence. With Vergennes's help and French money, Pierre-Augustin Caron de Beaumarchais set up Roderigue Hortalez and Company, the purpose of which was to disguise military supplies smuggled to the colonies as legitimate commerce. Congress sent Silas Deane to France in March 1776 to pursue French assistance, and Franklin and Lee had joined him by the end of the year.

The first official correspondence between the American commissioners and Vergennes came from the latter on December 23, 1776. "Sir," it began, "We beg leave to acquaint your Excellency that we are appointed and fully empowered by the Congress of the United States of America to propose and negotiate a treaty of amity and commerce between France and the United States." Franklin, Deane, and Lee asked for an audience. Vergennes received them respectfully five days later, but he could do little more than assure them of France's positive disposition to America. If France joined America, war would follow with England, and there were political elements in France wary of the expense and trouble that new hostilities would bring. France wanted to be certain that the 13 colonies had a chance of winning before it joined with them in a war, and it was not fully convinced of the possibility of victory until news of the defeat of the British Major General John Burgoyne at Saratoga reached France in December 1777. Until France officially allied itself with the United States in 1778, Vergennes was cautious about being seen with Franklin and the other commissioners too frequently, although he continually assured them of France's good disposition.

France and the United States signed a treaty of alliance on February 6, 1778. Congress recalled Deane the same year and replaced him with Adams. After Congress revoked the joint commission of Franklin, Adams, and Lee early in 1779, Franklin became the sole minister plenipotentiary to France, and the responsibility of working with Vergennes fell on him alone. Franklin and Vergennes worked together in all aspects of the war. They planned joint operations between French and American forces, helped organize exchanges of prisoners of war, and handled prize ships. Of the commissioners, Vergennes had always preferred Franklin, and the respect was mutual. Their harmonious working relationship was essential with regard to Franklin's most humiliating duty—asking Vergennes for more French money to pay the endless stream of bills that Congress sent to him. After one desperate request for money in 1780, Vergennes replied to Franklin: "You can easily imagine my astonishment at your request of the necessary funds to meet these drafts, since you perfectly well know the extraordinary efforts, which I have made thus far to assist you. . . . Nevertheless, Sir, I am very desirous of assisting you . . . and for this purpose I shall endeavor to procure for you, for the next year, the same aid that I have been able to furnish in the course of the present." In 1783 Franklin and Vergennes drew up an agreement that summarized French assistance to the United States and the terms for repayment.

In 1780 Adams, who had returned to France with a commission to negotiate any possible peace agreement, took the liberty of writing to Vergennes without consulting Franklin. Adams's letters offended Vergennes, who refused to have any further talks with him. Vergennes sent all of Adams's letters to Franklin with the request that Franklin transmit them to Congress. Adams did not trust Vergennes or the French, and he and other members of Congress thought that Franklin placed too much confidence in them. Franklin did indeed trust the French to follow through on what they promised. He wrote to Samuel Huntington in 1781: "[I] have had so much experience of his Majesty's goodness to us, in the aids afforded us from time to time, and of the sincerity of this upright and able minister, who never promised me anything which he did not punctually perform. . . . "

Affairs grew more complex after the surrender of General Charles Cornwallis at Yorktown in 1781. France and the United States had united under the common purpose of defeating England, but the two countries had different aims and considerations when it came to negotiating a peace treaty. Franklin was involved in informal and unofficial peace talks discussions with British envoys from March to October 1782, and during that time he more or less kept Vergennes up-to-date on their progress. According to Congress's instructions, the American commissioners were to treat with England with the participation of France. When Jay and later Adams, who were suspicious of France's aims with regard to boundaries and other matters, joined the negotiations, they insisted on proceeding with the official talks without consulting Vergennes. Franklin joined them in this violation of Congress's instructions, and Vergennes was shocked to learn in November 1782 that the commissioners had signed preliminary articles of agreement. Franklin assured Vergennes that the preliminary articles contained nothing contrary to the interest of France, and that France could remain assured of American loyalty. "Your observation is, however, apparently just," Franklin wrote, "that, in not consulting you before they were signed, we have been guilty in neglecting a point of *bienséance*." In a letter to the French minister in the United States, Vergennes excused Franklin's "irregular" conduct: "He has yielded too easily to the bias of his colleagues, who do not pretend to recognize the rules of courtesy in regard to us."

Franklin was troubled by Adams's distrust of Vergennes and in 1783 cautioned Robert R. Livingston in Congress about "the insinuations of [Adams] against this court, and the instances he supposes of their ill will to us, which I take to be as imaginary as I know his fancies to be, that the Count de V. and myself are continually plotting against him, and employing the newswriters of Europe to depreciate his character, &c." According to Franklin, Adams thought "the French minister one of the greatest enemies of our country."

Vergennes had always liked Franklin as well as his grandson, William Temple, who served as his grandfather's secretary and the secretary to the American commission during the peace negotiations. When Franklin received his long-awaited permission to return home in 1785, he wrote to Vergennes, "Permit me . . . to offer you my thankful acknowledgments for the protection and countenance you afforded me at my arrival, and your many favors during my residence here, of which I shall always retain the most grateful remembrance." Franklin's successor as minister plenipotentiary, Jefferson, noted that Vergennes spoke of Franklin in the most positive terms.

Upon hearing of Vergennes's death, Franklin wrote to Ferdinand Grand in 1787: "Your mention of the malady of M. de Vergennes afflicted me, and much more the news I since hear of his death. So wise and so good a man taken away from the station he filled, is a great loss not only to France, but to Europe in general, to America, and to mankind."

Related entries:
　Adams, John
　France
　Izard, Ralph
　Jay, John
　Jefferson, Thomas
　Journal of the Negotiation for Peace with Great Britain
　Lee, Dr. Arthur
　Revolutionary War
　Treaty of Alliance with France
　Treaty of Paris, 1783

Suggestions for further reading:
　Hale, Edward, and Edward E. Hale, Jr. 1969. *Franklin in France: From Original Documents, Most of Which Are Now Published for the First Time.* New York: Burt Franklin.
　"Journal of Negotiations for Peace with Great Britain," 1782 (Smyth, vol. VIII).
　Murphy, Orville Theodore. 1982. *Charles Gravier, Comte de Vergennes: French Diplomacy in the Age of Revolution, 1719–1787.* Albany: State University of New York Press.
　Schoenbrun, David. 1976. *Triumph in Paris: The Exploits of Benjamin Franklin.* New York: Harper & Row.
　"To Vergennes," May 26, 1780 (Labaree, et al., vol. 32).
　"To Vergennes," June 18, 1780 (Labaree, et al., vol. 32).

Volunteer Militia

*P*ennsylvania was seemingly frozen in its inability to form a plan for defense in several instances during Franklin's residence there. Pennsylvania politics were marked by several parties with contradictory interests. The first was a strong Quaker faction that refused to fight on religious principle and had to be persuaded to appropriate money for military purposes. The proprietors of Pennsylvania at this time were Thomas and Richard Penn, who had renounced their father's (William Penn's) Quaker religion and treated the province they inherited as a source of income. They owned vast estates in Pennsylvania and adamantly refused to allow them to be taxed, even in emergency situations when the province was threatened. Supporters of the Penns formed a second powerful faction. Other factions of merchants and townspeople resented the Quakers' refusal to fight, and they refused to take part in the defense of people who would not participate with them.

In the 1740s Franklin was not a member of the Assembly (he was the Assembly's clerk) and had no power to introduce legislation. The Quaker-dominated body refused to pass a defense bill in spite of the repeated urgings of the governor. Having lived in Pennsylvania for many years, Franklin said he was dissatisfied with only two things—the lack of a defense and the absence of a college. When Spanish and French privateers threatened the province during the years of King George's War, Franklin grew increasingly frustrated with the deadlock in the Assembly. He set his pen and press to work with a pamphlet entitled "Plain Truth" (1747), which called for "a voluntary association of the people" for the defense of Pennsylvania.

The pamphlet warned of the consequences of failing to organize a defense for the province and called for the warring political factions to put aside their differences for this important purpose. Franklin put the grave danger their undefended province faced in terms that everyone could relate to: "Those that are reputed rich will flee, through fear of torture, to make them produce more than they are able. The man that has a wife and children will find them hanging on his neck, beseeching him with tears to quit the city. . . ." The inhabitants of Pennsylvania were defenseless "through the dissensions of our leaders, through mistaken principles of religion, joined with a love of worldly power, on the one hand; through pride, envy, and implacable resentment on the other. . . ." Franklin promised his readership that, if in a few days they were interested, he would present them with a practical scheme for a voluntary association.

"The pamphlet had a sudden and surprising effect," Franklin wrote in his *Autobiography*. Franklin held meetings with influential men of the town and also discussed the plan at a larger meeting, where it was received with little objection. There were roughly 1,000 immediate subscribers, and their numbers later swelled to more than 10,000. The new militia armed itself and organized into companies and regiments. Its members chose officers and met every week for training. Women contributed silk colors painted with "different devices and mottos," supplied by Franklin. Philadelphia's regiment chose Franklin as their colonel, but Franklin believed that he was poorly qualified and suggested another man instead. Franklin thought that a lottery would help with the expense of building a battery below the town and supplying it with cannon. The battery was built and supplied with cannon bought from Boston. Meanwhile, more were on order from England, and a request for assistance was sent to the proprietaries, who were not likely to give it. Franklin went with a few others to New York to ask to borrow some cannon until those from England arrived. Governor George Clinton initially refused to lend the cannon, but after drinking a good amount of Madeira he finally consented to loan 18 of them.

They brought the cannon to the battery, where the soldiers kept a nightly watch until the war ended. "[A]mong the rest I regularly took my duty there as a common soldier," Franklin wrote. His son, William, went on an expedition to Canada with one of the companies. The governor appreciated Franklin's ingenuity with the militia and consulted him in matters relating to it. Franklin proposed a

Franklin directing the building of a stockade fort. Painting by Charles E. Mills, c. 1915.

day of fast, which was held on January 7, 1748, and was employed to draw up the proclamation, which was printed in English and German and distributed through Pennsylvania. It inspired more people to join the militia, but the war soon ended and with it the need for the large militia.

The French and Indian War brought fresh problems for Pennsylvania. Franklin had by this time been elected to the Assembly. The defeat and death of General Braddock on his way to Fort Duquesne in 1755 instilled fear in Pennsylvanians, as did reports of scalping of frontier settlers, but the same political quarrels prevented any effective mode of action. The proprietaries still refused to pay taxes on their estates; the Quakers would appropriate money if they could stay out of the fighting; and others refused to defend Quakers. The Assembly passed bills that would have appropriated money, but the governor continued to veto them because they did not exempt the proprietary estates from taxation. The Assembly, disgruntled Pennsylvanians, and some vocal critics in England (where the proprietaries lived) finally bullied the Penns into donating £5,000 for defense, and the Assembly succeeded in passing a £55,000 appropriations bill. "I had been active in modeling the bill and procuring its passage,

and had, at the same time, drawn a bill for establishing and disciplining a voluntary militia, which I carried through the House without much difficulty, as care was taken in it to leave the Quakers at their liberty," Franklin wrote in his *Autobiography.* The militia bill passed on November 2, 1755.

As he had done with the previous militia, he wrote a piece to promote the bill and placate angry townspeople who refused to enlist to defend Quakers. It was published in the *Pennsylvania Gazette* and entitled "A Dialogue between X, Y, and Z, Concerning the Present State of Affairs in Pennsylvania." In the dialogue, "X" tried to address every legal and personal objection that people might have against the bills. One of the primary objections was the refusal of some to enlist because the bill exempted Quakers from bearing arms. It was fair to exempt the Quakers, Franklin believed, because the charter of Pennsylvania granted "liberty of conscience" to its inhabitants. Furthermore, Quakers paid a significant amount of money in taxes—generally a greater amount than others in proportion to their numbers—for the king's service, which naturally included military service. "Z" objected: "For my part, I am no coward, but hang me if I'll fight to save the Quakers." "X" retorted: "That is to say, you won't pump ship, because 'twill save the rats, as well as yourself."

Again Franklin took an active role in the militia he had been instrumental in forming. The governor put him in charge of Pennsylvania's northwestern frontier, "infested by the enemy." Franklin was to construct a line of forts and raise troops to defend the inhabitants of that area. He commanded 560 troops, and his son William served as his aide-de-camp. Franklin assembled his men at Bethlehem. In January 1756 he marched with a portion of his men to Gnadenhutten, a Moravian town that had been attacked and burned by Shawnee Indians.

Franklin's men were poorly armed and found themselves marching in a January rain. They spent their first night huddled in the barn of a German settler. Ten of 11 farmers to whom Franklin had just given guns had perished in an Indian attack because their wet guns malfunctioned, and Franklin's company had been lucky to avoid the same fate. They arrived in Gnadenhutten the following day and began work on the fort. "[O]ur fort, if such a magnificent name may be given to so miserable a stockade, was finished in a week, though it rained so hard every other day that men could not work," Franklin said. Scouting parties found no Indians in the immediate vicinity, but they found abandoned spots from which Indians had observed the construction of the fort. The chaplain of Franklin's company, the Presbyterian Reverend Charles Beatty, complained that nobody came to his prayers. Franklin instructed him to give them their daily allowance of rum after the prayers, and the chaplain soon had full attendance. This method, Franklin thought, worked better than punishing his men for not attending prayers.

No sooner had Franklin finished constructing and supplying the fort (Fort Allen) than the governor requested his presence at the Assembly. He complied and commissioned the more experienced Colonel William Clapham in his place. Back in Philadelphia, Franklin found that the militia was doing well and getting organized. The other officers chose him as colonel of the Philadelphia Regiment. They paraded 1,200 "well-looking men, with a company of artillery, who had been furnished with six brass field pieces, which had become so expert in the use of as to fire twelve times in a minute." When the regiment fired shots outside his house to salute him, the shots "shook down and broke several glasses of my electrical apparatus." Franklin soon headed to Virginia on business for the post office. To his dismay, he was escorted out of town by mounted and uniformed men brandishing their swords. Thomas Penn, the proprietor and Franklin's arch political enemy, heard about the event and took offense because such high honors were normally reserved for royal visitors. He suspected Franklin of trying to make himself ruler of the province. Franklin's military career was short-lived, however. The militia bill was repealed in England, and all of the officers lost their commissions.

Franklin's third successful attempt at gathering men for defense was not to protect the English settlers but for the protection of some peaceable Indians living in the province. A gang of rioters known as the Paxton Boys had murdered a small band of peaceful Conestoga Indians in 1764 and now threatened this group, who were Moravian converts living under government protection in Philadelphia. Franklin hastily called for an association and succeeded in gathering nearly 1,000 men for their defense. He and several others rode out to meet the Paxton Boys and succeeded in convincing them that the Indians they sought were well protected.

These successes of the militia in Pennsylvania undoubtedly helped to prepare him for his role in the American Revolution, during which he and many others helped to supply and maintain an army for an entire nation.

Related entries:
French and Indian War
Native Americans
Pennsylvania Assembly

Suggestions for further reading:
"A Dialogue between X, Y, and Z, Concerning the Present State of Affairs in Pennsylvania," December 18, 1755 (Labaree et al., vol. 6).

Masur, Louis P., ed. 1993. *The Autobiography of Benjamin Franklin*. Boston: Bedford Books of St. Martin's Press.

Nolan, J. Bennett. 1936. *General Benjamin Franklin: The Military Career of a Philosopher.* Philadelphia: University of Pennsylvania Press.

"Plain Truth; Or, Serious Considerations on the Present State of the City of Philadelphia and Province of Pennsylvania," November 17, 1747 (Labaree et al., vol. 3).

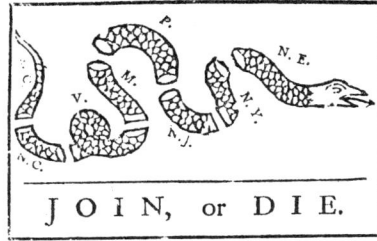

JOIN, or DIE.

W

Walpole Company

See **Grand Ohio Company.**

Washington, George (1732–1799)

*B*est remembered for his roles as the commander in chief of the American army during the Revolutionary War and the first president of the United States, George Washington played a central part in the formation of the new nation. He was born in Virginia, grew up on a plantation, and received less than ten years of formal education. In his early life he spent his time working on the family farms and exploring and surveying the frontier.

His distinguished military career began in 1753, just before the French and Indian War, when he was commissioned as a major in the Virginia militia. Later that year, the lieutenant governor sent Washington to warn the French that they were intruding in English territory in the Ohio Valley region. The French ignored the warning. He returned to the area for a second mission during which he was supposed to reinforce troops who were building a fort. Before he got there, however, the French had already captured the fort and renamed it Fort Duquesne. Washington and his men built Fort Necessity south of Fort Duquesne but were forced to surrender it to the French. In 1755 he became an aide-de-camp to British General Edward Braddock, who was soon to lead a disastrous expedition to Fort Duquesne that resulted in his death. Later that year, Washington was put in charge of defending Virginia's western frontier.

Franklin and Washington had both been involved in Braddock's campaign—Franklin obtained supplies for Braddock, and Washington was his aide-de-camp. In 1756 the two communicated to one another about maintaining an intercolonial postal route between Philadelphia and Winchester.

Washington's career in the Virginia House of Burgesses, in which revolutionary leaders like George Mason, Patrick Henry, and Thomas Jefferson also served, began in 1758. Like Franklin, he was not known for public oratory and spoke infrequently. He was among the many who strongly resented increasing British taxation and other restrictions on the colonies. Virginia sent him to both Continental Congresses as a delegate. The Second Continental Congress, in which Franklin also served, voted him commander in chief of the Continental army.

In September 1775 Franklin, Thomas Lynch, and Benjamin Harrison were sent to join Washington in Cambridge, Massachusetts, to determine the condition of the colonies

Silhouette of George Washington, etching in **The Columbian Magazine,** *March 1788.*

for battle. Washington reported a dismal state of affairs—troops were disorganized and undisciplined, and ammunition and other provisions were scarce. At the conference at Washington's camp, they agreed on methods for raising regiments, exchanging prisoners, paying troops, obtaining provisions, and other critical wartime issues.

After suffering some early defeats in the war, Washington led his troops on successful surprise attacks against British strongholds in Trenton and Princeton. British General William Howe advanced his troops toward Philadelphia, and Washington was unable to stop them. He and his troops passed the winter of 1777 in Valley Forge, Pennsylvania.

Franklin sent letters from France recommending foreign officers to Washington, including the Marquis de Lafayette, who became an intimate friend of Washington's and named his son after him. Franklin apologized for sending the general so many recommendations: "It is with regret that I give letters of introduction to foreign officers, fearing that you may be troubled with more than you can provide for, or employ to their and your own satisfaction." He assured Washington that he recommended only exceptional cases, and that he did not promise them any position when they got to America. Too many

foreign officers had in fact been sent to America, and both Congress and Washington requested that no more be recommended.

In 1778 British troops under Sir Henry Clinton clashed with Washington's forces at Monmouth, New Jersey, and the American troops again lost the battle. In 1780, 6,000 French troops commanded by the Comte de Rochambeau arrived to help Washington's forces. Also during that year, Washington wrote to Franklin to see if he would be able to obtain badly needed money for the American army. Franklin procured a gift of 6 million livres from the French king for supplies for the American army, to be handled by Washington. Washington and Rochambeau marched south from New York to Virginia. They joined forces with the Marquis de Lafayette and led a joint assault on Yorktown in 1781. British General Charles Cornwallis was surrounded and had no choice but to surrender.

Franklin received the articles of capitulation in Passy and wrote Washington a letter of congratulation in 1782. "All the world agree," he said, "that no expedition was ever better planned or better executed; it has made a great addition to the military reputation you had already acquired, and brightens the glory that surrounds your name, and that must accompany it to our latest posterity." Franklin wrote to him again a few days later and told him that he had managed to subdue not only the British generals but also their enemy politicians in Parliament.

When Franklin returned to Philadelphia from France in 1785, he sent a letter to Washington asking him to see Jean-Antoine Houdon, a French sculptor who wanted to make a bust of the general for Virginia. The sculptor went to Mount Vernon and created the bust.

When the government under the Articles of Confederation proved to be inadequate, a Constitutional Convention convened in 1787. Washington was elected president of the convention; Franklin was also a delegate. Washington became the first president of the

United States in 1788 and was reelected for a second term in 1792. Franklin was one of his many supporters. He wrote to his friend in France, Louis-Guillaume LeVeillard, "General Washington is the man that all our eyes are fixed on for President, and what little influence I may have, is devoted to him."

The two men deeply respected one another. They played two very different, but both important, roles during the war for American independence—Franklin's work was in the political arena and Washington's on the battlefield. Washington wrote to Franklin just before the latter's death: "If to be venerated for benevolence, if to be admired for talents, if to be esteemed for patriotism, if to be beloved for philanthropy, can gratify the human mind, you must have the pleasing consolation to know, that you have not lived in vain." Franklin said in his will: "My fine crab-tree walking stick, with a gold head curiously wrought in the form of the cap of liberty, I give to my friend, and the friend of mankind, General Washington. If it were a scepter, he has merited it, and would become it."

Franklin did not live to see most of Washington's presidency. As the first president, he created a cabinet, consisting in part of Thomas Jefferson as secretary of state, Henry Knox as secretary of war, Edmund Randolph as attorney general, and Alexander Hamilton as secretary of the treasury. In his farewell address he urged America to avoid "permanent alliances" with foreign powers, to promote educational institutions, to adhere to the Constitution, and to stay away from political partisanship. Washington left office in 1797 and spent the remainder of his life at Mount Vernon.

Related entries:
Constitutional Convention
Continental Congresses
France
Jefferson, Thomas
Lafayette, Marquis de
Revolutionary War

Suggestions for further reading:
"Minutes of the Conference between a

Committee of Congress, Washington, and Representatives of the New England Colonies," 1775 (Labaree et al., vol. 22).
"To George Washington," April 2, 1782 (Smyth, vol. VIII).
"To George Washington," September 15, 1789 (Smyth, vol. X).

Webster, Noah (1758–1843)

Franklin became acquainted with Noah Webster, who published his famed *American Dictionary of the English Language* in 1828, during the last few years of his life. Webster had proposed a scheme for an improved alphabet that Franklin said was very similar to the one he had suggested in 1768. After perusing Webster's proposal in 1786, he told Webster that their ideas were so similar and practical that they should get together and discuss them. According to Webster, Franklin had been ready to obtain types for his [Franklin's] new alphabet. Webster printed letters that Franklin and Polly Stevenson had exchanged in Franklin's new alphabet in his *Dissertations on the English Language* (1789) and dedicated the work to Franklin.

Webster graduated from Yale College, served in the American army during the Revolution, and became a Federalist after the war. He embraced American spellings and pronunciations rather than British ones. By 1785 he had completed *A Grammatical Institute of the English Language,* a three-part work on English spelling and grammar. He founded a daily newspaper in New York entitled *The Minerva* and wrote many other works in his lifetime, including *A Brief History of Epidemic and Pestilential Diseases.* Webster also helped to found Amherst College in Massachusetts.

Franklin took interest in the work of Webster, a skilled and careful writer from a young age. In a letter to him in 1789 Franklin commended him for his "zeal for preserving the purity of our language, both in its expressions and pronunciation, and in correcting the popular errors several of our states are continually falling into with respect to

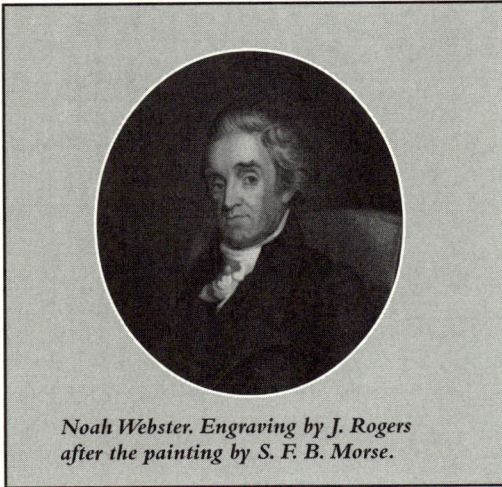
Noah Webster. Engraving by J. Rogers after the painting by S. F. B. Morse.

Suggestions for further reading:
"To Noah Webster," December 26, 1789 (Smyth, vol. X).
"To Noah Webster," July 9, 1786 (Smyth, vol. IX).
"To Noah Webster," June 18, 1786 (Smyth, vol. IX).

both." Three years later, Franklin complained to Webster about new usages of nouns as verbs. For example, variations of nouns such as "advocate," "progress," and "notice" were beginning to gain usage as verbs. Franklin suggested to Webster, "If you should happen to be of my opinion with respect to these innovations, you will use your authority in reprobating them."

Also annoying to Franklin were new printing styles. Printers had begun to use gray inks rather than the more easily read black inks. The letter "s" was shortened from "S" to "s," and the practice of capitalizing substantive nouns was eliminated. Franklin talked about the prominence of the French language in Europe and hoped that English would compete. The large number of good sermons, along with the extraordinary freedom of political writings, he thought, were sparking more interest in studying English in Europe. However, he believed that the new printing techniques rendered it more difficult for foreigners to study English.

Franklin was too old to pursue the phonetic alphabet or much other work with Webster. He died only a few months after he had written the 1789 letter.

Related entries:
Hewson, Mary (Polly) Stevenson
Printing

Weissenstein, Charles de

"Charles de Weissenstein" was the pseudonym of an unknown individual who briefly and indirectly became involved with Franklin (though they never met) while the latter was staying in Passy, France, during the Revolutionary War. A packet containing a letter and other documents was mysteriously dropped at Franklin's house, with instructions that only he was to read it. The documents contained plans for reconciliation of the colonies with Britain and promises of rewards for Americans who would help. Weissenstein identified himself as an Englishman who sympathized with some of the Americans' complaints against the Crown but did not think a war or independence was the answer to them. He stated his belief that the colonies could not trust the French.

Weissenstein's letter requested that Franklin's reply be delivered to a messenger who was to be waiting at the Church of Notre Dame. Franklin was incensed at the letter, which he believed came from George III, and his reply (which was never delivered to anyone but French authorities) was stinging. He asserted that the French were to be much more surely trusted by the American colonies than were the British.

Franklin was also offended by the offers to reward cooperative Americans. "As to my future fame," he wrote, "I am content to rest it on my past and present conduct, without seeking an addition to it in the crooked, dark paths you propose to me, where I should most certainly lose it." The very fact that Weissenstein, who he knew had not used his real name, would attempt to bribe him was a poor reflection on his character.

In the end the letter was never sent, and French police went to the place where Franklin was to meet the messenger. The messenger, who was not supposed to know anything about his mission, was followed, but nothing came of the incident.

Related entries:
Adams, John
France
Revolutionary War

Suggestion for further reading:
"To Charles de Weissenstein," July 1, 1778 (Labaree et al., vol. 27).

Williams, Jonathan, Jr. (1750–1815)

Jonathan Williams Jr. was Franklin's grandnephew, the son of one of his nieces in Boston. His father, Jonathan Williams Sr., married the daughter of Franklin's sister, Anne Franklin Harris, and was a Boston merchant. Franklin from the start liked the younger Williams, who with his musically inclined brother Josiah visited him in London in 1770 and 1771. In 1770 Franklin described him as "a very valuable young man, sober, regular, and inclined to industry and frugality, which are promising signs of success in business." He reported to the elder Williams the following year, "Jonathan seems to have an excellent turn for business, and to be a perfect master of accounts. In the latter he has been of great use to me, having put all mine in order for me."

During the American Revolution Williams, like Franklin, lived in France. He was an American commercial and financial agent at Nantes, where he handled sales of prize ships, sold American cargoes, and shipped goods to the United States. Williams worked with other American agents, such as John D. Schweighauser, John Ross, and Joseph Wharton, and he reported to Franklin, "I am treated here with as much respect, as if I were the nephew of a prince."

In 1779 Arthur Lee, serving with Franklin as an American commissioner to France, accused Williams of embezzling 100,000 livres of public money. Franklin asked other Nantes merchants to examine Williams's accounts, and he was later cleared, but Franklin did not renew his appointment as a public agent. Williams remained in France engaged in private business. The same year, Williams married Marianne Alexander, daughter of William Alexander, of Edinburgh. He returned to the United States with Franklin in 1785, and during the voyage he kept a journal of water and air temperatures for his uncle. After Franklin's death, John Adams, during his presidency, appointed him a major in the Second Regiment of Artillerists and Engineers. Williams later became the first superintendent of West Point.

Related entries:
France
Lee, Dr. Arthur
Revolutionary War

Suggestions for further reading:
"To Grace Williams," March 5, 1771 (Labaree et al., vol. 18).
"To Jonathan Williams, Jr.," March 16, 1779 (Labaree et al., vol. 29).
"To Jonathan Williams, Jr.," March 19, 1779 (Labaree et al., vol. 29).

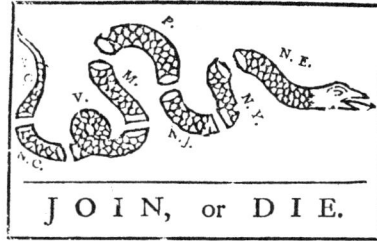

JOIN, or DIE.

SELECTED WRITINGS

The following selections from Franklin's writings, arranged in chronological order, represent a small fraction of his works. Some spellings and capitalization have been updated to modern usage. The location and date under each title indicate where and when Franklin wrote the piece or letter.

SILENCE DOGOOD, NO. 4
BOSTON, MAY 1722

The 14 "Silence Dogood" letters, published in James Franklin's *New England Courant* in 1722, are some of Franklin's earliest known writings. Franklin was apprenticed to his brother at the time and submitted the humorous letters secretly to the paper, using the pseudonym "Mrs. Silence Dogood." In 1753 he received an honorary master of arts from Harvard College.

An sum etiam nunc vel græce loqui vel Latinè docendus? CICERO

To the Author of the New-England Courant.
  Sir,
  Discoursing the other day at dinner with my reverend boarder, formerly mentioned, (whom for distinction sake we will call by the name of Clericus,) concerning the education of children, I asked his advice about my young son William, whether or no I had best bestow upon him academical learning, or (as our phrase is) "bring him up at our college:" he persuaded me to do it by all means, using many weighty arguments with me, and answering all the objections that I could form against it; telling me withal, that he did not doubt but that the lad would take his learning very well, and not idle away his time as too many there now-a-days do. These words of Clericus gave me a curiosity to inquire a little more strictly into the present circumstances of that famous seminary of learning; but the information which he gave me, was neither pleasant, nor such as I expected.

As soon as dinner was over, I took a solitary walk into my orchard, still ruminating on Clericus's discourse with much consideration, until I came to my usual place of retirement under the great apple-tree; where having seated myself, and carelessly laid my head on a verdant bank, I fell by degrees into a soft and undisturbed slumber. My waking thoughts remained with me in my sleep, and before I awaked again, I dreamt the following dream.

I fancied I was traveling over pleasant and delightful fields and meadows, and through many small country towns and villages; and as I passed along, all places resounded with the fame of the Temple of Learning: every peasant, who had wherewithal, was preparing to send one of his children at least to this famous place; and in this case most of them consulted their own purses instead of their children's capacities: so that I observed, a great many, yea, the most part of those who were traveling thither, were little better than dunces and blockheads. Alas! Alas!

At length I entered upon a spacious plain, in the midst of which was erected a large and stately edifice: it was to this that a great company of youths from all parts of the country were going; so stepping in among the crowd, I passed on with them, and presently arrived at the gate.

The passage was kept by two sturdy porters named Riches and Poverty, and the latter obstinately refused to give entrance to any who had not first gained the favor of the former; so that I observed, many who came even to the very gate, were obliged to travel back again as ignorant as they came, for want of this necessary qualification. However, as a spectator I gained admittance, and with the rest entered directly into the temple.

In the middle of the great hall stood a stately and magnificent throne, which was ascended to by two high and difficult steps. On the top of it sat Learning in awful state; she was appareled wholly in black, and surrounded almost on every side with innumerable volumes in all languages. She seemed very busily employed in writing something on half a sheet of paper, and upon enquiry, I understood she was preparing a paper, called, *The New-England Courant*. On her right hand sat English, with a pleasant smiling countenance, and handsomely attired; and on her left were seated several antique figures with their faces vailed. I was considerably puzzled to guess who they were, until one informed me, (who stood beside me,) that those figures on her left hand were Latin, Greek, Hebrew, &c. and that they were very much reserved, and seldom or never unvailed their faces here, and then to few or none, though most of those who have in this place acquired so much learning as to

distinguish them from English, pretended to an intimate acquaintance with them. I then enquired of him, what could be the reason why they continued vailed, in this place especially: he pointed to the foot of the throne, where I saw Idleness, attended with Ignorance, and these (he informed me) were they, who first vailed them, and still kept them so.

Now I observed, that the whole tribe who entered into the temple with me, began to climb the throne; but the work proving troublesome and difficult to most of them, they withdrew their hands from the plow, and contented themselves to sit at the foot, with Madam Idleness and her maid Ignorance, until those who were assisted by diligence and a docile temper, had well nigh got up the first step: but the time drawing nigh in which they could no way avoid ascending, they were fain to crave the assistance of those who had got up before them, and who, for the reward perhaps of a pint of milk, or a piece of plumb-cake, lent the lubbers a helping hand, and sat them in the eye of the world, upon a level with themselves.

The other step being in the same manner ascended, and the usual ceremonies at an end, every beetle-skull seemed well satisfied with his own portion of learning, though perhaps he was even just as ignorant as ever. And now the time of their departure being come, they marched out of doors to make room for another company, who waited for entrance: and I, having seen all that was to be seen, quitted the hall likewise, and went to make my observations on those who were just gone out before me.

Some I perceived took to merchandising, others to traveling, some to one thing, some to another, and some to nothing; and many of them from henceforth, for want of patrimony, lived as poor as church mice, being unable to dig, and ashamed to beg, and to live by their wits it was impossible. But the most part of the crowd went along a large beaten path, which led to a temple at the further end of the plain, called, the Temple of Theology. The business of those who were employed in this temple being laborious and painful, I wondered exceedingly to see so many go towards it; but while I was pondering this matter in my mind, I spied Pecunia behind a curtain, beckoning to them with her hand, which sight immediately satisfied me for whose sake it was, that a great part of them (I will not say all) traveled that road. In this temple I saw nothing worth mentioning, except the ambitious and fraudulent contrivances of Plagius, who (notwithstanding he had been severely reprehended for such practices before) was diligently transcribing some eloquent paragraphs out of Tillotson's works, &c. to embellish his own.

Now I bethought myself in my sleep, that it was time to be at home, and as I fancied I was traveling back thither, I reflected in my mind on the extreme folly of those parents, who, blind to their children's dullness, and insensible of the solidity of their skulls, because they think their purses can afford it, will needs send them to the Temple of Learning, where, for want of a suitable genius, they learn little more than how to carry themselves handsomely, and enter a room genteelly, (which might as well be acquired at a dancing school,) and from whence they return, after abundance of trouble and charge, as great blockheads as ever, only more proud and self-conceited.

While I was in the midst of these unpleasant reflections, Clericus (who with a book in his hand was walking under the trees) accidentally awaked me; to him I related my dream with all its particulars, and he, without much study, presently interpreted it, assuring me, that it was a lively representation of Harvard College, *et cetera*.

I remain, sir,
    your humble servant,
    Silence Dogood

ARTICLES OF BELIEF AND ACTS OF RELIGION, PART I
PHILADELPHIA, NOVEMBER 20, 1728

These articles were written when Franklin was 22 years old, around the time he became a "thorough deist." It served as his personal liturgy and devotion book. Part II is not known to exist.

Here will I hold. If there is a Power above us,
    (And that there is, all nature cries aloud,
    Through all her works), He must delight in virtue
    And that which He delights in must be happy.
                                                —Cato

First Principles
I believe there is one supreme most perfect Being, Author and Father of the gods themselves. For I believe that man is not the most perfect being but One, rather that as there are many degrees of beings his inferiors, so there are many degrees of beings superior to him.

Also, when I stretch my imagination through and beyond our system of planets, beyond the visible fixed stars themselves, into that space that is every way infinite, and conceive it filled with suns like ours, each with a chorus of worlds forever moving round him, then this little ball on which we move, seems, even in my narrow imagination, to be almost nothing, and my selfless than nothing, and of no sort of consequence.

When I think thus, I imagine it great vanity in me to suppose, that the Supremely Perfect, does in the least regard such an inconsiderable nothing as man. More especially, since it is impossible for me to have any positive clear idea of that which is infinite and incomprehensible, I cannot conceive otherwise, than that He the Infinite Father expects or requires no worship or praise from us, but that He is even infinitely above it.

But, since there is in all men something like a natural principle which inclines them to devotion, or the worship of some unseen power;

And since men are endued with reason superior to all other animals, that we are in our world acquainted with;

Therefore I think it seems required of me, and my duty as a man, to pay divine regards to something.

I conceive then, that the Infinite has created many beings or gods, vastly superior to man, who can better conceive His perfections than we, and return Him a more rational and glorious praise.

As, among men, the praise of the ignorant or of children is not regarded by the ingenious painter or architect, who is rather honored and pleased with the approbation of wise men and artists.

It may be that these created gods are immortal; or it may be that after many ages, they are changed, and others supply their places.

Howbeit, I conceive that each of these is exceeding wise and good, and very powerful; and that each has made for Himself, one glorious sun, attended with a beautiful and admirable system of planets.

It is that particular wise and good God, who is the author and owner of our system, that I propose for the object of my praise and adoration.

For I conceive that He has in Himself some of those passions He has planted in us, and that, since He has given us reason whereby we are capable of observing His wisdom in the creation, He is not above caring for us, being pleased with our praise, and offended when we slight Him, or neglect His glory.

I conceive for many reasons, that He is a good Being; and as I should be happy to have so wise, good, and powerful a Being my friend, let me consider in what manner I shall make myself most acceptable to Him.

Next to the praise resulting from and due to His wisdom, I believe He is pleased and delights in the happiness of those He has created; and since without virtue man can have no happiness in this world, I firmly believe He delights to see me virtuous, because He is pleased when He sees me happy.

And since He has created many things which seem purely designed for the delight of man, I believe He is not offended when He sees His children solace themselves in any manner of pleasant exercises and innocent delights; and I think no pleasure innocent that is to man hurtful.

I love Him therefore for His goodness and I adore Him for His wisdom.

Let me then not fail to praise my God continually, for it is His due, and it is all I can return for His many favors and great goodness to me; and let me resolve to be virtuous, that I may be happy, that I may please Him, who is delighted to see me happy. Amen!

Adoration

Prel. Being mindful that before I address the Deity, my soul ought to be calm and serene, free from passion and perturbation, or otherwise elevated with rational joy and pleasure, I ought to use a countenance that expresses a filial respect, mixed with a kind of smiling, that signifies inward joy, and satisfaction, and admiration.

O wise God, my good Father!

Thou beholdest the sincerity of my heart and of my devotion; Grant me a continuance of Thy favor!

(1) O Creator, O Father! I believe that Thou art good, and that Thou art pleased with the pleasure of Thy children. — Praised be Thy name forever!

(2) By Thy power hast Thou made the glorious sun, with his attending worlds; from the energy of Thy mighty will, they first received their prodigious motion, and by Thy wisdom hast Thou prescribed the wondrous laws, by which they move. —

Praised be Thy name forever!

(3) By Thy wisdom hast Thou formed all things. Thou hast created man, bestowing life and reason, and placed him in dignity superior to Thy other earthly creatures. —Praised be Thy name forever!

(4) Thy wisdom, Thy power, and Thy goodness are everywhere clearly seen; in the air and in the water, in the heaven and on the earth; Thou providest for the various winged fowl, and the innumerable inhabitants of the water; Thou givest cold and heat, rain and sunshine, in their season, and to the fruits of the earth increase. —Praised be Thy name forever!

(5) Thou abhorrest in Thy creatures treachery and deceit, malice, revenge, intemperance, and every other hurtful vice; but Thou art a lover of justice and sincerity, of friendship, and benevolence and every virtue. Thou art my Friend, my Father, and my Benefactor. —Praised be Thy name, O God, forever! Amen!

[After this, it will not be improper to read part of some such book as Ray's *Wisdom of God in the Creation,* or Blackmore on the Creation, or the Archbishop of Cambray's *Demonstration of the Being of a God,* &c., or else spend some minutes in a serious silence, contemplating on those subjects.]

Then sing

Milton's Hymn to the Creator

These are Thy glorious works, Parent of good!
Almighty, Thine this universal frame,
Thus wondrous fair! Thyself how wondrous then!
Speak ye who best can tell, ye sons of light,
Angels, for ye behold Him, and with songs,
And choral symphonies, day without night,
Circle His throne rejoicing you in heaven,
On earth, join all ye creatures to extol
Him first, Him last, Him midst, and without end.
"Fairest of stars, last in the train of night,
If rather thou belongst not to the dawn,
Sure pledge of day! Thou crownest the smiling morn
With thy bright circlet; praise Him in thy sphere
While day arises, that sweet hour of prime.
Thou sun, of this great world, both eye and soul,
Acknowledge Him thy greater; sound His praise
In thy eternal course; both when thou climbest,
And when high noon hast gained, and when thou fallest.
Moon! that now meetest the orient sun, now flyest
With the fixed stars, fixed in their orb that flies,
And ye five other wandering fires, that move
In mystic dance, not without song; resound
His praise, that out of darkness called up light.
Air! and ye elements! the eldest birth
Of nature's womb, that in quaternion run
Perpetual circle, multiform, and mix
And nourish all things, let your ceaseless change
Vary to our great Maker still new praise.
Ye mists and exhalations, that now rise
From hill or steaming lake, dusky or grey,
Till the sun paint your fleecy skirts with gold,
In honor to the world's Great Author rise;
Whether to deck with clouds the uncolored sky,
Or wet the thirsty earth with falling showers,
Rising or falling still advance His praise.

His praise, ye winds! that from 4 quarters blow,

Breathe soft or loud; and wave your tops, ye pines!

With every plant, in sign of worship wave.

Fountains! and ye that warble, as ye flow
Melodious murmurs, warbling tune His praise.

Join voices all ye living souls, ye birds!

That singing, up to heaven's high gate ascend,

Bear on your wings, and in your note his praise;

Ye that in waters glide! and ye that walk
The earth! and stately tread, or lowly creep;
Witness if I be silent, even or morn,
To hill, or valley, fountain, or fresh shade,
Made vocal by my song, and taught His praise.

[Here follows the reading of some book, or part of a book, discoursing on and exciting to moral virtue.]

Petition

Inasmuch as by reason of our ignorance we cannot be certain that many things, which we often hear mentioned in the petitions of men to the Deity, would prove real goods, if they were in our possession, and as I have reason to hope and believe that the goodness of my Heavenly Father will not withhold from me a suitable share of temporal blessings, if by a virtuous and holy life I conciliate His favor and kindness, therefore I presume not to ask such things, but rather humbly and with a sincere heart, express my earnest desires that he would graciously assist my continual endeavors and resolutions of eschewing vice and embracing virtue; which kind of supplications will at least be thus far beneficial, as they remind me in a solemn manner of my extensive duty.

That I may be preserved from atheism and infidelity, impiety, and profaneness, and, in my addresses to Thee, carefully avoid irreverence and ostentation, formality and odious hypocrisy, —Help me, O Father!

That I may be loyal to my prince, and faithful to my country, careful for its Good, valiant in its defense, and obedient to its laws, abhorring treason as much as tyranny, —Help me, O Father!

That I may to those above me be dutiful, humble, and submissive, avoiding pride, disrespect, and contumacy, —Help me, O Father!

That I may to those below me be gracious, condescending, and forgiving, using clemency, protecting innocent distress, avoiding cruelty, harshness, and oppression, insolence, and unreasonable severity, —Help me, O Father!

That I may refrain from censure, calumny and detraction; that I may avoid and abhor deceit and envy, fraud, flattery, and hatred, malice, lying, and ingratitude, —Help me, O Father!

That I may be sincere in friendship, faithful in trust, and impartial in judgment, watchful against pride, and against anger (that momentary madness), —Help me, O Father!

That I may be just in all my dealings, temperate in my pleasures, full of candor and ingenuity, humanity and benevolence, —Help me, O Father!

That I may be grateful to my benefactors, and generous to my friends, exercising charity and liberality to the poor, and pity to the miserable, —Help me, O Father!

That I may avoid avarice and ambition, jealousy and intemperance, falsehood, luxury and lasciviousness, —Help me, O Father!

That I may possess integrity and evenness of mind, resolution in difficulties, and fortitude under affliction; that I may be punctual in performing my promises, peaceable and prudent in my behavior, —Help me, O Father!

That I may have tenderness for the weak, and a reverent respect for the ancient; that I may be kind to my neighbors, good-natured to my companions, and hospitable to strangers, —Help me, O Father!

That I may be averse to talebearing, backbiting, detraction, slander, and craft, and overreaching, abhor extortion, perjury, and every kind of wickedness, —Help me, O Father!

That I may be honest and openhearted, gentle, merciful, and good, cheerful in spirit, rejoicing in the good of others, — Help me, O Father!

That I may have a constant regard to honor and probity, that I may possess a perfect innocence and a good conscience, and at length become truly virtuous and magnanimous, Help me, good God; — Help me, O Father!

And, forasmuch as ingratitude is one of the most odious of vices, let me not be unmindful gratefully to acknowledge the favors I receive from heaven.

Thanks

For peace and liberty, for food and raiment, for corn, and wine, and milk, and every kind of healthful nourishment, —Good God, I thank Thee!

For the common benefits of air and light, for useful fire and delicious water, —Good God, I thank Thee!

For knowledge, and literature, and every useful art, for my friends and their prosperity, and for the fewness of my enemies, — Good God, I thank Thee!

For all Thy innumerable benefits; for life, and reason, and the use of speech; for health, and joy, and every pleasant hour, —My good God, I thank Thee!

A PROPOSAL, FOR PROMOTING USEFUL KNOWLEDGE AMONG THE BRITISH PLANTATIONS IN AMERICA PHILADELPHIA, MAY 14, 1743

The American Philosophical Society, still in existence today, developed out of this proposal of Franklin's in 1743. Franklin sent it to his correspondents, and the society was founded the following year.

The English are possessed of a long tract of continent, from Nova Scotia to Georgia, extending north and south through different climates, having different soils, producing different plants, mines, and minerals, and capable of different improvements, manufactures, &c.

The first drudgery of settling new colonies, which confines the attention of people to mere necessaries, is now pretty well over; and there are many in every province in circumstances that set them at ease, and afford leisure to cultivate the finer arts and improve the common stock of knowledge. To such of these who are men of speculation, many hints must from time to time arise, many observations occur, which if well examined, pursued, and improved, might produce discoveries to the advantage of some or all of the British plantations, or to the benefit of mankind in general.

But as from the extent of the country such persons are widely separated, and seldom can see and converse or be acquainted with each other, so that many useful particulars remain uncommunicated, die with the discoverers, and are lost to mankind; it is, to remedy this inconvenience for the future, proposed,

That one society be formed of virtuosi or ingenious men, residing in the several colonies, to be called The American Philosophical Society, who are to maintain a constant correspondence.

That Philadelphia, being the city nearest the center of the continent colonies, communicating with all of them northward and southward by post, and with all the islands by sea, and having the advantage of a good growing library, be the center of the society.

That at Philadelphia there be always at least seven members, viz. a physician, a botanist, a mathematician, a chemist, a mechanician, a geographer, and a general natural philosopher, besides a president, treasurer, and secretary.

That these members meet once a month, or oftener, at their own expense, to communicate to each other their observations, and experiments, to receive, read, and consider such letters, communications, or queries as shall be sent from distant members; to direct the dispersing of copies of such communications as are valuable, to other distant members, in order to procure their sentiments thereupon.

That the subjects of the correspondence be: all new-discovered plants, herbs, trees, roots, their virtues, uses, &c.; methods of propagating them, and making such as are useful, but particular to some plantations, more general; improvements of vegetable juices, as ciders, wines, &c; new methods of curing or preventing diseases; all new-discovered fossils in different countries, as mines, minerals, and quarries; new and useful improvements in any branch of mathematics; new discoveries in chemistry, such as improvements in distillation, brewing, and assaying of ores; new mechanical inventions for saving labor; as mills and carriages, and for raising and conveying of water, draining of meadows, &c; all new arts, trades, and manufactures, that may be proposed or thought of; surveys, maps, and charts of particular parts of the sea-coasts or inland countries; course and junction of rivers and great roads, situation of lakes and mountains, nature of the soil and productions; new methods of improving the breed of useful animals; introducing other sorts from foreign countries; new improvements in planting, gardening, and clearing land; and all philosophical experiments that let light into the nature of things, tend to increase the power of man over matter, and multiply the conveniences or pleasures of life.

That a correspondence, already begun by some intended members, shall be kept up by this society with the Royal Society of London, and with the Dublin Society.

That every member shall have abstracts sent him quarterly, of every thing valuable communicated to the society's secretary at Philadelphia; free of all charge except the yearly payment hereafter mentioned.

That, by permission of the postmaster-general, such communications pass between the secretary of the society and the members, postage-free.

That, for defraying the expense of such experiments as the society shall judge proper to cause to be made, and other contingent charges for the common good, every member send a piece of eight per annum to the treasurer, at Philadelphia, to form a common stock, to be disbursed by order of the president with the consent of the majority of the members that can conveniently be consulted thereupon, to such persons and places where and by whom the experiments are to be made, and otherwise as there shall be occasion; of which disbursements an exact account shall be kept, and communicated yearly to every member.

That, at the first meetings of the members at Philadelphia, such rules be formed for regulating their meetings and transactions for the general benefit, as shall be convenient and necessary; to be afterwards changed and improved as there shall be occasion, wherein due regard is to be had to the advice of distant members.

That, at the end of every year, collections be made and printed, of such experiments, discoveries, and improvements, as may be thought of public advantage; and that every member have a copy sent him.

That the business and duty of the secretary be to receive all letters intended for the society, and lay them before the president and members at their meetings; to abstract, correct, and methodize such papers as require it, and as he shall be directed to do by the president, after they have been considered, debated, and digested in the society; to enter copies thereof in the society's books, and make out copies for distant members; to answer their letters by direction of the president, and keep records of all material transactions of the society.

Benjamin Franklin, the writer of this proposal, offers himself to serve the society as their secretary, till they shall be provided with one more capable.

To Mrs. Jane Mecom
Philadelphia, July 28, 1743

Jane Franklin Mecom was Franklin's youngest and favorite sister, who lived in Boston. The "book of devotions" referred to is likely Franklin's "Articles of Belief and Acts of Religion."

Dearest Sister Jenny,

I took your admonition very kindly, and was far from being offended at you for it. If I say any thing about it to you, it is only to rectify some wrong opinions you seem to have entertained of me; and this I do only because they give you some uneasiness, which I am unwilling to be the occasion of. You express yourself as if you thought I was against worshipping of God, and doubt good works would merit heaven; which are both fancies of your own, I think, without foundation. I am so far from thinking that God is not to be worshipped, that I have composed and wrote a whole book of devotions for my own use; and I imagine there are few if any in the world so weak as to imagine that the little good we can do here can merit so vast a reward hereafter.

There are some things in your New England doctrine and worship, which I do not agree with; but I do not therefore condemn them, or desire to shake your belief or practice of them. We may dislike things that are nevertheless right in themselves. I would only have you make me the same allowance, and have a better opinion

both of morality and your brother. Read the pages of Mr. [Jonathan] Edwards's late book entitled *Some Thoughts Concerning the Present Revival of Religion in New England,* from 367 to 375 and when you judge of others, if you can perceive the fruit to be good, don't terrify yourself that the tree may be evil; but be assured it is not so, for you know who has said, "Men do not gather grapes of thorns or figs of thistles." I have not time to add, but that I shall always be your affectionate brother,

B. Franklin

P.S. It was not kind in you, when your sister commended good works, to suppose she intended it a reproach to you. 'Twas very far from her thoughts.

The Speech of Polly Baker
Philadelphia, 1747

According to Thomas Jefferson, the Abbé Raynal included this fictitious speech as historical fact in his *Histoire des deux Indes.* Raynal was certain that the Polly Baker story was a true one. Franklin, amused, explained to him, "When I was a printer and editor of a newspaper, we were sometimes slack of news and to amuse our customers, I used to fill up our vacant columns with anecdotes and fables, and fancies of my own, and this of Polly Baker is a story of my own making, on one of those occasions." Raynal, with a laugh, replied, "Oh, very well, Doctor, I had rather relate your stories than other men's truths." One reader of *The Gentleman's Magazine,* in which the speech was published, claimed to have met Polly Baker in 1745.

The speech of Miss Polly Baker, before a court of judicature, at Connecticut near Boston in New England, where she was prosecuted the fifth time, for having a bastard child. Which influenced the court to dispense with her punishment, and induced one of her judges to marry her the next day—by whom she had fifteen children.

"May it please the honorable bench to indulge me in a few words: I am a poor, unhappy woman, who have no money to fee lawyers to plead for me, being hard put to it to get a living. I shall not trouble your honors with long speeches; for I have not the presumption to expect that you may, by any means, be prevailed on to deviate in your sentence from the law, in my favor. All I humbly hope is, that your honors would charitably move the governor's goodness on my behalf, that my fine may be remitted. This is the fifth time, gentlemen, that I have been dragged before your court on the same account; twice I have paid heavy fines, and twice have been brought to public punishment, for want of money to pay those fines. This may have been agreeable to the laws, and I don't dispute it; but since laws are sometimes unreasonable in themselves, and therefore repealed; and others bear too hard on the subject in particular circumstances, and therefore there is left a power somewhere to dispense with the execution of them; I take the liberty to say, that I think this law, by which I am punished, is both unreasonable in itself, and particularly severe with regard to me, who have always lived an inoffensive life in the neighborhood where I was born, and defy my enemies (if I have any) to say I ever wronged any man, woman, or child. Abstracted from the law, I cannot conceive (may it please your honors) what the nature of my offense is. I have brought five fine children into the world, at the risk of my life: I have maintained them well by my own industry, without burthening the township, and could have done it better, if it had not been for the heavy charges and fines I have paid. Can it be a crime (in the nature of things, I mean) to add to the king's subjects, in a new country, that really wants people? I own it, I should think it rather a praiseworthy than a punishable

action. I have debauched no other woman's husband, nor enticed any other youth; these things I never was charged with; nor has any one the least cause of complaint against me, unless, perhaps, the ministers, of justice, because I have had children without being married, by which they have missed a wedding fee. But can this be a fault of mine? I appeal to your honors. You are pleased to allow I don't want sense; but I must be stupefied to the last degree, not to prefer the honorable state of wedlock to the condition I have lived in. I always was, and still am, willing to enter into it; and doubt not my behaving well in it, having all the industry, frugality, fertility, and skill in economy appertaining to a good wife's character. I defy anyone to say I ever refused an offer of that sort: on the contrary, I readily consented to the only proposal of marriage that ever was made me, which was when I was a virgin, but too easily confiding in the person's sincerity that made it, I unhappily lost my honor by trusting to his; for he got me with child, and then forsook me.

"That very person, you all know, he is now become a magistrate of this county; and I had hopes he would have appeared this day on the bench, and have endeavored to moderate the court in my favor; then I should have scorned to have mentioned it; but I must now complain of it, as unjust and unequal, that my betrayer and undoer, the first cause of all my faults and miscarriages (if they must be deemed such), should be advanced to honor and power in the same government that punishes my misfortunes with stripes and infamy. I should be told, 'tis like, that were there no act of assembly in the case, the precepts of religion are violated by my transgressions. If mine is a religious offense, leave it to religious punishments. You have already excluded me from all the comforts of your church communion. Is not that sufficient? You believe I have offended heaven, and must suffer eternal fire: Will not that be sufficient? What need is there then of your additional fines and whipping? I own I do not think as you do, for, if I thought what you call a sin was really such, I would not presumptuously commit it. But how can it be believed that heaven is angry at my having children, when to the little done by me towards it, God has been pleased to add His divine skill and admirable workmanship in the formation of their bodies, and crowned it by furnishing them with rational and immortal souls?

"Forgive me, gentlemen, if I talk a little extravagantly on these matters; I am no divine, but if you, gentlemen, must be making laws, do not turn natural and useful actions into crimes, by your prohibitions. But take into your wise consideration the great and growing number of bachelors in the country, many of whom, from the mean fear of the expenses of a family, have never sincerely and honorably courted a woman in their lives; and by their manner of living leave unproduced (which is little better than murder) hundreds of their posterity to the thousandth generation. Is not this a greater offense against the public good than mine? Compel them, then, by law, either to marriage, or to pay double the fine of fornication every year. What must poor young women do, whom customs and nature forbid to solicit the men, and who cannot force themselves upon husbands, when the laws take no care to provide them any, and yet severely punish them if they do their duty without them; the duty of the first and great command of nature and of nature's God, increase and multiply; a duty, from the steady performance of which nothing has been able to deter me, but for its sake I have hazarded the loss of the public esteem, and have frequently endured public disgrace and punishment; and therefore ought, in my humble opinion, instead of a whipping, to have a statue erected to my memory."

ELECTRICAL KITE
PHILADELPHIA, OCTOBER 19, 1752

Franklin sent these instructions for performing the famous kite experiment to Peter Collinson in London. They were read at the Royal Society of London and printed in *The Gentleman's Magazine* in 1752.

As frequent mention is made in public papers from Europe of the success of the Philadelphia experiment for drawing the electric fire from clouds by means of pointed rods of iron erected on high buildings, &c., it may be agreeable to the curious to be informed, that the same experiment has succeeded in Philadelphia, though made in a different and more easy manner, which is as follows:

Make a small cross of two light strips of cedar, the arms so long as to reach to the four corners of a large thin silk handkerchief when extended; tie the corners of the handkerchief to the extremities of the cross, so you have the body of a kite; which being properly accommodated with a tail, loop, and string, will rise in the air, like those made of paper; but this being of silk, is fitter to bear the wet and wind of a thunder-gust without tearing. To the top of the upright stick of the cross is to be fixed a very sharp-pointed wire, rising a foot or more above the wood. To the end of the twine, next the hand, is to be tied a silk ribbon, and where the silk and the twine join, a key may be fastened. This kite is to be raised when a thunder-gust appears to be coming on, and the person who holds the string must stand within a door or window, or under some cover, so that the silk ribbon may not be wet; and care must be taken that the twine does not touch the frame of the door or window. As soon as any of the thunder clouds come over the kite, the pointed wire will draw the electric fire from them, and the kite, with all the twine, will be electrified, and the loose filaments of the twine will stand out every way, and be attracted by an approaching finger. And when the rain has wet the kite and twine, so that it can conduct the electric fire freely, you will find it stream out plentifully from the key on the approach of your knuckle. At this key the phial may be charged; and from electric fire thus obtained, spirits may be kindled, and all the other electric experiments be performed, which are usually done by the help of a rubbed glass globe or tube, and thereby the sameness of the electric matter with that of lightning completely demonstrated.

PLAN OF UNION, ADOPTED BY THE ALBANY CONGRESS
ALBANY, JULY 1754

In 1754, with the French and Indian War looming, the Lords of Trade in England ordered a congress convened at Albany with delegates from the colonies. The delegates were to meet with the chiefs of the Six Nations, an alliance of Iroquois tribes, and discuss the defense of their lands. The governor of Pennsylvania appointed Franklin as a delegate, and during his journey to New York he penned a plan of union. Franklin insisted that the colonies could not defend themselves effectively without some plan of union. The Albany Congress passed this amended version of his plan, but both colonial assemblies and England rejected it.

It is proposed that humble application be made for an act of the Parliament of Great Britain, by virtue of which one general government may be formed in America, including all the said colonies, within and under which government each colony may retain its present constitution, except in the particulars wherein a change may be directed by the said act, as hereafter follows.

President–General and Grand Council
That the said general government be administered by a President-General, to be appointed and supported by the crown; and a Grand Council, to be chosen by the representatives of the people of the several colonies met in their respective assemblies.

Election of Members
That within __ months after the passing of such act, the house of representatives, that happen to be sitting within that time, or that shall be specially for that purpose convened, may and shall choose members for the Grand Council in the following proportions, that is to say,

Massachusetts Bay	7
New Hampshire	2
Connecticut	5
Rhode Island	2
New York	4
New Jerseys	3
Pennsylvania	6
Maryland	4
Virginia	7
North Carolina	4
South Carolina	4
	48

Place of First Meeting
—who shall meet for the first time at the city of Philadelphia in Pennsylvania, being called by the President-General as soon as conveniently may be after his appointment.

New Election
That there shall be a new election of members of the Grand Council every three years; and, on the death or resignation of any member, his place should be supplied by a new choice at the next sitting of the Assembly of the colony he represented.

Proportion of Members after the First Three Years
That after the first three years, when the

proportion of money arising out of each colony to the general treasury can be known, the number of members to be chosen for each colony shall from time to time, in all ensuing elections, be regulated by that proportion, yet so as that the number to be chosen by any one province be not more than seven nor less than two.

Meetings of the Grand Council, and Call

That the Grand Council shall meet once in every year, and oftener if occasion require, at such time and place as they shall adjourn to at the last preceding meeting, or as they shall be called to meet at by the President-General on any emergency; he having first obtained in writing the consent of seven of the members to such call, and sent due and timely notice to the whole.

Continuance

That the Grand Council have power to choose their speaker; and shall neither be dissolved, prorogued, nor continued sitting longer than six weeks at one time, without their own consent or the special command of the crown.

Members' Allowance

That the members of the Grand Council shall be allowed for their service ten shillings sterling per diem, during their session and journey to and from the place of meeting; twenty miles to be reckoned a day's journey.

Assent of President-General and His Duty

That the assent of the President-General be requisite to all acts of the Grand Council, and that it be his office and duty to cause them to be carried into execution.

Power of President-General and Grand Council; Treaties of Peace and War

That the President-General, with the advice of the Grand Council, hold or direct all Indian treaties, in which the general interest or welfare of the colonies may be concerned; and make peace or declare war with Indian nations.

Indian Trade

That they make such laws as they judge necessary for regulating all Indian trade.

Indian Purchases

That they make all purchases, from Indians for the crown, of lands not now within the bounds of particular colonies, or that shall not be within their bounds when some of them are reduced to more convenient dimensions.

New Settlements

That they make new settlements on such purchases, by granting lands in the King's name, reserving a quitrent to the crown for the use of the general treasury.

Laws to Govern Them

That they make laws for regulating and governing such new settlements, till the crown shall think fit to form them into particular governments.

Raise Soldiers and Equip Vessels, &c.

That they raise and pay soldiers and build forts for the defense of any of the colonies, and equip vessels of force to guard the coasts and protect the trade on the ocean, lakes, or great rivers; but they shall not impress men in any colony, without the consent of the legislature.

Power to Make Laws, Lay Duties, &c.

That for these purposes they have power to make laws, and lay and levy such general duties, imposts, or taxes, as to them shall appear most equal and just (considering the ability and other circumstances of the inhabitants in the several colonies), and such as may be collected with the least inconvenience to the people, rather discouraging luxury, than loading industry with unnecessary burdens.

General Treasurer and Particular Treasurer

That they may appoint a General Treasurer and a Particular Treasurer in each government, when necessary; and from time to time may order the sums in the treasuries of each government into the general treasury; or draw on them for special payments, as they find most convenient.

Money, How to Issue

Yet no money to issue but by joint orders of the President-General and Grand Council; except where sums have been appropriated to particular purposes, and the President-General is previously empowered by an act to draw such sums.

Accounts

That the general accounts shall be yearly settled and reported to the several assemblies.

Quorum

That a quorum of the Grand Council, empowered to act with the President-General, do consist of twenty-five members; among whom there shall be one or more from a majority of the colonies.

Laws to Be Transmitted

That the laws made by them for the purposes aforesaid shall not be repugnant, but, as near as may be, agreeable to the laws of England, and shall be transmitted to the King in council for approbation, as soon as may be after their passing; and if not disapproved within three years after presentation, to remain in force.

Death of the President-General

That, in case of the death of the President-General, the Speaker of the Grand Council for the time being shall succeed, and be vested with the same powers and authorities, to continue till the King's pleasure be known.

Officers, How Appointed

That all military commission officers, whether for land or sea service, to act under this general constitution, shall be nominated by the President-General; but the approbation of the Grand Council is to be obtained, before they receive their commissions. And all civil officers are to be nominated by the Grand Council, and to receive the President-General's approbation before they officiate.

Vacancies, How Supplied

But, in case of vacancy by death or removal of any officer civil or military under this constitution, the Governor of the province in which such vacancy happens may appoint, till the pleasure of the President-General and Grand Council can be known.

Each Colony May Defend Itself on Emergency, &c.

That the particular military as well as civil establishments in each colony remain in their present state, the general constitution notwithstanding; and that on sudden emergencies any colony may defend itself, and lay the accounts of expense thence arising, before the President-General and Grand Council, who may allow and order payment of the same, as far as they judge such accounts just and reasonable.

THE WAY TO WEALTH
AT SEA, JULY 7, 1757

Published variously as "The Way to Wealth" and "Father Abraham's Speech," this piece was the preface to the final edition of *Poor Richard's Almanack* (1758). The speech collected into one piece sayings from the pages of the previous almanacs, which Franklin had published since 1732. During the American Revolution a French translation of the final preface, "La Science du

Bonhomme Richard," grew very popular in France.

Courteous Reader,

I have heard that nothing gives an author so great pleasure, as to find his works respectfully quoted by other learned authors. This pleasure I have seldom enjoyed; for though I have been, if I may say it without vanity, an eminent author of almanacs annually now a full quarter of a century, my brother authors in the same way, for what reason I know not, have ever been very sparing in their applauses, and no other author has taken the least notice of me, so that did not my writings produce me some solid pudding, the great deficiency of praise would have quite discouraged me.

I concluded at length, that the people were the best judges of my merit; for they buy my works; and besides, in my rambles, where I am not personally known, I have frequently heard one or other of my adages repeated, with, as Poor Richard says, at the end on it; this gave me some satisfaction, as it showed not only that my instructions were regarded, but discovered likewise some respect for my authority; and I own, that to encourage the practice of remembering and repeating those wise sentences, I have sometimes quoted myself with great gravity.

Judge, then how much I must have been gratified by an incident I am going to relate to you. I stopped my horse lately where a great number of people were collected at a vendue of merchant goods. The hour of sale not being come, they were conversing on the badness of the times and one of the company called to a plain clean old man, with white locks, "Pray, Father Abraham, what think you of the times? Won't these heavy taxes quite ruin the country? How shall we be ever able to pay them? What would you advise us to?" Father Abraham stood up, and

replied, "If you'd have my advice, I'll give it you in short, *for a word to the wise is enough,* and *many words won't fill a bushel,* as Poor Richard says." They joined in desiring him to speak his mind, and gathering round him, he proceeded as follows;

"Friends," says he, "and neighbors, the taxes are indeed very heavy, and if those laid on by the government were the only ones we had to pay, we might more easily discharge them; but we have many others, and much more grievous to some of us. We are taxed twice as much by our idleness, three times as much by our pride, and four times as much by our folly, and from these taxes the commissioners cannot ease or deliver us by allowing an abatement. However let us hearken to good advice, and something may be done for us; *God helps them that help themselves,* as Poor Richard says, in his almanac of 1733.

It would be thought a hard government that should tax its people one tenth part of their time, to be employed in its service. But idleness taxes many of us much more, if we reckon all that is spent in absolute sloth, or doing of nothing, with that which is spent in idle employments or amusements, that amount to nothing. Sloth, by bringing on diseases, absolutely shortens life. *Sloth, like rust, consumes faster than labor wears, while the used key is always bright,* as Poor Richard says. *But dost thou love life, then do not squander time, for that's the stuff life is made of,* as Poor Richard says. How much more than is necessary do we spend in sleep, forgetting that *The sleeping fox catches no poultry,* and that *There will be sleeping enough in the grave,* as Poor Richard says.

If time be of all things the most precious, wasting time must be, as Poor Richard says, *the greatest prodigality;* since, as he elsewhere tells us, *Lost time is never found again; and what we call time enough, always proves little enough:* Let us then up and be doing, and doing to the purpose; so by diligence shall we do more with less perplexity. *Sloth* makes all things difficult, but industry all easy, as Poor Richard says; and *He that riseth late must trot all day, and shall scarce overtake his business at night;* while *Laziness travels so slowly, that poverty soon overtakes him,* as we read in Poor Richard, who adds, *Drive thy business, let not that drive thee;* and *Early to bed, and early to rise, makes a man healthy, wealthy, and wise.*

So what signifies wishing and hoping for better times. We may make these times better, if we bestir ourselves. *Industry need not wish,* as Poor Richard says, *and he that lives upon hope will die fasting. There are no gains, without pains; then help hands, for I have no lands,* or if I have, they are smartly taxed. And, as Poor Richard likewise observes, *He that hath a trade hath an estate, and he that hath a calling, hath an office of profit and honor;* but then the trade must be worked at, and the calling well followed, or neither the estate nor the office will enable us to pay our taxes. If we are industrious, we shall never starve; for, as Poor Richard says, *At the working man's house hunger looks in, but dares not enter.* Nor will the bailiff or the constable enter, for *Industry pays debts, while despair increaseth them,* says Poor Richard. What though you have found no treasure, nor has any rich relation left you a legacy, *Diligence is the mother of good luck* as Poor Richard says *and God gives all things to industry. Then plough deep, while sluggards sleep, and you shall have corn to sell and to keep,* says Poor Dick. Work while it is called today, for you know not how much you may be hindered tomorrow, which makes Poor Richard say, *One today is worth two tomorrows,* and farther, *Have you somewhat to do tomorrow, do it today.* If you were a servant, would you not be ashamed that a good master should catch you idle? Are you then your own master, *be ashamed to catch yourself idle,* as Poor Dick says. When there is so much to be done for yourself, your family, your country, and your gracious King, be up by peep of day; *Let not the sun look down and say, inglorious here he*

lies. Handle your tools without mittens; remember that *The cat in gloves catches no mice,* as Poor Richard says. 'Tis true there is much to be done, and perhaps you are weak-handed, but stick to it steadily; and you will see great effects, for *Constant dropping wears away stones,* and by *diligence and patience the mouse ate in two the cable;* and *Little strokes fell great oaks,* as Poor Richard says in his almanac, the year I cannot just now remember.

Methinks I hear some of you say, *Must a man afford himself no leisure?* I will tell thee, my friend, what Poor Richard says, *Employ thy time well, if thou meanest to gain leisure; and, since thou art not sure of a minute, throw not away an hour.* Leisure, is time for doing something useful; this leisure the diligent man will obtain, but the lazy man never; so that, as Poor Richard says *A life of leisure and a life of laziness are two things.* Do you imagine that sloth will afford you more comfort than labor? No, for as Poor Richard says, *Trouble springs from idleness, and grievous toil from needless ease. Many without labor, would live by their wits only, but they break for want of stock.* Whereas industry gives comfort, and plenty, and respect: *Fly pleasures, and they'll follow you. The diligent spinner has a large shift; and now I have a sheep and a cow, everybody bids me good morrow;* all which is well said by Poor Richard.

But with our industry, we must likewise be steady, settled, and careful, and oversee our own affairs with our own eyes, and not trust too much to others; for, as Poor Richard says

    I never saw an oft-removed tree,
    Nor yet an oft-removed family,
    That throve so well as those that settled be.

And again, *Three removes is as bad as a fire;* and again, *Keep thy shop, and thy shop will keep thee;* and again, *If you would have your business done, go; if not, send.* And again,

    He that by the plough would thrive,
    Himself must either hold or drive.

And again, *The eye of a master will do more work than both his hands;* and again, *Want of care does us more damage than want of knowl-edge;* and again, *Not to oversee workmen, is to leave them your purse open.* Trusting too much to others' care is the ruin of many; for, as the almanac says, *In the affairs of this world, men are saved, not by faith, but by the want of it;* but a man's own care is profitable; for, saith Poor Dick, *Learning is to the studious,* and *riches to the careful,* as well as *power to the bold,* and *heaven to the virtuous.* And farther, *If you would have a faithful servant, and one that you like, serve yourself.* And again, he adviseth to circumspection and care, even in the smallest matters, because sometimes *A little neglect may breed great mischief;* adding, *for want of a nail the shoe was lost; for want of a shoe the horse was lost; and for want of a horse the rider was lost, being overtaken and slain by the enemy; all for want of care about a horse-shoe nail.*

So much for industry, my friends, and attention to one's own business; but to these we must add frugality, if we would make our industry more certainly success-ful. A man may, if he knows not how to save as he gets, *keep his nose all his life to the grindstone,* and die not worth a groat at last. *A fat kitchen makes a lean will,* as Poor Richard says; and

  Many estates are spent in the getting,
  Since women for tea forsook spinning and
knitting,
  And men for punch forsook hewing and
splitting.

If you would be wealthy, says he, in another almanac, *think of saving as well as of getting: The Indies have not made Spain rich, because her outgoes are greater than her incomes.* Away then with your expensive follies, and you will not have so much cause to complain of hard times, heavy taxes, and chargeable families; for, as Poor Dick says,

  Women and wine, game and deceit,
  Make the wealth small, and the wants great.

And farther, *What maintains one vice, would bring up two children.* You may think perhaps, that a little tea, or a little punch now and then, diet a little more costly, clothes a little finer, and a little entertain-ment now and then, can be no great matter; but remember what Poor Richard says, *Many a little makes a mickle;* and farther, *Beware of little expenses; A small leak will sink a great ship;* and again, *Who dainties love, shall beggars prove;* and moreover, *fools make feasts, and wise men eat them.*

Here you are all got together at this vendue of fineries and knicknacks. You call them goods; but if you do not take care, they will prove evils to some of you. You expect they will be sold cheap, and perhaps they may for less than they cost; but if you have no occasion for them, they must be dear to you. Remember what Poor Rich-ard says; *Buy what thou hast no need of, and ere long thou shalt sell thy necessaries.* And again, *At a great pennyworth pause a while:* He means, that perhaps the cheapness is apparent only; and not real; or the bargain, by straitening thee in thy business, may do thee more harm than good. For in another place he says, *Many have been ruined by buying good pennyworths.* Again, Poor Richard says, *'tis foolish to lay out money in a purchase of repentance;* and yet this folly is practiced every day at vendues, for want of minding the almanac. *Wise men,* as Poor Dick says, *learn by others' harms, fools scarcely by their own;* but, *felix quem faciunt aliena pericula cautum.* Many a one, for the sake of finery on the back, have gone with a hungry belly, and half starved their families. *Silks and satins, scarlet and velvets,* as Poor Richard says, *put out the kitchen fire.*

These are not the necessaries of life; they can scarcely be called the conve-niences; and yet only because they look pretty, how many want to have them! The artificial wants of mankind thus become more numerous than the natural; and, as Poor Dick says, *for one poor person, there are an hundred indigent.* By these, and other extravagancies, the genteel are reduced to poverty, and forced to borrow of those whom they formerly despised, but who through industry and frugality have maintained their standing; in which case it appears plainly, that *A ploughman on his legs is higher than a gentleman on his knees,* as Poor Richard says. Perhaps they have had a small estate left them, which they knew not the getting of; they think, *'tis day, and will never be night;* that a little to be spent out of so much, is not worth minding; *a child and a fool,* as Poor Richard says, *imagine twenty shillings and twenty years can never be spent* but, *always taking out of the meal-tub, and never putting in, soon comes to the bottom;* as Poor Dick says, *When the well's dry, they know the worth of water.* But this they might have known before, if they had taken his advice; *If you would know the value of money, go and try to borrow some; for, he that goes a borrowing goes a sorrowing;* and indeed so does he that lends to such people, when he goes to get it in again. Poor Dick farther advises, and says,

> *Fond pride of dress, is sure a very curse;*
> *E'er fancy you consult, consult your purse.*

And again, *Pride is as loud a beggar as want, and a great deal more saucy.* When you have bought one fine thing, you must buy ten more, that your appearance may be all of a piece; but Poor Dick says, *'Tis easier to suppress the first desire, than to satisfy all that follow it.* And 'tis as truly folly for the poor to ape the rich, as for the frog to swell, in order to equal the ox.

> *Great estates may venture more,*
> *But little boats should keep near shore.*

'Tis, however, a folly soon punished; for *Pride that dines on vanity, sups on contempt,* as Poor Richard says. And in another place, *Pride breakfasted with plenty, dined with poverty, and supped with infamy.* And after all, of what use is this pride of appearance, for which so much is risked so much is suffered? It cannot promote health, or ease pain; it makes no increase of merit in the person, it creates envy, it hastens misfortune.

> *What is a butterfly? At best*
> *He's but a caterpillar dressed*
> *The gaudy fop's his picture just,*

as Poor Richard says.

But what madness must it be to run in debt for these superfluities! We are offered, by the terms of this vendue, six months credit; and that perhaps has induced some of us to attend it, because we cannot spare the ready money, and hope now to be fine without it. But, ah, think what you do when you run in debt; *you give to another power over your liberty.* If you cannot pay at the time, you will be ashamed to see your creditor; you will be in fear when you speak to him; you will make poor pitiful sneaking excuses, and by degrees come to lose your veracity, and sink into base downright lying; for, as Poor Richard says *The second vice is lying, the first is running in debt.* And again, to the same purpose, *Lying rides upon debt's back.* Whereas a free-born Englishman ought not to be ashamed or afraid to see or speak to any man living. But poverty often deprives a man of all spirit and virtue: *'Tis hard for an empty bag to stand upright,* as Poor Richard truly says.

What would you think of that prince, or that government, who should issue an edict forbidding you to dress like a gentleman or a gentlewoman, on pain of imprisonment or servitude? Would you not say, that you are free, have a right to dress as you please, and that such an edict would be a breach of your privileges, and such a government tyrannical? And yet you are about to put yourself under that tyranny, when you run in debt for such dress! Your creditor has authority, at his pleasure to deprive you of your liberty, by confining you in goal for life, or to sell you for a servant, if you should not be able to pay him! When you have got your bargain, you may, perhaps, think little of payment; but *Creditors,* Poor Richard tells us, *have better memories than debtors;* and in another place says, *Creditors are a superstitious sect, great observers of set days and times.* The day comes round before you are aware, and the demand is made before you are prepared to satisfy it. Or if you bear your debt in mind, the term which at first seemed so long, will, as it lessens, appear extremely short. Time will seem to have added wings to his heels as well as shoulders. *Those have a short Lent,* saith Poor Richard, *who owe money to be paid at Easter.* Then since, as he says, *The borrower is a slave to the lender, and the debtor to the creditor,* disdain the chain, preserve your freedom; and maintain your independency: be industrious and free; be frugal and free. At present, perhaps, you may think yourself in thriving circumstances, and that you can bear a little extravagance without injury; but,

For age and want, save while you may;
No morning sun lasts a whole day,

as Poor Richard says. Gain may be temporary and uncertain, but ever while you live, expense is constant and certain; and *'tis easier to build two chimneys, than to keep one in fuel,* as Poor Richard says. So, *Rather go to bed supperless than rise in debt.*

Get what you can, and what you get hold;
'Tis the stone that will turn all your lead into gold,

as Poor Richard says. And when you have got the philosopher's stone, sure you will no longer complain of bad times, or the difficulty of paying taxes.

This doctrine, my friends, is reason and wisdom; but after all, do not depend too much upon your own industry, and frugality, and prudence, though excellent things, for they may all be blasted without the blessing of heaven; and therefore, ask that blessing humbly, and be not uncharitable to those that at present seem to want it, but comfort and help them. Remember, Job suffered, and was afterwards prosperous.

And now to conclude, *Experience keeps a dear school, but fools will learn in no other, and scarce in that;* for it is true, *we may give advice, but we cannot give conduct,* as Poor Richard says: However, remember this, *They that won't be counseled, can't be helped,* as Poor Richard says: and farther, that, *if you will not hear reason, she'll surely rap your knuckles."*

Thus the old gentleman ended his harangue. The people heard it, and approved the doctrine, and immediately practiced the contrary, just as if it had been a common sermon; for the vendue opened, and they began to buy extravagantly, notwithstanding, his cautions and their own fear of taxes. I found the good man had thoroughly studied my almanacs, and digested all I had dropped on those topics during the course of five and twenty years. The frequent mention he made of me must have tired any one else, but my vanity was wonderfully delighted with it, though I was conscious that not a tenth part of the wisdom was my own, which he ascribed to me, but rather the gleanings I had made of the sense of all ages and nations. However, I resolved to be the better for the echo of it; and though I had at first determined to buy stuff for a new coat, I went away resolved to wear my old one a little longer. Reader, if thou wilt do the same, thy profit will be as great as mine. I am, as ever, thine to serve thee,

Richard Saunders

TO JOHN PRINGLE
CRAVEN STREET, LONDON, DECEMBER 21, 1757

Sir John Pringle, a London physician and later president of the Royal Society of London, became one of Franklin's best friends in England, and the two traveled together in Europe on several occasions. The following letter to him describes Franklin's experiments with paralytics and electricity.

Sir,
In compliance with your request, I send you the following account of what I can at present recollect relating to the effects of electricity in paralytic cases, which have fallen under my observation.

Some years since, when the newspapers made mention of great cures performed in Italy or Germany, by means of electricity, a number of paralytics were brought to me from different parts of Pennsylvania, and the neighboring provinces, to be electrised, which I did for them at their request. My method was, to place the patient first in a chair on an electric stool, and draw a number of large strong sparks from all parts of the affected limb or side. Then I fully charged two six gallon glass jars, each of which had about three square feet of surface coated; and I sent the united shock of these through the affected limb or limbs, repeating the stroke commonly three times each day. The first thing observed, was an immediate greater sensible warmth in the lame limbs that had received the stroke, than in the others; and the next morning the patients usually related, that they had in the night felt a pricking sensation in the flesh of the paralytic limbs; and would sometimes shew a number of small red spots, which they supposed were occasioned by those prickings. The limbs, too, were found more capable of voluntary motion, and seemed to receive strength. A man, for instance, who could not the first day lift the lame hand from off his knee, would the next day raise it four or five inches, the third day higher; and on the fifth day was able, but with a feeble languid motion, to take off his hat. These appearances gave great spirits to the patients, and made them hope a perfect cure; but I do not remember that I ever saw any amendment after the fifth day; which the patients perceiving, and finding the shocks pretty severe, they became discouraged, went home, and in a short time relapsed; so that I never knew any advantage from electricity in palsies that was permanent. And how far the apparent temporary advantage might arise from the exercise in the patients' journey, and coming daily to my house, or from the spirits given by the hope of success, enabling them to exert more strength in moving their limbs, I will not pretend to say.

Perhaps some permanent advantage might have been obtained, if the electric shocks had been accompanied with proper medicine and regimen, under the direction of a skillful physician. It may be, too, that a few great strokes, as given in my method, may not be so proper as many small ones; since, by the account from Scotland of a case, in which two hundred shocks from a phial were given daily, it seems, that a perfect cure has been made. As to any uncommon strength supposed to be in the machine used in that case, I imagine it could have no share in the effect produced; since the strength of the shock from charged glass is in proportion to the quantity of surface of the glass coated; so that my shocks from those large jars must have been much greater than any that could be received from a phial held in the hand.

I am, with great respect, sir, your most obedient servant,

B. Franklin

To John Pringle
Craven Street, London, January 6, 1758

In the following letter to John Pringle, Franklin speculated on the positive side of global catastrophe.

Sir,

I return Mr. Mitchell's paper on the strata of the earth with thanks. The reading of it, and perusal of the draft that accompanies it, have reconciled me to those convulsions which all naturalists agree this globe has suffered. Had the different strata of clay, gravel, marble, coals, lime-stone, sand, minerals, &c. continued to lie level, one under the other, as they may be supposed to have done before those convulsions, we should have had the use only of a few of the uppermost of the strata, the others lying too deep and too difficult to be come at; but the shell of the earth being broke, and the fragments thrown into this oblique position, the disjointed ends of a great number of strata of different kinds are brought up to day, and a great variety of useful materials put into our power, which would otherwise have remained eternally concealed from us. So that what has been usually looked upon as a ruin suffered by this part of the universe, was, in reality, only a preparation, or means of rendering the earth more fit for use, more capable of being to mankind a convenient and comfortable habitation. I am, sir, with great esteem, yours, &c.

    B. F.

To Mary Stevenson
London, September 13, 1760

Mary (Polly) Stevenson was the daughter of Mrs. Margaret Stevenson, Franklin's landlady on Craven Street. After moving in with her aunt in 1759, she proposed that she and Franklin correspond on natural philosophy. The following is one of the letters Franklin wrote to her after her proposal. The philosophical letters ceased after she married William Hewson in 1770, but Polly and Franklin remained friends for the rest of Franklin's life. Her husband died in 1774, and she moved with her children to Philadelphia in 1786.

My dear friend,

I have your agreeable letter from Bristol, which I take this first leisure hour to answer, having for some time been much engaged in business.

Your first question, *What is the reason the water at this place, though cold at the spring, becomes warm by pumping?* it will be most prudent in me to forbear attempting to answer, till, by a more circumstantial account, you assure me of the fact. I own I should expect that operation to warm, not so much the water pumped, as the person pumping. The rubbing of dry solids together has been long observed to produce heat; but the like effect has never yet, that I have heard, been produced by the mere agitation of fluids, or friction of fluids

with solids. Water in a bottle, shook for hours by a mill hopper, it is said, discovered no sensible addition of heat. The production of animal heat by exercise is therefore to be accounted for in another manner, which I may hereafter endeavor to make you acquainted with.

This prudence of not attempting to give reasons before one is sure of facts, I learned from one of your sex, who, as Selden tells us, being in company with some gentlemen that were viewing and considering something which they called a Chinese shoe, and disputing earnestly about the manner of wearing it, and how it could possibly be put on; put in her word, and said modestly, *Gentlemen, are you sure it is a shoe? Should not that be settled first?*

But I shall now endeavor to explain what I said to you about the tide in rivers, and to that end shall make a figure, which, though not very like a river, may serve to convey my meaning. Suppose a canal 140 miles long, communicating at one end with the sea, and filled therefore with sea water. I choose a canal at first, rather than a river, to throw out of consideration the effects produced by the streams of fresh water from the land, the inequality in breadth, and the crookedness of courses.

Let A, C, be the head of the canal, C, D, the bottom of it; D, F, the open mouth of it, next the sea. Let the straight pricked line, B, G, represent low water mark, the whole length of the canal. A, F, high water mark: now if a person, standing at E, and observing, at the time of high water there, that the canal is quite full at that place

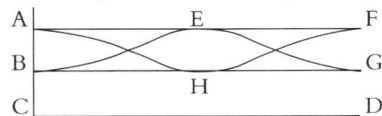

up to the line E, should conclude that the canal is equally full to the same height from end to end, and therefore there was as much more water come into the canal since it was down at the low water mark, as could be included in the oblong space A, B,

G, F, he would be greatly mistaken. For the tide is a wave, and the top of the wave, which makes high water, as well as every other lower part, is progressive; and it is high water successively, but not at the same time, in all the several points between G, F, and A, B. And in such a length as I have mentioned, it is low water at F, G, and also at A, B, at or near the same time with its being high water at E; so that the surface of the water in the canal, during that situation, is properly represented by the curve pricked line B, E, G. And on the other hand, when it is low water at E, H, it is high water both at F, G, and at A, B, at or near the same time; and the surface would then be described by the inverted curve, line A, H, F.

In this view of the case, you will easily see, that there must be very little more water in the canal at what we call high water, than there is at low water, those terms not relating to the whole canal at the same time, but successively to its parts. And, if you suppose the canal six times as long, the case would not vary as to the quantity of water at different times of the tide; there would only be six waves in the canal at the same time, instead of one, and the hollows in the water would be equal to the hills.

That this is not mere theory, but conformable to fact, we know by our long rivers in America. The Delaware, on which Philadelphia stands, is in this particular similar to the canal I have supposed of one wave; for, when it is high water at the capes or mouth of the river, it is also high water at Philadelphia, which stands about 140 miles from the sea; and there is at the same time a low water in the middle between the two high waters; where, when it comes to be high water, it is at the same time low water at the capes and at Philadelphia. And the longer rivers have, some a wave and half, some two, three, or four waves, according to their length. In the shorter rivers of this island, one may see the same thing in part; for instance, it is high water

at Gravesend an hour before it is high water at London Bridge; and 20 miles below Gravesend an hour before it is high water at Gravesend. Therefore at the time of high water at Gravesend the top of the wave is there, and the water is then not so high by some feet where the top of the wave was an hour before, or where it will be an hour after, as it is just then at Gravesend.

Now we are not to suppose that because the swell or top of the wave runs at the rate of 20 miles an hour, that therefore the current, or water itself of which the wave is composed, runs at that rate. Far from it. To conceive this motion of a wave, make a small experiment or two. Fasten one end of a cord in a window near the top of a house, and let the other end come down to the ground; take this end in your hand, and you may, by a sudden motion, occasion a wave in the cord that will run quite up to the window; but though the wave is progressive from your hand to the window, the parts of the rope do not proceed with the wave, but remain where they were, except only that kind of motion that produces the wave. So if you throw a stone into a pond of water when the surface is still and smooth, you will see a circular wave proceed from the stone as its center, quite to the sides of the pond; but the water does not proceed with the wave, it only rises and falls to form it in the different parts of its course; and the waves that follow the first, all make use of the same water with their predecessors.

But a wave in water is not indeed in all circumstances exactly like that in a cord; for, water being a fluid, and gravitating to the earth, it naturally runs from a higher place to a lower; therefore the parts of the wave in water do actually run a little both ways from its top towards its lower sides, which the parts of the wave in the cord cannot do. Thus when it is high and standing water at Gravesend, the water 20 miles below has been running ebb, or towards the sea for an hour, or ever since it was high water there; but the water at London Bridge will run flood, or from the sea yet another hour, till it is high water or the top of the wave arrives at that bridge, and then it will have run ebb an hour at Gravesend, &c. &c. Now this motion of the water, occasioned only by its gravity, or tendency to run from a higher place to a lower, is by no means so swift as the motion of the wave. It scarce exceeds perhaps two miles in an hour. If it went, as the wave does, 20 miles an hour, no ships could ride at anchor in such a stream, nor boats row against it.

In common speech, indeed, this current of the water both ways from the top of the wave is called the tide; thus we say, the tide runs strong, the tide runs at the rate of 1, 2, or 3 miles an hour, &c; and, when we are at a part of the river behind the top of the wave, and find the water lower than high-water mark, and running towards the sea, we say, the tide runs ebb; and when we are before the top of the wave, and find the water higher than low-water mark, and running from the sea, we say, the tide runs flood; but these expressions are only locally proper; for a tide, strictly speaking, is one whole wave, including all its parts higher and lower, and these waves succeed one another about twice in twenty four hours.

This motion of the water, occasioned by its gravity, will explain to you why the water near the mouths of rivers may be saltier at high water than at low. Some of the salt water, as the tide wave enters the river, runs from its top and fore side, and mixes with the fresh, and also pushes it back up the river.

Supposing that the water commonly runs during the flood at the rate of two miles in an hour, and that the flood runs 5 hours, you see that it can bring at most into our canal only a quantity of water equal to the space included in the breadth of the canal, ten miles of its length, and the depth between low and high water mark.

Which is but a fourteenth part of what would be necessary to fill all the space between low and high water mark, for 140 miles, the whole length of the canal.

And indeed such a quantity of water as would fill that whole space, to run in and out every tide, must create so outrageous a current, as would do infinite damage to the shores, shipping, &c., and make the navigation of a river almost impracticable.

I have made this letter longer than I intended, and therefore reserve for another what I have farther to say on the subject of tides and rivers. I shall now only add, that I have not been exact in the numbers, because I would avoid perplexing you with minute calculations, my design at present being chiefly to give you distinct and clear ideas of the first principles.

After writing 6 folio pages of philosophy to a young girl, is it necessary to finish such a letter with a compliment? Is not such a letter of itself a compliment? Does it not say, she has a mind thirsty after knowledge, and capable of receiving it; and that the most agreeable things one can write to her are those that tend to the improvement of her understanding? It does indeed say all this, but then it is still no compliment; it is no more than plain honest truth, which is not the character of a compliment. So if I would finish my letter in the mode, I should yet add something that means nothing, and is merely civil and polite. But, being naturally awkward at every circumstance of ceremony, I shall not attempt it. I had rather conclude abruptly with what pleases me more than any compliment can please you, that I am allowed to subscribe myself your affectionate friend

B. Franklin

To Deborah Franklin
London, April 6, 1766

Fear of crossing the ocean kept Deborah Franklin, Franklin's wife, in Philadelphia when the Pennsylvania Assembly sent her husband to England in 1764. Franklin rented rooms from Mrs. Margaret Stevenson, who frequently helped him choose gifts to send to Mrs. Franklin and their daughter, Sally. In 1766 Franklin testified before the House of Commons in favor of repealing the Stamp Act. He sent his wife a gown in honor of the repeal.

My Dear Child,

As the Stamp Act is at length repealed, I am willing you should have a new gown, which you may suppose I did not send sooner, as I knew you would not like to be finer than your neighbors, unless in a gown of your own spinning. Had the trade between the two countries totally ceased, it was a comfort to me to recollect, that I had once been clothed from head to foot in woollen and linen of my wife's manufacture, that I never was prouder of any dress in my life, and that she and her daughter might do it again if it was necessary. I told the Parliament that it was my opinion, before the old clothes of the Americans were worn out, they might have new ones of their own making. And indeed if they had all as many old clothes as your old man has, that would not be very unlikely, for I think you and George reckoned when I was last at home at least 20 pair of old breeches. Joking apart, I have sent you a fine piece of pompador satin, 14 yards cost 11 shillings per yard; a silk negligee and petticoat of brocaded lutestring for my dear Sally, with two dozen gloves, 4 bottles of lavender water, and two little reels. The reels are to screw on the edge of a table, when she would wind silk or thread. The skein is to be put over them, and winds better than if held in two hands. There is also an ivory knob to each, to which she may with a bit of silk cord hang a pinhook to fasten her plain work to, like the hooks on her weight. I send you also lace for two lappet caps, 3 ells of cambric (the cambric by Mr. Yates), 3 damask table cloths, a piece of crimson morin for curtains with tassels,

line and binding. A large true turkey carpet cost 10 guineas, for the dining parlor. Some oiled silk; and a gimcrack corkscrew, which you must get some brother gimcrack to show you the use of. In the chest is a parcel of books for my friend Mr. Coleman, and another for cousin Colbert. Pray did he receive those I sent him before? I send you also a box with three fine cheeses. Perhaps a bit of them may be left when I come home. Mrs. Stevenson has been very diligent and serviceable in getting these things together for you, and presents her best respects, as does her daughter, to both you and Sally. There are too boxes included in your bill of lading for Billy.

I received your kind letter of Feb. 20. It gives me great pleasure to hear, that our good old friend Mrs. Smith is on the recovery. I hope she has yet many happy years to live. My love to her. I fear, from the account you give of brother Peter, that he cannot hold it long. If it should please God, that he leaves us before my return, I would have the post office remain under the management of their son, till Mr. Foxcroft and I agree how to settle it.

There are some droll prints in the box, which were given me by the painter, and, being sent when I was not at home, were packed up without my knowledge. I think he was wrong to put in Lord Bute, who had nothing to do with the Stamp Act. But it is the fashion here to abuse that nobleman, as the author of all mischief. . . . I am, my dear Debby, your affectionate husband,
B. Franklin

To John Bartram
LONDON, JULY 9, 1769

John Bartram was an original member of the American Philosophical Society, one of America's earliest botanists, and American botanist to the king. While Franklin lived in England he often sent Bartram seeds to try in Pennsylvania.

Dear Friend,

It is with great pleasure I understand by your favor of April 10th, that you continue to enjoy so good a share of health. I hope it will long continue. And, although it may not now be suitable for you to make such wide excursions as heretofore, you may yet be very useful to your country and to mankind, if you sit down quietly at home, digest the knowledge you have acquired, and compile and publish the many observations you have made, and point out the advantages that may be drawn from the whole, in public undertakings or particular private practice. It is true, many people are fond of accounts of old buildings, and monuments; but there is a number, who would be much better pleased with such accounts as you could afford them. And, for one, I confess, that if I could find in any Italian travels a receipt for making Parmesan cheese, it would give me more satisfaction than a transcript of any inscription from any old stone whatever.

I suppose Mr. Michael Collinson, or Dr. Fothergill, has written to you what may be necessary for your information relating to your affairs here. I imagine there is no doubt but the King's bounty to you will be continued; and that it will be proper for you to continue sending now and then a few such curious seeds, as you can procure, to keep up your claim. And now I mention seeds, I wish you would send me a few of such as are least common, to the value of a guinea, which Mr. Foxcroft will pay you for me. They are for a particular friend, who is very curious. If in any thing I can serve you here, command freely. Your affectionate friend,

B. Franklin

To Benjamin Rush
London, July 14, 1773

Dr. Benjamin Rush was a Pennsylvania physician, abolitionist, and signer of the Dec-laration of Independence. This letter to him contains a summary of Franklin's sentiments on the causes of common colds. Franklin's belief that fresh air promoted health, and that spending time in cold weather or moist air did not necessarily cause colds, differed from the prevailing ideas of the time.

Dear Sir,

I received your favor of May 1st, with the pamphlet for which I am obliged to you. It is well written. I hope that in time the endeavors of the friends to liberty and humanity will get the better of a practice, that has so long disgraced our nation and religion.

A few days after I received your packet for M. [Barbeu] Dubourg, I had an opportunity of forwarding it to him by M. Poissonnière, physician of Paris, who kindly undertook to deliver it. M. Dubourg has been translating my book into French. It is nearly printed, and he tells me he purposes a copy for you.

I shall communicate your judicious remark, relating to the septic quality of the air transpired by patients in putrid diseases, to my friend Dr. [Joseph] Priestley. I hope that after having discovered the benefit of fresh and cool air applied to the sick, people will begin to suspect that possibly it may do no harm to the well. I have not seen Dr. Cullen's book, but am glad to hear that he speaks of catarrhs or colds by contagion. I have long been satisfied from observation, that besides the general colds now termed influenzas (which may possibly spread by contagion, as well as by a particular quality of the air), people often catch cold from one another when shut up together in small close rooms, coaches, &c., and when sitting near and conversing so as to breathe in each other's transpiration; the disorder being in a certain state. I think, too, that it is the frowzy, corrupt air from animal substances, and the perspired matter from our bodies, which, being long confined in beds not lately used, and clothes not lately worn, and books long shut up in close rooms, obtains that kind of putridity, which occasions the colds observed upon sleeping in, wearing, and turning over such bedclothes, or books, and not their coldness or dampness. From these causes, but more from too full living with too little exercise, proceed in my opinion most of the disorders, which for about one hundred and fifty years past the English have called colds.

As to Dr. Cullen's cold or catarrh *a frigore,* I question whether such an one ever existed. Traveling in our severe winters, I have suffered cold sometimes to an extremity only short of freezing, but this did not make me catch cold. And, for moisture, I have been in the river every evening two or three hours for a fortnight together, when one would suppose I might imbibe enough of it to take cold if humidity could give it; but no such effect followed. Boys never get cold by swimming. Nor are people at sea, or who live at Bermudas, or St. Helena, small islands, where the air must be ever moist from the dashing and breaking of waves against their rocks on all sides, more subject to colds than those who inhabit parts of a continent where the air is driest. Dampness may indeed assist in producing putridity and those miasmata which infect us with the disorder we call a cold; but of itself can never by a little addition of moisture hurt a body filled with watery fluids from head to foot.

With great esteem, and sincere wishes for your welfare, I am, sir, your most obedient humble servant,

B. Franklin

RULES BY WHICH A GREAT EMPIRE MAY BE REDUCED TO A SMALL ONE
LONDON, 1773

Along with the "Edict by the King of Prussia," this satire appeared in British newspapers in 1773. Franklin humorously tried to show that England, if it continued on its course of pursuing these "rules," would see the breakup of her empire. The "Edict" and the "Rules" were well received in America.

Presented to a late minister, when he entered upon his administration.

An ancient sage boasted that, though he could not fiddle, he knew how to make a great city of a little one. The science that I, a modern simpleton, am about to communicate, is the very reverse.

I address myself to all ministers who have the management of extensive dominions, which from their very greatness are become troublesome to govern, because the multiplicity of their affairs leaves no time for fiddling.

I. In the first place, gentlemen, you are to consider, that a great empire, like a great cake, is most easily diminished at the edges. Turn your attention, therefore, first to your remotest provinces; that, as you get rid of them, the next may follow in order.

II. That the possibility of this separation may always exist, take special care the provinces are never incorporated with the mother country, that they do not enjoy the same common rights, the same privileges in commerce, and that they are governed by severer laws, all of your enacting, without allowing them any share in the choice of the legislators. By carefully making and preserving such distinctions, you will (to keep to my simile of the cake) act like a wise gingerbread baker, who, to facilitate a division, cuts his dough half through in those places where, when baked, he would have it broken to pieces.

III. These remote provinces have perhaps been acquired, purchased, or conquered, at the sole expense of the settlers, or their ancestors, without the aid of the mother country. If this should happen to increase her strength, by their growing numbers, ready to join in her wars; her commerce, by their growing demand for her manufactures; or her naval power, by greater employment for her ships and seamen, they may probably suppose some merit in this, and that it entitles them to some favor; you are therefore to forget it all, or resent it, as if they had done you injury. If they happen to be zealous whigs, friends of liberty, nurtured in revolution principles, remember all that to their prejudice, and resolve to punish it; for such principles, after a revolution is thoroughly established, are of no more use; they are even odious and abominable.

IV. However peaceably your colonies have submitted to your government, shown their affection to your interests, and patiently borne their grievances; you are to suppose them always inclined to revolt, and treat them accordingly. Quarter troops among them, who by their insolence may provoke the rising of mobs, and by their bullets and bayonets suppress them. By this means, like the husband who uses his wife ill from suspicion, you may in time convert your suspicions into realities.

V. Remote provinces must have governors and judges, to represent the royal person, and execute everywhere the delegated parts of his office and authority. You ministers know, that much of the strength of government depends on the opinion of the people; and much of that opinion on the choice of rulers placed immediately over them. If you send them wise and good men for governors, who study the interest of the colonists, and advance their prosperity, they will think their King wise and good, and that he wishes the welfare of his subjects. If you send them learned and upright men for judges, they will think him a lover of justice. This may attach your provinces more to his government. You are therefore to be careful whom you recommend for those offices. If you can find prodigals, who have ruined their fortunes, broken gamesters or stockjobbers, these may do well as governors; for they will probably be rapacious, and provoke the people by their extortions. Wrangling proctors and pettifogging lawyers, too, are not amiss; for they will be for ever disputing and quarreling with their little parliaments. If withal they should be ignorant, wrong-headed, and insolent, so much the better. Attorneys' clerks and Newgate solicitors will do for chief justices, especially if they hold their places during your pleasure; and all will contribute to impress those ideas of your government, that are proper for a people you would wish to renounce it.

VI. To confirm these impressions, and strike them deeper, whenever the injured come to the capital with complaints of maladministration, oppression, or injustice, punish such suitors with long delay, enormous expense, and a final judgment in favor of the oppressor. This will have an admirable effect every way. The trouble of future complaints will be prevented, and governors and judges will be encouraged to further acts of oppression and injustice; and thence the people may become more disaffected, and at length desperate.

VII. When such governors have crammed their coffers, and made themselves so odious to the people that they can no longer remain among them, with safety to their persons, recall and reward them with pensions. You may make them baronets too, if that respectable order should not think fit to resent it. All will contribute to encourage new governors in the same practice, and make the supreme government detestable.

VIII. If, when you are engaged in war, your colonies should vie in liberal aids of men and money against the common enemy, upon your simple requisition, and give far beyond their abilities, reflect that a penny taken from them by your power is more honorable to you, than a pound presented by their benevolence; despise therefore their voluntary grants, and resolve to harass them with novel taxes. They will probably complain to your parliaments, that they are taxed by a body in which they have no representative, and that this is contrary to common right. They will petition for redress. Let the parliaments flout their claims, reject their petitions, refuse even to suffer the reading of them, and treat the petitioners with the utmost contempt. Nothing can have a better effect in producing the alienation proposed; for though many can forgive injuries, none ever forgave contempt.

IX. In laying these taxes, never regard the heavy burthens those remote people already undergo, in defending their own frontiers, supporting their own provincial governments, making new roads, building bridges, churches, and other public edifices, which in old countries have been done to your hands by your ancestors, but which occasion constant calls and demands on the purses of a new people. Forget the restraints you lay on their trade for your own benefit, and the advantage a monopoly of this trade gives your exacting merchants. Think nothing of the wealth those merchants and your manufacturers acquire by the colony commerce; their increased ability thereby to pay taxes at home; their accumulating, in the price of their commodities, most of those taxes, and so levying them from their consuming customers; all this, and the employment and support of thousands of your poor by the colonists, you are entirely to forget. But remember to make your arbitrary tax more grievous to your provinces, by public declarations importing that your power of taxing them has no limits, so that when you take from them without their consent one shilling in the pound, you have a clear right to the other nineteen. This will probably weaken every idea of security in their property, and convince them, that under such a government they have nothing they can call their own; which can scarce fail of producing the happiest consequences!

X. Possibly, indeed, some of them might still comfort themselves, and say, "Though we have no property, we have yet something left that is valuable; we have constitutional liberty, both of person and of conscience. This King, these Lords, and these Commons, who it seems are too remote from us to know us, and feel for us, cannot take from us our habeas corpus right, or our right of trial by a jury of our neighbors; they cannot deprive us of the exercise of our religion, alter our ecclesiastical constitution, and compel us to be papists, if they please, or Mahometans." To annihilate this comfort, begin by laws to perplex their commerce with infinite regulations, impossible to be remembered and observed; ordain seizures of their property for every failure; take away the trial of such property by jury, and give it to arbitrary judges of your own appointing, and of the lowest characters in the country, whose salaries and emoluments are to arise out of the duties or condemnations, and whose appointments are during pleasure. Then let there be a formal declaration of both houses, that opposition to your edicts is treason, and that any person suspected of treason in the provinces may, according to some obsolete law, be seized and sent to the metropolis of the empire for trial; and pass an act, that those there charged with certain other offenses, shall be sent away in chains from their friends and country to be tried in the same manner for felony. Then erect a new Court of Inquisition among them, accompanied by an armed force, with instructions to transport all such suspected persons; to be ruined by the expense, if they bring over evidences to prove their innocence, or be found guilty and hanged, if they cannot afford it. And, lest the people should think you cannot possibly go any farther, pass another solemn declaratory act, "that King, Lords, Commons had, hath, and of right ought to have, full power and authority to make statutes of sufficient force and validity to bind the unrepresented provinces in all cases whatsoever." This will include spiritual with temporal; and, taken together, must operate wonderfully to your purpose; by convincing them, that they are at present under a power something like that spoken of in the scriptures, which can not only kill their bodies, but damn their souls to all eternity, by compelling them, if it pleases, to worship the devil.

XI. To make your taxes more odious, and more likely to procure resistance, send from the capital a board of officers to superintend the collection, composed of the most indiscreet, ill-bred, and insolent you can find. Let these have large salaries out of the extorted revenue, and live in open, grating luxury upon the sweat and blood of the industrious; whom they are to worry continually with groundless and expensive prosecutions before the abovementioned arbitrary revenue judges; all at the cost of the party prosecuted, though acquitted, because the king is to pay no costs. Let these men, by your order, be exempted from all the common taxes and burthens of the province, though they and their property are protected by its laws. If any revenue officers are suspected of the least tenderness for the people, discard them. If others are justly complained of, protect and reward them. If any of the under officers behave so as to provoke the people to drub them, promote those to better offices: this will encourage others to procure for themselves such profitable drubbings, by multiplying and enlarging such provocations, and all will work towards the end you aim at.

XII. Another way to make your tax odious, is to misapply the produce of it. If it was originally appropriated for the defense of the provinces, and the better support of government, and the adminis- tration of justice, where it may be neces- sary, then apply none of it to that defense, but bestow it where it is not necessary, in augmented salaries or pensions to every governor, who has distinguished himself by his enmity to the people, and by calumni-

ating them to their sovereign. This will make them pay it more unwillingly, and be more apt to quarrel with those that collect it and those that imposed it, who will quarrel again with them, and all shall contribute to your main purpose, of making them weary of your government.

XIII. If the people of any province have been accustomed to support their own governors and judges to satisfaction, you are to apprehend that such governors and judges may be thereby influenced to treat the people kindly, and to do them justice. This is another reason for applying part of that revenue in larger salaries to such governors and judges, given, as their commissions are, during your pleasure only, forbidding them to take any salaries from their provinces; that thus the people may no longer hope any kindness from their governors, or (in crown cases) any justice from their judges. And, as the money thus mis-applied in one province is extorted from all, probably all will resent the misapplication.

XIV. If the parliaments of your provinces should dare to claim rights, or complain of your administration, order them to be harassed with repeated dissolutions. If the same men are continually returned by new elections, adjourn their meetings to some country village, where they cannot be accommodated, and there keep them during pleasure; for this, you know, is your prerogative; and an excellent one it is, as you may manage it to promote discontents among the people, diminish their respect, and increase their disaffection.

XV. Convert the brave, honest officers of your navy into pimping tide-waiters and colony officers of the customs. Let those, who in time of war fought gallantly in defense of the commerce of their country- men, in peace be taught to prey upon it. Let them learn to be corrupted by great and real smugglers; but (to shew their diligence) scour with armed boats every bay, harbor, river, creek, cove, or nook throughout the coast of your colonies; stop and detain every coaster, every wood-boat, every fisherman, tumble their cargoes and even their ballast inside out and upside down; and if a penn'orth of pins is found un-entered, let the whole be seized and confiscated. Thus shall the trade of your colonists suffer more from their friends in time of peace, than it did from their enemies in war. Then let these boats' crews land upon every farm in their way, rob the orchards, steal the pigs and the poultry, and insult the inhabitants. If the injured and exasperated farmers, unable to procure other justice, should attack the aggressors, drub them, and burn their boats; you are to call this high treason and rebellion, order fleets and armies into their country, and threaten to carry all the offenders three thousand miles to be hanged, drawn, and quartered. O! this will work admirably!

XVI. If you are told of discontents in your colonies, never believe that they are general, or that you have given occasion for them; therefore do not think of applying any remedy, or of changing any offensive measure. Redress no grievance, lest they should be encouraged to demand the redress of some other grievance. Grant no request that is just and reasonable, lest they should make another that is unreasonable. Take all your informations of the state of the colonies from your governors and officers in enmity with them. Encourage and reward these leasing-makers; secret their lying accusations, lest they should be confuted; but act upon them as the clearest evidence, and believe nothing you hear from the friends of the people: suppose all their complaints to be invented and promoted by a few factious demagogues, whom if you could catch and hang, all would be quiet. Catch and hang a few of them accordingly; and the blood of the martyrs shall work miracles in favor of your purpose.

XVII. If you see rival nations rejoicing at the prospect of your disunion with your provinces, and endeavoring to promote it; if they translate, publish, and applaud all the complaints of your discontented colonists, at the same time privately stimulating you to severer measures, let not that alarm or offend you. Why should it, since you all mean the same thing?

XVIII. If any colony should at their own charge erect a fortress to secure their port against the fleets of a foreign enemy, get your governor to betray that fortress into your hands. Never think of paying what it cost the country, for that would look, at least, like some regard for justice; but turn it into a citadel to awe the inhabitants and curb their commerce. If they should have lodged in such fortress the very arms they bought and used to aid you in your conquests, seize them all; it will provoke like ingratitude added to robbery. One admirable effect of these operations will be, to discourage every other colony from erecting such defenses, and so your enemies may more easily invade them; to the great disgrace of your government, and of course the furtherance of your project.

XIX. Send armies into their country under pretense of protecting the inhabitants; but, instead of garrisoning the forts on their frontiers with those troops, to prevent incursions, demolish those forts, and order the troops into the heart of the country, that the savages may be encouraged to attack the frontiers, and that the troops may be protected by the inhabitants. This will seem to proceed from your ill will or your ignorance, and contribute farther to produce and strengthen an opinion among them, that you are no longer fit to govern them.

XX. Lastly, invest the general of your army in the provinces, with great and unconstitutional powers, and free him from the control of even your own civil governors. Let him have troops enough under his command, with all the fortresses in his possession; and who knows but (like some provincial generals in the Roman Empire, and encouraged by the universal discontent you have produced) he may take it into his head to set up for himself? If he should, and you have carefully practiced these few excellent rules of mine, take my word for it, all the provinces will immediately join him; and you will that day (if you have not done it sooner) get rid of the trouble of governing them, and all the plagues attending their commerce and connection from henceforth and for ever.

Q. E. D.

AN EDICT BY THE KING OF PRUSSIA
LONDON, 1773

This satire of British policy in America appeared in several London papers in 1773. In the fictitious edict, the King of Prussia applied the same policies to England that England applied to the American colonies. The notion that England had no greater right to rule the American colonies arbitrarily than Saxony had to rule its ancient colonies in Britain grew popular in America in the years preceding the Revolution and was a premise of Thomas Jefferson's "Summary View of the Rights of British America" (1774).

Dantzic, September 5

We have long wondered here at the supineness of the English nation, under the Prussian impositions upon its trade entering our port. We did not, till lately, know the claims, ancient and modern, that hang over that nation; and therefore could not suspect that it might submit to those impositions from a sense of duty or from principles of equity. The following edict, just made public, may, if serious, throw some light upon this matter.

"Frederic, by the grace of God, King of Prussia, &c. &c. &c., to all present and to come, (à tous présens et à venir) health. The peace now enjoyed throughout our dominions, having afforded us leisure to apply ourselves to the regulation of commerce, the improvement of our finances,

and at the same time the easing our domestic subjects in their taxes: For these causes, and other good considerations us thereunto moving, we hereby make known, that, after having deliberated these affairs in our council, present our dear brothers, and other great officers of the state, members of the same, we, of our certain knowledge, full power, and authority royal, have made and issued this present edict, viz.

"Whereas it is well known to all the world, that the first German settlements made in the Island of Britain, were by colonies of people, subject to our renowned ducal ancestors, and drawn from their dominions, under the conduct of Hengist, Horsa, Hella, Uff, Cerdicus, Ida, and others; and that the said colonies have flourished under the protection of our august house for ages past; have never been emancipated therefrom; and yet have hitherto yielded little profit to the same: And whereas we ourselves have in the last war fought for and defended the said colonies, against the power of France, and thereby enabled them to make conquests from the said power in America, for which we have not yet received adequate compensation: And whereas it is just and expedient that a revenue should be raised from the said colonies in Britain, towards our indemnification; and that those who are descendants of our ancient subjects, and thence still owe us due obedience, should contribute to the replenishing of our royal coffers as they must have done, had their ancestors remained in the territories now to us appertaining: We do therefore hereby ordain and command, that, from and after the date of these presents, there shall be levied and paid to our officers of the customs, on all goods, wares, and merchandises, and on all grain and other produce of the earth, exported from the said island of Britain, and on all goods of whatever kind imported into the same, a duty of four and an half per cent *ad valorem,* for the use of us and our successors. And that the said duty may more effectually be collected, we do hereby ordain, that all ships or vessels bound from Great Britain to any other part of the world, or from any other part of the world to Great Britain, shall in their respective voyages touch at our port of Koningsberg, there to be unladen, searched, and charged with the said duties.

"And whereas there hath been from time to time discovered in the said island of Great Britain, by our colonists there, many mines or beds of iron stone; and sundry subjects, of our ancient dominion, skillful in converting the said stone into metal, have in time past transported themselves thither, carrying with them and communicating that art; and the inhabitants of the said island, presuming that they had a natural right to make the best use they could of the natural productions of their country for their own benefit, have not only built furnaces for smelting the said stone into iron, but have erected plating-forges, slitting-mills, and steel-furnaces, for the more convenient manufacturing of the same; thereby endangering a diminution of the said manufacture in our ancient dominion; we do therefore hereby further ordain, that, from and after the date hereof, no mill or other engine for slitting or rolling of iron, or any plating-forge to work with a tilt-hammer, or any furnace for making steel, shall be erected or continued in the said island of Great Britain: And the Lord Lieutenant of every county in the said island is hereby commanded, on information of any such erection within his county, to order and by force to cause the same to be abated and destroyed, as he shall answer the neglect thereof to us at his peril. But we are nevertheless graciously pleased to permit the inhabitants of the said island to transport their iron into Prussia, there to be manufactured, and to them returned, they paying our Prussian subjects for the workmanship, with all the costs of commis-sion, freight, and risk, coming and returning; any thing herein contained to the contrary notwithstanding.

"We do not, however, think fit to extend this our indulgence to the article of wool; but, meaning to encourage, not only the manufacturing of woollen cloth, but also the raising of wool, in our ancient dominions, and to prevent both, as much as may be, in our said island, we do hereby absolutely forbid the transportation of wool from thence, even to the mother country, Prussia; and that those islanders may be further and more effectually restrained in making any advantage of their own wool in the way of manufacture, we command that none shall be carried out of one county into another; nor shall any worsted, bay, or woollen yarn, cloth, says, bays, kerseys, serges, frizes, druggets, cloth-serges, shalloons, or any other drapery stuffs, or woollen manufactures whatsoever, made up or mixed with wool in any of the said counties, be carried into any other county, or be water-borne even across the smallest river or creek, on penalty of forfeiture of the same, together with the boats, carriages, horses, &c., that shall be employed in removing them. Nevertheless our loving subjects there are hereby permitted (if they think proper) to use all their wool as manure for the improvement of their lands.

"And whereas the art and mystery of making hats hath arrived at great perfection in Prussia, and the making of hats by our remoter subjects ought to be as much as possible restrained: And forasmuch as the islanders before mentioned, being in possession of wool, beaver and other furs, have presumptuously conceived they had a right to make some advantage thereof, by manufacturing the same into hats, to the prejudice of our domestic manufacture: We do therefore hereby strictly command and ordain, that no hats or felts whatsoever, dyed or undyed, finished or unfinished, shall be loaded or put into or upon any vessel, cart, carriage, or horse, to be transported or conveyed out of one county in the said island into another county, or to any other place whatsoever; by any person or persons whatsoever, on pain of forfeiting the same, with a penalty of five hundred pounds sterling for every offense. Nor shall any hat-maker, in any of the said counties, employ more than two apprentices, on penalty of five pounds sterling per month; we intending hereby, that such hatmakers, being so restrained, both in the production and sale of their commodity, may find no advantage in continuing their business. But, lest the said islanders should suffer inconvenience by the want of hats, we are further graciously pleased to permit them to send their beaver furs to Prussia; and we also permit hats made thereof to be exported from Prussia to Britain, the people thus favored to pay all costs and charges of manufacturing, interest, commission to our merchants, insurance and freight going and returning, as in the case of iron.

"And, lastly, being willing further to favor our said colonies in Britain, we do hereby also ordain and command, that all the thieves, highway and street robbers, house-breakers, forgerers, murderers, s--d--tes, and villains of every denomination, who have forfeited their lives to the law in Prussia; but whom we, in our great clemency, do not think fit here to hang, shall be emptied out of our gaols into the said island of Great Britain, for the better peopling of that country.

"We flatter ourselves, that these our royal regulations and commands will be thought just and reasonable by our much-favored colonists in England; the said regulations being copied from their statutes of 10 and 11 William III. c. 10, 5 Geo. II. c. 22, 23, Geo. II. c. 29, 4 Geo. I. c. 11, and from other equitable laws made by their parliaments; or from instructions given by their princes, or from resolutions of both houses, entered into for the good government of their own colonies in Ireland and America.

"And all persons in the said island are hereby cautioned not to oppose in any wise the execution of this our edict, or any part thereof, such opposition being high treason, of which all who are suspected shall be transported in fetters from Britain to Prussia, there to be tried and executed according to the Prussian law.

"Such is our Pleasure.

"Given at Potsdam, this twenty-fifth day of the month of August, one thousand seven hundred and seventy-three, and in the thirty-third year of our reign.

"By the King, in his Council.

"Rechtmaessig, Sec."

Some take this edict to be merely one of the King's *jeux d'esprit:* others suppose it serious, and that he means a quarrel with England; but all here think the assertion it concludes with, "that these regulations are copied from acts of the English Parliament respecting their colonies," a very injurious one; it being impossible to believe, that a people distinguished for their love of liberty, a nation so wise, so liberal in its sentiments, so just and equitable towards its neighbors, should, from mean and injudicious views of petty immediate profit, treat its own children in a manner so arbitrary and tyrannical!

To Joseph Priestley
Craven Street, London, April 10, 1774

Dr. Joseph Priestley and Franklin met in London in 1766, and Franklin encouraged him to experiment with electricity. In 1767 Priestley published *The History of Electricity* with Franklin's assistance. Priestley devoted much of his time to the study of gases and discovered oxygen, which he called "dephlogisticated air." In this letter, Franklin related to Priestley what he knew about what is now known as marsh gas, produced when matter decomposes in swamps.

Dear Sir,

In compliance with your request, I have

endeavored to recollect the circumstances of the American experiments I formerly mentioned to you, of raising a flame on the surface of some waters there.

When I passed through New Jersey in 1764, I heard it several times mentioned, that, by applying a lighted candle near the surface of some of their rivers, a sudden flame would catch and spread on the water, continuing to burn for near half a minute. But the accounts I received were so imperfect, that I could form no guess at the cause of such an effect, and rather doubted the truth of it. I had no opportunity of seeing the experiment; but, calling to see a friend who happened to be just returning home from making it himself, I learned from him the manner of it; which was to choose a shallow place, where the bottom could be reached by a walking-stick, and was muddy; the mud was first to be stirred with the stick, and, when a number of small bubbles began to arise from it, the candle was applied. The flame was so sudden and so strong, that it caught his ruffle and spoiled it, as I saw. New Jersey having many pine trees in many parts of it, I then imagined that something like a volatile oil of turpentine might be mixed with the waters from a pine-swamp, but this supposition did not quite satisfy me. I mentioned the fact to some philosophical friends on my return to England, but it was not much attended to. I suppose I was thought a little too credulous.

In 1765, the Reverend Dr. Chandler received a letter from Dr. Finley, president of the college in that province, relating the same experiment. It was read at the Royal Society, November 21st of that year, but not printed in the Transactions; perhaps because it was thought too strange to be true, and some ridicule might be apprehended, if any member should attempt to repeat it, in order to ascertain, or refute it. The following is a copy of that account.

"A worthy gentleman, who lives at a few miles distance, informed me, that in a certain small cove of a mill-pond, near his house, he was surprised to see the surface of the water blaze like inflamed spirits. I soon after went to the place, and made the experiment with the same success. The bottom of the creek was muddy, and when stirred up, so as to cause a considerable curl on the surface, and a lighted candle held within two or three inches of it, the whole surface was in a blaze, as instantly as the vapor of warm inflammable spirits, and continued, when strongly agitated, for the space of several seconds. It was at first imagined to be peculiar to that place; but upon trial it was soon found, that such a bottom in other places exhibited the same phenomenon. The discovery was accidentally made by one belonging to the mill."

I have tried the experiment twice here in England, but without success. The first was in a slow running water with a muddy bottom. The second in a stagnant water at the bottom of a deep ditch. Being some time employed in stirring this water, I ascribed an intermitting fever, which seized me a few days after, to my breathing too much of that foul air which I stirred up from the bottom, and which I could not avoid while I stooped, endeavoring to kindle it. The discoveries you have lately made, of the manner in which inflammable air is in some cases produced, may throw light on this experiment, and explain its succeeding in some cases, and not in others.

With the highest esteem, and respect
I am, dear sir, your most obedient humble servant,
B. Franklin

TO WILLIAM STRAHAN
PHILADELPHIA, JULY 5, 1775

William Strahan, a prominent London printer and member of the House of Commons, was one of Franklin's closest friends in

England. Franklin, angry at him over the misconceptions he held about America, wrote this letter just after he returned from London to Philadelphia, but he never sent it. The two men remained friends during the war.

Mr. Strahan,

You are a member of Parliament, and one of that majority which has doomed my country to destruction. You have begun to burn our towns, and murder our people. Look upon your hands! They are stained with the blood of your relations! You and I were long friends: You are now my enemy, and I am, yours,

B. Franklin.

THE SALE OF THE HESSIANS
PASSY, FRANCE, 1777

Americans widely resented King George III's hiring of German mercenaries, or Hessians, to fight in the colonies. Franklin wrote in 1777: "The conduct of those princes of Germany, who have sold the blood of their people, has subjected them to the contempt and odium of all Europe." This dark satire of the "princes of Germany" is generally believed to be Franklin's, written in France sometime after news reached him of George Washington's defeat of the Hessians at Trenton, New Jersey, on December 26, 1776.

From the Count de Schaumbergh to the Baron Hohendorf, Commanding the Hessian Troops in America

Rome, February 18, 1777

Monsieur Le Baron: —On my return from Naples, I received at Rome your letter of the 27th December of last year. I have learned with unspeakable pleasure the courage our troops exhibited at Trenton, and you cannot imagine my joy on being told that of the 1,950 Hessians engaged in the fight, but 345 escaped. There were just 1,605 men killed, and I cannot sufficiently commend your prudence in sending an exact list of the dead to my minister in London. This precaution was the more necessary, as the report sent to the English ministry does not give but 1,455 dead. This would make 483,450 florins instead of 643,500 which I am entitled to demand under our convention. You will comprehend the prejudice which such an error would work in my finances, and I do not doubt you will take the necessary pains to prove that Lord North's list is false and yours correct.

The court of London objects that there were a hundred wounded who ought not to be included in the list, nor paid for as dead; but I trust you will not overlook my instructions to you on quitting Cassel, and that you will not have tried by human succor to recall the life of the unfortunates whose days could not be lengthened but by the loss of a leg or an arm. That would be making them a pernicious present, and I am sure they would rather die than live in a condition no longer fit for my service. I do not mean by this that you should assassinate them; we should be humane, my dear Baron, but you may insinuate to the surgeons with entire propriety that a crippled man is a reproach to their profession, and that there is no wiser course than to let every one of them die when he ceases to be fit to fight.

I am about to send to you some new recruits. Don't economize them. Remember glory before all things. Glory is true wealth. There is nothing degrades the soldier like the love of money. He must care only for honor and reputation, but this reputation must be acquired in the midst of dangers. A battle gained without costing the conqueror any blood is an inglorious success, while the conquered cover themselves with glory by perishing with their arms in their hands. Do you remember that of the 300 Lacedæmonians who defended the defile of Thermopylæ, not one returned? How happy should I be could I say the same of my brave Hessians!

It is true that their king, Leonidas, perished with them: but things have changed, and it is no longer the custom for princes of the empire to go and fight in America for a cause with which they have no concern. And besides, to whom should they pay the thirty guineas per man if I did not stay in Europe to receive them? Then, it is necessary also that I be ready to send recruits to replace the men you lose. For this purpose I must return to Hesse. It is true, grown men are becoming scarce there, but I will send you boys. Besides, the scarcer the commodity the higher the price. I am assured that the women and little girls have begun to till our lands, and they get on not badly. You did right to send back to Europe that Dr. Crumerus who was so successful in curing dysentery. Don't bother with a man who is subject to looseness of the bowels. That disease makes bad soldiers. One coward will do more mischief in an engagement than ten brave men will do good. Better that they burst in their barracks than fly in a battle, and tarnish the glory of our arms. Besides, you know that they pay me as killed for all who die from disease, and I don't get a farthing for runaways. My trip to Italy, which has cost me enormously, makes it desirable that there should be a great mortality among them. You will therefore promise promotion to all who expose themselves; you will exhort them to seek glory in the midst of dangers; you will say to Major Maundorff that I am not at all content with his saving the 345 men who escaped the massacre of Trenton. Through the whole campaign he has not had ten men killed in consequence of his orders. Finally, let it be your principal object to prolong the war and avoid a decisive engagement on either side, for I have made arrangements for a grand Italian opera, and I do not wish to be obliged to give it up. Meantime I pray God, my dear Baron de Hohendorf, to have you in his holy and gracious keeping.

MODEL OF A LETTER OF RECOMMENDATION
PARIS, APRIL 2, 1777

As an American commissioner in France, Franklin was continually pressed by ambitious European officers for recommendations to the American army. Some of the officers he recommended, such as the Marquis de Lafayette and Baron von Steuben, proved to be of great service to the United States. However, Franklin grew weary of the requests, and Congress and George Washington did not have enough places for all of the officers who wished to serve. This "model letter" shows Franklin's frustration with the multitude of applications.

Sir,
The bearer of this, who is going to America, presses me to give him a letter of recommendation, though I know nothing of him, not even his name. This may seem extraordinary, but I assure you it is not uncommon here. Sometimes, indeed one unknown person brings another equally unknown, to recommend him; and sometimes they recommend one another! As to this gentleman, I must refer you to himself for his character and merits, with which he is certainly better acquainted than I can possibly be, I recommend him however to those civilities which every stranger, of whom one knows no harm, has a right to; and I request you will do him all the good offices, and show him all the favor that, on further acquaintance, you shall find him to deserve. I have the honor to be, etc. B.F.

TO MADAME BRILLON
PASSY, FRANCE, MARCH 10 (YEAR UNKNOWN)

The Brillons lived in Passy, France, where Franklin resided during the American Revolution. Franklin enjoyed socializing with the French ladies, and his two favorites were

Madame Helvétius, a widow, and Madame Brillon, who was married to a French treasury official. Madame Helvétius was not a letter-writer, but Madame Brillon exchanged playful and flirtatious letters with Franklin. The following is typical of their correspondence. The forwardness of the letter was part of their game, in which he asked and she refused.

I am charmed with the goodness of my spiritual guide, and resign myself implicitly to her conduct, as she promises to lead me to heaven in so delicious a road when I could be content to travel thither even in the roughest of all ways with the pleasure of her company.

How kindly partial to her penitent in finding him, on examining his conscience, guilty of only one capital sin and to call that by the gentle name of foible!

I lay fast hold of your promise to absolve me of all sins past, present, & future, on the easy & pleasing condition of loving God, America and my guide above all things. I am in rapture when I think of being absolved of the future.

People commonly speak of Ten Commandments. —I have been taught that there are twelve. The first was increase & multiply & replenish the earth. The twelfth is, a new commandment I give unto you, that you love one another. It seems to me that they are a little misplaced, and that the last should have been the first. However I never made any difficulty about that, but was always willing to obey them both whenever I had an opportunity. Pray tell me my dear casuist, whether my keeping religiously these two commandments though not in the Decalogue, may not be accepted in compensation for my breaking so often one of the ten, I mean that which forbids coveting my neighbor's wife, and which I confess I break constantly God forgive me, as often as I see or think of my lovely confessor, and I am afraid I should

never be able to repent of the sin even if I had the full possession of her.

And now I am consulting you upon a case of conscience I will mention the opinion of a certain father of the church which I find myself willing to adopt though I am not sure it is orthodox. It is this, that the most effectual way to get rid of a certain temptation is, as often as it returns, to comply with and satisfy it.

Pray instruct me how far I may venture to practice upon this principle?

But why should I be so scrupulous when you have promised to absolve me of the future?

Adieu my charming conductress and believe me ever with the sincerest esteem & affection.

Your most obed't hum. serv. B.F.

THE EPHEMERA
PASSY, FRANCE, 1778

While he lived in France, Franklin wrote short "bagatelles" to entertain his friends. "The Ephemera" was his first, written for Madame Brillon.

An Emblem of Human Life
You may remember, my dear friend, that when we lately spent that happy day in the delightful garden and sweet society of the Moulin Joly, I stopped a little in one of our walks, and stayed some time behind the company. We had been shown numberless skeletons of a kind of little fly, called an ephemera whose successive generations, we were told, were bred and expired within the day. I happened to see a living company of them on a leaf, who appeared to be engaged in conversation. You know I understand all the inferior animal tongues: my too great application to the study of them is the best excuse I can give for the little progress I have made in your charming language. I listened through curiosity

to the discourse of these little creatures; but as they, in their national vivacity, spoke three or four together, I could make but little of their conversation. I found, however, by some broken expressions that I heard now and then, they were disputing warmly on the merit of two foreign musicians, one a cousin, the other a mosquito; in which dispute they spent their time, seemingly as regardless of the shortness of life as if they had been sure of living a month. Happy people! thought I, you live certainly under a wise, just, and mild government, since you have no public grievances to complain of, nor any subject of contention but the perfections and imperfections of foreign music. I turned from them to an old gray-headed one, who was single on another leaf, and talking to himself. Being amused with his soliloquy, I put it down in writing, in hopes it will likewise amuse her to whom I am so much indebted for the most pleasing of all amusements, her delicious company and heavenly harmony.

"It was," says he, "the opinion of learned philosophers of our race, who lived and flourished long before my time, that this vast world, the Moulin Joly, could not itself subsist more than 18 hours; and I think there was some foundation for that opinion, since, by the apparent motion of the great luminary that gives life to all nature, and which in my time has evidently declined considerably towards the ocean at the end of our earth, it must then finish its course, be extinguished in the waters that surround us, and leave the world in cold and darkness, necessarily producing universal death and destruction. I have lived seven of those hours, a great age, being no less than four hundred twenty minutes of time. How very few of us continue so long! I have seen generations born, flourish, and expire. My present friends are the children and grandchildren of the friends of my youth, who are now, alas, no more! And I

must soon follow them; for, by the course of nature, though still in health, I cannot expect to live above seven or eight minutes longer. What now avails all my toil and labor, in amassing honey-dew on this leaf, which I cannot live to enjoy! What the political struggles I have been engaged in, for the good of my compatriot, inhabitants of this bush, or my philosophical studies for the benefit of our race in general! For, in politics, what can laws do without morals? Our present race of ephemeræ will in a course of minutes become corrupt, like those of other and older bushes, and consequently as wretched. And in philosophy how small our progress! Alas! Art is long, and life is short! My friends would comfort me with the idea of a name, they say, I shall leave behind me; and they tell me I have lived long enough to nature and to glory. But what will fame be to an ephemera who no longer exists? And what will become of all history in the eighteenth hour, when the world itself, even the whole Moulin Joly shall come to its end, and be buried in universal ruin?"

To me, after all my eager pursuits, no solid pleasures now remain, but the reflection of a long life spent in meaning well, the sensible conversation of a few good lady ephemeræ, and now and then a kind smile and a tune from the ever amiable Brillante.

To William Franklin
Passy, France, August 16, 1784

Franklin's only son, William, remained loyal to England during the Revolutionary War. He was the royal governor of New Jersey before the hostilities erupted, and the New Jersey Assembly ordered him arrested in 1776. William became president of a loyalist association and later moved to England. He breached the silence between himself and his father with a letter to him in France in 1784. The following was Franklin's reply.

Dear Son,

I received your letter of the 22nd past, and am glad to find that you desire to revive the affectionate intercourse, that formerly existed between us. It will be very agreeable to me; indeed nothing has ever hurt me so much and affected me with such keen sensations, as to find myself deserted in my old age by my only son; and not only deserted, but to find him taking up arms against me, in a cause, wherein my good fame, fortune and life were all at stake. You conceived, you say, that your duty to your king and regard for your country required this. I ought not to blame you for differing in sentiment with me in public affairs. We are men, all subject to errors. Our opinions are not in our own power; they are formed and governed much by circumstances, that are often as inexplicable as they are irresistible. Your situation was such that few would have censured your remaining neuter, though there are natural duties which precede political ones, and cannot be extinguished by them.

This is a disagreeable subject. I drop it. And we will endeavor, as you propose mutually to forget what has happened relating to it, as well as we can. I send your son over to pay his duty to you. You will find him much improved. He is greatly esteemed and beloved in this country, and will make his way anywhere. It is my desire, that he should study the law, as a necessary part of knowledge for a public man, and profitable if he should have occasion to practice it. I would have you therefore put into his hands those law-books you have, viz. Blackstone, Coke, Bacon, Viner, &c. He will inform you, that he received the letter sent him by Mr. [Joseph] Galloway, and the paper it enclosed, safe.

On my leaving America, I deposited with that friend for you, a chest of papers, among which was a manuscript of nine or ten volumes, relating to manufactures, agriculture, commerce, finance, &c., which cost me in England about 70 guineas; eight quire books, containing the rough drafts of all my letters while I lived in London. These are missing. I hope you have got them, if not, they are lost. Mr. [Benjamin] Vaughan has published in London a volume of what he calls my political works. He proposes a second edition; but, as the first was very incomplete, and you had many things that were omitted, (for I used to send you sometimes the rough drafts, and sometimes the printed pieces I wrote in London,) I have directed him to apply to you for what may be in your power to furnish him with, or to delay his publication till I can be at home again, if that may ever happen.

I did intend returning this year; but the Congress, instead of giving me leave to do so, have sent me another commission, which will keep me here at least a year longer; and perhaps I may then be too old and feeble to bear the voyage. I am here among a people that love and respect me, a most amiable nation to live with; and perhaps I may conclude to die among them; for my friends in America are dying off, one after another, and I have been so long abroad, that I should now be almost a stranger in my own country.

I shall be glad to see you when convenient, but would not have you come here at present. You may confide to your son the family affairs you wished to confer upon with me, for he is discreet. And I trust, that you will prudently avoid introducing him to company, that it may be improper for him to be seen with. I shall hear from you by him and any letters to me afterwards, will come safe under cover directed to Mr. Ferdinand Grand, banker at Paris. Wishing you health, and more happiness than it seems you have lately experienced, I remain your affectionate father,

B. Franklin

ON THE SLAVE TRADE
PHILADELPHIA, MARCH 23, 1790

Franklin wrote this piece as a parody of a speech delivered by Congressman James Jackson in favor of the slave trade. At this time, Franklin was the president of the Pennsylvania Society for the Abolition of Slavery. In the piece, a member of the Divan of Algiers uses the arguments of proponents of slavery in the United States to justify the enslavement of Europeans, over the objections of a group of abolitionists. The piece was written and published in the *Federal Gazette* less than a month before Franklin died.

To the editor of the Federal Gazette
Sir,

Reading last night in your excellent paper the speech of Mr. Jackson in Congress against their meddling with the affair of slavery, or attempting to mend the condition of the slaves, it put me in mind of a similar one made about 100 years since by Sidi Mehemet Ibrahim, a member of the Divan of Algiers, which may be seen in Martin's account of his consulship, anno 1687. It was against granting the petition of the sect called Erika, or Purists, who prayed for the abolition of piracy and slavery as being unjust. Mr. Jackson does not quote it; perhaps he has not seen it. If, therefore, some of its reasonings are to be found in his eloquent speech, it may only show that men's interests and intellects operate and are operated on with surprising similarity in all countries and climates, when under similar circumstances. The African's speech, as translated, is as follows.

"Allah Bismillah, &c. God is great, and Mahomet is His prophet.

"Have these Erika considered the consequences of granting their petition? If we cease our cruises against the Christians, how shall we be furnished with the commodities their countries produce, and which are so necessary for us? If we forbear to make slaves of their people, who in this hot climate are to cultivate our lands? Who are to perform the common labors of our city, and in our families? Must we not then be our own slaves? And is there not more compassion and more favor due to us as Mussulmen, than to these Christian dogs? We have now above 50,000 slaves in and near Algiers. This number, if not kept up by fresh supplies, will soon diminish, and be gradually annihilated. If we then cease taking and plundering the infidel ships, and making slaves of the seamen and passengers, our lands will become of no value for want of cultivation; the rents of houses in the city will sink one half; and the revenues of government arising from its share of prizes be totally destroyed! And for what? To gratify the whims of a whimsical sect, who would have us, not only forbear making more slaves, but even to manumit those we have.

"But who is to indemnify their masters for the loss? Will the state do it? Is our treasury sufficient? Will the Erika do it? Can they do it? Or would they, to do what they think justice to the slaves, do a greater injustice to the owners? And if we set our slaves free, what is to be done with them? Few of them will return to their countries; they know too well the greater hardships they must there be subject to; they will not embrace our holy religion; they will not adopt our manners; our people will not pollute themselves by intermarrying with them. Must we maintain them as beggars in our streets, or suffer our properties to be the prey of their pillage? For men long accustomed to slavery will not work for a livelihood when not compelled. And what is there so pitiable in their present condition? Were they not slaves in their own countries?

"Are not Spain, Portugal, France, and the Italian states governed by despots, who hold all their subjects in slavery, without exception? Even England treats its sailors as slaves; for they are, whenever the government pleases, seized, and confined in ships of war, condemned not only to work, but to fight, for small wages, or a mere subsistence, not better than our slaves are allowed by us. Is their condition then made worse by their falling into our hands? No; they have only exchanged one slavery for another, and I may say a better; for here they are brought into a land where the sun of Islamism gives forth its light, and shines in full splendor, and they have an opportunity of making themselves acquainted with the true doctrine, and thereby saving their immortal souls. Those who remain at home have not that happiness. Sending the slaves home then would be sending them out of light into darkness.

"I repeat the question, What is to be done with them? I have heard it suggested, that they may be planted in the wilderness, where there is plenty of land for them to subsist on, and where they may flourish as a free state; but they are, I doubt, too little disposed to labor without compulsion, as well as too ignorant to establish a good government, and the wild Arabs would soon molest and destroy or again enslave them. While serving us, we take care to provide them with every thing, and they are treated with humanity. The laborers in their own country are, as I am well informed, worse fed, lodged, and clothed. The condition of most of them is therefore already mended, and requires no further improvement. Here their lives are in safety. They are not liable to be impressed for soldiers, and forced to cut one another's Christian throats, as in the wars of their own countries. If some of the religious mad bigots, who now tease us with their silly petitions, have in a fit of blind zeal freed their slaves, it was not generosity, it was not humanity, that moved them to the action; it was from the conscious burthen of a load of sins, and hope, from the supposed merits of so good a work, to be excused damnation.

"How grossly are they mistaken in imagining slavery to be disallowed by the Alcoran! Are not the two precepts, to quote no more, 'Masters, treat your slaves with kindness; slaves, serve your masters with cheerfulness and fidelity,' clear proofs to the contrary? Nor can the plundering of infidels be in that sacred book forbidden, since it is well known from it, that God has given the world, and all that it contains, to his faithful Mussulmen, who are to enjoy it of right as fast as they conquer it. Let us then hear no more of this detestable proposition, the manumission of Christian slaves, the adoption of which would, by depreciating our lands and houses, and thereby depriving so many good citizens of their properties, create universal discontent, and provoke insurrections, to the endangering of government and producing general confusion. I have therefore no doubt, but this wise council will prefer the comfort and happiness of a whole nation of true believers to the whim of a few Erika, and dismiss their petition."

The result was, as Martin tells us, that the Divan came to this resolution; "The doctrine, that plundering and enslaving the Christians is unjust, is at best problematical; but that it is the interest of this state to continue the practice, is clear; therefore let the petition be rejected."

And it was rejected accordingly.

And since like motives are apt to produce in the minds of men like opinions and resolutions, may we not, Mr. Brown, venture to predict, from this account, that the petitions to the Parliament of England for abolishing the slave-trade, to say nothing of other legislatures, and the debates upon them, will have a similar conclusion? I am, sir, your constant reader and humble servant,

HISTORICUS

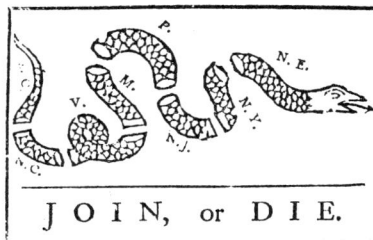

CHRONOLOGY

1706   Born in Milk Street in Boston to Josiah and Abiah Franklin; baptized at the Old South Church.

1714   Enters Boston grammar school.

1715   Father decides he cannot afford to send Franklin to the grammar school and withdraws him. Enters English and mathematics school and studies under George Brownell; excels in English, does poorly in math. Uncle Benjamin, for whom Franklin was named, moves to Boston from England and lives with the Franklins on Milk Street.

1716   Father withdraws him from the English school and puts him to work in his business, tallow-chandling and soap-boiling.

1717   Franklin strongly dislikes tallow-chandling and soap-boiling. Father considers apprenticing him to his cousin Samuel, a cutler; but monetary disagreements between his father and his cousin bring Franklin back home. James Franklin, an older brother, establishes a printing business in Boston.

1718   Signs as an apprentice to brother James in printing business. Writes two ballads, "The Lighthouse Tragedy" and "On the Taking of Teach or Blackbeard the Pirate." Around this time, gains greater access to books and begins to study and educate himself.

1721   James Franklin begins to publish the *New England Courant*.

1722   Secretly writes series of humorous letters to the *Courant* under the pseudonym "Mrs. Silence Dogood." Massachusetts Assembly jails James Franklin for ridiculing local officials, leaving the *Courant* under Franklin's care for nearly a month.

1723   Massachusetts Assembly forbids James Franklin to publish the *Courant;* James publishes the paper under Franklin's name. Franklin runs the paper while James is in hiding. Unhappy working under his brother, who treats him harshly, runs away to New York in September. Finds no work in New York and moves to Philadelphia. Hired by Samuel Keimer, who owns a printing shop. Lives with rival printer Andrew Bradford, then with John Read, father of Deborah Read, his future wife.

1724   Governor William Keith pushes Franklin to establish his own printing shop in Philadelphia. Returns to Boston to ask his father's help; father thinks Franklin is too young to set up his own business. Governor Keith promises to help him set up and sends him to London to procure materials. With friend James Ralph and merchant Thomas Denham, arrives in London and finds none of Keith's promised letters of recommendation or credit. Finds work at Palmer's printing house.

1725   Writes pamphlet, "A Dissertation on Liberty and Necessity, Pleasure and Pain," after setting type for William Wollaston's "The Religion of Nature

Delineated." Ashamed of printing the pamphlets, Franklin burns most of them. Pamphlet impresses William Lyons, a surgeon, who introduces him to some of his philosophical friends. Leaves Palmer's and finds work at Watts's printing house. Deborah Read marries John Rogers, who abandons her four months later.

1726 Returns to Philadelphia with Denham and briefly works in Denham's shop. Keeps records in *Journal of a Voyage from London to Philadelphia* during voyage home.

1727 Both Franklin and Denham fall ill; Franklin recovers, but Denham does not. Keimer hires him in his printing shop again. Organizes the Junto, a philosophical/political discussion club.

1728 Keimer and Franklin employed to print paper money for New Jersey. Quarrels with Keimer and leaves his shop. Sets up his own printing house with Hugh Meredith. Writes his personal devotion book, "Articles of Belief and Acts of Religion." Plans to publish a newspaper; George Webb, a member of the Junto, informs Keimer of Franklin's plan, and Keimer starts to publish *The Universal Instructor in All Arts and Sciences: and Pennsylvania Gazette.*

1729 Keimer's paper fails; Franklin and Meredith purchase it from him "for a trifle" and shorten the name to the *Pennsylvania Gazette.* The *Gazette* is soon successful. Writes pamphlet, "A Modest Enquiry into the Nature and Necessity of a Plentiful Paper Currency" to muster support for issuing more paper money in Pennsylvania.

1730 William Franklin, illegitimate son, born. Marries Deborah Read, but only able to form a common-law marriage, as the whereabouts of John Rogers are unknown. William lives with them.

1731 Becomes a member of the St. John's Lodge, established in Philadelphia the year before. Founds the Library Company of Philadelphia. Sends Thomas Whitemarsh to South Carolina under a printing partnership.

1732 Son Francis Folger Franklin born. Establishes short-lived *Philadelphische Zeitung,* the first German newspaper in the colonies. Prints first edition of *Poor Richard's Almanack.*

1733 Embarks on elaborate self-improvement scheme, identifying 13 virtues and grading himself on each. Louis Timothée replaces Whitemarsh, deceased, in South Carolina. Sees family in Boston and brother James in Rhode Island.

1734 Becomes grand master of Masons in Pennsylvania.

1735 Defends the Reverend Samuel Hemphill from attacks by Presbyterian clergy.

1736 Francis Folger Franklin dies of smallpox. Establishes Union Fire Company. Prints New Jersey's paper money with innovative anticounterfeiting images. Appointed clerk of Pennsylvania Assembly.

1737 Replaces rival printer, Andrew Bradford, as postmaster of Philadelphia.

1738 Falsely implicated in the death of a man during a mock Masonic ritual.

1739 The Reverend George Whitefield, Anglican evangelist of the Great Awakening, arrives in Philadelphia and befriends Franklin. Franklin prints his sermons.

1740 Plans to publish *The General Magazine and Historical Chronicle for All the British Plantations in America;* John Webbe discloses Franklin's plans to his rival, Bradford, who plans competing with *The American Magazine.*

1741 Both magazines begin publication; both fail within the year. Invents Franklin Stove.

1742 Enters into printing partnership with James Parker, who moves to New York and publishes the *New York Gazette.*

1743   Daughter Sarah (Sally) Franklin born. Circulates "A Proposal for Promoting Useful Knowledge among the British Plantations of America," out of which grows the American Philosophical Society. Meets Cadwallader Colden in New York and begins corresponding with him. Also begins corresponding with London printer William Strahan. Watches Dr. Adam Spencer perform electrical experiments "imperfectly" in Boston.

1744   At Franklin's encouragement, Strahan sends David Hall to Philadelphia. Franklin is pleased with Hall, who works for him in his shop.

1745   Josiah Franklin dies in Boston at age 87. Peter Collinson, a Quaker botanist and merchant in London, sends a glass tube used in electrical experiments to the Library Company. Begins his own electrical experiments.

1746   Travels to New England; devotes much of his time to electrical experiments.

1747   Writes and publishes "Plain Truth," calling for a volunteer militia to defend the province from French and Spanish privateers. Begins sending descriptions of electrical experiments to Collinson. The accounts are ignored and laughed at by members of the Royal Society of London.

1748   Enters into printing partnership with Hall, who effectively runs the business. Also enters into partnership with Thomas Smith, whom he sets up in a printing house in Antigua. Briefly becomes a soldier in one of the militia regiments he helped to organize. Elected to the Philadelphia Common Council.

1749   Becomes provincial grand master of the Masons. Appointed justice of the peace in Philadelphia; feels unqualified for the position and resigns. Writes "Proposals Relating to the Education of Youth in Pennsylvania," out of which eventually grows the University of Pennsylvania.

1750   First suggests the use of lightning rods to secure houses. Accidentally shocks himself instead of a turkey he is trying to electrocute.

1751   Helps Dr. Thomas Bond establish the Pennsylvania Hospital, raising private contributions and obtaining a matching amount from the Pennsylvania Assembly. Collinson and Dr. John Fothergill publish Franklin's letters on electricity as "Experiments and Observations on Electricity" in London. Thomas-François Dalibard translates the letters into French. Elected to the Pennsylvania Assembly and as alderman of Philadelphia.

1752   Mother, Abiah Franklin, dies in Boston at age 84. Draws electricity from a storm cloud with a kite and a key; sends instructions on how to repeat the experiment to Collinson in London. M. Delor performs Franklin's "Philadelphia experiments" for Louis XV, who is pleased and sends thanks to Collinson and Franklin at the Royal Society. Designs flexible catheter for brother, John Franklin, who suffers from a bladder stone. Sends nephew Benjamin Mecom to take over the printing house that Smith formerly managed in Antigua. In France, Delor and Dalibard draw electricity from clouds with lightning rods.

1753   Receives honorary master of arts degrees from Harvard and Yale Colleges during travels through New England. The Abbé Nollet, in France, publicly disputes Franklin's electrical theories; Franklin never answers him. The Royal Society of London, which had previously ignored his work in electricity, awards him the Sir Godfrey Copley medal. With William Hunter, appointed joint deputy postmaster general for America, the highest position in the post office in America. The two men begin an overhaul of the postal system. Helps negotiate a treaty with Six Nations and other Indians at Carlisle, Pennsylvania.

1754 Governor James Hamilton of Pennsylvania appoints Franklin as a delegate to the Albany Congress, convened on the order of the Lords of Trade in England for the purpose of discussing plans for defense with the chiefs of the Six Nations. To promote the idea of a colonial union, prints "Join or Die" cartoon, picturing a snake divided into different sections, each representing a colony. On the way to Albany, drafts a scheme for union; Albany Congress adopts an amended form of his plan. Colonial assemblies and England reject the plan. Writes letters to Governor William Shirley of Massachusetts arguing against the idea of allowing Parliament to tax the colonies. French and Indian War begins.

1755 Pennsylvania Assembly sends Franklin to establish postal routes for British General Edward Braddock, who plans to lead a campaign to capture Fort Duquesne. With son William, procures wagons and supplies for Braddock. An old dispute erupts again between the proprietaries, Thomas and Richard Penn, and the Pennsylvania Assembly, over the taxation of the Penns' estates. The Assembly refuses to vote money for defense unless the Penns contribute; the Penns refuse. Braddock mortally wounded in surprise attack on the way to Fort Duquesne. Franklin authors a militia bill, passed by Assembly.

1756 As a colonel, takes regiment to Gnadenhutten to construct forts on Pennsylvania's northwestern frontier. Assembly calls Franklin back to Philadelphia. Negotiates with Delaware Indians at Easton. Assembly finally passes his bill to provide for a town watch. Elected to the Royal Society of London and the Royal Society of Arts. William and Mary College awards Franklin an honorary master of arts degree.

1757 Assembly votes to send Franklin to England to petition for the right to tax the Penns' estates. Governor William Denny disobeys proprietary instructions and approves an Assembly bill taxing the Penns' estates. During voyage to England, writes "Father Abraham's Speech," the preface for the final edition of *Poor Richard's Almanack*. Engages in fruitless discussions with Thomas Penn over dispute between the Assembly and the proprietors. Rents rooms on Craven Street from Mrs. Margaret Stevenson, who nurses him through bouts of fever and cold. Finally meets longtime correspondents Strahan, Fothergill, and Collinson; befriends Dr. John Pringle, later Sir John Pringle.

1758 With son William, seeks information about ancestors at Banbury at Ectonshire. Attends informal discussion clubs; the Honest Whigs is his favorite.

1759 Meets Lord Kames, Adam Smith, William Robertson, David Hume, and others in Scotland. The University of St. Andrews awards him an honorary doctor of laws degree.

1760 With Richard Jackson, writes "The Interest of Great Britain Considered," suggesting that England should ask for Canada instead of the island of Guadeloupe in an upcoming treaty negotiation with France. Privy Council allows taxes on Penn lands to stand. Illegitimate son of William Franklin, William Temple Franklin, born to unknown mother.

1761 Travels to Belgium with son and Jackson. Returns in time to watch George III's coronation. Invents armonica, a musical instrument played by running a finger on the rim of a glass.

1762 William Franklin marries Elizabeth Downes and is appointed governor of New Jersey. Oxford University awards Franklin honorary doctorate of civil law. Returns to Philadelphia.

1763 Embarks on extensive inspection tour of colonial post offices.

1764 Writes "A Narrative of the Late Massacres in Lancaster County," condemning the Paxton Boys, a gang of men who murdered a band of peaceful Indians, and calling for justice against them. Organizes successful defense effort to protect another band of peaceful Indians from the rioters. Replaces Isaac Norris as speaker of the Assembly. Assembly resolves to petition the king to assume the government of the province from the Penns. Franklin loses seat in the Assembly after bitter election. Assembly returns him to England to present the petition, which he drafts. Moves back in with Mrs. Stevenson.

1765 Franklin and other colonial agents express their opposition to the Stamp Act to Sir George Grenville; Parliament passes the Stamp Act anyway. Americans universally resent the act, which is a tax imposed by a body in which they have no representatives. Franklin complies with Grenville's request to name a respectable agent in America, recommending John Hughes. In Pennsylvania, Franklin is accused of helping to pass the act; angry Pennsylvanians force Hughes to resign and hang him in effigy.

1766 Partnership with Hall ends. Testifies in favor of repeal of the Stamp Act before House of Commons; testimony is published and applauded in America. Parliament repeals the Stamp Act but reserves its right to tax the colonies. Travels to Germany with Pringle; the two men are elected to the Royal Academy of Sciences at Göttingen. Meets Baron von Münchhausen.

1767 Parliament passes the Townshend Duties, laying taxes on lead, paint, glass, tea, and other items. Americans are outraged. Franklin and Pringle travel to Paris, where they are presented to Louis XV. Sarah Franklin marries Richard Bache in Philadelphia.

1768 The Georgia Assembly appoints Franklin its agent. Writes "Causes of American Discontents before 1768."

1769 Benjamin Franklin Bache, grandson, born in Philadelphia. Joins Grand Ohio Company, which hopes to obtain grant of western lands from the Crown. New Jersey Assembly appoints him its agent.

1770 Massachusetts House of Representatives appoints Franklin its agent.

1771 Lord Hillsborough, secretary of state for American affairs, refuses to recognize the appointment, maintaining that the governor has not approved it. Begins *Autobiography* at home of Jonathan Shipley, the bishop of St. Asaph. Travels to Scotland and Ireland with Jackson; stays with David Hume and Lord Kames. Meets Richard Bache and his family at Preston in Lancashire.

1772 Elected to the French Academy of Sciences. Lord Hillsborough unsuccessfully tries to block the Grand Ohio Company's bid for western lands and resigns. Lord Dartmouth replaces him. Franklin mysteriously obtains letters written by Massachusetts Governor Thomas Hutchinson and Lieutenant Governor Andrew Oliver suggesting that England send troops to Massachusetts; sends letters to Boston.

1773 Writes satires on British policy in America to London newspapers, "Rules by Which a Great Empire May Be Reduced to a Small One" and "An Edict by the King of Prussia." Massachusetts instructs Franklin and other agents to present a petition for the removal of Hutchinson and Oliver.

1774 Summoned to the Cockpit at Whitehall on the pretense of considering the Massachusetts petition; asks to return later with counsel. Upon return, mercilessly denounced for conduct in obtaining Oliver-Hutchinson letters by Alexander Wedderburn, counsel for Hutchinson's and Oliver's agent, Israel Mauduit. First Continental Congress convenes in Philadelphia in response to the "Intolerable Acts," passed by Parliament to punish Massachusetts. Congress instructs Franklin and other

American agents to present its petition to the king; George III ignores it. Franklin becomes involved through mediators in secret negotiations with British officials. Deborah Franklin suffers stroke and dies five days afterward.

1775   Secret but futile negotiations continue. Meets with William Pitt, Earl of Chatham, who admires the Congress's petition. Pitt asks for Franklin's input and draws up conciliatory bill; he invites Franklin to attend when he presents it. Pitt's bill ignored. Parliament declares colonies in rebellion. Franklin, convinced that the Lords had "scarce discretion enough to govern a herd of swine," returns to Philadelphia. Takes seat in Second Continental Congress. Serves on committees to print colonial paper money, organize colonial post office, and establish contact with foreigners who might be friendly toward America. Travels to George Washington's camp in Massachusetts to determine needs of and establish rules for Continental army. George III follows Parliament, declaring colonies in rebellion. Also serves on the Pennsylvania Committee of Safety, charged with putting Pennsylvania into a state of defense. Favors independence before many others do.

1776   William Franklin, governor of New Jersey, arrested; he remains loyal to England during the war. Franklin resigns from Pennsylvania Assembly. Congress sends him on a futile mission to Canada to raise support for the colonies; his health suffers, and he returns early. Congress appoints him to committee to draft a declaration of independence; Thomas Jefferson writes the draft and asks Franklin and John Adams for input. Votes for independence on July 2. Travels with John Adams for futile negotiations with Lord Richard Howe at Staten Island. Congress appoints him commissioner to France; sets sail with two grandsons, William Temple Franklin and Benjamin

Franklin Bache. With other commissioners, Arthur Lee and Silas Deane, sends introductory note to the Comte de Vergennes, the French foreign minister.

1777   France begins granting secret aid to the United States. Settles in at Passy, a village outside of Paris, and befriends almost everyone who lives there. Enormously popular in France; closest friends include Anne-Louise Brillon de Jouy, Louis-Guillaume Le Veillard, and Anne-Catherine Helvétius. Sets up private printing press. Writes anti-British pieces and circulates them in Europe. The United States defeats Major General John Burgoyne at Saratoga, prompting a new French word, *burgoinised*. Elected to the Royal Society of Medicine as first foreign associate.

1778   France formally recognizes the United States and signs treaty of alliance and treaty of amity and commerce. John Adams replaces Silas Deane and lives with Franklin. Meets Voltaire at French Academy of Sciences and Nine Sisters Lodge. Congress revokes joint commission and appoints Franklin sole minister plenipotentiary. Writes first bagatelle, "The Ephemera," for Madame Brillon.

1779   Benjamin Vaughan publishes an edition of Franklin's works in England. Paper on aurora borealis read at the French Academy of Sciences. Investigates "igneous fluid" theories of future French revolutionary Jean-Paul Marat. Elected grand master of the Nine Sisters Lodge.

1780   Adams returns to France with a commission to negotiate any possible terms of peace with England and offends Vergennes with his letters; Adams travels to Holland to seek a loan. Vergennes insists that Franklin send Adams's letters to Congress.

1781   General Charles Cornwallis surrenders at Yorktown. Congress appoints Franklin, Adams, John Jay, Thomas

Jefferson, and Henry Laurens as commissioners to negotiate a peace treaty with England. Jay is in Spain, Adams in Holland, Laurens in England, and Jefferson in America.

1782   Begins informal peace negotiations with British emissaries. Jay and Adams arrive in France; the commissioners decide to violate Congress's instructions and negotiate without consulting Vergennes; they sign preliminary articles of peace with Richard Oswald, England's emissary.

1783   Convinces the Duc de La Rochefoucauld, a fellow Mason, to translate American constitutions into French. American commissioners sign final treaty with David Hartley. Witnesses first hot-air balloon flights.

1784   Thomas Jefferson arrives in France. Franklin is appointed to a commission to investigate Friedrich Anton Mesmer's "animal magnetism"; commission discredits Mesmer. With Jefferson and Adams, negotiates treaties of amity and commerce with other nations. Elected to the Royal Academy of History of Madrid. William Franklin, who has moved to England, writes to his father after long silence.

1785   Congress grants permission for Franklin to return home; appoints Jefferson minister plenipotentiary in his place. Signs treaty with Prussia before he leaves. Travels by a royal litter to Le Havre; meets Vaughan, the Shipleys, and son William at Southampton. Breaks promise to friends to work on his *Autobiography* on voyage home and instead writes three other pieces on smoky chimneys, maritime observations, and his pit-coal stove. Elected president of the Supreme Executive Council of Pennsylvania upon his return.

1786   Enlarges his house. Reelected president. Designs the "Long Arm" to assist him in taking down books from high shelves.

1787   Reelected president to serve third and final term. Society for Political Inquiries meets at his house. Serves as the oldest delegate to the Constitutional Convention; favors unsalaried government officials, proportional representation, and a single-house legislature. Becomes president of the Pennsylvania Society for Promoting the Abolition of Slavery.

1788   Retires from public office. Makes out will, leaving most of his estate to the family of his daughter Sarah.

1789   Drafts condemnation of slavery to send to Congress.

1790   Parodies pro-slavery speech delivered by Congressman James Jackson. Dies on April 17; buried next to Deborah Franklin in the Christ Church cemetery.

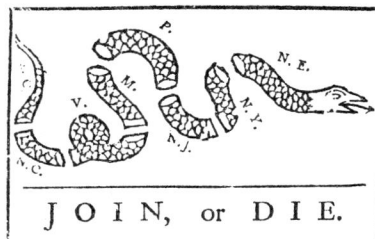

BIBLIOGRAPHY

COLLECTED WORKS

Bigelow, John, ed. *The Complete Works of Benjamin Franklin.* 10 vols. New York, 1887–1889. This edition of Franklin's works followed the Sparks collection of 1836–1840.

Franklin, William Temple, ed. *Memoirs of the Life and Writings of Benjamin Franklin.* 3 vols. London: H. Colburn, 1817–1818. Franklin's grandson, William Temple Franklin, inherited the bulk of his grandfather's papers and published this series after his death.

Labaree, Leonard W., et al., eds. *The Papers of Benjamin Franklin.* New Haven, Conn.: Yale University Press, 1959– . This collection is by far the best and most comprehensive set of Franklin's writings. In addition to Franklin's own writings, it contains letters others wrote to him and extensive explanatory notes. It is, however, not yet complete; the 32 volumes to date cover Franklin's life only through June 1780.

Lemay, J. A. Leo. *Benjamin Franklin: Writings.* New York: Literary Classics of the United States, 1987. This single-volume compilation contains a good representative selection of Franklin's letters, articles, pamphlets, and essays.

Smyth, Albert Henry, ed. *The Writings of Benjamin Franklin.* 10 vols. New York: Macmillan, 1905–1907. The Smyth collection is a respected ten-volume set of Franklin's writings with editorial notes and biographical information.

Sparks, Jared, ed. *The Works of Benjamin Franklin.* 10 vols. Boston: Hilliard, Gray, and Company, 1836–1840. Many scholars fault the Sparks collection for inaccuracies and alterations in the text of Franklin's writings.

OTHER WORKS

Abbott, John S. C. *Benjamin Franklin: A Picture of the Struggles of Our Infant Nation, One Hundred Years Ago.* New York: Dodd, Mead, 1876.

Adams, John. *Papers of John Adams.* Edited by Robert J. Taylor. Cambridge, Mass.: The Belknap Press of Harvard University Press, 1979.

———. *The Works of John Adams, Second President of the United States.* Boston: Little, Brown, 1850.

Adams, Samuel. *The Writings of Samuel Adams.* Edited by Harry Alonzo Cushing. New York: G. P. Putnam's Sons, 1906.

Aldridge, Alfred Owen. *Benjamin Franklin, Philosopher and Man.* Philadelphia: Lippincott, 1965.

———. *Franklin and His French Contemporaries.* New York: New York University Press, 1957.

Allen, Henry Butler. *Benjamin Franklin, Philosophical Engineer.* Princeton, N.J.: Princeton University Press, 1943.

Amacher, Richard E. *Benjamin Franklin.* New York: Twayne Publishers, 1962.

Aspinwall, A., ed. 1962–1970. *The Later Correspondence of George III*. Cambridge, England: Cambridge University Press.

Augur, Helen. *The Secret War of Independence.* New York: Duell, Sloan and Pearce, 1955.

Becker, Carl Lotus. *Benjamin Franklin: A Biographical Sketch.* Ithaca, N.Y.: Cornell University Press, 1946.

Bowen, Catherine Drinker. *The Most Dangerous Man in America: Scenes from the Life of Benjamin Franklin.* Boston: Little, Brown, 1974.

Brett-James, Norman G. *The Life of Peter Collinson.* London: E. G. Dunstan, 1926.

Brown, Ira V., ed. *Joseph Priestley: Selections from His Writings.* University Park, Pa.: The Pennsylvania State University Press, 1962.

Burlingame, Roger. *Benjamin Franklin, Envoy Extraordinary.* New York: Coward-McCann, 1967.

Buxbaum, Melvin H., ed. *Critical Essays on Benjamin Franklin.* Boston: G. K. Hall, 1987.

Carey, Lewis J. *Franklin's Economic Views.* Garden City, N.Y.: Doubleday, Doran & Company, 1928.

Carr, William George. *The Oldest Delegate: Franklin in the Constitutional Convention.* Newark, N.J.: University of Delaware Press, 1990.

Clark, Ronald William. *Benjamin Franklin: A Biography.* New York: Random House, 1983.

Clark, William Bell. *Ben Franklin's Privateers: A Naval Epic of the American Revolution.* Baton Rouge: Louisiana State University Press, 1956.

Cloyd, David Excelmons. *Benjamin Franklin and Education: His Ideal of Life and His System of Education for the Realization of That Ideal.* Boston: D. C. Heath Co., 1902.

Cochrane, James Aikman. *Dr. Johnson's Printer: The Life of William Strahan.* Cambridge, Mass.: Harvard University Press, 1964.

Cohen, I. Bernard. *Franklin and Newton: An Inquiry into Speculative Newtonian Experimental Science and Franklin's Work in Electricity as an Example Thereof.* Philadelphia: American Philosophical Society, 1956.

Colden, Cadwallader. *The History of the Five Indian Nations Depending on the Province of New-York in America.* Cornell University Press, 1969.

————. *The Letters and Papers of Cadwallader Colden, 1711–1775.* New York: New York Historical Society, 1918–1937.

Crane, Verner W. "The Club of Honest Whigs: Friends of Science and Liberty." 3 *William and Mary Quarterly*, XXIII, 1966, pp. 211–233.

Crane, Verner Winslow. *Benjamin Franklin and a Rising People.* Boston: Little, Brown, 1954.

————. *Benjamin Franklin, Englishman and American.* Providence, R.I.: Brown University, 1936.

Crowther, J. G. *Famous American Men of Science.* New York, W. W. Norton, 1937.

Currey, Cecil B. *Road to Revolution: Benjamin Franklin in England, 1765–1775.* Garden City, N.Y.: Anchor Books, 1968.

Davis, Harvey N. *Benjamin Franklin: A Bridge between Science and the Mechanic Arts.* New York: Newcomen Society of England, American Branch, 1949.

Donne, W. Bodham. 1971. *The Correspondence of King George the Third with Lord North, 1768 to 1783.* New York: Da Capo Press.

Dull, Jonathan R. *Franklin the Diplomat: The French Mission.* Philadelphia: American Philosophical Society, 1982.

Eliot, Charles William. *Four American Leaders.* Boston: American Unitarian Association, 1906.

Fay, Bernard. *Bernard Fay's the Two Franklins: Fathers of American Democracy.* Boston: Little, Brown, 1933.

Fisher, Sydney George. *The True Benjamin Franklin*. Philadelphia: J. B. Lippincott, 1899.

Fleming, Thomas J. *The Man Who Dared the Lightning: A New Look at Benjamin Franklin*. New York: Morrow, 1971.

Ford, Paul Leicester. *The Many-Sided Franklin*. Freeport, N.Y.: Books for Libraries Press, 1972.

Ford, Worthington Chauncy, ed. *Journals of the Continental Congress, 1774–1789*. Washington, D.C.: U.S. Government Printing Office, 1904–1937.

Fox, R. Hingston. *Dr. John Fothergill and His Friends: Chapters in Eighteenth Century Life*. London: Macmillan., 1919.

Franklin, Benjamin. *Autobiography and Other Writings*. Edited by Kenneth Silverman. New York: Penguin Books, 1986.

———. *Benjamin Franklin: His Life as He Wrote It*. Edited by Esmond Wright. Cambridge, Mass.: Harvard University Press, 1990.

———. *Some Account of the Pennsylvania Hospital*. Baltimore: Johns Hopkins Univeristy Press, 1954.

Franklin, Benjamin, and Jane Mecom. *The Letters of Benjamin Franklin and Jane Mecom*. Edited by Carl Van Doren. Princeton, N.J.: Princeton University Press, 1950.

George III, King of Great Britain. *The Correspondence of King George the Third with Lord North 1768 to 1783*. Edited by W. Bodham Donne. New York: Da Capo Press, 1971.

———. *The Later Correspondence of George III*. Edited by A. Aspinall. Cambridge, England: University Press, 1962–1970.

Granger, Bruce Ingham. *Benjamin Franklin, an American Man of Letters*. Norman: University of Oklahoma Press, 1976.

Grover, Eulalie Osgood. *Benjamin Franklin: The Story of Poor Richard*. New York: Dodd, Mead, 1953.

Hale, Edward, and Edward E. Hale, Jr. *Franklin in France: From Original Documents, Most of Which Are Now Published for the First Time*. New York: Burt Franklin, 1969.

Hanna, William S. *Benjamin Franklin and Pennsylvania Politics*. Stanford, Calif.: Stanford University Press, 1964.

Harris, Elizabeth M. *The Common Press: Being a Record, Description, and Delineation of the Early Eighteenth-Century Handpress in the Smithsonian Institution, with a History and Documentation of the Press*. Boston: D. R. Godine, 1978.

Hastings, George Everett. *The Life and Works of Francis Hopkinson*. Chicago: University of Chicago Press, 1926.

Historical Society of Pennsylvania. *Indian Treaties Printed by Benjamin Franklin*. Philadelphia: Historical Society of Pennsylvania, 1938.

Hornberger, Theodore. *Benjamin Franklin*. Minneapolis: University of Minnesota Press, 1962.

Huang, Nian-Sheng. *Benjamin Franklin in American Thought and Culture, 1790–1990*. Philadelphia: American Philosophical Society, 1994.

Jefferson, Thomas. *The Papers of Thomas Jefferson*. Edited by Julian P. Boyd. Princeton, N.J.: Princeton University Press, 1950.

Jenkins, Charles F. "The Historical Background of Franklin's Tree." *Pennsylvania Magazine of History and Biography*, vol. LVII, 1933, pp. 193–208.

Jennings, Francis. *Benjamin Franklin, Politician*. New York: W. W. Norton, 1996.

Johansen, Bruce E. *Forgotten Founders: Benjamin Franklin, the Iroquois, and the Rationale for the American Revolution*. Ipswich, Mass.: Gambit, 1982.

Kemp, Betty. *Sir Francis Dashwood: An Eighteenth Century Independent*. New York: St. Martin's Press, 1967.

Kershaw, Gordon E. *James Bowdoin II: A Patriot and Man of the Enlightenment*. Lanham, Md.: University Press of America, 1991.

Ketcham, Ralph Louis. *Benjamin Franklin*. New York: Washington Square Press, 1965.

Korty, Margaret Barton. *Benjamin Franklin and Eighteenth-Century American Libraries*. Philadelphia: American Philosophical Society, 1965.

Lemay, J. A. Leo. *Ebenezer Kinnersley, Franklin's Friend*. Philadelphia: University of Pennsylvania Press, 1964.

Lemay, J. A. Leo, ed. *The Oldest Revolutionary: Essays on Benjamin Franklin*. Philadelphia: University of Pennsylvania Press, 1976.

———. *Reappraising Benjamin Franklin: A Bicentennial Perspective*. Cranbury, N.J.: Associated University Presses, 1993.

Lettsom, John Coakley. *Memoirs of John Fothergill*. London, C. Dilly, 1786.

Lokken, Roy N., ed. *Meet Dr. Franklin*. Philadelphia: Franklin Institute Press, 1981.

Lopez, Claude-Anne. *Mon Cher Papa: Franklin and the Ladies of Paris*. New Haven, conn.: Yale University Press, 1966.

———. *The Private Franklin: The Man and His Family*. New York: W. W. Norton, 1975.

Masur, Louis P., ed. *The Autobiography of Benjamin Franklin*. Edited by Louis P. Masur. Boston: Bedford Books of St. Martin's Press, 1993.

Mather, Cotton. *Magnalia Christi Americana*. New York: Russell & Russell, 1967.

Meyer, Gladys. *Free Trade in Ideas: Aspects of American Liberalism Illustrated in Franklin's Philadelphia Career*. New York: King's Crown Press, 1941.

Meyerson, Martin, and Dilys Pegler Winegrad. *Gladly Learn and Gladly Teach: Franklin and His Heirs at the University of Pennsylvania, 1740–1976*. Philadelphia: University of Pennsylvania Press, 1978.

Middlekauff, Robert. *Benjamin Franklin and His Enemies*. Berkeley: University of California Press, 1996.

Miller, Clarence William. *Benjamin Franklin's Philadelphia Printing, 1728–1766: A Descriptive Bibliography*. Philadelphia: American Philosophical Society, 1974.

Morgan, David T. *The Devious Dr. Franklin, Colonial Agent: Benjamin Franklin's Years in London*. Macon, Ga.: Mercer University Press, 1996.

Murphy, Orville Theodore. *Charles Gravier, Comte de Vergennes: French Diplomacy in the Age of Revolution, 1719–1787*. Albany: State University of New York Press, 1982.

New York Historical Society. 1918–1937. *The Letters and Papers of Cadwallader Colden*. New York: New York Historical Society.

Newcomb, Benjamin H. *Franklin and Galloway: A Political Partnership*. New Haven, Conn.: Yale University Press, 1972.

Nolan, J. Bennett. *Benjamin Franklin in Scotland and Ireland, 1759 and 1771*. Philadelphia: University of Pennsylvania Press, 1938.

———. *General Benjamin Franklin: The Military Career of a Philosopher*. Philadelphia: University of Pennsylvania Press, 1936.

Oswald, John Clyde. *Benjamin Franklin: Printer*. Garden City, N.Y.: Doubleday, Page & Company, for the Associated Advertising Clubs of the World, 1917.

Pace, Antonio. *Benjamin Franklin and Italy*. Philadelphia: American Philosophical Society, 1958.

Paine, Thomas. *Common Sense*. Edited by Isaac Kramnick. Harmondsworth, England: Penguin, 1976.

Parton, James. *Life and Times of Benjamin Franklin*. New York: Mason Brothers, 1864.

Randall, Willard Sterne. *A Little Revenge: Benjamin Franklin and His Son*. Boston: Little, Brown, 1984.

Reed, William B. *Life and Correspondence of Joseph Reed, Military Secretary of Washington, at Cambridge; Adjutant-General of the Continental Army; Member of the Congress of the*

United States; and President of the Executive Council of the State of Pennsylvania. Philadelphia: Lindsay and Blakiston, 1847.

Roelker, William Greene, ed. *Benjamin Franklin and Catharine Ray Greene: Their Correspondence, 1755–1790*. Philadelphia: American Philosophical Society, 1949.

Rogers, George L., ed. 1986. *Benjamin Franklin's* The Art of Virtue: *His Formula for Successful Living*. Eden Prairie, MN: Acorn Publishing.

Rosengarten, J. G. *American History from German Archives, with Reference to the German Soldiers in the Revolution and Franklin's Visit to Germany*. Lancaster, Penn.: Pennsylvania-German Society, 1904.

Rush, Benjamin. *Letters.* Edited by L. H. Butterfield. Princeton:, N.J. Princeton University Press, 1951.

———. *The Selected Writings of Benjamin Rush.* Edited by Dagobert D. Runes. New York: Philosophical Library, 1947.

Russell, Phillips. *Benjamin Franklin, the First Civilized American.* New York: Brentano's, 1926.

Sanford, Charles L. *Benjamin Franklin and the American Character.* Boston: D. C. Heath, 1955.

Sappenfield, James A. *A Sweet Instruction: Franklin's Journalism as a Literary Apprenticeship.* Carbondale: Southern Illinois University Press, 1973.

Schoenbrun, David. *Triumph in Paris: The Exploits of Benjamin Franklin.* New York: Harper & Row, 1976.

Skemp, Sheila L. *William Franklin: Son of a Patriot, Servant of a King.* New York: Oxford University Press, 1990.

Smith, Jeffery Alan. *Franklin and Bache: Envisioning the Enlightened Republic.* New York: Oxford University Press, 1990.

Smythe, J. Henry, ed. *The Amazing Benjamin Franklin.* New York: Frederick A. Stokes Company, 1929.

St. John, Gerard J. "Ben and I: After 200 Years and a Few Unforeseen Difficulties, Benjamin Franklin's Bequest to Philadelphia Is Found Practicable." Philadelphia: Philadelphia Bar Association, 1993.

Steell, Willis. *Benjamin Franklin of Paris, 1776–1785.* New York: Minton, Balch, & Company, 1928.

Stephens, Brad. *The Pictorial Life of Benjamin Franklin, Printer, Typefounder, Ink Maker, Bookbinder, Copperplate Engraver and Printer, Stationer, Merchant, Bookseller, Author, Editor, Publisher, Inventor, Scientist, Philosopher, Diplomat, Philanthropist, and Statesman.* Philadelphia: Dill & Collins Company, 1923.

Stevens, Richard B., ed. *The Declaration of Independence and the Constitution of the United States.* Washington, D.C.: Georgetown University Press, 1984.

Stifler, James Madison. *"My Dear Girl": The Correspondence of Benjamin Franklin with Polly Stevenson, Georgiana and Catherine Shipley.* New York: George H. Doran, 1927.

———. *The Religion of Benjamin Franklin.* New York: D. Appleton and Company, 1925.

Stourzh, Gerald. *Benjamin Franklin and American Foreign Policy.* Chicago: University of Chicago Press, 1954.

Tagg, James. *Benjamin Franklin Bache and the "Philadelphia Aurora."* Philadelphia: University of Pennsylvania Press, 1991.

Thoms, Herbert. *Jared Eliot, Minister, Doctor, Scientist, and His Connecticut.* Hamden, Conn.: Shoe String Press, 1967.

Tourtellot, Arthur Bernon. *Benjamin Franklin, the Shaping of Genius: The Boston Years.* Garden City, N.Y.: Doubleday, 1977.

Van Doren, Carl. *Benjamin Franklin.* New York: Viking Press, 1938.

———. *Franklin's Autobiographical Writings.* New York: Viking Press, 1945.

———. *Jane Mecom, the Favorite Sister of Benjamin Franklin: Her Life Here First Fully

Narrated from Their Entire Surviving Correspondence. New York: Viking Press, 1950.

———. *Letters and Papers of Benjamin Franklin and Richard Jackson, 1753–1785.* Philadelphia: American Philosophical Society, 1947.

Washington, George. *The Papers of George Washington, Confederation Series.* Edited by W. W. Abbot and Dorothy Twohig. Charlottesville: University Press of Virginia, 1992–.

———. *The Papers of George Washington, Revolutionary War Series.* Edited by Philander D. Chase. Charlottesville: University Press of Virginia, 1985– .

Wolf, Edwin. *Franklin's Way to Wealth as a Printer.* Philadelphia, 1951.

Wright, Esmond. *Benjamin Franklin: A Profile.* New York: Hill and Wang, 1970.

———. *Franklin of Philadelphia.* Cambridge, Mass.: Belknap Press of Harvard University Press, 1986.

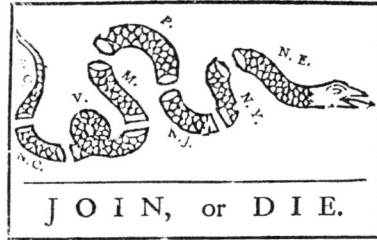

JOIN, or DIE.

ILLUSTRATION CREDITS

100	Library of Congress, LCUSZ62-15553
102	Library of Congress, LCUSZ62-45506
105	Library of Congress, LCUSZ62-28227
116	Library of Congress, LCUSZ62-42858
120	Library of Congress, LCUSZ62-28251
124	Library of Congress, LCUSZ62-3748
126	Library of Congress, LCUSZ62-30743
130	Library of Congress, LCUSZ62-44927
138	Library of Congress, LCUSZ62-48633
141	Library of Congress, LCUSZ6-116
143	Library of Congress, LCUSZ62-45113
147	From *The Writings of Benjamin Franklin,* Albert Henry Smyth, ed.
148	(left) Library of Congress, LCUSZ62-28246
148	(right) Library of Congress, LCUSZ62-28247
153	Library of Congress, LCUSZ62-49991
154	Rare Book Division, Library of Congress, LCUSZ62-28243
158	Rare Book Division, Library of Congress, LCUSZ62-1473
161	Rare Book Division, Libraryof Congress, LCUSZ62-28216
169	Library of Congress, LCUSZ62-10658
179	Library of Congress, LCUSZ62-56359
181	Library of Congress, LCUSZ62-9541
187	Library of Congress, LCUSZ62-72127
189	Library of Congress, LCUSZ62-28212
190	Library of Congress, LCUSZ62-46688
192	Library of Congress, LCUSZ62-54187
202	Library of Congress, LCUSZ62-24644
204	Library of Congress, LCUSZ62-96219
210	Library of Congress, LCUSZ62-1434
213	Library of Congress, LCUSZ62-54697
218	Library of Congress, LCUSZ62-16876
233	Library of Congress, LCUSZ62-48919
243	Library of Congress, LC-D416-28052 DLC
248	Library of Congress, LCUSZ62-45514
250	Library of Congress, LCUSZ62-5544

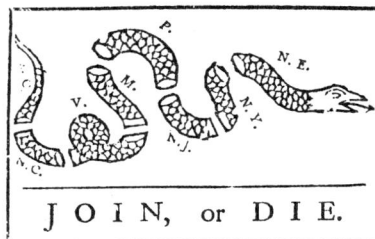

JOIN, or DIE.

INDEX

Note: Page numbers in **bold** indicate articles specifically dedicated to corresponding entries.